Learn Scala Programming

A comprehensive guide covering functional and reactive
programming with Scala 2.13, Akka, and Lagom

Slava Schmidt

BIRMINGHAM - MUMBAI

Learn Scala Programming

Commissioning Editor: Merint Mathew
Acquisition Editor: Shriram Shekhar
Content Development Editor: Manjusha Mantri
Technical Editor: Mehul Singh
Copy Editor: Safis Editing
Project Coordinator: Prajakta Naik
Proofreader: Safis Editing
Indexer: Priyanka Dhadke
Graphics: Jisha Chirayil
Production Coordinator: Nilesh Mohite

First published: October 2018

Production reference: 1311018

Published by Packt Publishing Ltd.
Livery Place
35 Livery Street
Birmingham
B3 2PB, UK.

ISBN 978-1-78883-630-2

www.packt.com

To my family – Tanja, Christina, and Marina – who made this book possible.

`mapt.io`

Mapt is an online digital library that gives you full access to over 5,000 books and videos, as well as industry leading tools to help you plan your personal development and advance your career. For more information, please visit our website.

Why subscribe?

- Spend less time learning and more time coding with practical eBooks and videos from over 4,000 industry professionals

- Improve your learning with skill plans designed especially for you

- Get a free eBook or video every month

- Mapt is fully searchable

- Copy and paste, print, and bookmark content

Packt.com

Did you know that Packt offers eBook versions of every book published, with PDF and ePub files available? You can upgrade to the eBook version at `www.packt.com` and, as a print book customer, you are entitled to a discount on the eBook copy. Get in touch with us at `customercare@packtpub.com` for more details.

At `www.packt.com`, you can also read a collection of free technical articles, sign up for a range of free newsletters, and receive exclusive discounts and offers on Packt books and eBooks.

Contributors

About the author

Slava Schmidt is a software developer living in Germany. During his career, he has used a wide spectrum of programming languages, ranging from Assembler to Haskell, and progressed from an intern programmer, via head of engineering, to a Scala contractor. In his current role, he helps to develop and bring into production a number of Scala projects of various sizes and complexities for customers from different industries.

He is a contributor to open source projects related to Scala and Akka. As a passionate conference speaker, he regularly gives talks about technologies to share his experiences with other developers.

I'd like to thank Tatjana Schmidt for making the images in this book look great, Mike Litvin for his timely support, Marco Borst for (in)validating lots of ideas (without necessarily knowing this) and the production team at Packt, especially Manjusha Mantri, for all of their advice and assistance.

About the reviewers

Rambabu Posa has 14 years of rich experience in Scala, Java, and BigData ecosystems. He has been working as Java developer since 2004 and Scala/BigData Developer since Mid of 2015. He loves functional programming in TDD (test-driven development) as a way of developing reactive microservices. He loves teaching, and has provided online training and written tutorials on Java, Scala, Cloud and BigData ecosystems. He loves developing Reactive systems using Lightbend's Reactive Platform technology stack, including Lagom Framework, ConductR, Scala, Akka Toolkit, Akka Streams, and Play Framework with AWS. He is a master of Apache Kafka (Kafka, KStreams, Connect, Schema Registry, Mirror Maker).

Mikhail Litvin is a passionate software engineer with more than 10 years experience in systems analysis, software design, and software architecture. During the day, Mikhail spends his time building highly scalable and resilient solutions for one of the leading Europe, e-commerce companies. Mikhail works with a variety of technologies such as, Scala, Akka, SQL/ NoSQL, AWS, Python, and others. He's interested in artificial intelligence and machine learning.
In a spare time, Mikhail enjoys riding his bicycle, fishing, and traveling.

Packt is searching for authors like you

If you're interested in becoming an author for Packt, please visit `authors.packtpub.com` and apply today. We have worked with thousands of developers and tech professionals, just like you, to help them share their insight with the global tech community. You can make a general application, apply for a specific hot topic that we are recruiting an author for, or submit your own idea.

Table of Contents

Preface

Today's Scala is quite different from its earlier versions.

The second version of the language is more than twelve years old, and underwent multiple changes related to supported features and library implementation. Many features then considered crucial, such as support for XML literals, Swing, and Actors, were moved from the language core to the external libraries or replaced by open source alternatives. Another functionality that makes Scala the programming language as we know it today were added directly, or by including yet another open source library in the distribution. The most notable example is adopting Akka in version 2.10.

Scala 2.13, with its focus on modularizing standard libraries and simplifying collections, entails a further change. The changes, however, do not only affect the technical side of Scala. Years of using it to solve real problems have helped us to collect more knowledge about structuring functional programs and using object-oriented features in new ways to our advantage. The same way as it was customary to use earlier versions of Scala as "Java without semicolons," it is now routine to build programs using monad transformers and type-level programming techniques.

This book addresses both technical and architectural changes by providing a comprehensive guide to the redesigned standard library and collections, as well as covering type systems and first-level support for functions in depth. It discusses implicits as a primary mechanism for building type classes and looks at different ways of testing Scala code. It covers in detail abstract building blocks used in functional programming, affording sufficient knowledge to pick up and use any existing functional programming library out there. It explores reactive programming by covering the Akka framework and reactive streams. Finally, it talks about microservices and how to implement them with Scala and the Lagom framework.

Who this book is for

As a software developer, you have a working knowledge of some imperative programming language, presumably Java.

You've got some basic Scala knowledge and a bit of experience of using it in actual projects. As a Scala beginner, you are surprised by the richness of its ecosystem, and the multiplicity of ways in which it allows you to solve problems, as well as the number of libraries available. You want to improve your Scala skills to be able to fully utilize the potential of the language and its reworked standard library, optimally use its rich type system to formulate your programs as closely as possible to the problem domain, and profit from its functional capabilities by understanding underlying paradigms, using relevant language features and open source libraries.

What this book covers

Chapter 1, *An Introduction to Scala 2.13,* walks the reader through Scala 2.13. Apart from helping readers who are new to Scala, the book will help developers who are already familiar with Scala to start using the new version and give them the motivation to migrate.

Chapter 2, *Understanding Types in Scala,* transforms the reader into a type master. It starts by describing different ways to define types in Scala, as well as refreshing the reader's memory about type bindings, variance, and bounds. This foundation will establish a stable groundwork for explaining how types can be combined to form patterns and the situations in which these patterns are applicable.

Chapter 3, *Deep Dive into Functions,* starts out by going over the different ways of defining a function in Scala. Then, it will cover intermediate aspects, such as higher-order functions, polymorphism, and recursion. Finally, it will discuss advanced aspects, such as trampolining and the object-oriented nature of functions in Scala.

Chapter 4, *Getting to Know Implicits and Type Classes,* teaches parts of the language related to implicits, in particular, different types of implicits, the order of implicit scope resolution, and context bounds. Moving on, the chapter will explain machinery that facilitates the use of modern functional programming in Scala as we know it – type classes.

Chapter 5, *Property-Based Testing in Scala,* touches upon different ways to style Scala test code and use its facilities to test asynchronous and concurrent functionality. The reader will be taken through the concept of property-based testing and its practical applications in depth.

Chapter 6, *Exploring Built-in Effects,* covers built-in Scala effects, such as Option, Either, Try, and Future. It describes the scenarios in which it is appropriate to use one or, other abstraction and reveals the proper ways to do so. Most importantly, it helps the reader discover similarities between these seemingly different abstractions.

Chapter 7, *Understanding Algebraic Structures,* begins by identifying common patterns in combining data. It teaches you how these patterns are named and demonstrate how they can be implemented in Scala using type classes.

Chapter 8, *Dealing with Effects,* deals with effects the same way we dealt with algebraic structures in the previous chapter. First, the chapter provides motivation in the form of real use cases for effects, and describes why they are useful and even crucial. Then, it extends this intuition by providing a formal description. Finally, it walks the reader through the example implementation.

Chapter 9, *Familiarizing Yourself with Basic Monads,* continues consolidating abstract concepts by combining algebraic data types and effects defined in the two previous chapters into yet another powerful concept – monads. It explains why monads are necessary, describes monadic laws, and shows example implementations for a small number of essential monads and monad transformers.

Chapter 10, *A Look at Monad Transformers and Free Monad,* outlines the problems introduced by monad transformers. It explores a free monad and the possibilities they provide. Finally, it gives due attention to the new kid on the block – an IO monad.

Chapter 11, *An Introduction to the Akka and Actor Models,* outlines the need for and principles of event-based programming. It then demonstrates how to implement a simple actor-based application using classical Akka. Finally, we drop the most important Akka modules into the mix and help to understand various testing techniques.

Chapter 12, *Building Reactive Applications with Akka Typed,* reveals an alternative way to build reactive applications with Akka. It introduces Akka Typed, compares classical and typed approaches, and shows the reader how the latter reduces a developer's choices but increases type safety and simplifies reasoning concerning actor-based programs.

Chapter 13, *Basics of Akka Streams,* describes yet another way to structure reactive programs – reactive streams. It catalogs the basic building blocks of typical Akka Stream applications and discusses techniques for wiring them together. Toward the end, it covers the topics of error handling and testing.

Chapter 14, *Project 1 - Building Microservices with Scala,* covers two topics. First, it substantiates the need for microservices and describes their advantages and building principles. It also uncovers technical and organizational challenges related to the microservice-based approach. Second, it uses the knowledge the reader has gained from previous chapters to build two actual projects from scratch. Both projects represent simple microservices implementing, CRUD API with access to a database, validation, and data transformation. The first project will be based on knowledge obtained from first and second sections of the book. We will build a microservice using the open source functional programming libraries, http4s, and circe, for client API, monocle to demonstrate the use of optics, and doobie for database access. The second project will be built using reactive programming libraries and techniques covered in the third section of the book, Akka, and Akka HTTP. For database access, well use Lightbend Slick, while marshalling and unmarshalling will be done using Spray-JSON.

Chapter 15, *Project 2 - Building Microservices with Lagom,* goes into the details of the Lagom framework by discussing its philosophy, the way Lagom applications are structured, available APIs and how to use them, and the topics of running and deployment. This knowledge will be used by the reader to build a project where they will create an application from scratch and deploy an example Lagom application.

Appendix A, *Preparing the Environment and Running Code Samples,* provides detailed installation instructions for Java and SBT for all major platforms. It also contains useful suggestions about checking out accompanying code from the Github repository as well as working with SBT shell and Scala REPL.

To get the most out of this book

1. We expect the reader to be comfortable with structuring and implementing simple programs in Scala and familiar with SBT and REPL. No previous knowledge of reactive programming, Akka, or microservices is required, but familiarity with the underlying concepts would be beneficial.
2. To work with the code examples in this book, Java 1.8+ and SBT 1.2+ need to be installed. The installation of Git is recommended to simplify checking out the source code from GitHub. For those readers who don't have the prerequisite software ready, we provide installation instructions for Java and SBT in Appendix A.

Download the example code files

You can download the example code files for this book from your account at
`www.packt.com`. If you purchased this book elsewhere, you can visit
`www.packt.com/support` and register to have the files emailed directly to you.

You can download the code files by following these steps:

1. Log in or register at `www.packt.com`.
2. Select the **SUPPORT** tab.
3. Click on **Code Downloads & Errata**.
4. Enter the name of the book in the **Search** box and follow the onscreen instructions.

Once the file is downloaded, please make sure that you unzip or extract the folder using the latest version of:

- WinRAR/7-Zip for Windows
- Zipeg/iZip/UnRarX for Mac
- 7-Zip/PeaZip for Linux

The code bundle for the book is also hosted on GitHub at `https://github.com/PacktPublishing/Learn-Scala-Programming`. In case there's an update to the code, it will be updated on the existing GitHub repository.

We also have other code bundles from our rich catalog of books and videos available at `https://github.com/PacktPublishing/`. Check them out!

Download the color images

We also provide a PDF file that has color images of the screenshots/diagrams used in this book. You can download it here:
`http://www.packtpub.com/sites/default/files/downloads/9781788836302_ColorImages.pdf`.

Conventions used

There are a number of text conventions used throughout this book.

`CodeInText`: Indicates code words in text, database table names, folder names, filenames, file extensions, pathnames, dummy URLs, user input, and Twitter handles. Here is an example: "In Scala 2.13, `StringOps` has been extended with option-returning methods for string literals parsing. Supported types include all numeric types and `Boolean`."

A block of code is set as follows:

```
object UserDb {
  def getById(id: Long): User = ???
  def update(u: User): User = ???
  def save(u: User): Boolean = ???
}
```

When we wish to draw your attention to a particular part of a code block, the relevant lines or items are set in bold:

```
scala> val user = User("John", "Doe", "jd@mail.me")
user: User = User(John, Doe, jd@mail.me)
scala> naiveToJsonString(user)
res1: String = { "name": "John", "surname": "Doe", "email": "jd@mail.me" }
```

Any command-line input or output is written as follows:

```
take
-S--c--a--l--a-- --2--.--1--3-
take
Lazy view constructed: -S-S-c-C-a-A-l-L-a-A- -
Lazy view forced: -S--c--a--l--a-- -List(S, C, A, L, A, )
Strict: List(S, C, A, L, A, )
```

Bold: Indicates a new term, an important word, or words that you see on screen.

Warnings or important notes appear like this.

Tips and tricks appear like this.

Get in touch

Feedback from our readers is always welcome.

General feedback: If you have questions about any aspect of this book, mention the book title in the subject of your message and email us at customercare@packtpub.com.

Errata: Although we have taken every care to ensure the accuracy of our content, mistakes do happen. If you have found a mistake in this book, we would be grateful if you would report this to us. Please visit www.packt.com/submit-errata, selecting your book, clicking on the Errata Submission Form link, and entering the details.

Piracy: If you come across any illegal copies of our works in any form on the internet, we would be grateful if you would provide us with the location address or website name. Please contact us at copyright@packt.com with a link to the material.

If you are interested in becoming an author: If there is a topic that you have expertise in, and you are interested in either writing or contributing to a book, please visit authors.packtpub.com.

Reviews

Please leave a review. Once you have read and used this book, why not leave a review on the site that you purchased it from? Potential readers can then see and use your unbiased opinion to make purchase decisions, we at Packt can understand what you think about our products, and our authors can see your feedback on their book. Thank you!

For more information about Packt, please visit packt.com.

An Introduction to Scala 2.13

At the moment of this writing, Scala 2.13 has reached its five-year milestone and approaches the first release candidate. At this point, its feature set is unlikely to change and it is safe to take a look at the new features of the update.

In this chapter, we will talk about the scope of the release, placing the main focus of the conversation on its centerpiece—the new collection library.

The following topics will be discussed in this chapter:

- Introduction to Scala 2.13
- New features of Scala 2.13
- The Scala 2.13 collection library

Technical requirements

- JDK 1.8+
- SBT 1.2+

The source code for this chapter is available under https://github.com/PacktPublishing/Learn-Scala-Programming/tree/master/Chapter01.

Introduction to Scala 2.13

Scala 2.13 is the latest minor update of the Scala programming language. Despite looking like a minor bump in the version number, this release is much more important than it might appear.

The reason for this is that its main focus is the reworked collection library, which is going to replace the current version introduced in version 2.8 and slightly redesigned in version 2.9.

The new collection framework is here to stay in Scala 2 and also will become a part of Scala 3.

As it is mostly a library release, the language itself is not changing a lot as compared to the previous version. Apart from the collections, the new version improves on three aspects:

- Minimizes the core library
- Speeds up the compiler
- Improves user-friendliness

These details are outside of the scope of this book and we will not discuss them further.

Besides that, there is an addition of literal and singleton types, which we will discuss in detail in Chapter 2, *Understanding Types in Scala*, and a few minor changes to the standard library which we'll look at next, before diving into the sea of maps and lists.

Eager to look into the future? We'll take you there!

New features of Scala 2.13

In this section, we will discuss a few small improvements in the new version, which are not related to the collections topic and don't really belong to some bigger topic, such as optional parsing for string literals, adding names-reporting functions to case classes, methods for chaining operations, and automatic resource-management.

Optional parsing for string literals

In Scala 2.13, StringOps has been extended with methods that return Option for string-literals parsing. Supported types include all numeric types and Boolean.

The new methods can greatly simplify the processing of user-provided data without the need to wrap the calls with the exception-handling, as shown in the following example:

```
scala> "10".toIntOption
res3: Option[Int] = Some(10)
scala> "TrUe".toBooleanOption
res4: Option[Boolean] = Some(true)
scala> val bool = "Not True"
bool: String = Not True
```

```
scala> bool.toBooleanOption
res5: Option[Boolean] = None
```

The optional `Boolean` parsing ignores the case of the argument the same way the exception-throwing `toBoolean` method does.

Products can report the names of their element

This feature probably will be mostly useful for the case classes as it makes possible some generic programming without the need to resort to reflection or macros.

The following examples demonstrate how the new `productElementName(idx)` method can be used to build a naive JSON serializer for simple case classes:

```
case class User(name: String, surname: String, email: String)

def naiveToJsonString(p: Product): String =
  (for { i <- 0 until p.productArity } yield
    s"""${p.productElementName(i)}": "${p.productElement(i)}"""")
    .mkString("{ ", ", ", " }")
```

Obviously, this simple iteration does not take nesting and escaping into account, but it already can produce valid results in elementary cases:

```
scala> val user = User("John", "Doe", "jd@mail.me")
user: User = User(John,Doe,jd@mail.me)
scala> naiveToJsonString(user)
res1: String = { "name": "John", "surname": "Doe", "email": "jd@mail.me" }
```

Unfortunately, the method taking an index of the element throws an exception in the case that the index is invalid:

```
scala> user.productElementName(3)
java.lang.IndexOutOfBoundsException: 3
 at User.productElementName(<console>:1)
 ... 38 elided
```

We will discuss why throwing exceptions is not the best approach, as well as viable alternatives, in `Chapter 6`, *Exploring Built-In Effects.*

Added methods for chaining operations

Via `import scala.util.chaining._`, it is now possible to add `tap` and `pipe` methods to instances of any type. The functionality is provided by an implicit conversion to `ChainingOps`. We will look at implicits in detail in `Chapter 4`, *Getting to Know Implicits and Type Classes*.

The `pipe` method applies a given function to the value and returns the result. It might be helpful in situations where it is desirable to convert nested function calls into the fluid-interface-like code. The following snippet shows an example of an imaginary user database with nested function calls chained via `pipe`.

Consider the following the database interface:

```
object UserDb {
  def getById(id: Long): User = ???
  def update(u: User): User = ???
  def save(u: User): Boolean = ???
}
```

We could apply all three actions to the user at once:

```
import UserDb._
val userId = 1L
save(update(getById(userId)))
```

`pipe` allows us to represent this in a more readable format:

```
getById(userId).pipe(update).pipe(save)
```

Arguably the same (or an even clearer) result could be achieved by combining functions before applying them:

```
val doEverything = (getById _).andThen(update).andThen(save)
doEverything(userId)
```

We will look at functions in general, and function composition in particular, in `Chapter 3`, *Deep Dive into Functions*.

`tap` applies a function given as an argument solely for the side-effects it produces and returns the original value. It might be useful, for example, for logging purposes and the simplest kind of performance measurements.

The next snippet demonstrates an elementary side-effect-causing performance-tracking implementation that utilizes a global variable:

```scala
scala> import scala.util.chaining._
import scala.util.chaining._
scala> val lastTick = new java.util.concurrent.atomic.AtomicLong(0)
lastTick: java.util.concurrent.atomic.AtomicLong = 0
scala> def measure[A](a: A): Unit = {
     |   val now = System.currentTimeMillis()
     |   val before = lastTick.getAndSet(now)
     |   println(s"$a: ${now-before} ms elapsed")
     | }
measure: [A](a: A)Unit
scala> def start(): Unit = lastTick.set(System.currentTimeMillis())
start: ()Unit
scala> start()
scala> val result =
scala.io.StdIn.readLine().pipe(_.toIntOption).tap(measure)
None: 291 ms elapsed
result: Option[Int] = None
scala> val anotherResult =
scala.io.StdIn.readLine().pipe(_.toIntOption).tap(measure)
Some(3456): 11356 ms elapsed
anotherResult: Option[Int] = Some(3456)
```

Here, we defined a global value of the `AtomicLong` type to store the last measured timestamp. Then we define a polymorphic `measure` method that captures the time between the moment of the last measurement and now, and a `start` method to reset the clock. After that, we can use the `tap` method to track the execution times of our actions.

We will talk about types and polymorphism in `Chapter 2`, *Understanding Types in Scala*, side-effects and more general concept of effects in `Chapter 8`, *Dealing with Effects*, and show drawbacks of having global variables and a global state in `Chapter 9`, *Familiarizing Yourself with Basic Monads*.

Automatic Resource Management

Scala 2.13 adds a practical way to automatically manage resources. We will discuss other ways to manage resources and implement dependency-injection in Chapter 9, *Familiarizing Yourself with Basic Monads* and 10. scala.util.Using allows us to do this in a familiar side-effecting way. All operations on the resource are wrapped in a Try, which we'll talk about in Chapter 6, *Exploring Built-In Effects*. If Exceptions is thrown, the first one is returned within a Try. The exception-handling is quite sophisticated in some corner cases and we invite the reader to consult ScalaDoc for a detailed description of it.

Using is a class that takes some resources as a by-name parameter. The resource can be anything that has a type class instance for scala.util.Resource available. Such an instance for java.lang.AutoCloseable is provided in the standard library. We will study type classes in Chapter 4, *Getting to Know Implicits and Type Classes*. Using also has a monadic interface, which allows us to combine multiple resources in for-comprehensions. We'll discuss monads in Chapter 9, *Familiarizing Yourself with Basic Monads*.

Here is an example of the practical application of Using. We will define a resource that implements AutoCloseable and a few of these resources in for-comprehension as a source of the data:

```scala
scala> import scala.util.{Try, Using}
import scala.util.{Try, Using}
scala> final case class Resource(name: String) extends AutoCloseable {
  | override def close(): Unit = println(s"Closing $name")
  | def lines = List(s"$name line 1", s"$name line 2")
  | }
defined class Resource
scala> val List(r1, r2, r3) = List("first", "2", "3").map(Resource)
r1: Resource = Resource(first)
r2: Resource = Resource(2)
r3: Resource = Resource(3)

scala> val lines: Try[Seq[String]] = for {
    | u1 <- Using(r1)
    | u2 <- Using(r2)
    | u3 <- Using(r3)
    | } yield {
    | u1.lines ++ u2.lines ++ u3.lines
    | }
Closing 3
Closing 2
Closing first
lines: scala.util.Try[Seq[String]] = Success(List(first line 1, first line 2, 2 line 1, 2 line 2, 3 line 1, 3 line 2))
```

The output in the console demonstrates that the result contains lines from all of the resources, and the resources themselves are automatically closed in the reverse order.

Now, after this small warm-up, we are ready to dive into the foundation of version 2.13—the new collection library.

The Scala 2.13 Collection Library

Scala 2.13 delivers a new collection library, for historical reasons it is also known as "collection - strawman". The refactoring of the library pursued a few main goals, such as fixing common gotchas of the previous version, simplifying its implementation and internal structure, as well as usage and backward-compatibility, achieving better integration with lazy collections and java streams and cleaner API separation between mutable and immutable collections, improving performance, and, last but not least, minimizing the migration effort from Scala 2.12's collections.

As a result, we have a library that is mostly source-compatible with the previous version, has many old methods and types (such as `Traversable`, `TraversableOnce`, and `Stream`) deprecated, and has a simpler internal hierarchy.

This book assumes that the reader has a rudimentary understanding of Scala collections. With this assumption, the next section will take a holistic approach and focus on giving a consistent overview of the new collection framework.

The next diagram represents the top-level hierarchy of the collection library:

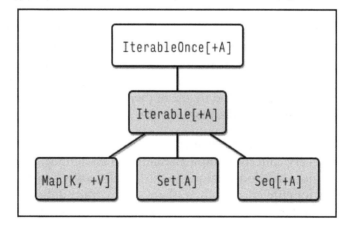

Here and further, we will pretend to always have `import scala.collections._` in the scope and use the following colour encoding in our diagrams:

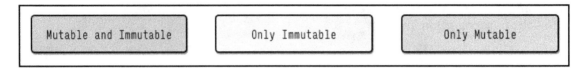

Each of the traits describes the structure, the *essence* of the collection. As the name suggests, `IterableOnce` can be iterated over only one time. `Iterable` softens this constraint so that it is possible to iterate over the collection multiple times. `Seq` adds a notion of succession to the elements of the collection, `Set` adds a constraint of the uniqueness of its elements, and `Map` changes the type of the collection from a single element, `A`, to a pair of key, `K`, and value, `V`.

As mentioned, in the spirit of the separation of concerns, these traits cover only the structural characteristics. The operations defined for the specific type are placed in the helper traits carrying the `Ops` suffix in the name. These traits form a hierarchical structure similar to the previous one, as shown here:

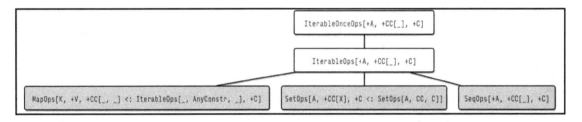

Where the "normal" traits had only one type parameter, the type of the element, the `Ops` have three of them. In addition to the type of the element, `A`, the `C` type describes the specific *representation* type of the collection this trait is mixed into and thus to the return type of the first-order methods defined on this collection. The `CC` type refers to the representation type that can be returned by the higher-order methods, or the type constructor. We will see later in this chapter how this works in practice.

Because the inheritance tree is structured as it is, `IterableOps` and `IterableOnceOps` are effectively mixed into every collection implementation in the library. Three traits on the bottom just add some more methods, unique to the specific collection type, and override some of the definitions for efficiency. Both `Iterable*Ops` traits define more than a hundred of methods and they are the reason the Scala collection library is very consistent and homogenous.

Because of the importance of `IterableOnceOps` and `IterableOps`, we will take a detailed look at them in the next section. After that, we will explore the unique features of the specialized collections.

IterableOnceOps

`IterableOnceOps` represents a blueprint for the collections that can be traversed one or multiple times. It defines a few abstract methods that must be implemented by every collection and a number of concrete methods implemented in terms of an iterator available from `IterableOnce`. The concrete methods provide default, if possible, lazy, implementations and fall into one of the following categories:

- **Size operations:** `isEmpty`, `nonEmpty`, `size`, `knownSize`, and `isTraversableAgain` check the collection for (non) emptiness or return its size. `knownSize` is an optimization that returns -1 if the size cannot be determined without iterating over the collection. `isTraversableAgain` returns `false` for `IterableOnce`.
- **Element tests:** `forall`, `exists`, and `count` check whether all, at least one, or some number of elements satisfy the given predicate.
- **String operations:** `mkString` and `addString`. These methods with different argument sets provide a possibility to build alternative string representation.
- **Conversions to another collections:** `copyToArray`, `toList`, `toMap`, `to`, `toSet`, `toSeq`, `toIndexedSeq`, `toBuffer`, and `toArray`. These methods copy or convert an `Iterable` into another collection. The `to` method is special in this list because it allows us to return any type of the collection that has a `Factory` available. We will look at it in more detail soon.
- **Fold and reduce:** `foldLeft`, `foldRight`, `reduce`, `reduceLeft`, `reduceRight`, `reduceOption`, `reduceLeftOption`, and `reduceRightOption` apply a binary operation to the elements of the collection. The `reduce*Option` methods handle the case of an empty collection gracefully by returning `None`.
- **Numeric combinations:** `sum` and `product` calculate the sum or product of the elements if there is an implicit `Numeric[B]` such that `B >: A` is available.
- **Ordering combinations:** `min`, `minOption`, `max`, `maxOption`, `maxBy`, `maxByOption`, `minBy`, and `minByOption` find an element of the collection that satisfies giving predicate if there is an implicit `Ordering[B]` with `B >: A` available. The `*Option` methods return `None` for an empty collection instead of throwing an exception.

- **Element retrieval:** `collectFirst` and `find`. Choose an element that satisfies a given condition.
- **Equality:** `corresponds` is an alternative way to compare collections. Satisfied if every element of this collection relates to matching element of another collection by given predicate.

Abstract methods fall into one of the following categories:

- **Subcollection retrieval:** `filter`, `filterNot`, `take`, `takeWhile`, `drop`, `dropWhile`, `slice`, and `span`. Take or discard elements that satisfy the given predicate or range, from the whole collection or beginning of it.
- **Mapping:** `map`, `flatMap`, `collect`, and `scanLeft`. Transforms elements of the collection by applying some function and possibly filtering the results.
- **Zippers:** `zipWithIndex` adds an index to all elements of the collection.

IterableOps

`IterableOps` extends `IterableOnceOps` and contains methods that is impossible to implement without a possibility to iterate over the collection multiple times.

They fall into the following categories:

- **Element retrieval:** `head`, `headOption`, `last`, and `lastOption` return the first or last element of the collection throwing `NoSuchElementException` or returning `None` for an empty collection.
- **Size:** `sizeCompare` is an optimization that allows us to efficiently compare the size of the collection with given value.
- **Subcollection retrieval:** `partition`, `partitionWith`, `splitAt`, `takeRight`, `dropRight`, `grouped`, `sliding`, `tail`, `init`, `groupBy`, `groupMap`, `groupMapReduce`, `tails`, and `inits`. These split the collection as defined by some predicate or index, take or drop elements from the end, group elements by some criteria or predicate possibly applying transformative function, and discard first or last elements.
- **Mapping:** `scanRight` produces a collection containing the cumulative results of applying the giving function starting from the end of the collection.
- **Addition:** `concat`, `++` returns another collection containing all elements of this collection and a collection provided as an argument.

- **Zippers:** `zip`, `zipAll`, `unzip`, and `unzip3` combine the elements of the collection with the elements of another collection into a product, or split them into separate collections.
- **Transformation:** `transpose` transforms the collection of collections by turning rows into columns and vice versa.

The following methods that defined the abstract in `IterableOnceOps` got a concrete default implementation in `IterableOps`: `filter`, `filterNot`, `take`, `takeWhile`, `span`, `drop`, `dropWile`, `slice`, `scanLeft`, `map`, `flatMap`, `flatten`, `collect`, and `zipWithIndex`. `isTraversableAgain` is overriden to return `true`.

It's worth noting that `Iterable` and `IterableOnce` do not support a general-equality operation, it is defined on specific collection subtypes. Because of this, it is impossible to compare these types directly using the equality operation, as the following example suggests:

```
scala> Set(1,2,3) == Seq(1,2,3)
res4: Boolean = false
```

Also there are three special methods that deserve our additional attention because they introduce types we haven't met yet:

- `def withFilter(p: A => Boolean): collection.WithFilter[A, CC]`
- `def iterableFactory: IterableFactory[CC]`
- `def view: View[A]`

Let's discuss them quickly before moving on to more specific collection types.

WithFilter

`WithFilter` is a template class that contains the `map`, `flatMap`, `foreach`, and `withFilter` methods of `Iterable`. It allows us to specialize mapping and filtering operations for distinguished collections.

Because of its technical nature, we won't go into further details here.

IterableFactory

`trait IterableFactory[+CC[_]]` is a base trait for companion objects for specific collections which provides a number of operations to create a specific collection with the type specified by the `CC` type constructor; this is sometimes called *target-type driven building* because the type of the source collection is ignored. Most of the companion objects in the collection library extend this trait, which makes it possible to use them in places where `IterableFactory` is expected.

As this is the main abstraction that allows to build a collection from scratch, it is useful to know which methods it supplies. All of them return `CC[A]`. The following table contains a short summary:

`def from[A](source: IterableOnce[A])`	Creates a target collection from existing `IterableOnce`.
`def empty[A]: CC[A]`	An empty collection, often defined as an object.
`def apply[A](elems: A*): CC[A]`	Creates a collection from the `elems` given as var-arg.
`def iterate[A](start: A, len: Int)(f: A => A): CC[A]`	Fills the collection with values taken from the result of the application of f on `start`, then on produced values and so on, `len` number of times.
`def range[A : Integral](start: A, end: A, step: A): CC[A]`	Collection containing increasing integers [`start`, `end`-1] with difference between successive numbers of `step`. There is also a version of this method with default value of `step` = 1.
`def fill[A](n: Int)(elem: => A): CC[A]`	Fills the collection with n evaluations of `elem`. There are variations of this function that go up to five dimensions.
`def tabulate[A](n: Int)(f: Int => A): CC[A]`	The same as `fill`, but using index as an argument for the evaluation. Similarly, there are variations of this function that go up to five dimensions.
`def concat[A](xss: Iterable[A]*): CC[A]`	Concatenates all argument collections into a single collection.
`def unfold[A, S](init: S)(f: S => Option[(A, S)]): CC[A]`	Calls f to produce the element of the collection using and modifying the internal state starting with the `init` state.

Arguably, `IterableFactory` provides a lot of different possibilities to create a collection of a desired type.

View

`View` has been reimplemented in the new version of the library. Now it represents a reified `Iterator` operations.

Reification is the process by which an abstract idea about a computer program is turned into an explicit data model or other object created in a programming language (https://en.wikipedia.org/wiki/Reification_(computer_science)).

This means that the `Iterator` methods are represented as a subclasses of `View` and encapsulate transformations to apply. The evaluation happens at the moment the view is converted to the strict collection type, or traversed, for example using the `foreach` method. Views don't *remember* the type of the source collection. This can be demonstrated by the following example. First, we define a generic transformation that might be strict or lazy, depending on the type of the collection given as an argument:

```
def transform[C <: Iterable[Char]](i: C): Iterable[Char] = i
map { c => print(s"-$c-"); c.toUpper }
take { println("\ntake");  6 }
```

Next, for each transformation step, we print out its result in the console at the moment the step happens. Now we can compare lazy and strict collection behaviors:

```
val str = "Scala 2.13"
val view: StringView = StringView(str)
val transformed = transform(view)      // A
val strict = transform(str.toList)    // B
print("Lazy view constructed: ")
transformed.foreach(print) // C
print("\nLazy view forced: ")
println(transformed.to(List)) // D
println(s"Strict: $strict") // E
```

This snippet produces the following output in the REPL:

```
take
-S--c--a--l--a-- --2--.--1--3-
take
Lazy view constructed: -S-S-c-C-a-A-l-L-a-A- -
Lazy view forced: -S--c--a--l--a-- -List(S, C, A, L, A, )
Strict: List(S, C, A, L, A, )
```

In the first line, we can see that the `take` method is always evaluated strictly regardless of the underlying collection type—this is commented as A in the preceding code. The second and third lines show the strict evaluation for `List[Char]`, line B in the code. Lines 4 and 5 demonstrate that `View[Char]` is then evaluated twice, each time at the moment it is forced, once by calling `foreach` (line C) and once by converting it to the `List` (line D). Also interesting is that `map` is only applied to the results of the `take` method even given the fact that `map` is the first transformation step in the chain.

Set

Set is a base trait for collections that have a notion of uniques of the elements. It is defined as trait Set[A] extends Iterable[A] with SetOps[A, Set, Set[A]] with Equals. We can see that it is effectively an Iterable that has some additional operations defined in SetOps and adds a notion of equality among sets. The sub-hierarchy of Set is represented in the following diagram:

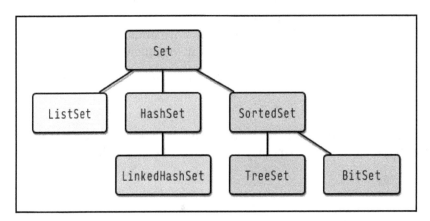

The previously mentioned SetOps adds a few methods on top of IterableOps. These methods are shown here:

- **Element retrieval:** contains and apply return true if this set contains a given element.
- **Equality:** subsetOf and subsets check whether this set is a subset of another set, or return all subsets of this set, possibly with a given size.
- **Combinations with another set:** intersect, &, diff, &~, concat, ++, union, and |. These methods compute the intersection, difference, or union of this and another set.

There are few classes in the hierarchy that augment Set with further properties:

- **SortedSet** extends Set with SortedOps[A, +C] and has two immutable and two mutable implementations—two TreeSets and two BitSets. SortedOps embodies following methods that depend on the notion of Ordering:
- **Key retrieval:** firstKey and lastKey return the first or last element of this collection.
- **Subcollection retrieval:** range, rangeFrom, rangeUntil, and rangeTo create a ranged projection of this collection, satisfying given criteria.

Because of the overloading, `SortedSet` has many overloaded methods defined twice, with and without ordering. If an operation is intended to be applied to the underlying unsorted `Set`, the type has to be coerced:

```scala
scala> import scala.collection.SortedSet
import scala.collection.SortedSet
scala> val set = SortedSet(1,2,3)
set: scala.collection.SortedSet[Int] = TreeSet(1, 2, 3)
scala> val ordered = set.map(math.abs)
ordered: scala.collection.SortedSet[Int] = TreeSet(1, 2, 3)
scala> val unordered = set.to(Set).map(math.abs)
unordered: scala.collection.immutable.Set[Int] = Set(1, 2, 3)
```

Please note that direct type-ascription will not work in the case of `Set` because its definition is invariant:

```scala
scala> val set1: Set[Int] = SortedSet(1,2,3)
                                     ^
        error: type mismatch;
         found : scala.collection.SortedSet[Int]
         required: Set[Int]
```

The invariance of `Set` is related to the fact that `Set[A]` extends a function, `A => Boolean`, that returns `true` if the set contains a given element. Thus, sets can be used in places where such one argument function is expected:

```scala
scala> ordered.forall(set)
res3: Boolean = true
```

There are four more specific set implementations in addition to `TreeSet` and `BitSet`:

- `ListSet` implements immutable sets using a list-based data structure.
- The immutable HashSet realizes immutable sets using a Compressed Hash-Array Mapped Prefix-tree (CHAMP)
- The mutable `HashSet` and `LinkedHashSet` implement mutable sets using a hash table, storing the data unordered and ordered, respectively.

The sets are closely related to `Map`, which represents a collection with elements represented as a pair of keys and values.

Map

`Map` is defined as `trait Map[K, +V] extends Iterable[(K, V)] with MapOps[K, V, Map, Map[K, V]] with Equals` which makes it an `Iterable` over pairs of key, `K`, and value, `V`. It also defines a notion of equality among maps. The class hierarchy for `Map` is represented on the following diagram:

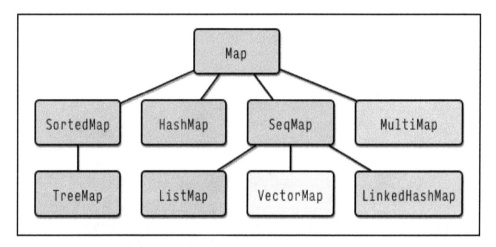

There are three different `MapOps`, one general for both mutable and immutable, and one specific for each of these forms.

`MapOps` extends `IterableOps` with the following specific operations:

- **Element retrieval:** `get`, `getOrElse`, `apply`, `applyOrElse`, `default`, `contains`, and `isDefinedAt`. These methods allow us to retrieve a value or check whether a value is present by a given key, optionally returning a default value or throwing an exception if the key can't be found.
- **Subcollection retrieval:** `keySet`, `keys`, `values`, `keysIterator`, and `valuesIterator` allow us to get a keys or values in different forms.
- **Mapping:** `map`, `flatMap`, and `collect` are transforming and optionally filtering the pairs of keys and values.
- **Addition:** `concat` returns a new collection with elements of both maps combined.

`immutable.MapOps` adds the following methods on top of `MapOps`:

- **Element removal**: `remove`, `removeAll`, `--` removes one or all given elements from the map returning new map.
- **Element updates**: `updated` and + update an element with the given key returning new map.
- **Mapping:** `transform` applies a given function to all elements, producing a new map with the returned results as values.

`mutable.MapOps` has a different set of methods as compared to the mutable one:

- **Element addition:** `put` adds a new value or updates existing one.
- **Element update:** `updated`, +, and `getOrElseUpdate` updates a value in place.
- **Element removal:** `remove` and `clear` remove one or all elements of the map.
- **Filtering:** `filterInPlace` retains only mappings that satisfy the predicate.
- **Mapping:** `mapValuesInPlace` applies a transformation to the values of the map, storing returned results as values.

The general `Map` definition has quite a few specialized subtypes, as shown in the preceding diagram. We will take a quick look at them now.

SortedMap

`SortedMap` is similar to `SortedSet`. It has a two implementations, a mutable and immutable `TreeMap`, and provides a few methods defined in terms of `SortedOps` such as:

- **Subcollection retrieval:**
  `iteratorFrom`, `keysIteratorFrom`, `valuesIteratorFrom`, and `rangeTo` give us a way to get elements of the map as an iterator.
- **Element retrieval:** `firstKey`, `lastKey`, `minAfter`, and `maxBefore` allow us to retrieve an element that satisfies some ordering condition.

HashMap

`HashMap` is also available in two flavors—immutable and mutable.

The immutable `HashMap` is implemented using a CHAMP tree.

The mutable `HashMap` implements mutable maps using a hashtable. A hash table stores its elements in an array. The hash code of the item is used to calculate the position in the array.

MultiMap

`MultiMap` is a trait for mutable maps that have multiple values assigned to a key.

It defines the `addBinding`, `removeBinding` and `entryExists` methods, which can be used to query or manipulate entries for a key.

SeqMap

`SeqMap` is a generic abstraction for ordered immutable maps. `SeqMap` itself exists in mutable and immutable forms. These forms have few different implementations:

- The immutable **ListMap** implements immutable maps using a list-based data structure. The methods traversing `ListMap` visit its elements in the order they were inserted.
- The mutable **ListMap** is a simple mutable map backed by a list. It preserves insertion order as its immutable sibling does.
- **VectorMap** exists only in immutable form. It is implemented using a vector/map-based data structure and preserves insertion order. It has constant lookup but slower other operations.
- **LinkedHashMap** is a mutable map whose implementation is based on a hashtable and preserves the insertion order if iterated over.

Seq

`Seq` is probably the most ubiquitous collection in the library. Like `Map`, it has a notion of succession of elements and the elements have indices. It is defined as `trait Seq[+A] extends Iterable[A] with PartialFunction[Int, A] with SeqOps[A, Seq, Seq[A]] with Equals`. Also similar to map, `Seq` specifies support for the equality relation and also extends `PartialFunction`, which accepts an index of the element as a parameter. As there are a lots of classes implementing `Seq`, we will take a gradual approach and look at them level by level. The direct children of `Seq` are shown in the following diagram:

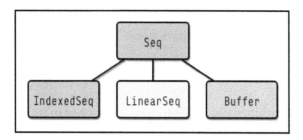

`scala.Seq`, known from previous Scala versions, is now replaced by `scala.collection.immutable.Seq`.

As with other collections, `SeqOps` extend `IterableOps` by adding quite a few methods:

- **Element retrieval:** `apply` retrieves an element with a given index.
- **Indexing and search:** `segmentLength`, `isDefinedAt`, `indexWhere`, `indexOf`, `lastIndexOf`, `lastIndexWhere`, `indexOfSlice`, `lastIndexOfSlice`, `containsSlice`, `contains`, `startsWith`, `endsWith`, `indices`, and `search`. These methods allow us to retrieve information about the presence or indexes of elements or subsequences given some predicate or element value.
- **Size:** `length` and `lengthCompare` provide efficient operations to retrieve the length of the collection.
- **Addition:** `prepend`, `+`, `appended`, `:+`, `prependAll`, `++`, `appendedAll`, `:++`, `concat`, and `union`. Can be used to append or prepend one or multiple elements to the collection.
- **Filtering:** `distinct` and `distinctBy` remove duplicates, possibly given some predicate.
- **Reversal:** `reverse` and `reverseIterator` return a new collection with elements in the reversed order.
- **Sorting:** `sorted`, `sortWith`, and `sortBy` sort this collection by some implicit `Ordering`, or by a given function, or both.
- **Equality:** `sameElements` and `corresponds` check whether this collection contains the same elements in the same order as given, using equality-checking or the provided comparison function.
- **Subcollection retrieval:** `permutations` and `combinations`. These methods allow us to retrieve a subcollection(s) that satisfies given conditions.
- **Updates:** `diff`, `intersect`, `patch`, `updated`, and `update` (mutable). Modify elements of this collection using another collection or element and returning another collection (except the last method defined on `mutable.Seq`, which update elements in place).

Each of the `Seq` direct descendants has its own specific properties and a subtree of implementations. We'll breeze through them now.

IndexedSeq

`IndexedSeq` does not introduce new operations, at least not in its immutable incarnation, but overrides a lots of methods defined in `SeqOps` to provide more efficient implementations. There are four classes implementing it:

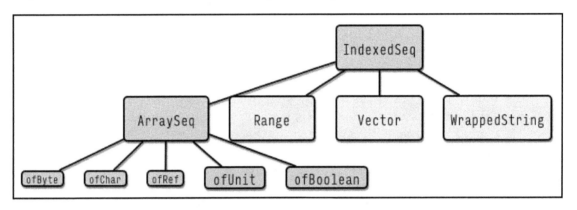

The `mutable`. **IndexedSeq** adds the following **mutation options**: `mapInPlace`, `sortInPlace`, `sortInPlaceWith`, and `sortInPlaceBy`.

The `mutable`. **ArraySeq** is a collection representing an `Array`. It defines an `array` method returning an underlying array, and an `elemTag` method that returns the tag of the element type needed to properly support different kinds of arrays as required by the JVM. Because of this requirement, it has separate implementations for all primitive types including numeric types (in addition to `ofByte`, there are implementations for all other numeric primitives, not shown on the diagram) and `Boolean`, `AnyRef` and `Unit`.

The `immutable`. **ArraySeq** was added in the version 2.13. It is an effectively an immutable sequence that wraps an array and is used to pass varargs parameters. It has the same descendants as its mutable cousin.

Range is an immutable structure that contains integer values. It is defined by `start`, `end`, and a `step`. There are two additional methods available: `isInclusive`, which is `true` for `Range.Inclusive` and `false` for `Range.Exclusive`, and `by`, which creates the new range with a different `step` but the same `start` and `end`.

Vector is an immutable structure that provides constant-time access and updates and fast append and prepend. Because of this, `Vector` is the default implementation for `IndexedSeq`, as demonstrated in the following snippet:

```
scala> IndexedSeq.fill(2)("A")
res6: IndexedSeq[String] = Vector(A, A)
```

`WrappedString` is an immutable wrapper over some `String`. It extends strings with all of the operations defined in `IndexedSeqOps`.

LinearSeq

Linear sequences have the notion of a head and a tail. The definition looks like `trait LinearSeq[+A] extends Seq[A] with LinearSeqOps[A, LinearSeq, LinearSeq[A]]` and the class diagram is shown here:

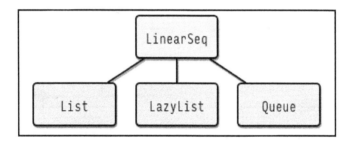

There are three representatives of `LinearSeq`, all are immutable:

- **List** defines three symbolic methods which provide a nice syntax for pattern-matching and building lists. `::` prepends element to the list, `:::` prepends all elements of a given list, and `reverse_:::` prepends all elements of a given list but in the reverse order.
- **LazyList** is a new immutable collection available since Scala 2.13. It implements a list with a `head` and a `tail`, which are not evaluated until needed. As it is superior to `Stream`, which is only lazy in the tail, `Stream` is now deprecated. `LazyList` has two additional methods, `force` which evaluates it, and `lazyAppendAll` which lazily appends a given collection to this list.
- **Queue** in this hierarchy is also immutable. It allows a first-in-first-out (FIFO) insertion and retrieval of the elements. For this functionality, it defines the `enqueue`, `enqueueAll`, `dequeue`, `dequeueOption`, and `front` methods.

Buffers

`Buffers` conclude our rush through the collection library. In essence, `Buffer` is just a `Seq` that can grow and shrink. This sub-hierarchy exists only in immutable form, though `IndexedBuffer` inherits from both Buffer and `IndexedSeq`, as shown by the next diagram:

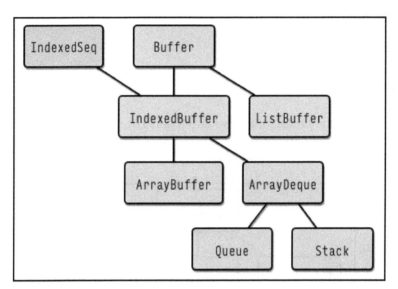

Let's take a look at the methods that these collections define, in addition to the definitions inherited from `SeqOps`:

- **Buffer** defines methods to add or remove one or more elements in place or returning new buffer: `prepend`, `append`, `appendAll`, `+=:`, `prependAll`, `++=:`, `insert`, `insertAll`, `remove`, `subtractOne`, `trimStart`, `trimEnd`, `patchInPlace`, `dropInPlace`, `dropRightInPlace`, `takeRightInPlace`, `sliceInPlace`, `dropWhileInPlace`, `takeWhileInPlace`, and `padToInPlace`.

- **ListBuffer** is a concrete buffer implementation baked by a `List`. In addition to other discussed methods, it provides `prependToList`, which allows us to prepend this collection to another list and a triple of `mapInPlace`, `flatMapInPlace`, and `filterInPlace`, giving us a possibility to modify elements in place.

- Take a `Buffer`, add an `IndexedSeq`, and you'll get an **IndexedBuffer**. Similar to `ListBuffer`, it provides the `flatMapInPlace` and `filterInPlace` methods.

- **ArrayBuffer** is a concrete implementation of `IndexedBuffer` that uses an array to store its elements and has a constant time for append, update, and random access. It has a `sizeHint` method, which can be used to enlarge the underlying array. It is a default implementation instantiated if `mutable.Seq` is created.

- **ArrayDeque** is another efficient collection that emerged in the 2.13 version. It implements a double-ended queue that internally uses a resizable circular buffer. This allows to have a constant time for append, prepend, remove first, remove last, and random-access operations. There are lots of additional methods available on this collection, mostly because of the notion of the second-end: `removeHeadOption`, `removeHead`, `removeLastOption`, `removeLast`, `removeAll`, `removeAllReverse`, `removeHeadWhile`, `removeLastWhile`, `removeFirst`, `removeAll`, `clearAndShrink`, `copySliceToArray`, and `trimToSize`.

- The **Queue** in this hierarchy is mutable. It is based on `ArrayDeque` and allows us to insert and retrieve elements in the FIFO manner. The following methods are available for that: `enqueue`, `enqueueAll`, `dequeue`, `dequeueFirst`, `dequeueAll`, and `dequeueWhile`.

- The **Stack** is similar to `Queue`, but it implements in last-in-first-out (LIFO) order instead of FIFO. The methods it defines are formulated in the corresponding terms: `push`, `pushAll`, `pop`, `popAll`, `popWhile`, and `top`.

Scala Collection Contrib library

Needless to say, the standard Scala collection library is very rich and provides collections for most of the common use cases. But of course, there are some other structures that might be useful in a number of specific situations. The Scala Collection `Contrib` module is Scala's way of having both a stable standard library and some extra features. In a sense, this module is an incubator for the new collection types; types that prove to be useful for a broad audience will presumably be incorporated into the standard library in further Scala versions.

Currently, there are four collection types available in the module, each both mutable and immutable:

- `MultiDict`
- `SortedMultiDict`
- `MultiSet`
- `SortedMultiSet`

Also this library provides a possibility to define additional operations on existing collections via an implicit enrichment. The following import is required to make it available:

```
import scala.collection.decorators._
```

And it delivers these methods:

- On Seq: `intersperse` and `replaced`
- On Map: `zipByKey`, `join`, `zipByKeyWith`, `mergeByKey`, `mergeByKeyWith`, `fullOuterJoin`, `leftOuterJoin`, and `rightOUterJoing`

Please consult the module documentation at `https://github.com/scala/scala-collection-contrib` for further details.

Summary

Scala 2.13 is a minor update of Scala with the main focus on the redesigned collection library. The few small additions to the standard library, such as automatic resource management, just accentuate this fact.

The new collection library mainly consists of two intermixed inheritance hierarchies with a similar shape. Members of the first hierarchy describe the structure of the collection and members of the second hierarchy—operations available on this collection type. Because of the inheritance relations, the collections situated lower in the tree define additional methods for more specific collections and override methods defined by the parent traits to provide more efficient implementation as required.

The three main collection types are `Seq`, `Set`, and `Map`. Each of these types has multiple implementations that are useful in specific situations. Set is also a function of one argument; `Seq` and `Map` are `PartialFunctions`.

Most of the collections are available in mutable and immutable forms.

In addition to the collection hierarchies, there is a concept of View, which is a reified definition of iterators' operations and can be used to lazily apply transformations to the collection. Another related abstraction is `IterableFactory`, which implements some general ways to create collection instances and to perform conversions between collection representations.

In the next chapter, we will shift our focus from the new features of version 2.13 to a general exploration of Scala, starting with its type system.

Questions

1. Describe two ways to make it possible for some resource, R, to use it together with `scala.util.Using` resource management utility.
2. How can an instance of a `Set` and an instance of a `List` be compared to each other?
3. Name the default concrete implementation for an immutable `Seq`.
4. Name the default concrete implementation for an immutable indexed `Seq`.
5. Name the default concrete implementation for a mutable `Seq`.
6. Name the default concrete implementation for a mutable indexed `Seq`.
7. It is sometimes said that `List.flatMap` is more powerful than it was expected to be. Can you explain why?
8. Describe a way to map over a collection multiple times using different functions but without producing intermediate collections.

Further reading

- Mads Hartmann, Ruslan Shevchenko, Professional Scala: Write concise and expressive, type-safe code in an environment that lets you build for the JVM, browser, and more.

- Vikash Sharma, *Learning Scala Programming: Learn how to write scalable and concurrent programs in Scala, a language that grows with you.*

Understanding Types in Scala 2

The strong type system is one of the most important parts of the Scala language. Like a double-edged sword, it helps the compiler to verify and optimize the code on one side, while at the same time guiding developers toward possible correct implementations and preventing them from making programming mistakes on another side. As with any sharp tool, it requires some skill so that it can be used for carving beautiful source code without cutting the user in the process.

In this chapter, we will improve this skill by recapping and summarizing basic type-related knowledge, taking a look at a new type that was introduced in Scala 2.13, and finally looking at some advanced usages of types.

The following topics will be covered in this chapter:

- Different ways to create a type
- Different ways to parameterize a type
- Kinds of types
- Using types to express domain constraints

Technical requirements

Before we begin, make sure you have the following installed:

- JDK 1.8+
- SBT 1.2+

The source code for this chapter is available under our GitHub repository at: `https://github.com/PacktPublishing/Learn-Scala-Programming/tree/master/Chapter02`.

Understanding types

The type of something is a summation of the information the compiler owns about this *something*. In the most general case, we're talking about the type of a variable; the knowledge of the compiler includes the methods that are available on this variable and the classes that the variable extends. A very convenient feature of Scala is that it tries to use type inference where possible, freeing the developer from the need to define types explicitly.

Let's take a structured look at Scala's type system, starting with a short recap of its basics.

Ways to create a type

There are four ways to define a type in Scala:

- By using a literal to define a singleton type
- By using the type keyword to define an alias for an abstract or concrete type
- By defining a class, object, or trait to create a concrete type
- By defining a method that creates a method type

Singleton types were introduced in Scala 2.13, and we'll look at them in detail later in this chapter. For now, let's try to define and refer to some concrete types in Scala REPL:

```
scala> class SomeClass
defined class SomeClass
scala> object SomeObject
defined object SomeObject
scala> :type SomeObject
SomeObject.type
scala> :type new SomeClass
SomeClass
scala> trait SomeTrait {
     | def usage(a: SomeClass, b: SomeObject.type): SomeTrait
     | }
defined trait SomeTrait
```

The type can be referred before it is fully defined, as shown by the example of `SomeTrait`.

When annotating types, traits and classes can be used directly, but the type of an object needs to be referenced by using its `type` operator. The `a.type` form in Scala describes a *singleton type*. Depending upon whether `p` conforms to `scala.AnyRef`, it denotes either a set of values, `[a, null]`, or just an `a`. As we usually don't use `null` in Scala programs, we can say that `a.type` denotes a type containing a single element, `a`. Normally, it is not used in *regular* code because it is easier to reference an object directly than to pass it as a parameter, but this style has found its use in some advanced libraries to implement parts of the internal DSL.

In Scala 2.13, there is a new marker trait `Singleton` that can be applied as an upper bound on a type parameter, which indicates that the singleton type should be inferred for this parameter:

```
scala> def singleIn[T <: Singleton](t: T): T = t
singleIn: [T <: Singleton](t: T)T

scala> final val t = singleIn(42)
t: 42 = 42
```

A *method type* does not denote a value, nor does it appear directly in the program. It is an internal representation of a method definition. It is represented as a sequence of parameter names with respective types and a return type of the method. The method type is important into know about because, if a method name is used as a value, its type is implicitly converted to the corresponding function type. As we defined in the `usage` method, the compiler internally created a method type called `(a: SomeClass, b: SomeObject.type)SomeTrait`.

Literal types

Scala 2.13 introduced a special kind of singleton type—the *literal type*. It denotes a single value of some literal and represents the most precise type of this literal. It is available for all types for which literal syntax is available (for example, `Boolean`, `Char`, `String`, and `Symbol`). It is impossible to define a literal type for `Unit` (by specification) and for `Byte` and `Short` (because there is no syntax to define literals of such types). This is how it works in practice:

```
scala> def bool2String(b: true) = "ja"
bool2String: (b: true)String
scala> bool2String(true)
res7: String = ja
scala> bool2String(false)
          ^
```

```
error: type mismatch;
found : Boolean(false)
required: true
```

There are two ways to define a variable of a literal type. The first way is by using an explicit type ascription, and the second way is by making it a non-lazy `final`:

```
scala> val a1: true = true
a1: true = true

scala> bool2String(a1)
res10: String = ja

scala> final val a2 = true
a2: Boolean(true) = true

scala> bool2String(a2)
res11: String = ja

scala> // but

scala> val a3 = true
a3: Boolean = true

scala> bool2String(a3)
                  ^
        error: type mismatch;
         found : a3.type (with underlying type Boolean)
         required: true
```

A literal type is erased to the normal type during compilation, and so it is not possible to override methods using literal types:

```
scala> object scope {
 | def bool2String(b: true) = "ja"
 | def bool2String(b: false) = "nein"
 | }
 def bool2String(b: false) = "nein"
 ^
On line 3: error: double definition:
 def bool2String(b: true): String at line 2 and
 def bool2String(b: false): String at line 3
 have same type after erasure: (b: Boolean)String
```

In the previous snippet, the compiler prevented us from declaring two methods with the same name, and so took a parameter with a different literal type because of the erasure.

The singleton type forming the .type operator can be used to specify that a function should return a literal type and not a normal type, as demonstrated by the type of t inferred by the compiler—42:

```scala
scala> def singleOut[T](t: T): t.type = t
singleOut: [T](t: T)t.type

scala> final val t = singleOut(42)
t: 42 = 42
```

Since Scala 2.13, there is a type class called scala.ValueOf[T] and an operator called scala.Predef.valueOf[T] that can be used to yield values for singleton types. This is how valueOf[T] is defined:

```scala
def valueOf[T](implicit vt: ValueOf[T]): T = vt.value
```

And this is how it can be used:

```scala
scala> final val a = valueOf[42]
a: 42 = 42
```

The pattern matching against literal types also works as expected, though the syntax is unusual and probably not very useful, as demonstrated by this first case:

```scala
scala> def int2str(i: Int) = i match {
     |   case t: 42 => "forty-two"
     |   case ii => ii.toString
     | }
int2str: (i: Int)String

scala> int2str(42)
res24: String = forhty-two

scala> int2str(43)
res25: String = 43
```

These literal types are probably not very interesting for day-to-day programming, but are very useful for type-level library development.

Compound (intersection) types

A compound type is defined as a combination of zero or more component types with a refinement. If no refinement is provided, an implicit empty one ({ }) is added by the compiler. Depending on the number of components, we can have the following cases:

- If just a refinement is given, the compound type is equivalent to extending AnyRef
- A single type is extended by using the corresponding extends keyword
- Two or more types are combined by interleaving them with the with keyword

In the case of a name clash in combined types and/or refinement, the usual override rules apply. This means that the rightmost type or refinement has the highest priority. This combination also represents an inheritance relation, and it is possible to access members of extended types with the use of the super keyword.

The compound type is easy to imagine as a layer of wrappers. Because of this, the process of resolving conflicting members in traits is called **trait linearisation**, while the decorator design pattern is called **stackable traits**. The following example demonstrates how layers of traits can access methods defined on subtypes of the compound type to implement a decorated toString representation:

```scala
scala> trait A { override def toString = "A" }
defined trait A

scala> trait B { override def toString = super.toString + "B" }
defined trait B

scala> trait C { override def toString = super.toString + "C" }
defined trait C

scala> class E extends A with B with C {
     | override def toString: String = super.toString + "D"
     | }
defined class E

scala> new E().toString
res28: String = ABCD
```

The definition of type contains just a refinement in the case of zero components being extended. This way of defining a type is known as a **structural type**. The use of structural types is generally discouraged in Scala because it can lead to a generation of bytecode that will access structurally defined members using reflection, which is significantly slower. Nevertheless, it is useful to define type lambdas, which we will take a look at near the end of this chapter.

Type constraints

Type constraints are rules associated with a type. They define a subset of all types that, for example, a variable can have. A type constraint takes the form of lower bound (subtype relation) or upper bound (supertype relation). It is possible to define multiple constraints for a single type. In this case, a type must satisfy both of them. Constraints are defined using the symbols >: (lower, unhappy bound) and <: (upper, happy bound), and the direction of the sign corresponds to the reversed direction of the arrow on the UML diagram, as shown in the following screenshot:

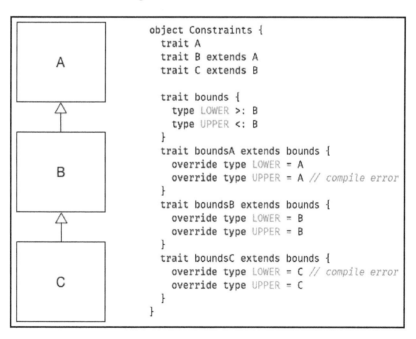

```
object Constraints {
  trait A
  trait B extends A
  trait C extends B

  trait bounds {
    type LOWER >: B
    type UPPER <: B
  }
  trait boundsA extends bounds {
    override type LOWER = A
    override type UPPER = A // compile error
  }
  trait boundsB extends bounds {
    override type LOWER = B
    override type UPPER = B
  }
  trait boundsC extends bounds {
    override type LOWER = C // compile error
    override type UPPER = C
  }
}
```

The type constraints are inclusive, which is why type B represents both the upper and lower bounds. Besides B in our type hierarchy, only A obeys the LOWER type constraint and only C obeys the UPPER constraint.

Scala's types hierarchy and special types

Type constraints in combination with Scala's type hierarchy give us a few interesting classes that are important to know about. To recap, the type hierarchy is represented in the following diagram:

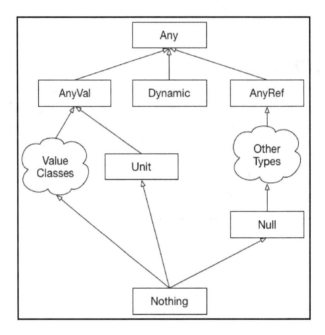

In Scala, all types have a maximum upper bound of **Any** and a lower bound of **Nothing**.

Value Classes is a Scala way to avoid allocating runtime objects. This works by wrapping JVM's primitive types. Scala already represents numeric types and `Boolean` and `Char` as **AnyVal**, and it is possible to implement custom value classes by extending **AnyVal** and obeying a few restrictions. An interesting subtype of **AnyVal** is a **Unit** type, which represents a case where something unimportant needs to be returned from a function or a method. It roughly corresponds to the void return type and has a single member, `()`.

AnyRef is a representation of any type that is allocated at runtime. In JVM, it is possible to have `null` in a place where an object reference is expected; the type of `null` is `Null`. The `Null` type has a single inhabitant, `null`, the same way `Unit` has a single value of `()`.

`Nothing` is a special subtype of every other type and has no members. Because of this, it is not possible to instantiate members of that type. As a result, it is useful to indicate that the only possibility for a method or function to terminate is to do this abnormally, usually by throwing an exception.

There are two traits that are not represented in the preceding diagram, `Serializable` and `Product`. The former marker trait is used to tell the JVM that some class should be serializable across platforms, and it just delegates to Java's interface, `java.io.Serializable`.

The `Product` stays for the Cartesian product, which is basically just an ordered set of pairs of named types. In Scala, `Product` is extended by tuples and case classes.

The `Self` type is another special notion in Scala that's used to define dependencies between traits without declaring an extension relation. This syntax allows you to bring in the scope of the trait members from other traits, as shown in the following code:

```
trait A { def a: String }
trait B { def b: String }
trait C { this: A => // override `this`
  def c = this.a
}
trait D { self: A with B => // any alias is allowed; mixed traits
  def d = this.a + this.b
}
```

The last member in our zoo of special types is `Dynamic`. This is a marker trait that allows you to use the dynamic invocation of methods (also known as **duck typing**).

It feels a bit inappropriate to go into the details of `Dynamic` here because Scala's strength is exactly the opposite—to express knowledge about the system statically using proper types. For curious readers, official documentation on this is available here: `https://www.scala-lang.org/api/current/scala/Dynamic.html`.

Type inference

The preceding type hierarchy is quite important for understanding how type inference works. Type inference is a mechanism that the compiler uses to guess the type of an expression or a method if the definition of its type is omitted. The same also applies to the type parameters of polymorphic methods or generic classes and sometimes to anonymous function parameter types as well. This inference aims to provide the most specific type possible while obeying all of the existing constraints. The compiler does this by walking the hierarchy tree and finding the *least upper bound*. Let's look at an example:

```
case class C(); class D(); case class E()

def iOrB(i: Int, s: Boolean)(b: Boolean): AnyVal = if (b) i else s
def iOrS(i: Int, s: String)(b: Boolean): Any = if (b) i else s

def sOrC(c: C, s: String)(b: Boolean): java.io.Serializable = if (b) c else
s
def cOrD(c: C, d: D)(b: Boolean): AnyRef = if (b) c else d
def cOrE(c: C, e: E)(b: Boolean): Product with Serializable = if (b) c else
e
```

Here, we specified the return types as the compiler infers them. For the first two cases, you can easily follow the hierarchy of Scala types to understand how the compiler did the inference. The last three are a bit more complicated:

- In sOrC, the inferred type is java.io.Serializable. The reason for this is that Scala's String is just an alias for java.lang.String, which extends java.io.Serializable. All case classes in Scala extend Product with Serializable by default and Serializable extends java.io.Serializable. Therefore, java.io.Serializable is the least upper bound in this case.
- In cOrD, D is not a case class, and therefore it does not extend anything but the AnyRef, which becomes an inferred type.
- In cOrE, both C and E are case classes, and so the compiler can infer the most specific type, that is, Product with Serializable.

In fact, the preciseness of the compiler can go quite far, as the following example demonstrates:

```
trait Foo { def foo: Int }
case class F() extends Foo {def foo: Int = 0}
case class G() extends Foo {def foo: Int = 0}

def fOrG(f: F, g: G)(b: Boolean):
  Product with Serializable with Foo = if (b) f else g
```

Here, we can see that the inferred type of `fOrG` is a compound type with three members.

Path-dependent types

Until now, we have avoided talking about paths, mostly because they are not types themselves. However, they can be a part of named types, and thus have an important role in Scala's type system.

A path can have one of the following forms:

- An empty path, denoted with ε. It cannot be written directly, but implicitly precedes any other path.
- `C.this`, where `C` is a reference class. This is the path that is constructed if `this` is used inside of a class.
- `C.super.x.` or `C.super[P].` refers to the member x of the superclass or designated parent class, `P` of `C`. It plays the same role as `this` for the class, but refers to the classes that are upper in the hierarchy.
- `p.x`, where `p` is a path and `x` is a stable member of `p`. The stable member is an object definition or a value definition for which it is possible for the compiler to tell that it will always be accessible (as opposed to the volatile type where it is not possible, for example, there is an abstract type definition that can be overridden by a subclass).

Types within the path can be referred to by two operators, # (hash) and . (dot). The former is known as **type projection**, and `T#m` refers to the type member m of the type `T`. We can demonstrate the difference between these operators by building a type-safe lock:

```
case class Lock() {
  final case class Key()
  def open(key: Key): Lock = this
  def close(key: Key): Lock = this
  def openWithMaster(key: Lock#Key): Lock = this
  def makeKey: Key = new Key
```

```
    def makeMasterKey: Lock#Key = new Key
}
```

Here, we defined a type, `Lock`, with a nested type, `Key`. The key can be referenced using its path, `Lock.Key`, or by using a projection, `Lock#Key`. The former denotes a type tied to a specific instance, and the latter denotes a type that is not. The specific types of key are returned by two different constructor methods. The `makeKey` return type is a `Key` that is a shortcut for `this.Key`, which in turn is an alias for `Lock.this.type#Key` and represents a *path-dependent type*. The latter is just a type projection, `Lock#Key`. Because the path-dependent type refers to the concrete instance, the compiler will only allow the use of the appropriate type to call the `open` and `close` methods:

```
val blue: Lock = Lock()
val red: Lock = Lock()
val blueKey: blue.Key = blue.makeKey
val anotherBlueKey: blue.Key = blue.makeKey
val redKey: red.Key = red.makeKey

blue.open(blueKey)
blue.open(anotherBlueKey)
blue.open(redKey) // compile error
red.open(blueKey) // compile error
```

The `masterKey` is not path-dependent, and so can be used to call methods on any instance in a typical way:

```
val masterKey: Lock#Key = red.makeMasterKey

blue.openWithMaster(masterKey)
red.openWithMaster(masterKey)
```

These path-dependent types conclude our journey regarding concrete types and can be used to describe values. All of the types we've seen so far (except method types) are named *value types* to reflect this fact. A named value type is called a **type designator**. All type designators are shorthand for type projections.

We will now switch gears and inspect how types can be used to narrate definitions of other types.

Types – all the way down

Up until now, we have only talked about concrete types. Despite being quite simple, they already allow for the expression of a lot of properties of a program on the type level and they have these properties verified at compile time. Scala gives the developer even more freedom by allowing them to use types as parameters while defining methods, classes, or other types. In the next section, we will look at different ways to do this, starting with basic type parameters and type member definition, and continuing with type constraints and variance topics. We'll conclude our discussion with higher kinded types and type lambdas.

Type parameters

Type parameters are defined using square brackets []. If applied to classes and methods, they must be declared before normal parameters, and the result is known as a **parameterized type**:

```
case class Wrapper[A](content: A) {
  def unwrap: A = content
}
def createWrapper[A](a: A):Wrapper[A] = Wrapper(a)
type ConcreteWrapper[A] = Wrapper[A]

val wInt: Wrapper[Int] = createWrapper[Int](10)
val wLong: ConcreteWrapper[Long] = createWrapper(10L)
val int: Int = wInt.unwrap
val long: Long = wLong.unwrap
```

The `Wrapper` class is parameterized by the `A` type. This type parameter is used to refer to the type of content in the `unwrap` method. The scope resolution rules apply to the type parameters the same way as they do to the normal parameters, as shown by the `unwrap` method definition.

The `createWrapper` method definition shows how the type parameter propagates to the implementation side—`Wrapper(a)` is parameterized with the `A` type by the compiler.

The `ConcreteWrapper` type definition shows that type aliases are parameterized in the same way that types are.

We then use our parameterized type to demonstrate that it is possible to provide explicit type parameters on the call side, as well as rely on type inference.

This type inference is in fact quite powerful. The compiler always tries to find the most specific type, as the following example reveals (I've provided the explicit type ascriptions, which reflect the types inferred by the compiler):

```
case class Abc[A](a: A, b: A, c: A)
val intA: Abc[Int] = Abc(10, 20, 30)
val longA: Abc[Long] = Abc(10L, 20L, 30L)
val whatA: Abc[AnyVal] = Abc(10, 20, true)
val whatB: Abc[io.Serializable] = Abc("10", "20", Wrapper(10))
val whatC: Abc[Any] = Abc(10, "20", Wrapper(10))
```

We discussed Scala's type hierarchy earlier, so it should be obvious how the compiler came up with the types shown in the preceding code snippet.

It is possible to restrict possible definitions of the type parameter by using type constraints, as shown in the following example:

```
trait Constraints[A <: AnyVal, B >: Null <: AnyRef] {
  def a: A
  def b: B
}

// compile error - type parameter bounds
// case class AB(a: String, b: Int) extends Constraints[String, Int]

case class AB(a: Int, b: String) extends Constraints[Int, String]
```

The compiler will check that the concrete definition conforms to the type parameter bounds.

Type members

A *type member* is similar to the type parameter, but it is defined as a type alias that's a member of an abstract class or trait. It can then be made concrete at the moment the abstract definition itself is made concrete. Let's look at the following few lines of code, which will show you how this works:

```
trait HolderA {
  type A
  def a: A
}
class A extends HolderA {
  override type A = Int
  override def a = 10
}
```

Here, we defined an abstract type member, A, and overrode it in the concrete implementation by binding it to the Int.

It is possible to define multiple type members, of course, and define constraints on them, including type members themselves as part of the constraint:

```
trait HolderBC {
  type B
  type C <: B
  def b: B
  def c: C
}
```

Type inference is not applied in this case, so the following code will not compile because the type definition is missing:

```
class BC extends HolderBC {
  override def b = "String"
  override def c = true
}
```

These type members can be defined using all language features that can be applied to other type definitions, including multiple type constraints and path-dependent types. In the following example, we demonstrate this by declaring type members in the HolderDEF and providing the concrete definition in the class DEF. Incompatible type definitions are noted as such and commented out:

```
trait HolderDEF {
  type D >: Null <: AnyRef
  type E <: AnyVal
  type F = this.type
  def d: D
  def e: E
  def f: F
}

class DEF extends HolderDEF {
  override type D = String
  override type E = Boolean

  // incompatible type String
  // override type E = String
  // override def e = true

  override def d = ""
  override def e = true
```

```
    // incompatible type DEF
    // override def f: DEF = this

    override def f: this.type = this
  }
```

It is also possible to combine type members and type parameters and use them later to further constrain possible definitions of the former:

```
abstract class HolderGH[G,H] {
  type I <: G
  type J >: H
  def apply(j: J): I
}
class GH extends HolderGH[String, Null] {
  override type I = Nothing
  override type J = String
  override def apply(j: J): I = throw new Exception
}
```

Type members and type parameters look very similar in their function—this is done to define abstract type definitions that can be refined later. Given this similarity, a developer can use one or another most of the time. Still, there are a couple of nuances regarding the situations in which you should prefer to use them.

These type parameters are usually more straightforward and easier to get right, so generally, they should be preferred. Type members are the way to go if you run into one of the following cases:

- If the concrete type definition should remain hidden
- If the intended way to provide the concrete definition of the type is via inheritance (overridden in subclasses or mixed-in via traits)

There is another simple rule that's easy to memorize—type parameters are used to define the types of parameters of the method and type members to define the result type of this method:

```
trait Rule[In] {
  type Out
  def method(in: In): Out
}
```

There is also another way to specify boundaries for type parameters and type members in Scala.

Generalized type constraints

In the previous two sections, we used type constraints provided by the language to precisely define type members and type parameters. There are also supplementary *generalized type constraints* defined in the standard library that allow you to define relations between types using type classes. We will look at type classes and implicits in detail in `Chapter 4`, *Getting to Know Implicits and Type Classes*, but we will give a brief introduction to generalized type constraints here.

The `<:<` constraint expresses the requirement that the left-side type is a subtype of the right-side type. Basically, having an instance of `A <:< B` is the same as having a definition of `A <: B`. But why is it needed, then? Because sometimes the language is not expressive enough. Let's look at an example:

```
abstract class Wrapper[A] {
  val a: A
  // A in flatten shadows A in the Wrapper
  // def flatten[B, A <: Wrapper[B]]: Wrapper[B] = a
  def flatten(implicit ev: A <:< Wrapper[B]): Wrapper[B] = a
}
```

It is not possible to express the `A <: Wrapper[B]` type constraint because the `A` in this definition will shadow the `A` type constraint in the definition of `Wrapper[A]`. The implicit, `ev`, solves this problem easily. `ev` will be available in scope if the compiler can prove that the subtype relation holds.

Another generalized type constraint available in the Scala standard library is `=:=`. So, `A =:= B` allows you to require that `A` and `B` are equal, the same way that `A <:< B` allows you to express subtyping relation. Due to restrictions on subclassing, it also witnesses that `A <:< B`, but not that `B <:< A`. We will take a look in detail how this equality relation can be used to express domain constraints at the end of this chapter.

The strange syntax of `A <:< B` and `A =:= B` brings us to the next section, *Infix types*.

Infix types

In the same way that Scala has infix operators, it has infix types. An infix type, such as `A Op B`, is just any type that has exactly two type operands. It is equivalent to the type defined as `Op[A, B]`. `Op` may be any valid identifier.

The type operators have the same associativity as term operators—they are left associative unless an operator ends in : (colon), in which case it is right associative. Consecutive infix operators must have the same associativity. Let's look at an example to understand what this means:

```
type Or[A, B]
type And[A, B]
type +=[A, B] = Or[A, B]
type =:[A, B] = And[A, B]

type CC = Or[And[A, B], C]
type DA = A =: B =: C
type DB = A And B And C

// type E = A += B =: C // wrong associativity
type F = (A += B) =: C
```

Here, we defined four types, all of which have two type parameters and so can be used as infix types. Then, we define a type called CC, which expresses some relation between the A, B, and C types. The DA and DB type definitions show what the type definition looks like in infix notation. The first attempt to define some type, E, to be the same as the C type fails because of the different associativity of the types, =+ and =:, and we have demonstrated how parentheses can be used to work around this rule.

If used properly, infix types can greatly improve the readability of the code:

```
type |[A, B] = Or[A, B]
type  [A, B] = And[A, B]
type G = A   B | C
```

Here, we can see how infix types allow you to define type relation in a way that looks similar to Boolean operations.

Variance

Variance is another aspect related to parameterized types. To understand why it is needed and how it works, let's have a drink. First, we will define a glass that can be (half) full or empty:

```
sealed trait Glass[Contents]
case class Full[Contents](contents: Contents) extends Glass[Contents]
case object Empty extends Glass[Nothing]
```

There can only be one empty glass filled with `Nothing`, and we model this case with a case object. A full glass can be filled with different contents. `Nothing` is a subclass of any class in Scala, so in our case it should be able to substitute any contents. We will now create the contents and we would like to be able to drink it. The implementation is not important in this case:

```
case class Water(purity: Int)
def drink(glass: Glass[Water]): Unit = ???
```

We now are able to drink from the full glass and are unable to do so from an empty one:

```
drink(Full(Water(100)))
drink(Empty) // compile error, wrong type of contents
```

But what if instead of drinking, we'd like to define `drinkAndRefill`, which should refill an empty glass?

```
def drinkAndRefill(glass: Glass[Water]): Unit = ???
drinkAndRefill(Empty) // same compile error
```

We would like our implementation to accept not only `Glass[Water]`, but also `Glass[Nothing]`, or more generally any `Glass[B]` if B <: Water. We can change our implementation accordingly:

```
def drinkAndRefill[B <: Water](glass: Glass[B]): Unit = ???
```

But what if we would like our `Glass` to work like this with any method, not only `drinkAndRefill`? Then we need to define how the relation between parameterizing types should affect the way the parameterized type works. This is done with variance. Our definition, `sealed trait Glass[Contents]`, is called **invariant**, and it means that the relation in the type that parameterizes `Glass` does not affect how glasses with different contents are related—they are not related at all. The *covariance* means that, in regards to the compiler, if type parameters are in a subclass relation, then the main types should be too. It is expressed with a + (plus) before the type constraint. Therefore, our definition of the glass becomes the following:

```
sealed trait Glass[+Contents]
```

And the rest of the code remains unchanged. Now, if we have contents that are related, we can drink them without facing the same problems we had before:

```
drink(Empty) // compiles fine
```

A typical use of covariance is with different kinds of immutable containers, where it is safe to have a more specific element in the container, like the one that is declared by the type.

It is not safe to do so with mutable containers, though. The compiler will not allow us to do this, but if it would, we might end up passing a container, C, with some subclass, B, to the method, expecting a container with superclass A. This method would then be able to replace the contents of C with A (as it is not even supposed to know about the existence of B), hence making future uses of C[B] impossible.

Now, let's imagine that our glass is supposed to interact with a drinker. We'll create a Drinker class for this, and the drinker is supposed to be able to drink the contents of Glass:

```
class Drinker[T] { def drink(contents: T): Unit = ??? }

sealed trait Glass[Contents] {
  def contents: Contents
  def knockBack(drinker: Drinker[Contents]): Unit = drinker.drink(contents)
}
case class Full[C](contents: C) extends Glass[C]
```

Now, let's inspect what happens if we have two different kinds of Water:

```
class Water(purity: Int)
class PureWater(purity: Int) extends Water(purity) {
  def shine: Unit = ???
}

val glass = Full(new PureWater(100))
glass.knockBack(new Drinker[PureWater])
```

PureWater is Water with some additional properties. We can create a glass full of it and let it fill a drinker. Obviously, if somebody can drink just water, they should be able to drink pure water as well:

```
glass.knockBack(new Drinker[Water]) // compile error
```

To fix this, we need to use *contravariance*, which is denoted by the – (minus sign) before the type parameter. We fix our Drinker like so, and our example starts to compile:

```
class Drinker[-T] { def drink(contents: T): Unit = ??? }
glass.knockBack(new Drinker[Water]) // compiles
```

It is important to notice that co- and contravariance do not define the type itself, but only the type parameters. This is very important for functional programming in Scala because it allows defining functions as first-class citizens. We will look at function definition in more detail in the next chapter, but to give you some indication, here is what it is about.

If we want to pass over to the caller a function, that is, `f(water: Water): Water`, what kind of substitute would be safe to pass instead? It would not be safe to pass a function that accepts `PureWater` because the caller won't be able to call it with such an argument. But it will be safe for the function to accept `Water` and any superclass of it that describes contravariance. For the result, it would be unacceptable for our replacement function to return anything higher in the hierarchy than `f` because the caller expects the result to be at least as specific as `f`. It would be no problem if our substitute was more specific, though. Therefore, we end up with covariance. Hence, we can define `f` as `f[-Parameter,+Result]`.

Existential types

Existential types come into play if we stop caring about the specifics of type parameters. Taking our previous example, if we have a method that expects a glass of something, but inside the method, we do not actually care what this something is, then we get the following:

```
def drink[T <: Water](g: Glass[T]): Unit = { g.contents; () }
```

In this definition, we actually don't need to know what `T` is, we just want to make sure that it is some kind of `Water`. Scala allows you to have an underscore as a placeholder, in the same way it can be utilized to denote unused variables:

```
def drink[_ <: Water](g: Glass[_]): Unit = { g.contents; () }
```

This is a placeholder syntax for *existential type*s. As we saw previously, if the upper bound is omitted, `scala.Any` is assumed. In the case that the lower bound hasn't been defined, the compiler will implicitly add `scala.Nothing`.

This syntax is just a shorter version of the more powerful syntax `T forSome { Q }`, where `Q` is a sequence of type declarations, for example:

```
import scala.language.existentials
val glass = Full[T forSome { type T <: Water }](new Water(100))
```

Existential types are considered to be an advanced language feature and so need a respective import to be in scope or to be enabled as a compiler option.

Higher kinded types

Our example of the glass has become a bit boring. To make it fascinating again, we'll add another abstraction, a jar. This is how our model will look after that:

```
sealed trait Contents
case class Water(purity: Int) extends Contents
case class Whiskey(label: String) extends Contents
sealed trait Container[C <: Contents] { def contents: C }
case class Glass[C<: Contents](contents: C) extends Container[C]
case class Jar[C <: Contents](contents: C) extends Container[C]
```

The glass and the jar can both be filled with any contents. For instance, this is how it can be done:

```
def fillGlass[C <: Contents](c: C): Glass[C] = Glass(c)
def fillJar[C <: Contents](c: C): Jar[C] = Jar(c)
```

As we can see, both methods look identical with respect to the type used to construct the result. The parameterized type that is used to construct types is called a **type constructor**. As a consistent language, Scala allows you to abstract over type constructors in the same way it allows you to abstract over functions via higher order functions (more about this in the next chapter). This abstraction over type constructors is called **higher kinded types**. The syntax requires us to use an underscore to denote the expected type parameter on the definition side. The implementation should then use the type constructor without type constraints.

We can use a type constructor to provide a generic filling functionality. Of course, we can't get rid of the specific knowledge about how to fill our containers, but we can move it to the type level:

```
sealed trait Filler[CC[_]] {
  def fill[C](c: C): CC[C]
}
object GlassFiller extends Filler[Glass] {
  override def fill[C](c: C): Glass[C] = Glass(c)
}
object JarFiller extends Filler[Jar] {
  override def fill[C](c: C): Jar[C] = Jar(c)
}
```

In the preceding code, we're using the type constructor CC[_] to denote both Glass and Jar in the Filler trait. We can now use created abstractions to define a generic filling functionality:

```
def fill[C, G[_]](c: C)(F: Filler[G]): G[C] = F.fill(c)
```

The `G[_]` type is a type constructor for glass and jar, and `Filler[G]` is a higher order type that uses this type constructor to build a full `G[C]` for any content, `C`. This is how the generic fill method can be used in practice:

```
val fullGlass: Glass[Int] = fill(100)(GlassFiller)
val fullJar: Jar[Int] = fill(200)(JarFiller)
```

This might not look like a huge win over the specific methods for now because we've provided our type constructors explicitly. The real advantage will become obvious the moment we start talking about implicits in `Chapter 4`, *Getting to know Implicits and Type Classes*.

Type lambdas

As a next step, let's imagine that we have a generic `Filler` that is capable of filling different containers with different kinds of contents, as shown in the following code snippet:

```
sealed trait Contents
case class Water(purity: Int) extends Contents
case class Whiskey(label: String) extends Contents

sealed trait Container[C] { def contents: C }
case class Glass[C](contents: C) extends Container[C]
case class Jar[C](contents: C) extends Container[C]

sealed trait Filler[C <: Contents, CC <: Container[C]] {
  def fill(c: C): CC
}
```

What could we do if we had a requirement to provide a method that should only accept one type of container or content? We would need to fix the second type parameter in a similar fashion to how we would partially apply a function if given one of the arguments. A type alias can be used to do this on the type level:

```
type WaterFiller[CC <: Container[Water]] = Filler[Water, CC]

def fillWithWater[CC <: Container[Water]](container: CC)(filler:
WaterFiller[CC]) = ???
```

But it feels a bit verbose to define a type alias just to be used once in the definition of the function parameter. **Type lambda** is a syntax that allows us to do such partial type application in-place:

```
def fillWithWater[CC <: Container[Water], F: ({ type T[C] = Filler[Water,
C] })#T[CC]](container: CC)(filler: F) = ???
```

The type lambda can also be used to define a parameter type directly:

```
def fillWithWater[CC <: Container[Water]](container: CC)(filler: ({ type
T[C] = Filler[Water, C] })#T) = ???
```

The internal definition of `T[C]` is analogous to the type alias we defined previously. The added part is the type projection, `()#T[C]`, that allows us to reference the type we've just defined.

Using types to define domain constraints

We've already seen how simple types can be used to express domain constraints, as discussed in the *Path-dependent types* section. We implemented a lock that guaranteed at compile time that it is only possible to open and close it with the key created for this specific lock. We will conclude our study of type parameters and higher kinded types with two examples.

The first example will demonstrate an application of phantom types to create another version of the lock, which can guarantee the safety of state transitions at compile time without the use of inheritance.

The second example will show how self-recursive types can help to constrain possible subtyping.

Phantom types

The *phantom type* in Scala is a type that is never instantiated at runtime. Because of this, it is only useful at compile time to express domain constraints similar to (generalized) type constraints. To get a feeling for how this works, let's imagine the following situation—we have an abstraction of `Lock`, that has already been implemented in different ways via the use of inheritance:

```
sealed trait Lock
class PadLock extends Lock
class CombinationLock extends Lock
```

We would like to encode in the type system that only the following state transitions are allowed for any locks:

- open -> closed
- closed -> open
- closed -> broken
- open -> broken

As we already have an existing hierarchy, we cannot easily model these state transitions with inheritance by extending `Lock` with `ClosedLock`, `OpenLock`, and `BrokenLock`. Instead, we will use the phantom types `Open`, `Closed`, and `Broken` to model the states (we will define `Lock` from scratch later, just to avoid cluttering the example with unnecessary details):

```
sealed trait LockState
sealed trait Open extends LockState
sealed trait Closed extends LockState
sealed trait Broken extends LockState
```

Now, we can assign this `State` to a `Lock`:

```
case class Lock[State <: LockState]()
```

And define our state transitioning methods using type constraints:

```
def break: Lock[Broken] = Lock()
def open[_ >: State <: Closed](): Lock[Open] = Lock()
def close[_ >: State <: Open](): Lock[Closed] = Lock()
```

We can bring any lock to the broken state so that the `break` method does not have any constraints defined on it.

The transition to the `Open` state is only available from the `Closed` state, and we encode this fact with the existential type (that, nevertheless, should be available for successful compilation), which is a subclass of the current `State` of the lock and a superclass of `Closed`. The only possibility to satisfy type constraint is for `State` to be equal to `Closed`. This is done in the same way that it is only possible way to call the `close` method and satisfy type constraints by having `Lock` in the `Open` state. Let's see how the compiler reacts in different cases:

```
scala> val openLock = Lock[Open]
openLock: Lock[Open] = Lock()
scala> val closedLock = openLock.close()
closedLock: Lock[Closed] = Lock()
scala> val broken = closedLock.break
```

```
broken: Lock[Broken] = Lock()
scala> closedLock.close()
       ^
  error: inferred type arguments [Closed] do not conform to method close's
type parameter bounds [_ >: Closed <: Open]
scala> openLock.open()
       ^
  error: inferred type arguments [Open] do not conform to method open's type
parameter bounds [_ >: Open <: Closed]
scala> broken.open()
       ^
  error: inferred type arguments [Broken] do not conform to method open's
type parameter bounds [_ >: Broken <: Closed]
```

The compiler refuses to accept calls that would lead to inappropriate state transitions.

We can also provide an alternative implementation by using generalized type constraints:

```
def open(implicit ev: State =:= Closed): Lock[Open] = Lock()
def close(implicit ev: State =:= Open): Lock[Closed] = Lock()
```

It is arguable that the generalized syntax conveys the intention much better as it almost reads as State should be equal to Closed in the first case or State should be equal to Open in the second case.

Let's see how the compiler reacts to our new implementation:

```
scala> val openLock = Lock[Open]
openLock: Lock[Open] = Lock()

scala> val closedLock = openLock.close
closedLock: Lock[Closed] = Lock()

scala> val lock = closedLock.open
lock: Lock[Open] = Lock()

scala> val broken = closedLock.break
broken: Lock[Broken] = Lock()

scala> closedLock.close
                 ^
       error: Cannot prove that Closed =:= Open.

scala> openLock.open
               ^
       error: Cannot prove that Open =:= Closed.

scala> broken.open
```

```
          ^
     error: Cannot prove that Broken =:= Closed.
```

Obviously, the error messages are also better for the implementation with generalized type constraints.

Self-recursive types

Let's recall different implementations inheriting from a single trait from the previous example:

```
sealed trait Lock
class PadLock extends Lock
class CombinationLock extends Lock
```

We will now extend `Lock` with an `open` method, which should return the same type of `Lock` and let our implementations serve as type parameters:

```
sealed trait Secret[E]
sealed trait Lock[E] { def open(key: Secret[E]): E = ??? }
case class PadLock() extends Lock[PadLock]
case class CombinationLock() extends Lock[CombinationLock]
```

The realization is not very interesting for now—the important part is that it returns the same type as the instance it was called on.

Now, with this implementation, there is an issue that we can use it with something that is not a `Lock` at all:

```
case class IntLock() extends Lock[Int]
lazy val unlocked: Int = IntLock().open(new Secret[Int] {})
```

Naturally, we don't want to allow this! We want to constrain our type parameter so that it is a subtype of `Lock`:

```
sealed trait Lock[E <: Lock]
```

But unfortunately, this won't compile because the `Lock` takes a type parameter that is absent in the preceding definition. We need to provide that type parameter. What should it be? Logically, the same type as we used to parameterize the `Lock`—E:

```
sealed trait Lock[E <: Lock[E]] {
  def open(key: Secret[E]): E = ???
}
```

The type parameter looks a bit weird because it refers to itself recursively. This way of defining a type is called a **self-recursive type parameter** (or sometimes an F-bounded type polymorphism).

Now, we can only parameterize `Lock` by the type, which is itself a `Lock`:

```
scala> case class IntLock() extends Lock[Int]
                                            ^
        error: illegal inheritance;
         self-type IntLock does not conform to Lock[Int]'s selftype Int
scala> case class PadLock() extends Lock[PadLock]
defined class PadLock
```

But unfortunately, we can still mess things up by defining the wrong subtype as a type parameter:

```
scala> case class CombinationLock() extends Lock[PadLock]
defined class CombinationLock
```

Therefore, we need to define another constraint that will say that the type parameter should refer to the type itself, not just any `Lock`. We already know that there is a self-type that can be used for that:

```
sealed trait Lock[E <: Lock[E]] { self: E =>
  def open(key: Secret[E]): E = self
}

scala> case class CombinationLock() extends Lock[PadLock]
                                                ^
        error: illegal inheritance;
         self-type CombinationLock does not conform to Lock[PadLock]'s
selftype PadLock
scala> case class CombinationLock() extends Lock[CombinationLock]
defined class CombinationLock
scala> PadLock().open(new Secret[PadLock]{})
res2: PadLock = PadLock()
scala> CombinationLock().open(new Secret[CombinationLock]{})
res3: CombinationLock = CombinationLock()
```

Nice! We've just defined a `Lock` trait that can only be parameterized with classes that extend this trait and only by the class itself. We've done this by using a combination of the self-recursive type parameter and the self-type.

Summary

The type system is one of the key components of the Scala language. It allows the developer to express expectations about the behavior of the program, which can then be checked at compile time. This reduces the number of tests needed to verify the correctness of the solution and the possibility of runtime errors.

Usually, strictly typed languages are associated with verbose code. Normally, this is not the case with Scala because of its powerful type inference mechanism.

Scala allows you to define very narrow types containing a single value as well as much wider types, even those represented as a combination of other types.

The type definition can be made more precise by using type constraints, type parameters, and variance.

We also looked at some examples of how the type system can be used to express domain constraints.

Needless to say, Scala's ecosystem is much richer than what we have covered here. Some open source libraries offer advanced type constraints that are expressed as refined types, fixpoint types, or tagged types. Other libraries, such as shapeless, provide the possibility for type-level programming, which allows you to express and verify quite complex program logic at compile time.

Questions

1. Which type constraints can you name?
2. What implicit type constraints are added to a type if there are no type constraints defined on it by the developer?
3. Which operators can be used to refer to the nested type of some type?
4. Which type can be used as an infix type?
5. Why is the use of structural types discouraged in Scala?
6. What is expressed via variance?

Further reading

- Mads Hartmann, and Ruslan Shevchenko, *Professional Scala*: You will learn how to write type-safe code concisely and expressively in an environment that lets you build for the JVM, browser, and more.

- Vikash Sharma, *Learning Scala Programming: Learn how to write scalable and concurrent programs in Scala,* a language that grows with you.

Deep Dive into Functions

3

Scala combines both object-oriented and functional programming paradigms. In particular, functions are a first-class language concept. They can be defined in a variety of ways, assigned to variables, passed as parameters, and stored in data structures. Scala gives a lot of flexibility with regard to how these actions can be performed.

We'll start this chapter by looking in detail at different flavors of defining a function. We'll then go on and apply the knowledge about types from the previous chapter to make our functions polymorphic and higher order. We'll study recursion, tail recursion, and trampolining as important aspects of functional programming for the JVM. Finally, we'll evaluate peculiarities related to the fact that functions in Scala are implemented in an object-oriented way.

The following topics will be covered in this chapter:

- Ways to define a function
- Polymorphic functions
- Higher order functions
- Recursion
- Trampolining
- Object-oriented aspects of functions

Technical requirements

- JDK 1.8+
- SBT 1.2+

The source code for this chapter is available under `https://github.com/PacktPublishing/Learn-Scala-Programming/tree/master/Chapter03`.

Ways to define a function

To provide some common ground for the readers with different levels of Scala knowledge, let's recap how a function can be defined. We'll start with the basic approaches such as defining a method and placing it in different scopes to create a local function. Then we'll look at more interesting aspects, for example closing over scope, partial application, different ways to specify function literals, and, finally, currying.

Function as a method

Most Scala developers came to it from Java. Because of this, probably the most common way is to define a method inside of a class, trait, or an object, like in the following familiar example:

```
class MethodDefinition {
   def eq(arg1: String, arg2: Int): Boolean = ! nonEqual(arg1, arg2)
   private def nonEq(a: String, b: Int) = a != b.toString
}
```

By convention, we've explicitly defined a return type for the public method in the same way that we would do for the return type in Java. For the non recursive function, the result type can be omitted. We've done this for the private method.

The type declaration for the value parameters is mandatory.

Each value parameter can have one default value assigned to it:

```
def defaultValues(a: String = "default")(b: Int = 0, c: String =
a)(implicit d: Long = b, e: String = a) = ???
```

The preceding snippet also demonstrates that it is possible to define multiple groups of value parameters. The parameters from the last group can be implicit and also can be provided with default values. The default values from consecutive groups can refer to the parameters defined in previous groups as e refers to the default value of c, which is a.

The type of the value parameter prefixed with => means that this parameter should not be evaluated at the moment the method is called, but instead each time the parameter is referenced in the body of the method. Such arguments are called *by-name parameters* and basically, they represent a zero-argument method with the argument's return type:

```
scala> def byName(int: => Int) = {
     | println(int)
     | println(int)
     | }
```

```
byName: (int: => Int)Unit
scala> byName({ println("Calculating"); 10 * 2 })
Calculating
20
Calculating
20
```

In this example, we can see how the passed block of code is executed twice, matching the number of usages inside the method's body.

The * (star) can be added as a suffix to the name of the type of the last value parameter to denote that this is a *repeated parameter* and it takes a number of arguments of the defined type. The given arguments are then available in the method body as a `collection.Seq` of the specified type:

```
def variable(a: String, b: Int*): Unit = {
   val bs: collection.Seq[Int] = b
}

variable("vararg", 1, 2, 3)
variable("Seq", Seq(1, 2, 3): _*)
```

It is illegal to pass the `Seq` direct in place of repeated parameters. The last line in the previous snippet shows the `:_*` syntax to mark the last parameter as a *sequence argument*. The repeated parameter can't take default values.

Arguments in the method definition have names. These names can be used to call the method by providing arguments in any order (as opposed to the order specified in the definition of the method):

```
def named(first: Int, second: String, third: Boolean) = s"$first, $second, $third"

named(third = false, first = 10, second = "Nice")
named(10, third = true, second = "Cool")
```

The named and normal arguments can be mixed, as shown in the last line of the previous code. In this case, the positional arguments must be specified first.

Until now, we defined our examples in the scope of the enclosing class or object. But Scala gives more flexibility in this regard. A method can be defined in any valid scope. This makes it local to the enclosing block and thus limits its visibility.

Local functions

Here is an example of two functions that are local to the enclosing method:

```
def average(in: Int*): Int = {
  def sum(in: Int*): Int = in.sum
  def count(in: Int*): Int = in.size
  sum(in:_*)/count(in:_*)
}
```

In this example, we have both `sum` and `count` defined inside of the `average` definition, which makes them inaccessible from the outside:

```
scala> :type sum
        ^
       error: not found: value sum

scala> :type count
        ^
       error: not found: value count
```

As already mentioned, the function does not need to be nested in another method. The enclosing block can be of any kind, for example, a variable definition. For instance, consider if the `average` function from the previous example was only defined in order to calculate a single average:

```
val items = Seq(1,2,3,4,5)
val avg = average(items:_*)
```

We could rewrite both code blocks as follows:

```
val items = Seq(1,2,3,4,5)
val avg = {
  def sum(in: Int*): Int = in.sum
  def count(in: Int*): Int = in.size
  sum(items:_*)/count(items:_*)
}
```

The scope visibility rules apply for methods the same way as for other language constructs. Because of this, the parameters of the `outer` method are visible to the inner functions and don't need to be passed explicitly. We can rewrite our first example again using this rule, as follows:

```
def averageNoPassing(in: Int*): Int = {
  def sum: Int = in.sum
  def count: Int = in.size
  sum /count
}
```

There is a special name for the functions that refer to the definitions from the enclosing block, *closures*. Let's discuss them a little more deeply.

Closures

In our function definitions, we've referred to two different types of variables: the ones that are provided as parameters (*bound variables*) and others, which were defined in the enclosing block (*free variables*). The free variable is named so, because the function itself does not give any meaning to it.

A function that does not refer to any free variable is self-sufficient and the compiler can translate it to the bytecode in any context. Another way to state this is to say that this definition is closed in itself. It is named, accordingly, a *closed term*. A function referring to the free variables, on the other hand, can only be compiled in a context where all of these variables are defined. Therefore it is called *open term* and it closes over the free variables at the moment it is compiled, hence the name *closure* (over the free variables).

The usual scope resolution rules apply for closures in the same way that they apply for variables and other definitions as demonstrated by the next snippet:

```
scala> def outerA = {
     | val free = 5
     | def innerA = {
     | val free = 20
     | def closure(in: Int) = free + in
     | closure(10)
     | }
     | innerA + free
     | }
outerA: Int

scala> outerA
res3: Int = 35
```

The res3 is calculated as outerA.free (5) + innerA.free (20) + closure.in(10).

The free variable must be defined before the closure, otherwise, the compiler will complain:

```
scala> def noReference(in: Int) = {
     |   def closure(input: Int) = input + free + in
     | }
           def closure(input: Int) = input + free + in
                                             ^
On line 2: error: not found: value free

scala> def forwardReference(in: Int) = {
     |   def closure(input: Int) = input + free + in
     |   val free = 30
     | }
           def closure(input: Int) = input + free + in
                                             ^
On line 2: error: forward reference extends over definition of value free
```

The first try fails because we forgot to define a free variable. The second is still unsuccessful because the free variable is defined after the closure.

Partial application and functions

Until now, the methods and variables were handled the same way by the compiler. Can we exploit the similarities further and return a method as a result of another method and store it into the variable? Let's give it a try:

```
scala> object Functions {
     |   def method(name: String) = {
     |     def function(in1: Int, in2: String): String = name + in2
     |     function
     |   }
     |   val function = method("name")
     | }
           function
           ^
On line 4: error: missing argument list for method function
       Unapplied methods are only converted to functions when a function
type is expected.
       You can make this conversion explicit by writing `function _` or
`function(_,_)` instead of `function`.
```

Unfortunately, it didn't work. We tried to create and return a function from within a method and assign this function to a variable, but the compiler does not allow this. However, it gives us a useful hint about what we are doing wrong!

It turns out that functions and methods are different for the compiler and methods can only be passed in the form of an instance of the enclosing class. This distinction is related to the fact that everything in the JVM is represented as an instance of some class. Because of this, the methods we define become methods of the class, and methods are not first-class citizens in the JVM. Scala works around this approach by having a hierarchy of classes representing functions of different arities. Thus, in order for us to be able to return a method from another method, the former must become a function. And the compiler gave us a hint as to how to achieve this: by using _ (underscore) in the place where the parameters are expected.

```
scala> object Functions {
     |  def method(name: String) = {
     |  def function(in1: Int, in2: String): String = name + in2
     |  function _
     |  }
     |  val function = method("name")
     |  }
defined object Functions
```

The partial application can have two forms: a single underscore replacing the whole parameter list, or a single underscore replacing each parameter. Thus, for the partial application of the function we've just defined, both `function _` or `function(_,_)` would be appropriate.

The partial application syntax can be used to create *shortcuts* for functions defined elsewhere, by importing and partially applying them at the same time:

```
val next = Math.nextAfter _
next(10f, 20f)
val /\ = Math.hypot (_, _)
/\ (10 , 20)
```

In general, for the function of N parameters, the partial application means specifying $0 =< M < N$ parameters and leaving the rest undefined, basically applying the function to some part of the parameter list. This partial application gives a function of (N-M) parameters and the same type of result as the original function back. In our previous example, we defined M to be zero and thus the signature of the resulting function remained unchanged. But the very fact of there being a partial application has converted our method into the function, which allowed us to further work with it as with a value.

In the case, if 0< M <N, the underscores go into the place of the parameters that are not applied at the moment:

```
def four(one: String, two: Int, three: Boolean, four: Long) = ()
val applyTwo = four("one", _: Int, true, _: Long)
```

We applied the first and third arguments and left the second and fourth unapplied. The compiler requires us to provide a type ascription for missing parameters in order to use it while inferring the type of the resulting function.

The parameter names defined for methods are lost during the partial application and so are default values. The repeated parameters are converted to the Seq.

Function literals

We can inspect the type of the applyTwo function using REPL:

```
scala> :type Functions.applyTwo
(Int, Long) => Unit
```

This is what the type of a first-class function looks like! In general, the type of function has right and left parts separated by the =>. The left part defines the types of the arguments, the right part—the type of the result. The implementation follows the same pattern and is called *function literal*. Here is an example of the full definition for a function of four arguments:

```
val hash: (Int, Boolean, String, Long) => Int = (a, b, c, d) => {
  val ab = 31 * a.hashCode() + b.hashCode()
  val abc = 31 * ab + c.hashCode
  31 * abc + d.hashCode()
}
```

On the implementation side, we have a code block which consists of three expressions and therefore is wrapped in curly braces. Please note that we define our function as a val.

Usually, the function literal can be defined using simplified syntax. For instance, the type inference allows leaving the definition of the result type. The type definition, in this case, disappears altogether, because the type definitions for the parameters will move close to the parameter names exactly as in the definition of a method:

```
val hashInferred = (a: Int, b: Boolean, c: String, d: Long) =>
  // ... same implementation as before
```

On the application side, the compiler can help us to simplify the definition even more. Let's consider an example:

```
def printHash(hasher: String => Int)(s: String): Unit =
  println(hasher(s))
```

We could have the following equal definitions for the `hasher` function. The full definition looks like the next code block:

```
val hasher1: String => Int = s => s.hashCode
val hasher2 = (s: String) => s.hashCode
printHash(hasher1)("Full")
printHash(hasher2)("Inferred result type")
```

This snippet illustrates four different ways to represent a function literal:

- Defined inline: `printHash((s: String) => s.hashCode)("inline")`
- Defined inline with type inference for the function parameter: `printHash((s: String) => s.hashCode)("inline")`
- Defined inline with type inference for the function parameter (this is known as *target typing*): `printHash((s) => s.hashCode)("inline")`
- The parentheses around single argument can be omitted: `printHash(s => s.hashCode)("single argument parentheses")`
- In the case, if an argument is used in the implementation of the function, at most once we can go further and use placeholder syntax: `printHash(_.hashCode)("placeholder syntax")`

In fact, the placeholder syntax is quite powerful and can also be used to define functions of multiple parameters as well as functions that are not in the target typing position. Here is an example of a function that calculates a hash code for four instances of `Int` using the placeholder syntax:

```
scala> val hashPlaceholder =
(_: Int) * 31^4 + (_: Int) * 31^3 + (_: Int) * 31^2 + (_: Int) * 31

scala> :type hashPlaceholder
(Int, Int, Int, Int) => Int
```

This syntax looks close to the partial application syntax, but represents a completely different language feature.

Currying

Speaking about partial application, we have not referred to one special case of this, *currying*. Currying is in a sense a partial application where we take a function of N arguments and apply partial application for each argument in a row each time, to produce a function that takes one argument less. We repeat this process until we're left with N functions, each taking one argument. If it sounds complicated, consider the next example of a function of two arguments:

```
def sum(a: Int, b: Int) = a + b
```

Using two parameter lists, we can rewrite it as follows:

```
def sumAB(a: Int)(b: Int) = a + b
```

The type of this method is `(a: Int)(b: Int): Int` or expressed as a function:

```
:type sumAB _
Int => (Int => Int)
```

This is a function that takes an `Int` and returns a function from `Int` to `Int`! The number of arguments is not limited to just two of course:

```
scala> val sum6 = (a: Int) => (b: Int) => (c: Int) => (d: Int) => (e: Int)
=> (f: Int) => a + b + c + d+ e + f
sum6: Int => (Int => (Int => (Int => (Int => (Int => Int)))))
```

The placeholder syntax will give us the same functionality, but in *uncurried* form:

```
scala> val sum6Placeholder = (_: Int) + (_: Int) + (_: Int) + (_: Int) +
(_: Int) + (_: Int)
sum6Placeholder: (Int, Int, Int, Int, Int, Int) => Int
```

Currying is not very important in Scala compared to some other functional programming languages, but it is good to know as a useful functional programming concept.

Polymorphism and higher order functions

Until now, we've played with functions that operate on only one type of data (*monomorphic functions*). Now, we will finally apply our type system knowledge to build functions that work for multiple types. Functions that take type parameters are called *polymorphic functions* similar to polymorphic methods implemented in an object-oriented hierarchy of classes (*subtype polymorphism*). For functions in Scala, it is called *parametric polymorphism*.

Polymorphic functions

We have already used polymorphic functions when we played with `Glass` examples in the previous chapter:

```
sealed trait Glass[+Contents]
case class Full[Contents](c: Contents) extends Glass[Contents]
case object EmptyGlass extends Glass[Nothing]
case class Water(purity: Int)

def drink(glass: Glass[Water]): Unit = ???

scala> :type drink _
Glass[Water] => Unit
```

The `drink` method is monomorphic and thus can only be applied to the argument of the type `Glass[Water]`, not even for an `EmptyGlass`. Of course, we don't want to implement a separate method for every possible type of content out there. Instead, we implement our functions in a polymorphic way:

```
def drinkAndRefill[C](glass: Glass[C]): Glass[C] = glass
drinkAndRefill: [C](glass: Glass[C])Glass[C]

scala> :type drinkAndRefill _
Glass[Nothing] => Glass[Nothing]

scala> :type drinkAndRefill[Water] _
Glass[Water] => Glass[Water]
```

The type parameter is available in the body of the method. In this case, we specify that the result should have the same type of content as the argument.

Of course, it is possible to further constrain type parameter as we did before:

```
def drinkAndRefillWater[B >: Water, C >: B](glass: Glass[B]): Glass[C] =
glass

scala> :type drinkAndRefillWater[Water, Water] _
Glass[Water] => Glass[Water]
```

Here, our method accepts any glass as long as it is a glass of water and allows anything more specific than water to be filled in it.

Both examples also demonstrate that we can specify a type parameter during the partial application in order to have a monomorphic function of some specific type. Otherwise, the compiler applies the bottom type parameter the same way as it does when we define a polymorphic function using a function literal:

```
scala> def drinkFun[B] = (glass: Glass[B]) => glass
drinkFun: [B]=> Glass[B] => Glass[B]

scala> :type drinkFun
Glass[Nothing] => Glass[Nothing]

scala> drinkFun(Full(Water))
res17: Glass[Water.type] = Full(Water)
```

The inferred result type is correct at the moment of function application.

Higher-order functions

So far, we have discussed function literals and we've created a `printHash` function, which we used to demonstrate different forms of passing functions into methods:

```
scala> def printHash(hasher: String => Int)(s: String): Unit =
    println(hasher(s))
printHash: (hasher: String => Int)(s: String)Unit
```

The `printHash` takes two parameters: the `hasher` function and a string to hash. Or, in functional form:

```
scala> :type printHash _
(String => Int) => (String => Unit)
```

Our function is `curried` as it takes one argument (a `String => Int` function) and returns another function, `String => Unit`. The fact that `printHash` takes a function as an argument is reflected by saying that `printHash` is a **higher order function** (HOF). There is nothing else special about HOFs except the fact that one or multiple parameters are functions. They work just as normal functions, can be assigned and passed over, partially applied and be polymorphic:

```
def printHash[A](hasher: A => Int)(s: A): Unit = println(hasher(s))
```

In fact, HOFs usually apply function(s) given as parameter(s) to another parameter in some creative ways and therefore are almost always polymorphic.

Let's take another look at our `printHash` example. There is nothing in particular that requires a `hasher` function to calculate a hash; the function carried out by the `hasher` is independent of the logic of the `printHash`. Interestingly, this is the case more often than one would expect and it leads to the definition of HOF, for example:

```
def printer[A, B, C <: A](f: A => B)(a: C): Unit = println(f(a))
```

Our printing logic does not require the given function to have any specific type of an argument or result. The only limitation we need to enforce is that it is possible to call the function with the given argument, which we formulate with the type constraint `C <: A`. The nature of the function and an argument can also be anything, and it is common to use short neutral names when defining a HOF because of this. This is how our new definition can be used in practice:

```
scala> printer((_: String).hashCode)("HaHa")
2240498
scala> printer((_: Int) / 2)(42)
21
```

The compiler needs to know the type of the function, and therefore we need to define it as a part of the placeholder syntax. We can help the compiler by changing the order of the parameters of the function:

```
def printer[A, B, C <: A](a: C)(f: A => B): Unit = println(f(a))
```

With this definition, it will be possible to infer the `C` first and then use the inferred type to enforce the type of `f`:

```
scala> printer("HoHo")(_.length)
4
scala> printer(42)(identity)
42
```

The `identity` function is defined as `def identity[A](x: A): A = x` in the standard library.

Recursion and trampolining

There is a special case of a function calling another function—the function calling itself. Such functions are called *recursive*. Recursive functions can be head-recursive or tail-recursive. There is also an approach to model recursive calls in an object-oriented way called *trampolining*. Recursion is very convenient and often uses the technique in functional programming, so let's take a close look at these concepts.

Recursion

Recursion is used to implement recurring logic without relying on loops and the internal states associated with them. The recursive behavior is defined by two properties:

- **Base case**: The simplest terminating case, in which no recursive calls are needed anymore
- **Recursive case**: The set of rules describing how to reduce any other state to the base case

One of the possible examples for recursive implementation can be reversing a string. The two recursive properties would be:

- The base case is an empty or single-char string. In this case, the reversed string is just the same string as given.
- The recursive case for the string of length N can be reduced to the case of a string of length N-1 by taking the first char of the string and appending it to the reversed tail of the given string.

This is how we implement this logic in Scala:

```
def reverse(s: String): String = {
  if (s.length < 2) s
  else reverse(s.tail) + s.head
}
```

So, this is easier implemented than explained, right?

One important aspect of our implementation in a recursive case is that it first makes the recursive call and then adds the rest of the string to the result. Such functions are head-recursive (but usually just called recursive) in the sense that the recursive call stays in the head of the computation. This works in a similar way to the depth-first algorithm, with the implementation first going down to the terminal case and then building up the result from the bottom up:

```
scala> println(reverse("Recursive function call"))
llac noitcnuf evisruceR
```

The nested function calls are naturally kept in the stack during runtime. Because of this, functions that work fine for inputs of smaller size might blow up the stack for bigger inputs, crashing the whole application:

```
scala> println(reverse("ABC" * 100000))
java.lang.StackOverflowError
  at scala.collection.StringOps$.slice$extension(StringOps.scala:548)
```

```
at scala.collection.StringOps$.tail$extension(StringOps.scala:1026)
at ch03.Recursion$.reverse(Recursion.scala:7)
at ch03.Recursion$.reverse(Recursion.scala:7)
at ch03.Recursion$.reverse(Recursion.scala:7)
...
```

It is possible to increase the size of memory reserved for a stack in JVM, but often there is a better solution—tail recursion.

Tail recursion

In the tail-recursive function, the recursive call is done as the very last activity. Because of this, it is possible to "finish" all the "preparations" for the call and then just "jump" back to the beginning of the function with new arguments. The Scala compiler rewrites tail-recursive calls as loops and hence such recursive invocations do not consume the stack at all. Usually, to make a recursive function tail-recursive, either some kind of state or some sort of and/or local helper function is introduced.

Let's rewrite our reverse function in the tail-recursive way:

```
def tailRecReverse(s: String): String = {
  def reverse(s: String, acc: String): String =
    if (s.length < 2) s + acc
    else reverse(s.tail, s.head + acc)
  reverse(s, "")
}
```

In this implementation, we've defined a local tail-recursive function, `reverse`, which shadows the argument s so that we do not unintentionally reference it, and also introduces an `acc` argument, which is needed to carry over the remaining part of the string. Now the reverse is called after the head of the string and `acc` are glued together. To return the result, we call the helper function with the original argument and an empty accumulator.

This implementation does not consume the stack, which we can check by throwing an exception in the base case and inspecting the stack trace:

```
scala> println(inspectReverse("Recursive function call"))
java.lang.Exception
  at $line19.$read$$iw$$iw$.reverse$1(<console>:3)
  at $line19.$read$$iw$$iw$.inspectReverse(<console>:5)
```

At the moment we're finishing the reversing of the string, we still have just a single recursive call in the stack. Sometimes it confuses the developer as it appears as if the recursive call would not be made. In this case, it is possible to disable tail-call optimization by using the **notailcalls** compiler option.

Sometimes the opposite is happening and a (presumably) tail-recursive call overflows the stack at runtime because the developer overlooked a recursive call in the head position. To eliminate the possibility for such kinds of error there is a special annotation for tail-recursive calls, `@scala.annotation.tailrec`:

```
def inspectReverse(s: String): String = {
  @scala.annotation.tailrec
  def reverse(s: String, acc: String): String = ...
}
```

The compiler will fail to compile head-recursive functions with this annotation:

```
scala> @scala.annotation.tailrec
     | def reverse(s: String): String = {
     | if (s.length < 2) s
     | else reverse(s.tail) + s.head
     | }
           else reverse(s.tail) + s.head
                                  ^
On line 4: error: could not optimize @tailrec annotated method reverse: it
contains a recursive call not in tail position
```

It seems as if we're on the safe side with properly annotated tail-recursive functions? Well, not 100%, because there is also a possibility that some functions cannot be made tail-recursive at all.

One of the examples, when tail recursion cannot be implemented, is mutual recursion. Two functions are mutually recursive if the first calls the second, and the second calls the first.

 In mathematics, a Hofstadter sequence is a member of a family of related integer sequences defined by nonlinear recurrence relations. You can learn more about them in Wikipedia at `https://en.wikipedia.org/wiki/Hofstadter_sequence#Hofstadter_Female_and_Male_sequences`.

One of the examples of such functions is `Hofstadter` Female and Male sequences, defined as follows:

```
def F(n:Int): Int = if (n == 0) 1 else n - M(F(n-1))
def M(n:Int): Int = if (n == 0) 0 else n - F(M(n-1))
```

Another example of a non-tail-recursive function is an Ackerman function (more about it can be found at `https://en.wikipedia.org/wiki/Ackermann_function`) with the following definition:

```
val A: (Long, Long) => Long = (m, n) =>
  if (m == 0) n + 1
  else if (n == 0) A(m - 1, 1)
  else A(m - 1, A(m, n - 1))
```

It is very simple, but not primitive recursive, it is stack-hungry, and it overflows the stack even with moderate values of m and n:

```
scala> A(4,2)
java.lang.StackOverflowError
  at .A(<console>:4)
  at .A(<console>:4)
...
```

There is a special technique called trampolining to implement non-tail-recursive functions on JVM.

Trampolining

In essence, *trampolining* is replacing recursive function calls with objects representing these calls. This way the recursive computation is built up in the heap instead of the stack, and it is possible to represent much deeper recursive calls just because of the bigger size of the heap.

The Scala `util.control.TailCalls` implementation provides a ready-to-use abstraction for trampolined recursive calls. Remember that we have two general cases in recursion that break down to three concrete cases? These are:

- The base case
- The recursive case, which can be:
    - Head recursion
    - Tail recursion

The representation reflects them by following three protected case classes:

```
case class Done[A](value: A) extends TailRec[A]
case class Call[A](rest: () => TailRec[A]) extends TailRec[A]
case class Cont[A, B](a: TailRec[A], f: A => TailRec[B]) extends TailRec[B]
```

As these are protected, we can't use them directly, but are expected to use special helper methods instead. Let's take a look at them by re implementing our Ackerman function:

```scala
import util.control.TailCalls._

def tailA(m: BigInt, n: BigInt): TailRec[BigInt] = {
  if (m == 0) done(n + 1)
  else if (n == 0) tailcall(tailA(m - 1, 1))
  else tailcall(tailA(m, n - 1)).flatMap(tailA(m - 1, _))
}
def A(m: Int, n: Int): BigInt = tailA(m, n).result
```

We wrap our recursive calls into the `tailcall` method, which creates an instance of a `Call`. The recursive call is a bit more complex than the base case because we first need to recursively wrap the internal call and then use the `flatMap` method provided by the `TailRec` to pass the result into the outer recursive call.

The `A` is just a helper method to unlift the result of the calculation from the `TailRec`. We're using `BigInt` to represent the result because now, as the implementation is stack safe, it can return quite huge numbers:

```scala
scala> Trampolined.A(4,2).toString.length
```

Now, as we've seen how to represent recursive functions as objects, it is time to reveal another truth about Scala functions.

Object-oriented aspects of functions

We mentioned that Scala is a fusion of object-oriented and functional paradigms. Because of this, Scala has functions as a first-class element of the language. Also because of this, everything is an object in Scala. This is partly related to the fact that everything is an object or a primitive type in the JVM, but Scala goes further and also hides primitives behind objects.

It turns out that functions are also objects! Depending on the number of arguments, they extend one of the special traits. Also because of their object-oriented nature, it is possible to implement additional features by defining additional methods on the implementing class. This is how partial function is implemented. It is also natural to utilize companion objects to define common logic for functions so that it can be easily reused. It's even possible to write some custom implementation of a function, though it is seldom a good idea.

Chapter 3

Each of these aspects is worth a deep dive, but to really understand them, we need to start with some implementation details.

Functions are traits

Each function in Scala implements a `FunctionN` trait, where N is an arity of the function. The zero-argument function is translated by the compiler to the implementation of `Function0`, of one argument—to `Function1` and so on, up to `Function22`. This complexity is needed because of the static nature of the language. Does it mean it is not possible to define functions of more than 22 arguments? Well, it is always possible to define a function using currying or multiple parameter lists, so this is not really a limitation.

Function literals are just a syntactic sugar accepted by the compiler for developers' convenience. This is how the desugared signature of our previously defined Ackerman function looks:

```
val A: Function2[Long, Long, Long] = (m, n) =>
  if (m == 0) n + 1
  else if (n == 0) A.apply(m - 1, 1)
  else A.apply(m - 1, A.apply(m, n - 1))
```

And the (simplified) definition of `Function2` in the standard library is like this:

```
trait Function2[-T1, -T2, +R] extends AnyRef { self =>
  def apply(v1: T1, v2: T2): R
  ...
}
```

Remember our co- and contravariance discussion in the previous chapter? Here we have it in action; the arguments are contravariant and the result type is covariant.

It turns out that the compiler rewrites our definition as an instance of an anonymous class implementing this trait:

```
val objectOrientedA: Function2[Long, Long, Long] =
  new Function2[Long, Long, Long] {
    def apply(m: Long, n: Long): Long =
      if (m == 0) n + 1
      else if (n == 0) objectOrientedA(m - 1, 1)
      else objectOrientedA(m - 1, objectOrientedA(m, n - 1))
  }
```

And the instance of this class can then be passed over, assigned to a variable, stored into data structures, and so on. The `FunctionN` trait also defines a few helper methods that implement function-related functionality at the library level, as opposed to the language syntax. One example is a conversion of a normal function into the `curried` form, which for `Function2[T1,T2,R]` is defined as `def curried: T1 => T2 => R = (x1: T1) => (x2: T2) => apply(x1, x2)`

```scala
scala> objectOrientedA.curried
res9: Long => (Long => Long)
```

This method is available for any function.

Partial functions

The possibility of having additional methods gives a way do define concepts that would be hard to state otherwise, at least without extending the language itself. One such example is *partial functions*. A partial function is a function that is undefined for some values of its arguments. The classical example is a division that is not defined, for the divider equals zero. But actually, it is possible to have arbitrary domain rules that make some function partial. For instance, we could decide that our string reverse function should be undefined for empty strings.

There are a couple of possibilities for implementing such constraints in a program:

- Throw an exception for arguments for which the function is not defined
- Constrain the type of an argument so that it is only possible to pass a valid argument to the function, for example using refined types
- Reflect the partiality in the return type, for example using `Option` or `Either`

There are obvious tradeoffs related to each of these approaches and in Scala, the first one is preferred as most natural. But, to better model the partial nature of the function, there is a special trait available in the standard library:

```scala
trait PartialFunction[-A, +B] extends (A => B)
```

The key difference to normal function is that there is an additional method available that allows us to check whether the function is defined for some argument or not:

```scala
def isDefinedAt(x: A): Boolean
```

This allows the user of the function to do something different for "invalid" input values.

For example, let's imagine we've invented a very efficient method to check if a string is a palindrome. Then we could define our reverse function as two partial functions, one that is only defined for palindromes and does nothing and another that is defined only for non-palindromes and does the actual reverse action:

```scala
val doReverse: PartialFunction[String, String] = {
  case str if !isPalindrome(str) => str.reverse
}
val noReverse: PartialFunction[String, String] = {
  case str if isPalindrome(str) => str
}
def reverse = noReverse orElse doReverse
```

Here we're using syntactic sugar again to define our partial functions as a pattern match and compiler creates `isDefinedAt` method for us. Our two partial functions are combined into the total function using the `orElse` method.

Function object

The `orElse` method for partial function and `curried` method for a normal function earlier are just two examples of function-related methods predefined in the standard library.

Similar to the `curried` method defined for every function instance (except `Function0` and `Function1`) there is another one, `tupled`, which converts a function of N arguments into the function of one argument which is a `TupleN`.

Besides that, there is a companion object, `scala.Function`, that incorporates a few methods that are useful for higher order functional programming, most notably a `const` function, which always returns its argument, and a `chain` function, which combines a list of functions into a single function as in the following example:

```scala
val upper = (_: String).toUpperCase
def fill(c: Char) = c.toString * (_: String).length
def filter(c: Char) = (_: String).filter(_ == c)

val chain = List(upper, filter('L'), fill('*'))
val allAtOnce = Function.chain(chain)

scala> allAtOnce("List(upper, filter('a'), fill('C'))")
res11: String = ****
```

`allAtOnce` is a function that is similar to the one that could be constructed by combining our three original functions with `andThen` (which is defined in the `FunctionN` trait):

```
val static = upper andThen filter('a') andThen fill('C')
```

But `allAtOnce` is built in a dynamic manner.

Extending functions

Nothing prevents a developer from extending a `FunctionN` trait the same way it is done with `PartialFunction`, though it seldom makes sense because of the limitations imposed by the referential transparency constraint. This means that such an implementation of the function should not have a shared state, nor should it mutate state.

It might be tempting, for example, to implement a loaner pattern as a function, so that a used resource would be automatically closed after function application, but it won't be referentially transparent and thus won't satisfy the requirements for a function.

Here is how the implementation could look:

```
class Loan[-T <: AutoCloseable, +R](app: T => R) extends (T => R) {
  override def apply(t: T): R = try app(t) finally t.close()
}
```

And this is what happens if we call it:

```
scala> new Loan((_: java.io.BufferedReader).readLine())(Console.in)
res13: String = Hello

scala> [error] (run-main-0) java.io.IOException: Stream Closed
[error] java.io.IOException: Stream Closed
[error] at java.io.FileInputStream.read0(Native Method)
[error] at java.io.FileInputStream.read(FileInputStream.java:207)
[error] at
jline.internal.NonBlockingInputStream.read(NonBlockingInputStream.java:245)
...
```

Unfortunately, it is not even possible to test whether the second call would produce the same result (obviously it will not) because we broke the REPL by closing the `Console.in`.

Summary

Functions represent another side of the blend of object-oriented and functional features in Scala. They can be defined in a number of ways, including the partial application of methods, function literals, and partial functions. Functions can be defined in any scope. If a function closes over variables available in scope, it is called **closure**.

Polymorphic functions implement an idea similar to polymorphism in object orientation, but apply that idea for types of parameters and of the result. This is called parametric polymorphism. It is especially useful when defining functions accepting other functions as arguments, so-called higher order functions.

There are two ways to implement recursion and only tail-recursive functions are stack safe in the JVM. For the functions which cannot be made tail-recursive, there is a way to represent the call chain in the heap by encoding it as objects. This approach is called trampolining and it is supported in the standard library.

Functions are first-class values in Scala because they are implemented as anonymous classes extending `FunctionN` traits. This not only makes it possible to work with functions as with normal variables, but it also allows for the provision of extended function implementations with additional properties, for example, a `PartialFunction`.

Questions

1. What will be a type of following function in `curried` form: `(Int, String) => (Long, Boolean, Int) => String`?
2. Describe the difference between a partially applied function and a partial function
3. Define a signature and implement a function `uncurry` for a `curried` function of three arguments `A => B => C => R`
4. Implement a head-recursive function for factorial calculation n! = n * (n-1) * (n-2) * ... * 1
5. Implement a tail-recursive function for factorial calculation
6. Implement a recursive function for factorial calculation using trampolining

Further reading

Mads Hartmann and Ruslan Shevchenko, *Professional Scala*: Write the type-safe code concise and expressive in an environment that lets you build for the JVM, browser, and more.

Vikash Sharma, *Learning Scala Programming*: Learn how to write scalable and concurrent programs in Scala, a language that grows with you.

4
Getting to Know Implicits and Type Classes

We are already familiar with two cornerstones of Scala—its type system and first-class functions. Implicits is the third one. Implicits enable elegant designs and probably no state-of-the-art Scala library is possible without them.

In this chapter, we will start with a systematic overview of different types of implicits and recap the implicit scope resolution rules. After taking a short look at context bounds, we'll move on to type classes, the central implementation mechanism that's utilized in modern functional programming libraries.

The following topics will be covered in this chapter:

- Types of implicits
- Context bounds
- Type classes
- Type classes and recursive resolution
- Type class variance
- Implicit scope resolution rules

Technical requirements

Before we begin, make sure you have the following installed:

- JDK 1.8+
- SBT 1.2+

The source code for this chapter is available under our GitHub repository at `https://github.com/PacktPublishing/Learn-Scala-Programming/tree/master/Chapter04`.

Types of implicits

In Scala, there are a couple of different mechanisms hidden behind the keyword `implicit`. This list contains implicit parameters, implicit conversions, and implicit classes. They have slightly different semantics and it is important to know in which situations which one is the best fit. Each of these three types deserves a brief overview.

Implicit conversions

The first type of implicit in our list is implicit conversion. They allow you automatically to convert values of one type into values of another type. This implicit conversion is defined as a one-argument method that's marked with the `implicit` keyword. Implicit conversions are considered to be a somewhat controversial language feature (we will take a look at why in a moment), so we need to enable them explicitly with a compiler flag or by importing the corresponding language feature:

```
import scala.language.implicitConversions
```

`Predef` contains a number of implicit conversions for Java-specific classes and primitives. For example, this is how *autoboxing* and *autounboxing* is defined for Scala's `Int` and Java's `Integer`:

```
// part of Predef in Scala
implicit def int2Integer(x: Int): java.lang.Integer =
x.asInstanceOf[java.lang.Integer]
implicit def Integer2int(x: java.lang.Integer): Int = x.asInstanceOf[Int]
```

These two methods are used by the compiler in cases where a value of type `Int` is expected, but the value with the type `java.lang.Integer` is provided and vice versa. Assuming that we have a Java method returning a random `Integer`, we would have implicit conversion applied in the following scenario:

```
val integer: Integer = RandomInt.randomInt()
val int: Int = math.abs(integer)
```

`math.abs` expects `Int`, but an `Integer` is provided, so the compiler applies the implicit conversion `Integer2int`.

Identical principles apply to the return types in the same way that they apply to the parameters. If the compiler finds a method call on a type that does not have this method, it will look for an implicit conversion so that the original return type can be converted to the type that suits this method. This allows you to implement a pattern called **extension methods**. A `String` type in Scala is a perfect example. It is defined as a type alias for Java's `String`:

```
type String = java.lang.String
```

But it is possible to call methods such as `map`, `flatMap`, `append`, `prepend`, and many others, which are not defined in the original `String`. This is achieved by converting a `String` into `StringOps` every time such a method is called:

```
@inline implicit def augmentString(x: String): StringOps = new StringOps(x)

scala> "I'm a string".flatMap(_.toString * 2) ++ ", look what I can do"
res1: String = II''mm aa ssttrriinngg, look what I can do
```

The implicit conversion can be type-parameterized, but cannot be nested or directly chained. The compiler will only apply one implicit conversion at a time:

```
case class A[T](a: T)
case class B[T](a: T)

implicit def a2A[T](a: T): A[T] = A(a)
implicit def a2B[T](a: T): B[T] = B(a)

def ab[C](a: B[A[C]]): Unit = println(a)
```

The compiler will accept the call with `A` because of implicit conversion `t2B` being in scope, but will reject everything that is neither `A` nor `B`:

```
scala> ab(A("A"))
B(A(A))

scala> ab("A")
          ^
        error: type mismatch;
         found  : String("A")
         required: B[A[?]]
```

Sometimes, it is possible to enforce one of the conversions so that the compiler can then apply the other. Here, we tell the compiler to apply a conversion from `String` to `A[String]` by providing a type ascription. The conversion from A to B[A] then happens like it did previously:

```scala
scala> ab("A" : A[String])
B(A(A))
```

Quite handy, isn't it?

Why are implicit conversions considered disputable, then? Because sometimes they can be applied without the developer knowing that and can change semantics in unexpected ways. This can be especially bad in situations where conversions for two types exist for both directions (like in our Int/Integer example) or when pre-existing types are involved. This classical example is based on having some implicit conversions in scope and type coercions later:

```scala
scala> implicit val directions: List[String] = List("North", "West",
"South", "East")
directions: List[String] = List(north, west, south, east)
scala> implicit val grades: Map[Char, String] = Map('A' -> "90%", 'B' ->
"80%", 'C' -> "70%", 'D' -> "60%", 'F' -> "0%")
grades: Map[Char,String] = ChampHashMap(F -> 0%, A -> 90%, B -> 80%, C ->
70%, D -> 60%)
scala> println("B" + 42: String)
B42
scala> println(("B" + 42): String)
B42
scala> println("B" + (42: String))
java.lang.IndexOutOfBoundsException: 42
  at scala.collection.LinearSeqOps.apply(LinearSeq.scala:74)
  at scala.collection.LinearSeqOps.apply$(LinearSeq.scala:71)
  at scala.collection.immutable.List.apply(List.scala:72)
  ... 38 elided
scala> "B" + 'C'
res3: String = BC
scala> "B" + ('C': String)
res4: String = B70%
scala> "B" + (2: String)
res5: String = BSouth
```

Here, we can see two examples of this behavior: one with a semantically similar `String` plus `Int` concatenation producing different results, and another crafted in the same way but for `String` and `Char`.

The reason for strange results and `IndexOutOfBoundsException` is that `Map` and `List` both implement `PartialFunction`, and thus just `Function1`. In our case, it's `Int =>` `String` for the `List` and `Char => String` for the `Map`. Both are defined as implicit, and at the moment one of both type conversions is required, the corresponding function is applied.

Because of this unpredictability, the use of implicit conversions is discouraged in modern Scala, though they are not removed from the language or deprecated, because a lot of existing implementations depend on them. They are mostly used to add methods to the existing classes or to add trait implementations for the new traits.

Implicit parameters

Implicit parameters use the same syntax as implicit conversions, but provide different functionality. They allow you to pass arguments into a function automatically . The definition of implicit parameters is done as a separate argument list in the definition of the function with a leading `implicit` keyword. Only one implicit argument list is allowed:

```
case class A[T](a: T)
case class B[T](a: T)

def ab[C](name: String)(a: A[C])(implicit b: B[C]): Unit =
  println(s"$name$a$b")
```

Implicit arguments do not require any special imports or compiler options to be activated. The preceding example shows that they also can be type-parameterized. If there is no value for the implicit argument *visible* at the moment the method is called, the compiler will report an error:

```
scala> ab("1")(A("A"))
              ^
    error: could not find implicit value for parameter b: B[String]
```

This error can be fixed by providing the required implicit value:

```
scala> implicit val b = B("[Implicit]")
b: B[String] = B([Implicit])

scala> ab("1")(A("A"))
1A(A)B([Implicit])
```

If there are multiple implicit values in scope, the compiler will return an error:

```
scala> implicit val c = B("[Another Implicit]")
c: B[String] = B([Another Implicit])

scala> ab("1")(A("A"))
              ^
        error: ambiguous implicit values:
          both value b of type => B[String]
          and value c of type => B[String]
          match expected type B[String]
```

The solution to this problem is to remove all but one of the ambiguous implicit values or make one of the values *more specific*. We will look at how this can be done in a moment. Yet another approach is to provide the implicit value explicitly:

```
scala> ab("1")(A("A"))(b)
1A(A)B([Implicit])

scala> ab("1")(A("A"))(c)
1A(A)B([Another Implicit])
```

The implicit parameter does not need to be a value—it can be defined as a method. Having impure implicit methods can lead to *random* behavior, especially in the case of the type of implicit parameter being somewhat general:

```
scala> implicit def randomLong: Long = scala.util.Random.nextLong()
randomLong: Long

scala> def withTimestamp(s: String)(implicit time: Long): Unit =
println(s"$time: $s")
withTimestamp: (s: String)(implicit time: Long)Unit

scala> withTimestamp("First")
-3416379805929107640: First

scala> withTimestamp("Second")
8464636473881709888: Second
```

Because of this, there is a general rule that implicit parameters must have possibly specific types. Following this rule also allows you to avoid confusing the compiler with recursive implicit parameters like the following:

```
scala> implicit def recursiveLong(implicit seed: Long): Long =
scala.util.Random.nextLong(seed)
recursiveLong: (implicit seed: Long)Long
```

```
scala> withTimestamp("Third")
                     ^
        error: diverging implicit expansion for type Long
        starting with method recursiveLong
```

Done right, implicit parameters can be very useful and can provide configuration parameters for the implementations. Usually, it is done top-down and affects all layers of the program:

```
object Application {
  case class Configuration(name: String)
  implicit val cfg: Configuration = Configuration("test")
  class Persistence(implicit cfg: Configuration) {
    class Database(implicit cfg: Configuration) {
      def query(id: Long)(implicit cfg: Configuration) = ???
      def update(id: Long, name: String)(implicit cfg: Configuration) = ???
    }
    new Database().query(1L)
  }
}
```

In this example, the configuration is defined once in the top layer and automatically passed down to the methods in the lowest layer. As a result, the calling of the function becomes more readable.

These configuration settings are just a special case of a more general use case—context passing. The context is usually stable compared to normal arguments and it is because of this that it makes sense to pass it implicitly. The classic example of this is an ExecutionContext, which is required for most of the Future methods (we'll take a detailed look at this in Chapter 6, *Exploring Built-In Effects*):

```
def filter(p: T => Boolean)(implicit executor: ExecutionContext): Future[T]
  = ...
```

The execution context usually doesn't change as opposed to the filtering logic, and therefore is passed implicitly.

Another use case is to verify types. We already saw an example of this in Chapter 2, *Understanding Types in Scala* when we discussed generalized type constraints.

Implicit classes

So far, we have discussed implicit conversions and the extension methods pattern. The implementation is usually done in such a way that the old type is wrapped in an instance of a new type, which then provides the additional methods. We looked at `StringOps` as an example, but let's try to come up with a homegrown implementation of this pattern. We'll have a type, A, and we want it to be able to do some operation, b:

```
case class A[T](a: T) { def doA(): T = a }
A("I'm an A").doB() // does not compile
```

We can fix the compile error by defining a class, with the required operation, and by providing an implicit conversion from A to B:

```
case class B[T](b: T) { def doB(): T = b }

import scala.language.implicitConversions
implicit def a2b[T](a: A[T]): B[T] = B(a.a)

A("I'm an A").doB() // works
```

This approach is so common that Scala has a special syntax for that called **implicit classes**. It combines defining a class and an implicit conversion into one definition of the class. The extended type becomes an argument for the constructor of the new class just as, in the previous code and in the following example:

```
implicit class C[T](a: A[T]) { def doC(): T = a.a }
A("I'm an A").doC()
```

It's cleaner and it does not require a `scala.language.implicitConversions` import.

The reason for this is that there is a subtle but significant difference between plain implicit conversions and implicit classes. While an implicit conversion can represent any kind of change, including already existing and/or primitive types, an `implicit` class is something that is created with the typed conversion in mind. The fact that it accepts the initial type as a constructor parameter makes it parameterized by this type—in a sense. All in all, it is safer to use implicit classes than implicit conversions.

View and context bounds

Implicit conversions and implicit parameters we discussed previously, and they are so ubiquitous that there is a special language syntax for them, that is, view and context bounds. View bounds have been deprecated since Scala 2.11, but we believe that knowing about them will help you understand context bounds, so we'll cover both, though in different degrees of details.

View bounds

The *view bound* is a syntactic sugar for the implicit parameter, which represents conversion between two types. It allows you to write a method signature with such implicit arguments in a slightly shorter form. We can see the difference between these two approaches by developing a method that will compare two unrelated types if there is a conversion to the third specific type for both of them:

```
case class CanEqual(hash: Int)

def equal[CA, CB](a: CA, b: CB)(implicit ca: CA => CanEqual, cb: CB =>
CanEqual): Boolean = ca(a).hash == ca(a).hash
```

The version with view bounds (similar to the upper bound and lower bound, which we discussed in Chapter 2, *Understanding Types in Scala*) has a shorter definition:

```
def equalsWithBounds[CA <% CanEqual, CB <% CanEqual](a: CA, b: CB): Boolean
= {
  val hashA = implicitly[CA => CanEqual].apply(a).hash
  val hashB = implicitly[CB => CanEqual].apply(b).hash
  hashA == hashB
}
```

The implicit method we are using here is a `helper` method, which is defined in Predef as the following:

```
@inline def implicitly[T](implicit e: T) = e
```

This allows us to summon an implicit value of type `T`. We're not providing this implicit value explicitly, and so we need to help the compiler figure out the sequence of calls by using the apply method on the summoned conversion.

If the implementation is more complex as compared to the original version, why would we want to use it? The answer is this—it becomes much better if the implicit parameters were just passed over to some internal function:

```
def equalsWithPassing[CA <% CanEqual, CB <% CanEqual](a: CA, b: CB):
Boolean = equal(a, b)
```

Like we said previously, view bounds have been deprecated since Scala 2.11, so we won't go into further details. Instead, we'll give our attention to context bounds.

Context bounds

There is a yet another special case with implicit parameters where they are parameterized with the types of normal parameters. In this case, our previous example could be rewritten as follows:

```
trait CanEqual[T] { def hash(t: T): Int }

def equal[CA, CB](a: CA, b: CB)(implicit ca: CanEqual[CA], cb:
CanEqual[CB]): Boolean =
  ca.hash(a) == cb.hash(b)
```

As we have already mentioned, there is also some syntactic sugar for this case named *context bounds*. With context bounds, our example can be simplified as follows:

```
def equalBounds[CA: CanEqual, CB: CanEqual](a: CA, b: CB): Boolean = {
  val hashA = implicitly[CanEqual[CA]].hash(a)
  val hashB = implicitly[CanEqual[CB]].hash(b)
  hashA == hashB
}
```

As in the previous case, this syntax becomes concise in the case of the implicit parameters being passed over to the internal function:

```
def equalDelegate[CA: CanEqual, CB: CanEqual](a: CA, b: CB): Boolean =
equal(a, b)
```

Now, this is short and readable!

What is missing is the implementation of the implicit parameters for the different CA and CB. For String, it might be implemented as follows:

```
implicit val stringEqual: CanEqual[String] = new CanEqual[String] {
  def hash(in: String): Int = in.hashCode()
}
```

The implementation for `Int` is done in a very similar way. Using single abstract method syntax, we can replace the class definition with a function:

```
implicit val intEqual: CanEqual[Int] = (in: Int) => in
```

We can do this with even shorter code by using the identity in curried form:

```
implicit val intEqual: CanEqual[Int] = identity _
```

Now, we can use our implicit values to call functions with context bounds:

```
scala> equal(10, 20)
res5: Boolean = false
scala> equalBounds("10", "20")
res6: Boolean = false
scala> equalDelegate(10, "20")
res7: Boolean = false
scala> equalDelegate(1598, "20")
res8: Boolean = true
```

In the previous snippet, the compiler resolves different implicits for different types of parameters, and these implicits are used to compare the arguments of the function.

Type classes

The previous example demonstrated that we need three parts for context bounds to work:

1. A parameterized type, T, which is defined as an implicit parameter of the function we're going to call
2. One or more operations (methods) which are defined on T, and which will be available after the conversion
3. Implicit instances that implement T

In the case of the type referred to of the method definition being an abstract one and the mentioned method being implemented in different ways in instances, we're talking about *ad-hoc polymorphism* (as opposed to parametric polymorphism for functions, and subtype polymorphism for subclasses). Here, we will explore how this concept is implemented with type classes, how the compiler finds suitable instances if needed, and how variance applies in ad hoc polymorphic cases.

Type classes

Ad-hoc polymorphism is especially useful in languages that aren't object-oriented and thus can't have subtype polymorphism. One example of such a language is Haskell. The pattern we're discussing is named *type classes* in Haskell and this name also came over to Scala. Type classes are widely used in `stdlib` and open source libraries and are fundamental for functional programming in Scala.

 The name *type classes* sound very familiar for an object-oriented developer because of the notion of classes. Unfortunately, it has nothing to do with classes in the OO sense and is just confusing. It helped me to think about type classes as a *class of types* instead in order to rewire my brain for this pattern.

Let's compare it to the traditional object-oriented approach and a type class that is used to define a set of USB cables. With OO, we would have the following definition:

```
trait Cable {
  def connect(): Boolean
}
case class Usb(orientation: Boolean) extends Cable {
  override def connect(): Boolean = orientation
}
case class Lightning(length: Int) extends Cable {
  override def connect(): Boolean = length > 100
}
case class UsbC(kind: String) extends Cable {
  override def connect(): Boolean = kind.contains("USB 3.1")
}
def connectCable(c: Cable): Boolean = c.connect()
```

Each of the subclasses implements the `connect` method by overriding the base traits' method. The `connectCable` just delegates the call to the instance, and proper implementation is called using dynamic dispatch:

```
scala> connectCable(Usb(false))
res9: Boolean = false
scala> connectCable(Lightning(150))
res10: Boolean = true
```

The type class version looks slightly different. The classes do not need to extend the `Cable` any more (and thus are free to be a part of a different class hierarchy). We've also made a `UsbC` type generic, just for fun:

```
case class Usb(orientation: Boolean)
case class Lightning(length: Int)
case class UsbC[Kind](kind: Kind)
```

The connection logic has moved into the type class that's been parameterized by the type of the cable:

```
trait Cable[C] {
  def connect(c: C): Boolean
}
```

It is implemented in the respective type class instances:

```
implicit val UsbCable: Cable[Usb] = new Cable[Usb] {
  override def connect(c: Usb): Boolean = c.orientation
}
```

Or in the same approach using single abstract method syntax:

```
implicit val LightningCable: Cable[Lightning] = (_: Lightning).length > 100
```

We can't just define an implicit instance for our recently parameterized `UsbC` as we can't provide a generic implementation for *any* type parameter. The instance for the `UsbC[String]` (the same as in the OO version) can be easily implemented through the following:

```
implicit val UsbCCableString: Cable[UsbC[String]] =
  (_: UsbC[String]).kind.contains("USB 3.1")
```

The `connectCable` is implemented with the context bound and uses ad-hoc polymorphism to select a proper delegate method:

```
def connectCable[C : Cable](c: C): Boolean =
implicitly[Cable[C]].connect(c)
```

This method can be called in the same way we called its OO sibling:

```
scala> connectCable(Usb(false))
res11: Boolean = false
scala> connectCable(Lightning(150))
res12: Boolean = true
scala> connectCable(UsbC("USB 3.1"))
res13: Boolean = true
```

On the call side, we have the same syntax, but the implementation is different. It is completely decoupled—our case classes don't know anything about the connection logic. In fact, we could have implemented this logic for the classes defined in another, closed source library!

Type class recursive resolution

In our previous example, we haven't implemented the connection functionality for the parameterized `UsbC` type, and our solution was only limited to `UsbC[String]`.

We could improve our solution by further delegating the connection logic. Say that we have an implicit function, `T => Boolean`, available—we could say that this is the logic the user of our library wants to use to describe the connection method.

 This is an example of a *bad* use of implicits. This does not only include *primitive* `Boolean` types; it is highly probable that it will refer to another predefined type at the moment the implicit conversion will be defined. We provide this example exactly as it is mentioned—as an illustration of the bad design to be avoided!

This is what our delegate method could look like:

```
implicit def usbCCableDelegate[T](implicit conn: T => Boolean):
Cable[UsbC[T]] = (c: UsbC[T]) => conn(c.kind)
```

It literally reflects the intuition we had for the delegating function—the compiler will create an instance of `Cable[UsbC[T]]` if there is an implicit conversion of `T => Boolean` available.

This is how this could be used:

```
implicit val symbolConnect: Symbol => Boolean =
  (_: Symbol).name.toLowerCase.contains("cable")

scala> connectCable(UsbC('NonameCable))
res18: Boolean = true
scala> connectCable(UsbC('FakeKable))
res19: Boolean = false
```

But then, we have to deal with all of the dangers of the implicit conversion we're delegating to. For example, having the following unrelated conversions in scope:

```
implicit val isEven: Int => Boolean = i => i % 2 == 0
implicit val hexChar: Char => Boolean = c => c >= 'A' && c <='F'
```

Would suddenly allow us to connect cables in unexpected ways:

```
scala> connectCable(UsbC(10))
res23: Boolean = true
scala> connectCable(UsbC(11))
res24: Boolean = false
scala> connectCable(UsbC('D'))
res25: Boolean = true
```

It might look like it is a dangerous approach to have an implicit definition that relies on the existence of another implicit in order to produce the required implicit value, but this is exactly what gives type classes their power.

To demonstrate this, let's imagine that we'd like to implement a USB adapter that should connect two USB devices with different standards. We could do this easily by representing our adapter as a pair of cable ends to connect, and delegating the real connection to the respective end of the cable:

```
implicit def adapt[A, B](implicit ev1: Cable[A], ev2: Cable[B]): Cable[(A,
B)] = new Cable[(A, B)] {
  def connect(ab: (A, B)): Boolean =
    ev1.connect(ab._1) && ev2.connect(ab._2)
}
```

Or, we could use context bounds and SAM syntax:

```
implicit def adapt[A: Cable, B: Cable]: Cable[(A, B)] =
  (ab: (A, B)) =>
    implicitly[Cable[A]].connect(ab._1) &&
    implicitly[Cable[B]].connect(ab._2)
```

Now, we can use this implicit to call our existing `connectCable` method, but with the adapter logic:

```
scala> val usb2usbC = (Usb(false), UsbC('NonameCable))
usb2usbC: (Usb, UsbC[Symbol]) = (Usb(false),UsbC('NonameCable))

scala> connectCable(usb2usbC)
res33: Boolean = false

scala> val lightning2usbC = (Lightning(150), UsbC('NonameCable))
lightning2usbC: (Lightning, UsbC[Symbol]) =
(Lightning(150),UsbC('NonameCable))

scala> connectCable(lightning2usbC)
res34: Boolean = true
```

Impressive, isn't it? Just imagine how much effort would be needed to add this functionality to the OO version!

The fun does not stop here! Because of the recursive nature of the context bound resolution, we can now build a chain of any length and the compiler will recursively check if it is possible to build the required adapter at compile time:

```scala
scala> val usbC2usb2lightning2usbC = ((UsbC('NonameCable), Usb(false)),
(Lightning(150), UsbC("USB 3.1")))
usbC2usb2lightning2usbC: ((UsbC[Symbol], Usb), (Lightning, UsbC[String])) =
((UsbC('NonameCable),Usb(false)),(Lightning(150),UsbC(USB 3.1)))

scala> connectCable(usbC2usb2lightning2usbC)
res35: Boolean = false

scala> val noUsbC_Long_Cable = (UsbC('NonameCable), (Lightning(150),
UsbC(10L)))
noUsbC_Long_Cable: (UsbC[Symbol], (Lightning, UsbC[Long])) =
(UsbC('NonameCable),(Lightning(150),UsbC(10)))

scala> connectCable(noUsbC_Long_Cable)
                    ^
        error: could not find implicit value for evidence parameter of type
Cable[(UsbC[Symbol], (Lightning, UsbC[Long]))]
```

We can improve the error message a bit by applying a special annotation on our type class definition:

```scala
@scala.annotation.implicitNotFound("Cannot connect cable of type ${C}")
trait Cable[C] {
  def connect(c: C): Boolean
}
```

Then, our last unsuccessful attempt will explain the reason for the failure a bit better:

```scala
scala> connectCable(noUsbC_Long_Cable)
                    ^
        error: Cannot connect cable of type (UsbC[Symbol], (Lightning,
UsbC[Long]))
```

Unfortunately, this is only as far as we can get in this case. The compiler can't currently figure out that the real reason for the failure is just `UsbC[Long]` and not the whole type.

The compiler will always try to infer the most specific implicit value with respect to subtyping and variance. This is why it is possible to combine subtype polymorphism and ad-hoc polymorphism.

Type class variance

To see how this combination works, let's imagine that our USB cables represent a hierarchy with a common ancestor:

```
abstract class UsbConnector
case class Usb(orientation: Boolean) extends UsbConnector
case class Lightning(length: Int) extends UsbConnector
case class UsbC[Kind](kind: Kind) extends UsbConnector
```

How will this affect our type class definition? Well, of course, our previous version with every subtype implemented separately will work fine. But what if we would like to provide a generic type class instance for the whole `UsbConnector` hierarchy as shown in the following example?

```
implicit val usbCable: Cable[UsbConnector] = new Cable[UsbConnector] {
  override def connect(c: UsbConnector): Boolean = {
    println(s"Connecting $c")
    true
  }
}
```

We would not be able to connect our cables anymore:

```
scala> connectCable(UsbC("3.1"))
                  ^
       error: could not find implicit value for evidence parameter of type
Cable[UsbC[String]]
```

This happens because the definition of our type class is invariant—thus, we are expected to provide an instance of `Cable[T]` with `T <:< UsbC[String]`. Is the `usbCable` a good fit? It turns out that it is not because its return type is `Cable[UsbConnector]` and we're expected to provide a `UsbC[String]`.

We can fix this in two ways, depending upon whether we want our type class to work the same way for any class hierarchy or whether each class hierarchy that needs general treatment has to define it separately.

In the first case, we need to make sure that the compiler understands the following:

```
Cable[UsbConnector] <:< Cable[UsbC[String]]
```

We can check that this is currently not the case in the REPL:

```
implicitly[Cable[UsbConnector] <:< Cable[UsbC[String]]]
           ^
        error: Cannot prove that Cable[UsbConnector] <:<
Cable[UsbC[String]]
```

But we already know what we need to change in order to make it pass—our `Cable` should become contravariant:

```
trait Cable[-C] {
  def connect(c: C): Boolean
}
```

As soon as we have proper variation in the definition of the `Cable`, everything falls into place, and the compiler can resolve all required implicits:

```
scala> implicitly[Cable[UsbConnector] <:< Cable[UsbC[String]]]
res1: TypeClassVariance.Cable[TypeClassVariance.UsbConnector] <:<
TypeClassVariance.Cable[TypeClassVariance.UsbC[String]] = generalized
constraint

scala> connectCable(UsbC("3.1"))
Connecting UsbC(3.1)
```

Unfortunately, if we decide that we need a special handling just for some of the classes from our hierarchy, we won't be able to reuse our implementation by defining a *more specific* type class instance:

```
implicit val usbCCable: Cable[UsbC[String]] = new Cable[UsbC[String]] {
  override def connect(c: UsbC[String]): Boolean = {
    println(s"Connecting USB C ${c.kind}")
    true
  }
}

scala> connectCable(UsbC("3.1"))
Connecting UsbC(3.1)
```

This test shows that the generic instance is still used and that the specific one is ignored.

Luckily, we have another option that is feasible in the case that we can afford that each hierarchy takes care of subtyping resolution on its own. In this case, we keep our type class invariant but change the type class instance to be of a specific type instead of a general one:

```
implicit def usbPolyCable[T <: UsbConnector]: Cable[T] = new Cable[T] {
  override def connect(c: T): Boolean = {
    println(s"Poly-Connecting $c")
```

```
      true
    }
  }
```

We need to change `val` to a `def` in order to be able to parameterize it. Our generalized constraint starts to fail again for the invariant type class:

```
scala> implicitly[Cable[UsbConnector] <:< Cable[UsbC[String]]]
         ^
  error: Cannot prove that Cable[UsbConnector] <:< Cable[UsbC[String]].
```

Nevertheless, we can connect the cable:

```
scala> connectCable(UsbC("3.1"))
Poly-Connecting UsbC(3.1)
```

Now, the compiler is able to choose the most specific instance available for our type class! If we bring the definition of `implicit val usbCCable` back into scope, we'll see that the output changes:

```
scala> connectCable(UsbC("3.1"))
Connecting USB C 3.1
```

This shows how *static overloading resolution* works. But this is only part of the picture. Let's clarify how and where the compiler looks for implicits if it needs them.

Implicit scope resolution

In order to put the implicits in the places where they are required, the compiler first has to find them. This process is called **implicit scope resolution** and has well-defined rules in order to guarantee that implicits are determined as expected by the language specification and the developer using them. Implicit scope resolution is a three-step process.

 Or four-step, if we count the case where the implicit parameter is provided explicitly as an argument to the method. We'll consider this case as number zero and won't take it into the account because it has the highest precedence and does not involve implicit lookup.

We'll provide a short overview of these steps so that we have them in one place for easy reference and then go into the details of each on the list:

- The current invocation (or lexical) scope. It has precedence over the implicit scope and encloses implicits that are accessible directly by their names without prefix, such as the following:
  - Local declarations
  - Outer scope declarations
  - Package objects
  - Inheritance chain
  - Import statements
- The implicit scope. It is looked up recursively and includes the following:
  - Companion object of the parameters
  - Companion object of super types
  - Companion object of mixin types (supertraits)
  - Companion object of the type
  - Companion object of the type parameters
  - Companion object of the type constructor
- Static overloading rules in the case of multiple implicits being found on one of the scopes.

Lexical scope

Let's start with the *lexical scope*. The lexical scope defines how variables are resolved in nested language constructs such as methods, functions, and other structured blocks. In general, the definitions of outer blocks are visible from inside the inner block (unless they are shadowed).

The following listing shows all possible conflicts during implicit resolution in this scope:

```
package object resolution {
  implicit val a: TS = new TS("val in package object") // (1)
}

package resolution {
  class TS(override val toString: String)
  class Parent {
    // implicit val c: TS = new TS("val in parent class") // (2)
  }
  trait Mixin {
```

```
      // implicit val d: TS = new TS("val in mixin") // (3)
    }
    // import Outer._ // (4)
    class Outer {
      // implicit val e: TS = new TS("val in outer class") // (5)
      // import Inner._ // (6)

      class Inner(/*implicit (7) */ val arg: TS = implicitly[TS]) extends
  Parent with Mixin {
        // implicit val f: TS = new TS("val in inner class") (8)
        private val resolve = implicitly[TS]
      }
      object Inner {
        implicit val g: TS = new TS("val in companion object")
      }
    }
    object Outer {
      implicit val h: TS = new TS("val in parent companion object")
    }
  }
```

The possible conflicts are underlined. It is easy to see that implicit values in the package object, outer and inner scope, as well as those brought into the inner or outer scope, are of the same weight. The parameter to the class constructor (7) will lead to the conflict as well, if it is declared implicit.

Implicit scope

Now, let's move on to an example for the *implicit scope*, which has lower precedence than the lexical scope. The implicit scope usually includes (if applicable) the companion object of the type, the implicit scope of an argument's type, the implicit scope of type argument(s), and for nested types, outer objects.

The following example demonstrates the first three cases in action:

```
import scala.language.implicitConversions

trait ParentA { def name: String }
trait ParentB
class ChildA(val name: String) extends ParentA with ParentB

object ParentB {
  implicit def a2Char(a: ParentA): Char = a.name.head

}
```

```scala
object ParentA {
  implicit def a2Int(a: ParentA): Int = a.hashCode()
  implicit val ordering = new Ordering[ChildA] {
    override def compare(a: ChildA, b: ChildA): Int =
      implicitly[Ordering[String]].compare(a.name, b.name)
  }
}
object ChildA {
  implicit def a2String(a: ParentA): String = a.name
}

trait Test {
  def test(a: ChildA) = {
    val _: Int = a // companion object of ParentA
    val _: String = a // companion object of ChildA
    val _: Char = a // companion object of ParentB
  }
  def constructor[T: Ordering](in: T*): List[T] = in.toList.sorted //
companion object of type constructor
  constructor(new ChildA("A"), new ChildA("B")).sorted // companion object
of type parameters
}
```

Here, we spread a few implicit conversions in a class hierarchy to show how the lookup goes over companion objects of the argument and its supertypes, including supertraits. The last two lines demonstrate how the implicit scope includes type parameters of both the constructor and parameter type of the `sorted` method.

Unlike the first example, all implicits we defined in this one are unambiguous. If they aren't, the compiler would apply the static resolution rules to try to figure out the most specific implicit.

Static overloading rules

The definition of static overloading rules is quite long and complicated (it can be found in the official documentation at https://www.scala-lang.org/files/archive/spec/2.13/06-expressions.html#overloading-resolution). It specifies a number of rules that the compiler uses to decide which alternative implicit is chosen. This decision is based on the relative weight of the alternatives. The higher weight means that the alternative A is more specific than B, and A wins.

The relative weight of A over B is calculated as a sum of two numbers:

- If A is defined in a class or object which is derived from the class or object defining B (simplified, A is derived from B if A is a subclass or companion object of a subclass of B, or B is a companion object of a superclass of A)
- If A is as specific as B (simplified, this means that if A is a method, it can be called with the same arguments as B; for polymorphic methods, this also means more specific type constraints)

These two rules allow you to calculate relative weights for two implicit conversions or parameters between 0 and 2 and to select the more suitable alternative in the case of the weights being different. If the weights are equal, the compiler will report ambiguous implicit values.

Summary

We have discussed three types of implicits in this chapter. These include implicit conversions, implicit classes, and implicit parameters.

We also discussed the syntactic sugar that's provided by the language in the form of view bounds and context bounds. We've seen how the former allows for defining implicit conversions in a somewhat concise way and that the latter does the same for type classes.

We compared object-oriented and type class based approaches in regards to polymorphic behavior. To depend on our knowledge of the topic, we worked through the recursive resolution of case classes and showed an example of type class variance.

In conclusion, we studied how the three levels of implicit scope resolution work. We've shown that all implicits in the lexical scope have the same precedence. The implicit scope is only looked at by the compiler if no suitable implicit can be found in the lexical scope. If there are multiple implicits in the scope, the static overloading rules are used to resolve possible conflicts.

This chapter concludes part of the book dedicated to Scala language constructs. In the following chapters, we'll move over to more complex concepts. But before doing this, in the next chapter, we'll take a brief digression into property-based testing to learn about some of the techniques we'll use to validate assumptions about the code we'll write in the second part of this book.

Questions

1. Describe a case where an implicit parameter is also an implicit conversion.
2. Replace the following definition that uses view bounds with one using context bounds: `def compare[T <% Comparable[T]](x: T, y: T) = x < y`?
3. Why are type classes sometimes said to separate behavior and data?
4. It is easy to change the example of possible conflicts in lexical scope so that one of the implicits wins over others and so that all others can be uncommented without having conflicts anymore. Can you change this?

Further reading

Mads Hartmann, Ruslan Shevchenko, *Professional Scala*: Writing concise and expressive, type-safe code in an environment that lets you build for the JVM, browser, and more.

Vikash Sharma, *Learning Scala Programming*: Learn how to write scalable and concurrent programs in Scala, a language that grows with you.

5
Property-Based Testing in Scala

Unit testing is a daily activity of many programmers. It is performed in order to verify the behavior of the software under development. Property-based testing is an alternative and supplementary approach to unit testing. It allows for the description of the expected properties of software and for their verification, if these properties hold using automatically generated data.

In this chapter, we'll discuss the situations in which property-based testing can be especially useful, and look at how the expected properties can be formulated and the test data can be produced.

The following topics will be covered in this chapter:

- The concept of property-based testing
- Properties
- Generators
- Shrinkers
- Properties as laws

Technical requirements

- JDK 1.8+
- SBT 1.2+

The source code for this chapter is available under: `https://github.com/PacktPublishing/Learn-Scala-Programming/tree/master/Chapter05`.

Introduction to property-based testing

The concept of unit testing should be well-known by any professional developer. A unit test usually contains a number of test cases. Each test case describes the expected behavior of a part of the program. The description is usually formulated in the form: *for this unit of code in that specific state we expect given input to produce the following output*. The developer then replicates such test cases with some deviations in the initial state and/or input data and expectations of the result in order to cover different code paths.

The specification of the test case is represented in the form of a test code relying on a testing framework. As at the moment of this writing, there are two popular testing frameworks for Scala projects, `ScalaTest` and `Specs2`. It is arguable that at least one of them should be familiar to any Scala developer, so we won't cover them in this book.

Instead, we'll take a look at alternative ways to formulate expectations about the behavior of the program.

From unit tests to properties

It turns out that testing scenarios (sometimes also called example-based tests) are just one of the many ways to define how the system is expected to work. Examples just describe some properties of the software having a specific state. The state usually affects the output in response to a provided input.

Generally speaking, in addition to properties described via examples, there are other types of properties which characterize software, such as:

- Universally quantified properties
- Conditional properties

With them we can tell something about the system which should hold for any valid input and possibly for all possible states. This form of testing is called **property-based testing (PBT)**. In contrast to the concrete scenario in a unit-testing case, the property is an abstract specification.

The same way that unit-testing frameworks provide functionality to structure tests and to formulate the expectations in the forms of unit tests, there is a Scala framework for PBT.

ScalaCheck

ScalaCheck (http://www.scalacheck.org) is a framework for automated PBT in Scala. It works great with SBT or IntelliJ IDEA and also has a built-in test runner and can be used standalone because of this. It also integrates well with ScalaTest and specs2.

ScalaCheck is an external dependency, so we need to add it to the build.sbt:

```
libraryDependencies += "org.scalacheck" %% "scalacheck" % "1.14.0" % Test
```

In order to be able to play with the code in REPL, we'll need to add it to the default scope (by removing the % Test part (this is already done in the chapter's code) and start the REPL with SBT dependencies. If you don't know how to do this, please refer to the Appendix A, *Preparing the Environment and Running Code Samples*, where we explain it in detail.

Now, we can define and verify our first property:

```
scala> import org.scalacheck.Prop.forAll
import org.scalacheck.Prop.forAll

scala> val stringLengthProp = forAll { (_: String).length >= 0 }
stringLength: org.scalacheck.Prop = Prop

scala> stringLengthProp.check
+ OK, passed 100 tests.
```

We just defined and verified that all Strings have non-negative lengths! Confused a bit? Let's take a closer look how it was done.

In the first line, we imported a forAll property factory. In essence, its purpose is to convert functions into properties.

In our case, in the second line the function is of a type String => Boolean. Naturally, there is some implicit magic in play. Among other things, there is an implicit conversion Boolean => Property and an Arbitrary[String] which provides a test data, in our case, random strings.

In the third line we call a `check` method available on the `Prop` (`ScalaCheck` uses this name as an abbreviation for `"property"`) among other combination and execution methods to execute our test using the default configuration. Hence, it runs with 100 random strings as an input data.

Now that we've got a feeling for how the PBT looks in general, we'll rigorously approach each aspect of it, starting with properties.

Properties

Defining properties is the most important aspect of PBT. It is impossible to test a system properly without having good properties definition. The transition from testing scenarios to properties is usually the hardest part for developers starting to adopt PBT.

Therefore, it is useful to have some kind of system which would help to approach the task of defining a property in a systematic manner. Often, the first step in systematizing something is classification.

Types of properties

We already said that there are universally quantified and conditional properties, depending upon if some property holds always or just for some subset of all possible inputs. Now, we want to break down properties in different dimensions—by how they are defined. Let's see how we could describe some operations in general terms.

Commutativity

If order operands do not matter, we say that the operation is commutative. The most trivial examples would be addition and multiplication. The property should be universal for both of these operations. In the following code, we're creating two properties, one for addition and one for multiplication, and checking that our assumption is correct by comparing results of computations with the changed order of operands:

```
scala> forAll((a: Int, b: Int) => a + b == b + a).check
+ OK, passed 100 tests.
scala> forAll((a: Int, b: Int) => a * b == b * a).check
+ OK, passed 100 tests.
```

For strings, the addition is defined as a concatenation but is not commutative in general:

```
scala> forAll((a: String, b: String) => a + b == b + a).check
! Falsified after 1 passed tests.
> ARG_0: "\u0001"
> ARG_0_ORIGINAL
> ARG_1: "\u0000"
> ARG_1_ORIGINAL: "賺"
```

In this example, we can also see how `ScalaCheck` generates random inputs and finds some minimal failing case. If at least one of the strings is empty, the property becomes commutative which can be demonstrated with the following modification of the previous test where b is assigned an empty string:

```
scala> forAll((a: String) => a + "" == "" + a).check
+ OK, passed 100 tests.
```

This is an example of a conditional test for string concatenation.

Associativity

The associativity is the same for operators as commutativity is for operands—if there are multiple operations, then the order in which operations are performed does not matter as long as the order of operands does not change.

The associativity properties for multiplication and addition again look very similar, as in the following example where we have three properties, each comparing results of two computations with a different order of operations:

```
scala> forAll((a: Int, b: Int, c: Int) => (a + b) + c == a + (b + c)).check
+ OK, passed 100 tests.
scala> forAll((a: Int, b: Int, c: Int) => (a * b) * c == a * (b * c)).check
+ OK, passed 100 tests.
scala> forAll((a: String, b: String, c: String) =>
   (a + b) + c == a + (b + c)).check
+ OK, passed 100 tests.
```

The last line demonstrates that string concatenation is associative as well.

Identity

The identity property of some operation states that if one of the operands is the identity value, then the result of the operation will be equal to another operand. For multiplication, the identity value is one; for addition, it is zero. Because of the commutativity of both multiplication and addition, the identity value can appear in any position. For example, in the next snippet the identity element appears as the first and as the second operand for all of them:

```scala
scala> forAll((a: Int) => a + 0 == a && 0 + a == a).check
+ OK, passed 100 tests.
scala> forAll((a: Int) => a * 1 == a && 1 * a == a).check
+ OK, passed 100 tests.
scala> forAll((a: String) => a + "" == a && "" + a == a).check
+ OK, passed 100 tests.
```

For string concatenation, the identity is an empty string. It turns out our conditional commutativity property for strings was just a manifestation of the universal identity property!

Invariants

Invariant properties are those which should never change in the context of the operation. For example, sorting the contents of the string or changing the case of it should never change its length. The next property demonstrates that it holds for normal as well as for uppercase strings:

```scala
scala> forAll((a: String) => a.sorted.length == a.length).check
+ OK, passed 100 tests.
scala> forAll((a: String) => a.toUpperCase().length == a.length).check
! Falsified after 50 passed tests.
> ARG_0: "ﬄ"
> ARG_0_ORIGINAL: "滇屾梗Ｊ丁肧裋裋伊墻轄玟潑"
```

Or well, for `toUpperCase` at least it should work if the locale matches the contents of the string or the string only contains ASCII symbols:

```scala
scala> forAll(Gen.asciiStr)((a: String) => a.toUpperCase().length ==
a.length).check
+ OK, passed 100 tests.
```

Here we went a bit ahead of ourselves and used `Gen.asciiStr` to generate strings which only contain ASCII chars.

Idempotence

Idempotent operations only change their operand once. After the initial change, any follow-up application should leave the operand unchanged. Sorting and uppercasing the contents of the string are good examples of idempotent operations. Please note that the same operations had the length property invariant in the previous example.

We can demonstrate that operations `toUpperCase` and sorted are idempotent by applying them a different number of times and expecting that the result is the same as after the first application:

```
scala> forAll((a: String) =>
  a.toUpperCase().toUpperCase() == a.toUpperCase()).check
+ OK, passed 100 tests.
scala> forAll((a: String) => a.sorted.sorted.sorted == a.sorted).check
+ OK, passed 100 tests.
```

For multiplications, the natural idempotent element is by definition the identity element. But it is also a zero:

```
scala> forAll((a: Int) => a * 0 * 0 == a * 0) .check
+ OK, passed 100 tests.
```

The logical AND and OR are idempotent for the Boolean values `false` and `true`, respectively.

Induction

Inductive properties reflect those of their operand(s). They are usually formulated for the inductive case.

For example, the factorial function for any argument should obey the factorial definition:

```
scala> def factorial(n: Long): Long = if (n < 2) n else n * factorial(n-1)
factorial: (n: Long)Long

scala> forAll((a: Byte) => a > 2 ==>
  (factorial(a) == a * factorial(a - 1))).check
+ OK, passed 100 tests.
```

Which is, of course, a conditional property for $n > 2$, which we specify using the implication operator ==> (more about this operator later).

Symmetry

Symmetry is a type of invariance. It states that the operand will have its original form after the application of some ordered set of operations . Often this set is limited to a pair of operations or even to a single symmetric operation.

For our usual experimental string, there is a symmetric operation `reverse`; for numbers, we could define a pair of addition and subtraction:

```
scala> forAll((a: String) => a.reverse.reverse == a).check
+ OK, passed 100 tests.
scala> forAll((a: Int, b: Int) => a + b - b == a).check
+ OK, passed 100 tests.
```

It is possible to define another pair with multiplication and division as operands (with respect to division by zero, overflow, and precision).

The symmetry property is often called a **round-trip** property. For a single operation it must hold for any inversible function.

Test Oracle

Strictly speaking, the test oracle does not belong to this list because it does not specify an intrinsic quality of the operation. Still, it is a useful and convenient way to pinpoint an expected behavior.

The principle is simple and especially useful during a refactoring or rewriting of the existing system. It uses given trusted implementation to verify the behavior of the new code. Back to our string examples, we might use Java's Array as a test oracle for the sorting of the contents of the string, by expecting that the results of sorting the string and an array, which consists of its elements, would be the same:

```
scala> forAll { a: String =>
     | val chars = a.toCharArray
     | java.util.Arrays.sort(chars)
     | val b = String.valueOf(chars)
     | a.sorted == b
     | }.check
+ OK, passed 100 tests.
```

But, of course, in the real refactoring scenario on the place of an array, the existing implementation would be used.

Defining a property

We've defined all different type's properties in the same way, using the most concise version of the `forAll` constructor and a `check` method. There are some ways to customize them.

Checking property

The `check()` method accepts `Test.Parameters`, which allow for the configuration of a few aspects of how the check is executed. The most useful describe a minimum number of successful tests, the number of workers to run in parallel, a test callback to execute after each test, the maximum discard ratio between passed and discarded tests for conditional tests, and an initial seed which can help to make the property evaluation deterministic. It is also possible to limit the time the test is allowed to execute. Here is an example, which uses both test parameters and a time limit:

```
scala> val prop = forAll { a: String => a.nonEmpty ==> (a.reverse.reverse
== a) }
prop: org.scalacheck.Prop = Prop

scala> val timed = within(10000)(prop)
timed: org.scalacheck.Prop = Prop

scala> Test.check(timed) {
     |
_.withMinSuccessfulTests(100000).withWorkers(4).withMaxDiscardRatio(3)
     | }
res47: org.scalacheck.Test.Result =
Result(Failed(List(),Set(Timeout)),0,0,Map(),10011)
```

Here we used the `Test.check` method, which executes a property with given parameters and returns test statistics back. We can see that our test has failed because of the timeout.

Besides `within`, there are other wrapper methods defined on `Prop`. For instance, it is possible to convert exceptions thrown by the property into test failures, to evaluate properties lazily, or to collect data for the test report:

```
scala> forAll { a: String =>
     |   classify(a.isEmpty, "empty string", "non-empty string") {
     |     a.sorted.length ?= a.length
```

```
|    }
| }.check()
+ OK, passed 100 tests.
> Collected test data:
96% non-empty string
4% empty string
```

The difference between == and ?= used in the previous code is subtle—the == compares two values and returns a Boolean, which is then implicitly converted to the `Prop`; the ?= creates a `Prop` directly and sometimes it can be useful in the situations where properties are combined, as we'll see further.

A property can also be labelled, which makes it easier to spot in the results:

```
scala> val prop2 = "Division by zero" |: protect(forAll((a: Int) => a / a
== 1))
prop2: org.scalacheck.Prop = Prop

scala> prop2.check()
! Exception raised on property evaluation.
> Labels of failing property:
Division by zero
> ARG_0: 0
> Exception: java.lang.ArithmeticException: / by zero
$line74.$read$$iw$$iw$$iw$$iw$$iw$$iw$$iw$$iw$.$anonfun$prop2$2(<console>:2
   3)
...
```

Here we also used the `protect` method to convert the exception into the test failure.

Combining properties

Until now, we were talking about single, isolated properties. Sometimes, it is useful, or even required, to make sure that some combination of properties holds. For instance, we might want to define a property which holds if and only if all other properties hold. Or we might want to have a property which is true if at least one property from a set of properties is true. There are combination methods defined on `Prop` exactly for such use cases. The result is just another property which can be checked the same way we already did:

```
forAll { (a: Int, b: Int, c: Int, d: String) =>
  val multiplicationLaws = all(
    "Commutativity" |: (a * b ?= b * a),
    "Associativity" |: ((a * b) * c ?= a * (b * c)),
    "Identity" |: all(a * 1 ?= a, 1 * a ?= a)
  ) :| "Multiplication laws"
```

```
        val stringProps = atLeastOne(d.isEmpty, d.nonEmpty)
        all(multiplicationLaws, stringProps)
    }.check()

+ OK, passed 100 tests.
```

This is a nested combination of properties. The topmost one holds if both `multiplicationLaws` and `stringProps` hold. The `stringProps` verifies that any `String` is either empty or non-empty; only one of these properties can be true at the same time. For `multiplicationLaws`, all nested properties must hold.

There are also more specific combinators, for example `someFailing` and `noneFailing` which hold in the case if some underlying properties are failing or none are failing respectively.

Generators

We have had a detailed discussion of properties, but haven't mentioned yet where the input data for these properties comes from. Let's correct this omission and give generators the care they deserve.

The idea of the generator comes from the general concept of types. In a sense, a type is a specification of possible values complying to that type. In other words, types describe the rules that values must comply to. These rules give us the possibility to generate ranges of data values for given types.

For some types there are more values; for others, there are less. As we already know, there are literal types which contain a single value. The same applies for `Unit` type with its `()` value. For `Boolean`, there are two values that exist: `true` and `false`. Two values would also exist for an imaginary equality relation type—equal and non-equal. With the same principle, we can say that full ordering takes one of three values: less than, equal, or greater than.

Properties defined in terms of types with such limited sets of possible values are called *provable*. This is because it is possible to try out all values of a given type (or combinations, if there are multiple parameters) and prove that the program is correct for all possible inputs.

The other type of properties are *falsifiable* properties. It is not possible (or does not make sense) to try out all possible values of input parameters, hence it is only possible to tell that the functionality under test works for some subset of all inputs.

To make falsifiable properties more trustworthy, existing `ScalaCheck` generators for `Byte`, `Short`, `Int`, and `Long` place additional weight on `zero`, `+1`, `-1`, and both `minValue` and `maxValue` for the type.

Let's take a look at which generators are included in the `ScalaCheck` and how we can use them to create new generators for the data types specific for our code. We'll also briefly touch the topic of gradually reducing the test data for failing cases known as shrinking.

Existing generators

Speaking about existing generators, ScalaCheck provides a lot of them out of the box, such as all subtypes of `AnyVal`, `Unit`, `Function0`, chars and strings with different contents (`alphaChar`, `alphaLowerChar`, `alphaNumChar`, `alphaStr`, `alphaUpperChar`, `numChar`, `numStr`), containers, lists and maps (`containerOf`, `containerOf1`, `containerOfN`, `nonEmptyContainerOf`, `listOf`, `listOf1`, `listOfN`, `nonEmptyListOf`, `mapOf`, `mapOfN`, `nonEmptyMap`), numbers (`chooseNum`, `negNum`, `posNum`), duration, `Calendar`, `BitSet`, and even `Test.Parameters`!

If there is no generator suitable for the testing purposes available, it is possible to create a custom generator by implementing a `Gen` class:

```
sealed abstract class Gen[+T] extends Serializable { self =>
  ...
  def apply(p: Gen.Parameters, seed: Seed): Option[T]
  def sample: Option[T]
  ...
}
```

This is an abstract class, which is basically just a function taking test parameters and returning an optional value of the required type.

It is partially implemented, but still, it's a bit mundane to extend it manually. Hence new generators are usually implemented by reusing already existing ones. As an exercise, let's implement a generator for literal types:

```
def literalGen[T <: Singleton](t: T): Gen[T] = Gen.const(t)
implicit val myGen: Arbitrary[42] = Arbitrary(literalGen(42))
val literalProp = forAll((_: 42) == 42).check
```

In the first line, we're creating a generator factory for literal types by delegating the value generation to the `Gen.const`. This is safe to do because, by definition, literal types contain just a single value. The second line creates an `implicit Arbitrary[42]`, which is expected to be in scope by the `forAll` property.

Combining generators

Though it is not very hard to create a custom one, the absolute majority of generators is built by combining existing implementations. `Gen` offers a couple of methods that are very useful in such scenarios. The classic example is to use the `map` and `flatMap` methods to create a generator for a case class.

Let's demonstrate this with an example of playing cards:

```
sealed trait Rank
case class SymRank(s: Char) extends Rank {
  override def toString: String = s.toString
}
case class NumRank(n: Int) extends Rank {
  override def toString: String = n.toString
}
case class Card(suit: Char, rank: Rank) {
  override def toString: String = s"$suit $rank"
}
```

First, we need some generators for suits and ranks which we can create by reusing existing `oneOf` and `choose` constructors:

```
val suits = Gen.oneOf('♡', '◇', '♤', '♧')
val numbers = Gen.choose(2, 10).map(NumRank)
val symbols = Gen.oneOf('A', 'K', 'Q', 'J').map(SymRank)
```

Now, we can combine our generators into the card generator using `for` comprehension:

```
val full: Gen[Card] = for {
  suit <- suits
  rank <- Gen.frequency((9, numbers), (4, symbols))
} yield Card(suit, rank)
```

We also use `Gen.frequency` in order to have a proper distribution of numbers and symbols produced by our combined generator.

It is easy to change this generator to only make cards for a pique pack by using the `suchThat` combinator:

```
val piquet: Gen[Card] = full.suchThat {
  case Card(_, _: SymRank) => true
  case Card(_, NumRank(n)) => n > 5
}
```

We can check that our generators produce trustworthy values by using the `Prop.collect` method:

```
scala> forAll(piquet) { card =>
     | Prop.collect(card)(true)
     | }.check
+ OK, passed 100 tests.
> Collected test data:
8% ♡ J
6% ◇ 7
6% ♡ 10
... (couple of lines more)
scala> forAll(full) { card =>
     | Prop.collect(card)(true)
     | }.check
+ OK, passed 100 tests.
> Collected test data:
6% ♡ 3
5% ◇ 3
... (a lot more lines)
```

Of course, it is also possible to generate a handfull of cards from the deck using one of the container generator methods:

```
val handOfCards: Gen[List[Card]] = Gen.listOfN(6, piquet)
```

And use it as before:

```
scala> forAll(handOfCards) { hand: Seq[Card] =>
     | Prop.collect(hand.mkString(","))(true)
     | }.check
! Gave up after only 58 passed tests. 501 tests were discarded.
> Collected test data:
2% ♤ 8,♤ 10,♤ 8,♤ 7,♡ Q,◇ 8
```

Oh, we have duplicate cards in our hand. It turns out that we need to use a more general form of the container generator, which takes both the type of the container and the type of the element as type parameters:

```
val handOfCards = Gen.containerOfN[Set, Card](6, piquet)
scala> forAll(handOfCards) { hand =>
     | Prop.collect(hand.mkString(","))(true)
     | }.check
! Gave up after only 75 passed tests. 501 tests were discarded.
> Collected test data:
1% ♡ A,♤ J,♡ K,◇ 6,♧ K,♧ A
1% ♤ 9,♧ A,♧ 8,♧ 9
```

That is better, but now it seems that the duplicate elements have just disappeared so that we still don't have an expected behavior. Moreover, another issue is obvious—a lot of tests are discarded. This happens because our `piquet` generator is defined in terms of filtering the output of the more general `full` generator. `ScalaCheck` notices that there are too many tests which do not qualify as a valid input and gives up earlier.

Let's fix our `piquet` generator and an issue with missing cards. For the first one, we will use the same approach as we've used for the `full` generator. We'll just change the number used for the rank:

```
val piquetNumbers = Gen.choose(6, 10).map(NumRank)

val piquet: Gen[Card] = for {
  suit <- suits
  rank <- Gen.frequency((5, piquetNumbers), (4, symbols))
} yield Card(suit, rank)
```

Please note how the frequency changed in respect to the changed set of possible values.

To fix the second issue, we will repeatedly generate the set of cards until it has an expected size using `retryUntil` combinator:

```
val handOfCards = Gen.containerOfN[Set, Card](6, piquet).retryUntil(_.size == 6)

scala> forAll(handOfCards) { hand =>
     |   Prop.collect(hand.mkString(","))(true)
     | }.check
+ OK, passed 100 tests.
> Collected test data:
1% ♠ 9,◇ 9,♣ 9,◇ Q,♣ J,♠ 10
. . .
```

Now, our hands are generated as expected.

Of course, there are even more useful combinator methods, which can be used to create other sophisticated generators. Please refer to the documentation (https://github.com/rickynils/scalacheck/blob/master/doc/UserGuide.md) or the source code for further details.

Shrinkers

We have looked at two cornerstones of PBT—properties and generators. There is still one aspect we should take a look at before considering ourselves done.

In PBT, the test data comes from generators and it is kind of random. Given this fact, we could expect that it might be hard to find out why a test is failing. Consider the following example:

```
scala> forAllNoShrink { num: Int =>
     |  num < 42
     |  }.check
! Falsified after 0 passed tests.
> ARG_0: 2008612603
```

Here, we can see that our property was falsified by the number 2008612603, which is arguably not very useful. It is more or less obvious for an `Int`, but consider a case with a list of many elements and a property formulated for these elements:

```
scala> forAllNoShrink(Gen.listOfN(1000, Arbitrary.arbString.arbitrary)) {
     |  _.forall(_.length < 10)
     |  }.check
! Falsified after 10 passed tests.
> ARG_0: List ("烱麐侼頜",·"ú惡鴬瀜",·"商裘→嬰口",·"螢貌棠豐綪娚",
  "配口",·"ↄ滎德π撲澠",·"廸磬惛
    ",
... // a lot of similar lines
```

Obviously, it is near to impossible to find out which of 1,000 strings had a wrong length in this test.

At this moment, the new component comes into play: the `Shrink`. The job of the shrinker is to find a minimal test data with which the property does not hold. In two previous examples, we used a `forAllNoShrink` property constructor and thus had no shrinker active. This is how the result will look like if we change the definition to the normal `forAll`:

```
scala> forAll(Gen.listOfN(1000, Arbitrary.arbString.arbitrary)) {
     |  _.forall(_.length < 10)
     |  }.check
! Falsified after 10 passed tests.
> ARG_0: List("")
> ARG_0_ORIGINAL: // a long list as before
```

Here, we can see that the minimal list, which falsifies our property, is the list with one empty string. The original failing input is shown as `ARG_0_ORIGINAL` and it is of a similar length and complexity as we've seen before.

The `Shrink` instances are passed as implicit parameters, so we can summon one to see how they work. We'll do this with our failing value for `Int` property:

```
val intShrink: Shrink[Int] = implicitly[Shrink[Int]]
scala> intShrink.shrink(2008612603).toList
res23: List[Int] = List(1004306301, -1004306301, 502153150, -502153150,
251076575, -251076575, 125538287, -125538287, 62769143, -62769143,
31384571, -31384571, 15692285, -15692285, 7846142, -7846142, 3923071,
-3923071, 1961535, -1961535, 980767, -980767, 490383, -490383, 245191,
-245191, 122595, -122595, 61297, -61297, 30648, -30648, 15324, -15324,
7662, -7662, 3831, -3831, 1915, -1915, 957, -957, 478, -478, 239, -239,
119, -119, 59, -59, 29, -29, 14, -14, 7, -7, 3, -3, 1, -1, 0)
```

The `shrink` method generates a stream of values and we evaluate it by converting it to the list. It is easy to see the pattern—the values produced by the `Shrink` lie symmetrically to the **central** value of 0 (zero), starting from the initial failing value, and then are each time divided by two until they converge to the zero. This is pretty much how it is implemented for numbers, including hardcoded values of +-`two`, +-`one`, and `zero`.

It is easy to see that numbers produced by the `Shrink` will depend on the initial failing argument. This is why for the first property the returned value will differ each time:

```
scala> forAll { (_: Int) < 42 }.check
! Falsified after 0 passed tests.
> ARG_0: 47
> ARG_0_ORIGINAL: 800692446

scala> forAll { (_: Int) < 42 }.check
! Falsified after 0 passed tests.
> ARG_0: 54
> ARG_0_ORIGINAL: 908148321

scala> forAll { (_: Int) < 42 }.check
! Falsified after 2 passed tests.
> ARG_0: 57
> ARG_0_ORIGINAL: 969910515

scala> forAll { (_: Int) < 42 }.check
! Falsified after 6 passed tests.
> ARG_0: 44
> ARG_0_ORIGINAL: 745869268
```

As we can see, the resulting failing value depends on the original failing value and is never 43, but sometimes it lies quite close.

Shrinkers are essential at the time there are some properties which do not hold, especially if the input data is of significant size.

Summary

Property-based testing is a supplementary technique to the traditional unit testing and behavior-driven development. It allows one to describe program properties in the form of an abstract specification, and the test data in the form of rules to apply for its generation.

Properly generated data includes edge cases, which are often ignored during example-based testing, and allows for higher code coverage.

The `ScalaCheck` is a framework for property-based testing with Scala. It has three main components—properties, generators, and shrinkers.

Universally quantified properties must hold for any test data in any state of the program. Conditional properties are defined for some subset of the data or specific states of the system.

`ScalaCheck` provides a lots of generators for standard types out of the box. The best way to create generators for custom types is by combining existing generators using suitable methods defined on them.

The role of an optional shrink is to reduce a test data set for a failing property, helping to identify a minimal failing test case.

There are a few extension libraries available which allow one to generate arbitrary case classes and ADTs (`scalacheck-shapeless`), cats type class instances (`cats-check`), and other common cases (`scalacheck-toolbox`).

Now, we are properly equipped to start our journey into the land of functional programming concepts, which we will cover in the next part of the book. We will start by examining some types present in the standard library, which are known as effects, such as `Option`, `Try`, `Either`, and `Future`.

Questions

1. Define an invariant property for sorting a list
2. Define an idempotent property for sorting a list
3. Define an inductive property for sorting a list
4. Define a generator for a `List[Lists[Int]]`, such that elements of the nested list are positive
5. Define a generator for a `Map[UUID, () => String]`

6
Exploring Built-In Effects

Sometimes, computers do things differently compared to what the developer expects. Sometimes, a function can't return a value for a given set of arguments, a device is not available at runtime, or calling an external system takes much longer than expected.

Functional approaches strive to capture these aspects and express them with types. This allows for precise reasoning about the program and helps to avoid surprises at runtime.

In this chapter, we will study how the mentioned aspects are covered by Scala's standard library. We'll take a look at the following:

- Foundations of encoding runtime aspects with types
- Option
- Either
- Try
- Future

Technical requirements

Before we begin, make sure you have the following installed:

- JDK 1.8+
- SBT 1.2+

The source code for this chapter is available under our GitHub repository at: `https://github.com/PacktPublishing/Learn-Scala-Programming/tree/master/Chapter06`.

Introduction to effects

Scala code compiles to the Java bytecode and runs on the JVM (Java Virtual Machine). As the name suggests, the JVM was not built specifically for Scala. Because of this, there is a mismatch between what is expressible with the Scala language and what the JVM supports. The consequences are twofold:

- The compiler converts Scala features that are not supported by the JVM into the proper bytecode, mostly by creating wrapper classes. As a result, the compilation of a simple Scala program might lead to the creation of dozens or hundreds of classes, which in turn leads to decreased performance and a higher garbage footprint. These negative consequences, in essence, are just an implementation detail. As the JVM improves, it is possible to optimize the bytecode produced by the compiler for the newer versions of Java without any efforts from the application developer.
- Looking in the opposite direction, there are some features of the platform that are not especially consistent with Scala. Support for them is required, though, partly for Scala-Java interoperability reasons, and partly because if something happens in the underlying runtime, it needs to be expressible in the language.

For us, as users of the language, the first class of differences is more of a theoretical interest as it is comfortable to assume that the compiler developers are doing their best to generate the bytecode which is of the best standards for the current version of the JVM, so we can just rely on them. Consequences of the second kind concern us more directly because they might influence the way we structure our code, and they definitely affect the code we write to interact with existing libraries, especially Java libraries.

Here, we're talking about features that might negatively impact on our possibility to reason about the code, especially those which break their referential transparency.

To illustrate the last point, let's take a look at the following code:

```scala
scala> import java.util
import java.util
scala> val map = new util.HashMap[String, Int] { put("zero", 0) }
map: java.util.HashMap[String,Int] = {zero=0}
scala> val list = new util.ArrayList[String] { add("zero") }
list: java.util.ArrayList[String] = [zero]
scala> println(map.get("zero"))
0
scala> println(list.get(0))
zero
```

We've defined a Java `HashMap`, an `ArrayList`, put some items in them, and got these back as expected. So far, so good.

Let's push this a bit further:

```
scala> println(map.get("one"))
null
scala> :type null
Null
```

For an element that can't be found in the `map`, we got a `null`: `Null` back, which is a bit unexpected. Is it really so bad? Well, it probably is:

```
scala> println(map.get("one").toString)
java.lang.NullPointerException
   ... 40 elided
```

We've got a `NullPointerException` which would crash our program at runtime if not caught!

OK, but we *can* check if the returned element is `null`. We just need to remember to do this each time we call a function that can potentially return `null`. Let's do this with the `list`:

```
scala> list.get(1) match {
     | case null => println("Not found")
     | case notNull => println(notNull)
     | }
java.lang.IndexOutOfBoundsException: Index: 1, Size: 1
  at java.util.ArrayList.rangeCheck(ArrayList.java:653)
  at java.util.ArrayList.get(ArrayList.java:429)
  ... 49 elided
```

Oh, the list does not return `null` for absent elements, it just throws the `IndexOutOfBoundsException` straight away! Looks like we need to add a `catch` clause to our call so that we can make it safe...

At this moment, our point is already clear – it is hard or impossible to reason about what the possible result of execution of some code written in this style is without looking at the JavaDocs, and eventually at the implementations' source code. The reason for this is that the functions we're calling can return the result in a way that's not encoded in their types. In the first example, the function returns a special `null` value for the case where there's no element in the collection. But this special value could also be something different! Another example is −1 for the `indexOf` method that's defined on the `ArrayList`. Yet another case is the indication of the impossibility to perform an operation, which is done by throwing an exception.

In a way, the functions we've called altered the environment they were executed in. In the case of an exception, the execution path of the program changed to propagate the exception, and in the case of `null` being returned, the caller's expectations had changed, unfortunately not at compile time but at runtime.

In functional programming, we call such a behavior an *effect*, and strive to express this effect at the type level. Effects in functional programming (FP) overlap with *side-effects*, but represent a wider concept. For example, an effect of optionality (returning `null`) of the result is not a side-effect.

Effects have the advantage that they don't need to be implemented on the language level. Because of this, the same effect can be designed in different ways, depending on the goals and architectural considerations of the library author. Most importantly, they can be extended and combined, which allows us to represent complex sets of effects in a structured and type-safe way.

In further sections of this chapter, we will take a look at four different kinds of effects that are available in the standard library, starting with `Option`.

Option

`Option` is probably the first effect that a novice Scala developer gets familiar with. It encodes the situation that the function might return no result. Simplified, it is represented in `stdlib` as an algebraic data type, as shown in the following code:

```
sealed abstract class Option[+A]
case object None extends Option[Nothing]
final case class Some[+A](value: A) extends Option[A]
```

`None` represents the case of an absent result, while `Some(value)` represents the case where a result exists. Next, we'll look at a three-step approach to gain more understanding of how to work with an `Option`—how to create it, read the value from it (if there is one) and which possibilities emerge from the fact that `Option` is an effect.

Creating an Option

An `Option` can be created in a variety of ways. The most straightforward, though not recommended, is to use the constructor of the case class or to return `None` directly:

```
val opt1 = None
val opt2 = Some("Option")
```

This is not recommended because it is absolutely possible to return `null` wrapped in `Option` again, thus defeating the purpose of it:

```
val opt3 = Some(null)
```

Because of this, we need to check whether the constructor argument is `null` first:

```
def opt4[A](a: A): Option[A] = if (a == null) None else Some(a)
```

In fact, this pattern is so common that the `Option` companion object provides the corresponding constructor:

```
def opt5[A](a: A): Option[A] = Option(a)
```

The companion object defines a few more constructors which allow you to refrain from direct use of `Some` or `None` altogether:

```
val empty = Option.empty[String]
val temperature: Int = 26
def readExactTemperature: Int = 26.3425 // slow and expensive method call
val temp1 = Option.when(temperature > 45)(readExactTemperature)
val temp2 = Option.unless(temperature < 45)(readExactTemperature)
```

The first constructor creates the type `None`, and the second and third return `Some`, but only if the condition is `true` or `false`, respectively. The second argument is a by-name parameter and is only calculated if the condition holds.

Reading from an Option

Now we have an `Option` and need to take the value out of it. The most obvious way to do this is in a "null-checking" style:

```
if (opt1.isDefined) println(opt1.get)
if (opt1.isEmpty) println("Ooops, option is empty") else println(opt1.get)
```

Here, we're using one of two emptiness checks and in this case, if an `Option` is non-empty, we call `.get` to retrieve its value. Besides being quite verbose, the main disadvantage of this approach is that it is easy to forget to check if an option has been defined. If `None.get` gets called, it will throw a `NoSuchElementException`:

```
scala> None.get
java.util.NoSuchElementException: None.get
  at scala.None$.get(Option.scala:378)
  ... 40 elided
```

There are a few more methods that allow you to check whether the contents of the option satisfy a given criteria, but they all suffer in the same way:

```
if (option.contains("boo")) println("non-empty and contains 'boo'")
if (option.exists(_ > 10)) println("non-empty and greater then 10")
if (option.forall(_ > 10)) println("empty or greater then 10")
```

The `contains` method compares its argument with the contents of the option if it has been defined. `exists` takes a predicate that is applied to the value of an option if it is non-empty. Compared to the other methods, `forall` is special because it returns `true` if a predicate applied to the argument holds for a non-empty option or if an option is empty.

Another way to get a value out of `Option` is to deconstruct it:

```
if (opt.isDefined) { val Some(value) = opt }
```

You can also use pattern matching to avoid checking for non-emptiness completely:

```
opt match {
  case Some(value) => println(value)
  case None => println("there is nothing inside")
}
```

Sometimes, all that is needed for the caller is a "default" value if an `Option` is empty. There is a special method for this called `getOrElse`:

```
val resultOrDefault = opt.getOrElse("No value")
```

Another similar method is `orNull`. It is not very useful in Scala code, but is very convenient for Java interoperability and is available for `Option[AnyRef]`. It returns `null` in the case of an empty option or the option's value otherwise:

```
scala> None.orNull
res8: Null = null
```

The `foreach` method feels quite different from what we've seen so far as it executes a function on a value of an `Option` in the case it is defined:

```
scala> val opt2 = Some("I'm a non-empty option")
opt2: Some[String] = Some(I'm a non-empty option)
scala> opt2.foreach(println)
I'm a non-empty option
```

The reason why it is special compared to the other methods we've seen so far is that it does not treat the option as a special value. Instead, it is semantically formulated as a callback – "if this effect has (had) place, execute the following code on it."

This view of an `Option` offers another possibility so that we can work with it – to provide higher order functions that will be executed in the case of an empty or non-empty option. Let's see how this works in detail.

Option as an effect

The first consequence of the aforementioned approach is that it is possible to constrain the possible values of the `Option` (and convert it to `None` if the conditions don't hold) without inspecting its contents. Here is an example of filtering options further containing a number bigger or less than `10`, respectively:

```
val moreThen10: Option[Int] = opt.filter(_ > 10)
val lessOrEqual10: Option[Int] = opt.filterNot(_ > 10)
```

It is also possible to use a partial function as a filter. This allows you to filter and transform the value at the same time. For example, you can filter numbers bigger than `10` and convert them into a `String`:

```
val moreThen20: Option[String] = opt.collect {
  case i if i > 20 => s"More then 20: $i"
}
```

Functionally, the `collect` method can be seen as a combination of `filter` and `map`, where the latter can be used separately to transform the contents of a non-empty option. For instance, let's imagine a chain of calls we'd need to make in order to catch a fish:

```
val buyBait: String => Bait = ???
val castLine: Bait => Line = ???
val hookFish: Line => Fish = ???

def goFishing(bestBaitForFish: Option[String]): Option[Fish] =
  bestBaitForFish.map(buyBait).map(castLine).map(hookFish)
```

Here, we're buying some bait, casting the line, and hooking the fish at the appropriate moment. The argument for our implementation is optional because we might not know what the best bite for a fish would be.

There is an issue with this implementation, though. We're ignoring the fact that our functions will have no results for the given parameters. The fishing store might be closed, the cast might break, and the fish can slip out. It turns out that we violate our own rules about expressing effects with types that we defined a couple of pages ago!

Let's fix that by making our functions return `Option`. We'll start with `hookFish`:

```
val hookFish: Line => Option[Fish]

def goFishingOld(bestBaitForFish: Option[String]): Option[Option[Fish]] =
  bestBaitForFish.map(buyBait).map(castLine).map(hookFish)
```

But now our function returns a nested `Option`, which is hard to work with. We can address this by flattening the result using the corresponding method:

```
def goFishingOld(bestBaitForFish: Option[String]): Option[Fish] =
  bestBaitForFish.map(buyBait).map(castLine).map(hookFish).flatten
```

Now, we can also make the `castLine` return `Option`:

```
val castLine: Bait => Option[Line]
val hookFish: Line => Option[Fish]

def goFishingOld(bestBaitForFish: Option[String]): Option[Fish] =
  bestBaitForFish.map(buyBait).map(castLine).map(hookFish).flatten
```

Unfortunately, this implementation ceases to compile:

```
error: type mismatch;
  found : FishingOptionExample.this.Line =>
Option[FishingOptionExample.this.Fish]
  required: Option[UserExample.this.Line] => ?
```

To deal with chained, non-empty options, there is a `flatMap` method, which accepts a function returning an `Option` and flattens the result before returning it. With `flatMap`, we can implement our chain of calls without the need to call `flatten` at the end:

```
val buyBait: String => Option[Bait]
val makeBait: String => Option[Bait]
val castLine: Bait => Option[Line]
val hookFish: Line => Option[Fish]

def goFishingOld(bestBaitForFish: Option[String]): Option[Fish]
bestBaitForFish.flatMap(buyBait).flatMap(castLine).flatMap(hookFish)
```

Having `map` and `flatMap` also allows us to use `Option` in `for` comprehensions. For instance, we can rewrite the preceding example like so:

```
def goFishing(bestBaitForFish: Option[String]): Option[Fish] =
  for {
    baitName <- bestBaitForFish
    bait <- buyBait(baitName).orElse(makeBait(baitName))
    line <- castLine(bait)
    fish <- hookFish(line)
  } yield fish
```

Here, we also added a fallback case for the situation of the fishing shop being closed, and when you need to make the bait by hand. This demonstrates that empty options can also be chained. The `orElse` method resolves a series of options until the first one that's defined is found or returns the last `Option` in the chain, regardless of its contents:

```
val opt5 = opt0 orElse opt2 orElse opt3 orElse opt4
```

There is a possibility to map over the `Option` and provide a default value for the empty case. This is done with the `fold` method, which accepts the default value as a first argument list and a mapping function as a second one:

```
opt.fold("Value for an empty case")((i: Int) => s"The value is $i")
```

The last pair of methods available for an `Option` are `toRight` and `toLeft`. They return instances of the next effect we want to take a look at, `Either`. `toRight` returns `Left`, which contains its argument for `None`, or `Right`, containing the value of `Some`:

```
opt.toRight("If opt is empty, I'll be Left[String]")
```

`toLeft` does the same but returns on different sides of `Either`, respectively:

```
scala> val opt = Option.empty[String]
opt: Option[String] = None

scala> opt.toLeft("Nonempty opt will be Left, empty - Right[String]")
res8: Either[String,String] = Right(Nonempty opt will be Left, empty -
Right[String])
```

But what are these `Left` and `Right` options we are talking about?

Either

`Either` represents the possibility of a function having one of two alternative results which can't be represented by a single type.

For example, let's imagine that we have a new simulation system that replaced an old one. The new system is very popular, and so is constantly under load and thus not always available. The old one is kept as a fallback for this reason. Unfortunately, the results of the simulation have very different formats for both systems. Hence, it makes sense to represent them as `Either`:

```
type OldFormat
type NewFormat

def runSimulation(): Either[OldFormat, NewFormat]
```

If this example gives you the feeling that types of alternatives must be related, then you are getting the wrong feeling. Usually, the types of the results would be completely unrelated. To illustrate this, let's consider another example.

As we're fishing, there is the possibility of us catching very different kinds of fish. Yet another possibility is to pull something completely different—an old boot that was lost by a tourist two years ago, or potential evidence that had been concealed by a criminal:

```
def catchFish(): Either[Boot, Fish]
```

Traditionally, the right side is preferred to represent the more desirable, *right* outcome, the left side is less desirable.

The simplified definition of `Either` looks like this in the Scala library:

```
sealed abstract class Either[+A, +B]
final case class Left[+A, +B](value: A) extends Either[A, B]
final case class Right[+A, +B](value: B) extends Either[A, B]
```

It takes two type parameters for the left and right sides, and there are two case classes representing these sides. Let's dive a bit deeper using the same approach that we did with `Option` – create an effect, read from the effect, and abstract over it.

Creating Either

Again, as in the case of `Option`, an obvious way to create an instance of `Either` is to use the constructor of the respective case class:

```
scala> Right(10)
res1: scala.util.Right[Nothing,Int] = Right(10)
```

The caveat is that the preceding definition leaves us with an `Either` whose left side is of the type `Nothing`. This probably wasn't our intention. Therefore, it is desirable to provide type parameters for both sides:

```
scala> Left[String, Int]("I'm left")
res2: scala.util.Left[String,Int] = Left(I'm left)
```

This is arguably a bit cumbersome.

Again, similar to `Option`, the `Either` companion object offers a helpful constructor which takes a predicate and two by-name constructors for the right and left sides:

```
scala> val i = 100
i: Int = 100
scala> val either = Either.cond(i > 10, i, "i is greater then 10")
either: scala.util.Either[String,Int] = Right(100)
```

If the condition holds, the `Right` with a given argument is constructed, otherwise a `Left` is created. Because both sides are defined, the compiler can inference the resulting type of `Either` properly.

There are two helper methods that are defined on both the `Left` and `Right` that help to upcast the previously defined side to full `Either`:

```
scala> val right = Right(10)
right: scala.util.Right[Nothing,Int] = Right(10)
scala> right.withLeft[String]
res11: scala.util.Either[String,Int] = Right(10)
scala> Left(new StringBuilder).withRight[BigDecimal]
res12: scala.util.Either[StringBuilder,BigDecimal] = Left()
```

Here, we upcast `Right[Nothing,Int]` to `Either[String, Int]` and do the same with `Left`, which produces the resulting value of the type `Either[StringBuilder,BigDecimal]`.

Reading values from Either

`Either` is different from `Option` in the sense that it represents two possible values instead of one. Accordingly, we can't just check if `Either` contains a value. We have to specify which side we're talking about:

```
if (either.isRight) println("Got right")
if (either.isLeft) println("Got left")
```

They are of little use if compared to the Option's approach because `Either` does not offer a method to extract the value from it. In the case of `Either`, pattern matching is a way to go:

```
either match {
  case Left(value)  => println(s"Got Left value $value")
  case Right(value) => println(s"Got Right value $value")
}
```

The predicate functions are also available with semantics similar to `Option`, with `None` represented by `Left` and `Some` by `Right`:

```
if (either.contains("boo")) println("Is Right and contains 'boo'")
if (either.exists(_ > 10)) println("Is Right and > 10")
if (either.forall(_ > 10)) println("Is Left or > 10")
```

This special treatment of `Right` as a default side makes `Either` *right-biased*. Another example of this bias is the `getOrElse` function, which also returns the contents of the `Right` side or the default value provided as an argument in the case of `Left`:

```
scala> val left = Left(new StringBuilder).withRight[BigDecimal]
res14: scala.util.Either[StringBuilder,BigDecimal] = Left()

scala> .getOrElse("Default value for the left side")
res15: String = Default value for the left side
```

The right bias plays very well for the conversion to `Option`, with `Some` representing the right side and `None` the left side, regardless of the `value` of `Left`:

```
scala> left.toOption
res17: Option[BigDecimal] = None
```

Similarly, `toSeq` represents `Right` as a `Seq` of one element and `Left` as an empty `Seq`:

```scala
scala> left.toSeq
res18: Seq[BigDecimal] = List()
```

In the case of there being a `Left` that we'd like to be `Right` or vice versa, there is a `swap` method whose sole purpose is to changes sides:

```scala
scala> left.swap
res19: scala.util.Either[BigDecimal,StringBuilder] = Right()
```

This can help to apply the right-biased methods if a value that needs to be applied is on the left side.

Either as an Effect

Naturally, methods defined in terms of an effect are also right-biased for `Either`. So is, for example, the callback method `foreach`, which we already know from `Option`:

```scala
scala> val left = Left("HoHoHo").withRight[BigDecimal]
left: scala.util.Either[String,BigDecimal] = Left(HoHoHo)
scala> left.foreach(println)
scala> left.swap.foreach(println)
HoHoHo
```

In the preceding example, the callback is not executed for the `left`, but is called as soon as it becomes `Right` after we call `swap` on it. The filtering has a bit of a different definition, as it accepts a predicate to filter the right side, and a value to return as a `Left` if the predicate does not hold:

```scala
scala> left.swap.filterOrElse(_.length > 10, "Sorry, too short")
res27: ... = Left(Sorry, too short)
```

`map` and `flatMap` allow you to transform the right side if you provide the appropriate functions. `flatMap` expects the result of the function to have a type of `Either` as well. To demonstrate this, we'll reuse our `Option` example:

```scala
val buyBait: String => Bait = ???
val makeBait: String => Bait = ???
val castLine: Bait => Line = ???
val hookFish: Line => Fish = ???
```

But this time we'll start with `bestBaitForFish`, which is the result of us asking about this other fisherman. The fisherman may be in a bad mood and we might hear them cursing instead of the hint we're expecting to get. These are both of the `String` type, but we absolutely want to differentiate between them:

```
def goFishing(bestBaitForFishOrCurse: Either[String, String]):
Either[String, Fish] =
  bestBaitForFishOrCurse.map(buyBait).map(castLine).map(hookFish)
```

Again, we're not living up to the standards we've defined for ourselves. We might get an explanation from the seller in the shop as to why we can't have the bait we want to buy. In the case that we fail to make bait, cast a line, or hook a fish, we might express ourselves verbally as well with some text that we will not put in the examples of this book. It makes sense to express the possibility that our functions return this verbal feedback if something goes wrong:

```
val buyBait:  String => Either[String, Bait]
val makeBait: String => Either[String, Bait]
val castLine: Bait => Either[String, Line]
val hookFish: Line => Either[String, Fish]
```

Now, we can rewrite the code that used `map` with `flatMap`. It makes sense to write it as a `for` comprehension:

```
def goFishing(bestBaitForFishOrCurse: Either[String, String]):
Either[String, Fish] = for {
  baitName <- bestBaitForFishOrCurse
  bait <- buyBait(baitName).fold(_ => makeBait(baitName), Right(_))
  line <- castLine(bait)
  fish <- hookFish(line)
} yield fish
```

The calls will be carried over until the last one succeeds or one of them produces a `Left`. In the second case, the first `Left` we meet will be returned as the result of the function call.

In the preceding example, we used the `fold` method, which allows us to apply the given functions to one side of `Either`. In our use case, we did this to ignore any eventual error message that will be returned by the seller in the shop and to make the bait ourselves. If we succeed, we wrap the bait into the `Right` before returning it so that we have proper type alignment.

The `fold` method is *unbiased* as it treats the left and right sides of `Either` equally.

In the last example we looked at, the model we represented with `Either` had its left side dedicated to the description of failures that happened during its operation. It is always useful to have the type of the error more specific than `String`. Often, especially in cases involving integration with Java, the most suitable choice would be to represent errors as subtypes of the `Exception`. In fact, this is so ubiquitous that there is a special effect available for this in Scala called `Try`. An `Either` having a type of its left side inheriting from a `Throwable` can be converted into a `Try` with the respective method:

```
def toTry(implicit ev: A <:< Throwable): Try[B] = this match {
  case Right(b) => Success(b)
  case Left(a)  => Failure(a)
}
```

Let's examine cases in which `Try` is a better choice then `Either` and learn how to use it.

Try

In the same way that `Either` stands for an effect of possible alternative results, `Try` denotes the effect of throwing an `Exception` by the function. In a sense, it is just a subset of `Either`, but it is so common that it has its own implementation. Unsurprisingly, the simplified representation of it looks quite familiar:

```
sealed abstract class Try[+T]
final case class Success[+T](value: T) extends Try[T]
final case class Failure[+T](exception: Throwable) extends Try[T]
```

Obviously, `Success` represents the happy-path outcome of the operation, and `Failure` is for exceptional conditions. The type for the contents of the `Failure` is fixed to be a subclass of `Throwable`, so we're back to the single type parameter for the whole ADT, which is similar to `Option`.

We'll study `Try` in the same way as we did with `Option` and `Either` – by creating, reading from, and abstracting over the effect.

Creating a Try

The definition of `Try` is already familiar because of its similarity to `Either`, and so are the ways of creating an instance of it. For starters, we can use the constructors of the case classes to create instances directly:

```
scala> import scala.util._
import scala.util._
scala> Success("Well")
res1: scala.util.Success[String] = Success(Well)
scala> Failure(new Exception("Not so well"))
res2: scala.util.Failure[Nothing] = Failure(java.lang.Exception: Not so
well)
```

The idea behind `Try` is that it can be used in scenarios where an exception would normally be thrown. Hence, the constructors we just mentioned would normally form the following pattern:

```
try Success(System.console().readLine()) catch {
  case err: IOError => Failure(err)
}
```

This will end with the result of the `try` block being wrapped in `Success` and the `catch` exception wrapped in `Failure`. Again, `stdlib` already has this pattern implemented in the companion object of `Try`. The `apply` method takes a single by-name parameter for the `try` block, like so:

```
Try(System.console().readLine())
```

And then catches all `NonFatal` exceptions.

> `NonFatal` represents a class of exceptions that the developer is able to deal with. It does not include fatal errors such as `OutOfMemoryError`, `StackOverflowError`, `LinkageError`, or `InterruptedException`. It does not make sense to deal with these programmatically. Another group of Throwables not matched by `NonFatal` is `scala.util.control.ControlThrowable`, which is used internally to control program flow and thus should not be used in a catch exception either.

It is common to provide multiline blocks wrapped in curly braces as a parameter for the `Try` constructor to makes it appear like it's a language feature:

```scala
scala>val line = Try {
  val line = System.console().readLine()
  println(s"Got $line from console")
  line
}
```

This constructor is so common that it covers the absolute majority of use cases.

Now, let's take a look at how we can get back the value from an instance of `Try`.

Reading values from Try

There are multiple ways to approach this task. It is possible to use methods similar to `isDefined` and `isEmpty` for `Option`, which allow for a null-pointer checking style:

```scala
if (line.isSuccess) println(s"The line was ${line.get}")
if (line.isFailure) println(s"There was a failure")
```

Obviously, this approach suffers from the same issue that `Option` does – if we forget to check that the result is a `Success` before extracting it, calling `.get` will throw an exception:

```scala
scala> Try { throw new Exception("No way") }.get
java.lang.Exception: No way
  at .$anonfun$res34$1(<console>:1)
  at scala.util.Try$.apply(Try.scala:209)
  ... 40 elided
```

To avoid throwing an exception just after catching it, there is a version of `get` that allows us to provide a default argument for the case if `Try` is a `Failure`:

```scala
scala> Try { throw new Exception("No way") }.getOrElse("There is a way")
res35: String = There is a way
```

Unfortunately, there are no predicate-taking methods like there were for `Option`. The reason for this is that `Try` was adopted from Twitter's implementation and was first added to Scala's standard library in version 2.10.

The `foreach` callback is still available, though, and allows us to define a function that will be executed on the value of the `Success`:

```scala
scala> line.foreach(println)
Hi, I'm the success!
```

The `foreach` method brings our discussion to the effect side of `Try`.

Try as an effect

`Try` offers the same functionality as an `Option` in terms of filtering its results with a predicate. If the predicate does not hold, the result is represented as a `Failure[NoSuchElementException]`. Taking the `line` definition from our previous example, like so:

```
scala> line.filter(_.nonEmpty)
res38: scala.util.Try[String] = Success(Hi, I'm the success!)
scala> line.filter(_.isEmpty)
res39: scala.util.Try[String] = Failure(java.util.NoSuchElementException:
Predicate does not hold for Hi, I'm the success!)
```

`collect` works in the same way, but it takes a partial function and allows us to filter and transform the contents of the `Try` at the same time:

```
scala> line.collect { case s: String => s * 2 }
res40: scala.util.Try[String] = Success(Hi, I'm the success!Hi, I'm the
success!)
scala> line.collect { case s: "Other input" => s * 10 }
res41: scala.util.Try[String] = Failure(java.util.NoSuchElementException:
Predicate does not hold for Hi, I'm the success!)
```

The `filter` and `collect` functions are `Success` biased, and so are `map` and `flatMap`. Let's reimplement the fishing example in this situation, where our parameter is of type `Try[String]`, and the exceptions are replacing strings as the problem descriptions we had in our example of `Either`:

```
def goFishing(bestBaitForFishOrCurse: Try[String]): Try[Fish] =
  bestBaitForFishOrCurse.map(buyBait).map(castLine).map(hookFish)
```

The operations are chained on the `Success`. Yet again, we have to fix the signatures of our functions so that they encode the possibility of an error in every step in the type of the result:

```
val buyBait: String => Try[Bait]
val makeBait: String => Try[Bait]
val castLine: Bait => Try[Line]
val hookFish: Line => Try[Fish]
```

Now, we have to use `flatMap` instead of `map` to align the types. Again, it is more readable if represented as a `for` comprehension:

```
def goFishing(bestBaitForFishOrCurse: Try[String]): Try[Fish] = for {
  baitName <- bestBaitForFishOrCurse
  bait <- buyBait(baitName).fold(_ => makeBait(baitName), Success(_))
  line <- castLine(bait)
  fish <- hookFish(line)
} yield fish
```

This implementation is almost identical to the one we have for `Either`, with the exception that we now have to wrap successful calls into `Success` and not into `Right` (we have to use a different constructor for an effect).

The `fold` is one of the methods that is unbiased for `Try`. It takes arguments to transfer both `Success` and `Failure`, as shown in the preceding code. Another unbiased method is `transform`, which is similar to `fold`, but takes functions for returning `Try` as parameters. In a sense, `transform` could be called `flatFold`:

```
scala> line.transform((l: String) => Try(println(l)), (ex: Throwable) =>
Try(throw ex))
Hi, I'm the success!
res45: scala.util.Try[Unit] = Success(())
```

There are also a few functions that are `Failure` biased.

`recover` and `recoverWith` apply the given partial function to the `Failure`. They are basically duals of `map` and `flatMaps`, but for the exception side:

```
line.recover {
  case ex: NumberFormatException => Math.PI
}
line.recoverWith {
  case ex: NoSuchElementException => Try(retryAfterDelay)
}
```

The `orElse` method allows us to chain Failures in the same way we did with `None`:

```
val result = firstTry orElse secondTry orElse failure orElse success
```

As we can see, `Try` is similar to `Option` and `Either`, and it should not come as a surprise that it can be converted to both `Option` and `Either[Throwable, _]`:

```
scala> line.toOption
res51: Option[String] = Some("Hi, I'm the success!")
scala> line.toEither
res53: scala.util.Either[Throwable,String] = Right("Hi, I'm the success!")
```

There is one more effect in the standard library that is a bit different from the three we just looked at because it takes into account a more subtle aspect of calling a function – the time it is going to take to return the result.

Future

Sometimes, the functions we call take time to return results of the computation. Often, the cause is side-effects like reading from a disk or calling a slow remote API. At times, the operation itself just requires a lot of CPU time to finish. In both cases, the main flow of the program is stopped until the function returns the result. It might be acceptable in the latter case to wait for the result if it is required immediately after calculation (though even in this case it is suboptimal because it makes the system unresponsive), but it is undesirable in the former case because it means that our program consumes CPU while doing nothing (well, waiting for other subsystems of the computer to return the result, but still nothing related to the CPU). Often, such long-running operations are executed in a separate thread of execution.

As a functional programmer, we would like to express these—two aspects, that is, the duration of the call and the fact that the code is executed in a separate thread, as an effect. This is what `Future` does. To be more specific, it does not represent the duration of the call explicitly, but encodes it in a binary form—an operation either takes long and possibly runs in a separate thread or it doesn't.

The `Future` is a very interesting concept and deserves a full chapter on its own. Here, we'll just take a brief look at some of its aspects. We highly recommend referring to the official documentation for more details. Let's apply our ubiquitous three-step approach one more time, this time for `Future`.

Creating a Future

The `Future` is not encoded as an ADT and thus we have to use a constructor that's provided by the companion object to construct it. Because the code we'll be providing will be executing in a separate thread, the `Future` has to have a way to obtain this `Thread`. This is done implicitly by having an `ExecutionContext` in scope, which we import in two steps. First, we'll import the whose `scala.concurrent` package in scope and the `ExecutionContext` from it:

```
scala> import scala.concurrent._
import scala.concurrent._
scala> import ExecutionContext.Implicits.global
import ExecutionContext.Implicits.global
```

The `ExecutionContext` is basically a factory for `Threads`. It can be configured as needed for specific use cases. For demonstration purposes, we're using global context, but in general, this is not recommended. Please refer to the ScalaDocs under https://www.scala-lang.org/api/current/scala/concurrent/ExecutionContext.html for further details.

Having this context in scope, we can construct a `Future` by providing a by-name parameter to its constructor:

```
val success = Future("Well")
val runningForever = Future {
  while (true) Thread.sleep(1000)
}
```

The `Future` starts executing immediately after it is created, with respect to the time needed to obtain a thread from the executor.

Sometimes, we just want to wrap a value at hand into the `Future` for the code which expects some `Future` as a parameter. In this case, we don't need an execution context because we don't need to calculate anything. We can use one of the special constructors that help to create it successfully: `failed` and a `Future` from `Try`, respectively:

```
scala> val success = Future.successful("Well")
success: scala.concurrent.Future[String] = Future(Success(Well))
scala> val failure = Future.failed(new IllegalArgumentException)
failure: scala.concurrent.Future[Nothing] =
Future(Failure(java.lang.IllegalArgumentException))
scala> val fromTry = Future.fromTry(Try(10 / 0))
fromTry: scala.concurrent.Future[Int] =
Future(Failure(java.lang.ArithmeticException: / by zero))
```

There is also a predefined `Future[Unit]` that can be used as an indirect constructor by mapping over it:

```scala
scala> val runningLong = Future.unit.map { _ =>
  | while (math.random() > 0.001) Thread.sleep(1000)
  | }
runningLong: scala.concurrent.Future[Unit] = Future(<not completed>)
```

Now, since we have a value inside of the `Future`, let's take a look at the possible ways to get it out.

Reading values from a Future

As the `Future` is not implemented as an ADT, we can't directly pattern-match on it as we did with other the effects that we looked at in this chapter.

Instead, we can use the null-checking style:

```scala
scala> if (runningLong.isCompleted) runningLong.value
res54: Any = Some(Success(()))
```

Luckily, the `value` method returns an `Option` that will be `None` until the future completes, so we can use this in a pattern match:

```scala
scala> runningForever.value match {
  | case Some(Success(value)) => println(s"Finished successfully with
$value")
  | case Some(Failure(exception)) => println(s"Failed with $exception")
  | case None => println("Still running")
  | }
Still running
```

Of course, the most useful methods are defined not in relation to the value of the `Future`, but in terms of `Future` as an effect.

Future as an effect

`Future` has all of the usual suspects that have been made known to us from this chapter so far. `foreach` allows us to define a callback to execute after the `Future` successfully completes:

```scala
scala> runningLong.foreach(_ => println("First callback"))
scala> runningLong.foreach(_ => println("Second callback"))
```

```
scala> Second callback
First callback
```

The order of execution is not guaranteed, as shown in the previous example.

There is another callback that is called for any completed feature, regardless of its success. It accepts a function, taking `Try` as a parameter:

```
scala> runningLong.onComplete {
     | case Success(value) => println(s"Success with $value")
     | case Failure(ex) => println(s"Failure with $ex")
     | }
scala> Success with ()
```

The `transform` method is also applied in both cases. There are two flavors of it. One takes two functions, for `Success` and `Failure`, accordingly, and another takes one function, `Try => Try`:

```
stringFuture.transform(_.length, ex => new Exception(ex))
stringFuture.transform {
  case Success(value) => Success(value.length)
  case Failure(ex) => Failure(new Exception(ex))
}
```

In both cases, we transform the string to its length in the case of success and wrap an exception in the case of failure. The second variant is more flexible, though, as it allows us to convert success to failure and vice versa.

This filtering is also done in the same way as with other effects, that is, with the `filter` and `collect` methods:

```
stringFuture.filter(_.length > 10)
stringFuture.collect {
  case s if s.length > 10 => s.toUpperCase
}
```

The former just converts a `Success` into `Failure(NoSuchElementException)` (or leaves the existing `Failure` in place) if the predicate does not hold. The latter also modifies the contents to upper case for `Success`.

And of course, `map` and `flatMap` are available. We'll let our user service use Futures as an effect – this time to denote that every action, including our research for the best bite name for the fish, takes some time to finish:

```
val buyBait: String => Future[Bait]
val makeBait: String => Future[Bait]
```

```
val castLine: Bait => Future[Line]
val hookFish: Line => Future[Fish]
```

This brings us to the following, already familiar, implementation:

```
def goFishing(bestBaitForFish: Future[String]): Future[Fish] = for {
  baitName <- bestBaitForFish
  bait <- buyBait(baitName).fallbackTo(makeBait(baitName))
  line <- castLine(bait)
  fish <- hookFish(line)
} yield fish
```

It is easy to see that besides changes in the effect type, the only difference to the previous implementations is the use of the fallback method to provide an alternative in the case of an unsuccessful call of the buyBait method.

There is a lot more to cover about the Future and its dual Promise. We encourage you to take a look at the official documentation and related blog posts (for example https:// viktorklang.com/blog/Futures-in-Scala-2.12-part-9.html) for some examples of advanced usage.

Summary

In this chapter, we discussed the effects defined in the standard library. First, an Option which represents a case where it might be impossible for the function to return the result. Then the Try which extends the optionality with the possibility to return an error description in the failure case. Next was Either which further extends the concept of Try by allowing it to provide an arbitrary type as a description of an *unsuccessful* path. Finally, the Future which stays a bit aside in this list and represents the notion of long and possibly executed in separate context computations

We noticed that these effects have different constructors tailored to the situations that require the creation of the respective instances. In accordance, they offer slightly different ways to access values that are stored inside the container.

We paid attention to the fact that having effects as a first-class concept allows us to define methods not only in terms of contained values but also in terms of the effect itself, which often leads to more expressive code.

Most importantly, we realized that many methods such as
`filter`, `collect`, `map`, `flatMap`, and so, are on identical from the user's perspective and induce identical, higher level implementations for different kinds of effects. We demonstrated this by implementing four uniform examples for catching a fish in a few steps, encoded in terms of different effects.

Later in this book, we will identify the underlying concepts that lead to these kinds of similarities.

We'll also approach the topic of combining different kinds of effects, which we left out of scope for now.

Questions

1. What would be the proper effect to represent getting the first element of a list, such as a list of tweets? What about a user's information from the database for a given `userId`?

2. What are the range of possible values of the following expression: `Option(scala.util.Random.nextInt(10)).fold(9)(_-1)`?

3. What will be the result of the following expression?

```
Try[Int](throw new OutOfMemoryError()).filter(_ > 10).recover {
  case _: OutOfMemoryError => 100
}
```

4. Describe the result of the following expression:

```
Future[Int](throw new OutOfMemoryError()).filter(_ > 10).recover {
  case _: OutOfMemoryError => 100
}(20)
```

5. Given the following function, what would be the result of the following call: `either(1)`?

```
def either(i: Int): Boolean =
  Either.cond(i > 10, i * 10, new IllegalArgumentException("Give me
more")).forall(_ < 100)
```

7
Understanding Algebraic Structures

In the previous chapter, we looked at some standard Scala effects and identified lots of similarities among them. We also promised to dive deeper and find out what principles underly these commonalities.

Before diving deep into the ocean of abstractions, let's fish for the simpler concepts first to gain some familiarity and skill working with them.

In this chapter, we'll take a look at a few abstract algebraic structures—structures that are fully identified by the laws defining them. We will start with a simpler yet usable abstraction and advance to more complex topics.

In this chapter, we will take a look at the following topics:

- Semigroup
- Monoid
- Foldable
- Group

Technical requirements

Before we begin, make sure you have the following installed:

- Java 1.8+
- SBT 1.2+

The source code for this chapter is available under our GitHub repository at: `https://github.com/PacktPublishing/Learn-Scala-Programming/tree/master/Chapter07`.

Introduction to abstract algebraic structures

An abstract algebraic structure is something that is fully defined by a set of laws. Abstract algebraic structures have their roots in category theory, a branch of mathematics dedicated to studying them.

The "abstractness" of the topic has two consequences for us. First, we need to get into a specific state of mind and talk about things in general as opposed to the concrete implementations that we were discussing up until now. Second, the structures we'll be looking at, the semigroup, monoid, group, and foldable, are applicable to a wide spectrum of cases, and each case can lead to the implementation of the abstract concept at hand. If this sounds too theoretical, don't worry; we'll get practical in a moment with `Semigroup`.

Semigroup

Semigroup is probably the simplest yet most useful algebraic structure. It is fully defined by two qualities:

- It is defined for some (possibly infinite) set of elements
- It has a binary operation defined for any pairs of elements in this set

It also has the following two properties:

- The operation is closed, which means that the result of the operation belongs to the same set as its operands
- The operation is associative, meaning that multiple operations should produce the same result, regardless of the order in which they are applied

We can translate these definitions into the Scala code almost literally:

```scala
trait Semigroup[S] {
  def op(l: S, r: S): S
}
```

S denotes the type that the set elements belong to, and op denotes the operation. The result type is also S—we have defined the property of closeness of the operation on the type level. Formally, it is said that S *forms a semigroup under op*.

Readers that are familiar with Chapter 5, *Property-Based Testing in Scala*, will also remember that we talked about associativity as one of the ways to formulate ScalaCheck properties. It is very easy to define this property to check the second semigroup law in the same way we mentioned earlier:

```
import org.scalacheck._
import org.scalacheck.Prop._
def associativity[S : Semigroup : Arbitrary]: Prop =
  forAll((a: S, b: S, c: S) => {
    val sg = implicitly[Semigroup[S]]
    sg.op(sg.op(a, b), c) == sg.op(a, sg.op(b, c))
  })
```

We need the S type to have a Semigroup and Arbitrary, the former of which we need to get the implementation we want to check and the latter to be able to generate random data for S.

The property itself, sg.op(sg.op(a, b), c) == sg.op(a, sg.op(b, c)), just verify that operations that are applied in a different order produce the same result—exactly as specified verbally.

Please note that properties we define in this chapter can also be executed by running tests in SBT directly. To do this, it is enough to start the SBT session and type **test** followed by the *Enter* key.

OK, we now have a definition of a semigroup for S and a way to check that the semigroup is properly implemented, but what are these S's? Well, this is the beauty of the abstract algebraic data structure. The S can be absolutely anything as long as semigroup laws hold. As an example, we can stick to our figure of speech regarding fishing.

We can specify at least two `eat` operations for S that are defined on all of the fish. The *the big fish eats the little fish* operation is defined on two fish with the result that the bigger fish has a volume equal to the sum of the volumes of both fish participating in the operation. Similarly, *the heavy fish eats the light fish* is defined by the same principle but in terms of the fish's weight. It's easy to see that the first property of this semigroup holds by definition. The following diagrams represent the proof for the second property. The first diagram illustrates the associativity of the *Big eats small/Heavy eats light* operation on the fish:

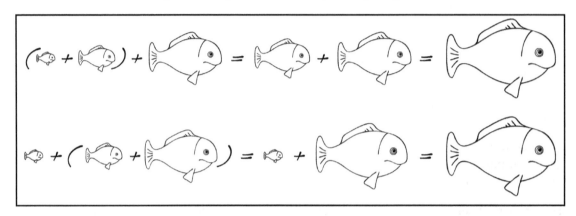

Figure 1: Big fish eats small fish/Heavy fish eats light fish

The following diagram illustrates the same property for the *More teeth win* rule:

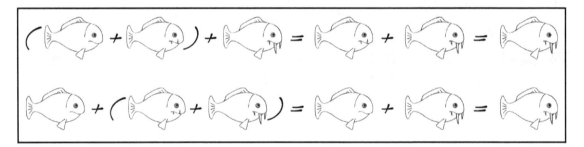

Figure 2: More teeth win

This final illustration shows that associativity also holds for the property of toxicity:

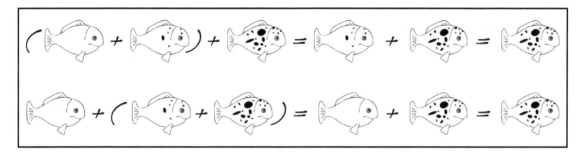

Figure 3. Combinations of toxic fish

The semigroup operation does not need to be an addition. For instance, we can define it so that, from both participants, the most poisonous fish is on the left as a result. This book has no age restriction, so we should pretend that the second fish was scared away in the process. But experienced fishers know the creatures—instead, we have to constrain the semigroup for this operation to the set of all *living* fish, which allows us to avoid ambiguity for the result of the operation.

As per our analogy, we could define another operation in terms of teeth—the fish with the bigger teeth is on the left as a result of the operation. Again, to avoid ambiguity, our semigroup is formed by *solid*, living fish under this operation.

In order to implement the semigroups we just defined, we need a definition of fish. Let's have it represented as a case class:

```
final case class Fish(volume: Int, size: Int, teeth: Int, poisonousness: Int)
```

The relevant properties are represented as fields.

Let's start with the big and small fish semigroup. The law checking property we defined previously requires an implicit semigroup in scope, so we'll mark our instance as `implicit`:

```
implicit val volumeSemigroup: Semigroup[Fish] = (l: Fish, r: Fish) => {
  val result = if (l.volume >= r.volume) l else r
  result.copy(volume = r.volume + l.volume)
}
```

We can check which fish wins by comparing their volumes. The bigger fish incorporates the volume of the fish eaten during the operation.

At the moment, some of you must be scratching your heads, trying to remember why this structure looks so familiar. The astute reader will have already recognized the *type class pattern* we talked about in Chapter 4, *Getting to Know Implicits and Type Classes*. Good job, astute reader!

Our implementation is so simple that it cannot be incorrect, but for completeness' sake, let's define a property for it. First, we need a generator for Fish:

```
val fishGen: Gen[Fish] = for {
  weight <- Gen.posNum[Int]
  volume <- Gen.posNum[Int]
  poisonousness <- Gen.posNum[Int]
  teeth <- Gen.posNum[Int]
} yield Fish(volume, weight, teeth, poisonousness)

implicit val arbFish: Arbitrary[Fish] = Arbitrary(fishGen)
```

We implement it by combining generators for single properties, exactly as we did in Chapter 4, *Getting to Know Implicits and Type Classes*. Now, defining the check itself boils down to importing the proper implicit and delegating to the property we defined previously:

```
property("associativity for fish semigroup under 'big eats little'") = {
  associativity[Fish]
}
```

The definitions of the properties in this chapter cannot be pasted in REPL because they need to be placed in a test wrapper. Please see the accompanying code to see how it is done.

Running this property is also done in the same way as in Chapter 4, *Getting to Know Implicits and Type Classes*, so there should be no surprises here:

```
scala> associativity[Fish]
res1: org.scalacheck.Prop = Prop
scala> .check
! Falsified after 3 passed tests.
> ARG_0: Fish(2,3,2,1)
> ARG_1: Fish(2,3,3,3)
> ARG_2: Fish(3,2,3,2)
```

Ouch, it turns out there are surprises! Our implementation does not satisfy the associativity requirements for the case where the fish have the same volume!

This little case demonstrates how important it is to check that an implementation of an abstract algebraic structure obeys the laws defined for it for all possible input values. In our case, we don't actually have a proper semigroup implementation yet. Let's fix that by pretending that the bigger fish incorporates all of the properties of the eaten one. This might look strange for the number of teeth and venom, but we're talking about abstractions, after all:

```
final case class Fish(volume: Int, weight: Int, teeth: Int, poisonousness:
Int) {
  def eat(f: Fish): Fish = Fish(volume + f.volume, weight + f.weight, teeth
+ f.teeth, poisonousness + f.poisonousness)
}
```

This gives us a slightly simpler semigroup implementation:

```
implicit val volumeSemigroup: Semigroup[Fish] = (l: Fish, r: Fish) =>
  if (l.volume > r.volume) l.eat(r) else r.eat(l)
```

In the case of the fish being of an equal volume, the right fish wins. This is a random choice, but this makes our semigroup right-biased.

Let's retry our check (if you're playing with the code in REPL, you'll need to paste the definition of `fishGen` and `arbFish` again to apply them to the new definition of the `Fish`):

```
scala> associativity[Fish]
res10: org.scalacheck.Prop = Prop
scala> .check
+ OK, passed 100 tests.
```

This states that we are on the right track—it passes.

We can define and check other semigroups by analogy:

```
implicit val weightSemigroup: Semigroup[Fish] = (l: Fish, r: Fish) =>
  if (l.weight > r.weight) l.eat(r) else r.eat(l)

implicit val poisonSemigroup: Semigroup[Fish] = (l: Fish, r: Fish) =>
  if (l.poisonousness > r.poisonousness) l else r

implicit val teethSemigroup: Semigroup[Fish] = (l: Fish, r: Fish) =>
  if (l.teeth > r.teeth) l else r
```

This code reflects our earlier discussion about how different attributes of the fish work during the operation. The definition is basically always the same; it just refers to the different properties of the fish! We omitted the definition of the ScalaCheck properties because they are identical to the ones we already looked at.

It would be a disappointment if semigroups were only useful in the realm of fishing. Let's take a look at another example—mixing colored shapes:

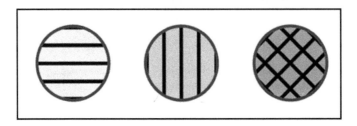

Figure 3: Colored circles with different transparency levels

We can pick one of the following operations to work with:

- Combine transparency
- Combine shapes
- Combine colors (represented as textures on the image)

These are represented in the following diagrams. The first addresses the transparency:

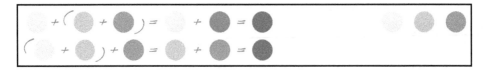

Figure 4: Combining transparencies

The second is about combining shapes in a consistent way:

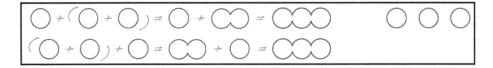

Figure 5: Combining shapes

This final diagram shows us that combining colors (fillings) produces the same result as well:

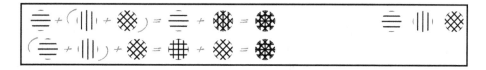

Figure 6: Combining colors (fillings)

The preceding diagrams provide proof that the associative law holds and that the closure property again holds by definition.

Have you noticed the commonality between both the fishing and shapes examples? We pick a numeric property of the entity and apply an operation to this property. For instance, all of our fishing examples can be reduced to just two cases: integer addition (for volume and weight) and integer comparison (for teeth and poisonousness).

Of course, we also can specify semigroups for these cases. The numbers form a semigroup under addition as well as under multiplication. We can demonstrate this with an example of the Int type:

```
implicit val intAddition: Semigroup[Int] = (l: Int, r: Int) => l + r
implicit val intMultiplication: Semigroup[Int] = (l: Int, r: Int) => l * r

property("associativity for int under addition") = {
  import Semigroup.intAddition
  associativity[Int]
}
property("associativity for int under multiplication") = {
  import Semigroup.intMultiplication
  associativity[Int]
}
```

This definition is completely analogous to what we had before, and so is the result of the execution of the test command in SBT:

```
+ Semigroup.associativity for int under addition: OK, passed 100 tests.
+ Semigroup.associativity for int under multiplication: OK, passed 100
tests.
```

Strings form semigroups under concatenation:

```
implicit val stringConcatenation: Semigroup[String] =
  (l: String, r: String) => l + r
```

```
property("associativity for strings under concatenation") = {
  import Semigroup.stringConcatenation
  associativity[String]
}
```

This semigroup is implemented entirely like the others, but conceptually this is a bit different from what we had before. In the case of a `String`, the operation is defined not in terms of some property but in terms of content. In a sense, we're defining a semigroup for the container of chars and the operation is specified as bringing the contents of both containers together in an ordered fashion.

In our fishing realm, a similar example would be a combination of two fish: one with caviar and one with milk, which would spawn a number of smaller fish as a result. This can't be an example of a semigroup as long as we're talking about single fish because the operation is not closed—we expect a single fish as a result, but the operation returns many of them. We can turn the situation around if we start to talk about buckets of fish. Combining two buckets, each with a single fish, will produce a bucket full of small fish. This operation is closed and if we can prove that it is associative, this would be a valid example of a semigroup.

Switching perspectives from a single item to a container has another subtle effect: it is now possible to have an empty container (bucket) for any operation. In the situation where one of the operands is an empty container, the operation just returns another operand as a result. This makes our abstraction more powerful. It turns a semigroup into a monoid.

Monoid

A monoid is a semigroup with an *identity* element. Formally, the identity element z is an element for which an equation, $z + x = x + z = x$, holds for any x. This equation is called identity property. Both closure and associativity properties that are defined for semigroups are also required to hold for a monoid.

The existence of the identity property requires us to implement the monoid, as follows:

```
trait Monoid[S] extends Semigroup[S] {
  def identity: S
}
```

The check we specified for the semigroup also needs to be augmented for the monoid to verify that the new property holds:

```
def identity[S : Monoid : Arbitrary]: Prop =
  forAll((a: S) => {
```

```
    val m = implicitly[Monoid[S]]
    m.op(a, m.identity) == a && m.op(m.identity, a) == a
})

def monoidProp[S : Monoid : Arbitrary]: Prop = associativity[S] &&
identity[S]
```

Now, we can define our first monoid, which will put all of the fish from the two buckets into a single bucket:

```
type Bucket[S] = List[S]

implicit val mergeBuckets: Monoid[Bucket[Fish]] = new Monoid[Bucket[Fish]]
{
  override def identity: Bucket[Fish] = List.empty[Fish]
  override def op(l: Bucket[Fish], r: Bucket[Fish]): Bucket[Fish] = l ++ r
}
```

Here, we represent a `Bucket` with a `List` and just merge two buckets to denote that the contents of both have been put together. Are you curious to check if this implementation is a monoid? The property definition is unspectacular as it just delegates to the `monoidProp` we defined before:

```
implicit val arbBucketOfFish: Arbitrary[Bucket[Fish]] =
Arbitrary(Gen.listOf(fishGen))

property("bucket of fish monoid") = {
  import Monoid.mergeBuckets
  monoidProp[Bucket[Fish]]
}
```

But, there is a bit of machinery underneath. First, we need to define a generator for buckets of fish so that we can use it to formulate a combined property of associativity and identity. Luckily, the property holds:

```
scala> implicit val arbBucketOfFish: Arbitrary[Bucket[Fish]] =
Arbitrary(Gen.listOf(fishGen))
arbBucketOfFish: org.scalacheck.Arbitrary[Monoid.Bucket[Fish]] =
org.scalacheck.ArbitraryLowPriority$$anon$1@3dd73a3d
scala> monoidProp[Bucket[Fish]]
res13: org.scalacheck.Prop = Prop
scala> .check
+ OK, passed 100 tests.
```

Are monoids only defined for containers? No, they're definitely not. Containers are just a special, comfortable case, because, in the majority of cases, it is obvious what should be an identity element of the corresponding monoid.

Looking away from containers and back to the colors example from the previous section, we can also pick an identity element for the operations we defined there to extend semigroups to monoids:

- Combining transparency would require a fully transparent identity element
- Combining shapes has an identity without a shape—a dot
- Combining colors might have a white color as an identity (this identity element will make the color less saturated, but it won't change the color itself)

We could even be creative and specify an identity element that's suitable for all of these operations—a fully transparent white-colored dot.

How about the other semigroups we've defined so far? From math, we know that natural numbers have identity elements for addition and multiplication, that is, zero and one, respectively. This allows us to upgrade the semigroups we implemented for ints to monoids:

```
implicit val intAddition: Monoid[Int] = new Monoid[Int] {
  override def identity: Int = 0
  override def op(l: Int, r: Int): Int = l + r
}

implicit val intMultiplication: Monoid[Int] = new Monoid[Int] {
  override def identity: Int = 1
  override def op(l: Int, r: Int): Int = l * r
}
```

This definition is similar to the one we had for the semigroup—we've just added the identity element to it. The implementation of the property check is also identical to what we had before.

Obviously, strings also form a monoid under concatenation and, as we noticed before, the identity element would be an empty container—a blank `String`:

```
implicit val stringConcatenation: Monoid[String] = new Monoid[String] {
  override def identity: String = ""
  override def op(l: String, r: String): String = l + r
}
```

Another nice thing about containers is that it is actually possible to not only define an algebraic structure in terms of the container as a whole, but to the reuse existing algebraic structures that have been defined for its elements.

This is the real power of abstract algebraic structures—they compose!

To demonstrate this, let's cheat a bit and define a weightless and toothless non-poisonousness fish with zero volume as an identity element for our fishing examples. Here is a definition for the *big fish eats little fish* monoid:

```
val ZeroFish = Fish(0,0,0,0)

implicit val weightMonoid: Monoid[Fish] = new Monoid[Fish] {
  override def identity: Fish = ZeroFish
  override def op(l: Fish, r: Fish): Fish =
    if (l.weight > r.weight) l.eat(r) else r.eat(l)
}
```

The monoids for the other three cases are implemented similarly by adding a `ZeroFish` as an identity element to all of them.

Having this definition in scope, we can now implement the survival logic for two buckets of fish. First, we'll form a pair of fish from both buckets, and then one fish from the pair should survive:

```
implicit def surviveInTheBucket(implicit m: Monoid[Fish]):
Monoid[Bucket[Fish]] =
  new Monoid[Bucket[Fish]] {
    override def identity: Bucket[Fish] = List.fill(100)(ZeroFish)
    override def op(l: Bucket[Fish], r: Bucket[Fish]): Bucket[Fish] = {
      val operation = (m.op _).tupled
      l zip r map operation
    }
  }
```

Here, we define our monoid in terms of a simpler monoid. The operation itself is built from the original operation converted to the tuple form and is applied to the pairs of fish from both buckets. This is defined for buckets of size less or equal than `100` because the identity bucket for this operation needs to contain enough `ZeroFish` in the case that the buckets we're combining have a different number of elements.

Now, we can test out different survival strategies just by having an instance of the desired monoid in scope:

```
property("props for survival in the bucket for most poisonousness") = {
    import Monoid.poisonMonoid
    import Monoid.surviveInTheBucket
    monoidProps[Bucket[Fish]]
}
```

We need to import both monoids in scope so that the implicit resolution works properly. In this example, from every pair of fish, the more toxic fish will survive. This can easily be changed by bringing a different monoid into scope, for example, the `weightMonoid` gives heavier fish a chance of survival:

```
scala> {
     | import ch07.Monoid.weightMonoid
     | import ch07.Monoid.surviveInTheBucket
     | monoidProp[Bucket[Fish]]
     | }
res3: org.scalacheck.Prop = Prop

scala> .check
+ OK, passed 100 tests.
```

We can check and see that the properties of the derived monoid hold. This can even be proved mathematically—by zipping two monoids, we created a product monoid, which has been proven to obey monoid laws.

Another interesting aspect of monoids and semigroups is their ability to be used to reduce any iterable collection to a single value.

For instance, the following is the `reduce` method that was defined for `IterableOnce` from the standard library:

```
def reduce[B >: A](op: (B, B) => B): B
```

This takes an associative binary operator and applies it between all elements of the collection. The type signature tells us that it is a good application for a semigroup as its operation satisfies the requirements of this function:

```
scala> val bucketOfFishGen: Gen[List[Fish]] = Gen.listOf(fishGen)
bucketOfFishGen: org.scalacheck.Gen[List[Fish]] =
org.scalacheck.Gen$$anon$1@34d69633

scala> val bucket = bucketOfFishGen.sample.get
bucket: List[Fish] = List(Fish(98,44,11,22), Fish(69,15,57,18), ...

scala> bucket.reduce(poisonSemigroup.op)
res7: Fish = Fish(25,6,29,99)
```

In the preceding snippet, we generated a random bucket of fish and then applied the `poisonSemigroup` to it by specifying its operation as an argument for the `reduce` method.

Obviously, any semigroup operation is a perfect fit as soon as types match.

Unfortunately, the implementation of `reduce` throws an `UnsupportedOperationException` for empty collections, which makes it unsuitable for real functional programming:

```
scala> List.empty[Fish].reduce(poisonSemigroup.op)
java.lang.UnsupportedOperationException: empty.reduceLeft
  at scala.collection.IterableOnceOps.reduceLeft(IterableOnce.scala:527)
  at scala.collection.IterableOnceOps.reduceLeft$(IterableOnce.scala:524)
  at scala.collection.AbstractIterable.reduceLeft(Iterable.scala:759)
  at scala.collection.IterableOnceOps.reduce(IterableOnce.scala:496)
  at scala.collection.IterableOnceOps.reduce$(IterableOnce.scala:496)
  at scala.collection.AbstractIterable.reduce(Iterable.scala:759)
  ... 40 elided
```

There is a sibling of `reduce` called `reduceOption` that returns `None` for empty collections instead of throwing an exception, but this makes the whole result type optional.

There are a couple of similar methods defined on `IterableOnce`. Grouping them together would allow us to represent the "reducibility" property as a standalone concept:

```
trait Reducible[A] {

  @throws("UnsupportedOperationException ")
  def reduceLeft(op: (A, A) => A): A

  @throws("UnsupportedOperationException ")
  def reduceRight(op: (A, A) => A): A
```

```
@throws("UnsupportedOperationException ")
def reduce(op: (A, A) => A): A = reduceLeft(op)

def reduceLeftOption(op: (A, A) => A): Option[A]

def reduceRightOption(op: (A, A) => A): Option[A]

def reduceOption(op: (A, A) => A): Option[A] = reduceLeftOption(op)

}
```

This does not look very nice because, as we have already discussed, the methods either throw an exception or introduce an effect of optionality. How could we improve this implementation? We could make use of the monoids' identity property!

Foldable

The monoid identity property allows us to handle empty collections in a general way. So, instead of having the following:

```
def reduceLeft(op: (A, A) => A): A
```

We'll have a definition that takes an identity element as another parameter. By convention, this approach is called `fold`:

```
def foldLeft(identity: A)(op: (A, A) => A): A
```

The reason for the name `foldLeft` is that the identity element is used as an initial argument for reducing the collection, which leads to the following sequence of calls:

```
op(op(op(op(identity, a1), a2), a3), a4), ...
```

Optionally, it is represented in postfix-notation:

```
(((identity op a1) op a2) op a3) ...
```

Which is, well, kind of folding the collection, starting with the identity and the first element of it.

The associativity of the operation and the identity element tells us that another approach is also possible, starting from the identity and the last element of the collection and then moving toward its head:

```
(a1 op (a2 op (a3 op identity))) ...
```

Folding in this direction is naturally called `foldRight`:

```
def foldRight(identity: A)(op: (A, A) => A): A
```

The same properties also give us the ability to fold the collection, starting from any place! This is particularly useful in a balanced fold, which works from both ends:

```
(a1 op (a2 op identity)) op ((a3 op identity) op a4)
```

Interestingly, both sides can be dealt with recursively, in that we can split each of them into two parts and use a balanced fold again. Even more interestingly, as the left and right sides are folded independently from each other, the folding can be done in parallel!

In the same way, as we did for `Reducible`, we can group these functions into yet another abstraction, `MonoidFoldable`:

```
trait MonoidFoldable[A, F[_]] {
  def foldRight(as: F[A])(i: A, op: (A,A) => A): A
  def foldLeft(as: F[A])(i: A, op: (A,A) => A): A
  def foldBalanced(as: F[A])(i: A, op: (A,A) => A): A
}
```

This time, we define it as a type class that is capable of folding collections of type F with elements of type A. For most of the existing collections, instances of this type class should be able to delegate the `foldLeft` and `foldRight` implementations to the F. Let's demonstrate this with an instance of `ListMonoidFoldable`:

```
implicit def listMonoidFoldable[A : Monoid]: MonoidFoldable[A, List] = new
MonoidFoldable[A, List] {
  private val m = implicitly[Monoid[A]]
  override def foldRight(as: List[A])(i: A, op: (A, A) => A): A =
as.foldRight(m.identity)(m.op)

  override def foldLeft(as: List[A])(i: A, op: (A, A) => A): A =
as.foldLeft(m.identity)(m.op)

  override def foldBalanced(as: List[A])(i: A, op: (A, A) => A): A = as
match {
    case Nil => m.identity
    case List(one) => one
    case _ => val (l, r) = as.splitAt(as.length/2)
      m.op(foldBalanced(l)(m.identity, m.op), foldBalanced(r)(m.identity,
m.op))
  }
}
```

First of all, we require that type A is a monoid. Then, we get an instance of it by using the usual approach of calling implicitly. Then, we implement `foldRight` and `foldLeft` by calling the corresponding methods on the underlying `List`. Finally, we implement `foldBalanced` in a head-recursive manner. This implementation splits the list into two halves and folds them independently, exactly as we reasoned before. It is not done in parallel, though.

We can improve on that aspect by utilizing the `Future` we discussed in the previous chapter. We introduced a new method, `foldPar`, which takes an additional implicit `ExecutionContext`:

```
def foldPar(as: F[A])(i: A, op: (A,A) => A)(implicit ec: ExecutionContext):
A
```

The execution context needs to pass over the moment we create a `Future` for our parallel computation. The structure of the method is similar to the `balancedFold`, since we have to split the collection into two parts and fold it recursively. This time, we limit the minimal number of items in the collection to be folded in parallel because it might be more computationally expensive to create a `Future` than to fold a handful of elements in a sequential manner:

```
private val parallelLimit = 8
override def foldPar(as: List[A])(i: A, op: (A, A) => A)(implicit ec:
ExecutionContext): Future[A] = {
  if (as.length < parallelLimit) Future(foldBalanced(as)(i, op))
  else {
    val (l, r) = as.splitAt(as.length/2)
    Future.reduceLeft(List(foldPar(l)(m.identity, m.op),
foldPar(r)(m.identity, m.op)))(m.op)
  }
}
```

For simplicity, we've hardcoded the minimal number of elements eligible for parallel computation, but it can be passed over as a parameter. In the method itself, we either spawn a balanced fold in a separate thread if the collection is shorter than the limit or we initiate two parallel folds the same way we did before, but this time we use `Future.reduceLeft` to combine them together at the moment both computations are finished.

We expect `foldPar` to be quicker than other folds. Let's write a property for that. This endeavor will be more involved than before. The reason for this is that the monoids we've to build so far are very simple and, because of that, very fast. Because of this, we won't be able to see the advantages of parallelization—the price of spawning a `Future` will outweigh the folding itself. For our purposes, we'll make our monoid a bit slower by adding a small delay to it:

```
implicit val slowPoisonMonoid: Monoid[Fish] = new Monoid[Fish] {
  override def identity: Fish = ZeroFish
  override def op(l: Fish, r: Fish): Fish = {
    Thread.sleep(1)
    if (l.poisonousness > r.poisonousness) l else r
  }
}
```

Another point is that the list should be long enough, otherwise we won't be really testing the parallelization feature. We need to create a dedicated generator for lists between 100 and 1,000 in length:

```
val bucketOfFishGen: Gen[List[Fish]] = for {
  n <- Gen.choose(100, 1000)
  gen <- Gen.listOfN(n, fishGen)
} yield gen

implicit val arbBucketOfFish: Arbitrary[Bucket[Fish]] =
Arbitrary(bucketOfFishGen)
```

We also need a `helper` method to measure the execution time of the code block:

```
def withTime(block: => Fish): (Fish, Long) = {
  val start = System.nanoTime()
  val result = block
  (result, (System.nanoTime() - start) / 1000000)
}
```

For `foldPar`, we also need an implicit execution context. We'll use the global one as it is good enough for our purposes:

```
import scala.concurrent.ExecutionContext.Implicits.global
```

With all the preparations out of the way, we can formulate our property:

```
property("foldPar is the quickest way to fold a list") = {
  import Monoid.slowPoisonMonoid
  val foldable = MonoidFoldable.listMonoidFoldable[Fish]

  forAllNoShrink((as: Bucket[Fish]) => {
```

```
        . . .
    })
  }
```

In the body, we'll first measure the execution time of different folding approaches:

```
val (left, leftRuntime) = withTime(foldable.foldLeft(as))
val (right, rightRuntime) = withTime(foldable.foldRight(as))
val (balanced, balancedRuntime) = withTime(foldable.foldBalanced(as))
val (parallel, parallelRuntime) =
withTime(Await.result(foldable.foldPar(as), 5.seconds))
```

`foldPar` returns a `Future[Fish]` as the result, so we're waiting for it to complete. Finally, we check that the result of all of folds is the same and that the parallel folding does not take more time than the other approaches. We label these properties appropriately:

```
  s"${as.size} fishes: $leftRuntime, $rightRuntime, $balancedRuntime,
$parallelRuntime millis" |: all(
    "all results are equal" |: all(left == right, left == balanced, left ==
parallel),
    "parallel is quickest" |: parallelRuntime <= List(leftRuntime,
rightRuntime, balancedRuntime).min
  )
})
```

Now, we can run our test and check that our implementation lives up to our expectations if tested in SBT session:

```
+ MonoidFoldable.foldPar is the quickest way to fold a list: OK, passed 100
tests.
```

It turns out that it does!

Needless to say that it is possible to define other instances of the `MonoidFoldable` type class. Moreover, the collection does not need to be linear. As soon as it is possible to iterate over its elements, any structure will do—a binary tree, a map, a bag, or anything even more sophisticated. This possibility of being able to abstract over different data structures and to parallelize computations is what makes monoids especially useful in big data and distributed scenarios.

Having said that, we need to emphasize that `MonoidFoldable` can be made even more flexible and general-purpose. To understand how this can be done, we need to look once again at the definition of the fold process we gave earlier:

```
(((identity op a1) op a2) op a3) ...
```

We can notice from this that the recursive operation takes two arguments and returns a result that becomes the first argument for the next iteration. This observation leads to the conclusion that the folding function does not need to have both arguments of the same type. As long as the return type is the same as the type of the first argument and the same as the type of the identity element, any function will be good for folding. This allows us to define a more generic `Foldable` abstraction that can convert elements of the collection and combine them at the same time:

```
trait Foldable[F[_]] {
  def foldLeft[A,B](as: F[A])(z: B)(f: (B, A) => B): B
  def foldRight[A,B](as: F[A])(z: B)(f: (A, B) => B): B
}
```

This approach allows us to use any function, not only monoids, for folding. Of course, it is still possible to use existing monoid definitions, for example, by defining a method that would accept a monoid as an implicit parameter:

```
def foldMap[A,B : Monoid](as: F[A])(f: A => B): B = {
  val m = implicitly[Monoid[B]]
  foldLeft(as)(m.identity)((b, a) => m.op(f(a), b))
}
```

This definition relies on the existence of some complementary function, `f`, which converts elements of the collection into the appropriate type before they can be combined using the monoid operation.

Looking in the opposite direction, abstract algebraic structures do not end with monoids. In fact, there are a lot of more advanced definitions out there like the group, abelian group, and ring.

We'll take a short look at the implementation of the group just to reinforce our understanding of the topic of algebraic structures.

Group

A group adds an invertibility property to the properties of the monoid, which means that for every element, `a`, from the set, `S`, on which the group is defined, there is an inverse element so that the result of the operation on both of them is an identity element.

Formalized in the code, it looks like the following:

```
trait Group[S] extends Monoid[S] {
  def inverse(a: S): S
}
```

The `ScalaCheck` property for this new law looks similar to the properties we defined for semigroup and monoid:

```
def invertibility[S : Group : Arbitrary]: Prop =
  forAll((a: S) => {
    val m = implicitly[Group[S]]
    m.op(a, m.inverse(a)) == m.identity && m.op(m.inverse(a), a) ==
m.identity
  })
```

Like we did previously, we can define an overarching check that aggregates single properties:

```
def groupProp[S : Group: Arbitrary]: Prop = monoidProp[S] &&
invertibility[S]
```

By adding a `commutative` *property* to the group, we'll get an abelian group. The `commutative` property states that for any two input elements, the order of arguments does not matter. For a group to be abelian, it does not need to implement anything; all it needs to do is satisfy this additional property!

We can extend our check definitions to incorporate this:

```
def commutativity[S : Group : Arbitrary]: Prop =
  forAll((a: S, b: S) => {
    val m = implicitly[Group[S]]
    m.op(a, b) == m.op(b, a)
  })

def abelianGroupProp[S : Group: Arbitrary]: Prop =
  groupProp[S] && commutativity[S]
```

Again, we also define a single comprehensive property to check all of the laws of the abelian group at once.

One example of the abelian group is integer under addition. It can be implemented by extending the monoid we defined previously:

```
implicit val intAddition: Group[Int] = new Group[Int] {
  override def identity: Int = 0
  override def op(l: Int, r: Int): Int = l + r
```

```
      override def inverse(a: Int): Int = identity - a
   }
```

The properties we defined previously can help to ensure that this is indeed a valid abelian group implementation:

```
property("ints under addition form a group") = {
   import Group.intAddition
   groupProp[Int]
}

property("ints under addition form an abelian group") = {
   import Group.intAddition
   groupProp[Int]
}
```

We will leave the reader with the task of executing these properties to check that our implementation is correct.

Summary

The definition of the abelian group concludes our discussion of abstract algebraic structures; that is, the structures solely defined by the laws they satisfy.

We looked at three such structures: semigroup, monoid, and group. The semigroup is defined by a binary operation that is closed and associative. The monoid adds to this an identity element so that the operation applied to it and another argument returns the second argument unchanged. The group extends monoids with an invertibility law, stating that for each element there should be another element so that the operation applied on them returns an identity element. If the operation defined by the group is commutative, the group is called abelian.

We provided an example implementation for all these algebraic equations, along with `ScalaCheck` properties for verifying that our implementations are sane.

Needless to say, our code is for demonstration purposes only, and because of this, it is quite simplistic.

There are at least two major functional programming libraries in the Scala ecosystem in which the concepts we discussed are implemented more rigorously—cats (`https://typelevel.org/cats/`), and scalaz (`https://github.com/scalaz/scalaz`). They are well-documented and regularly blogged and talked about, and provide a solid grounding for readers who are curious about using the notions we've talked about in real-life projects.

In the next chapter, we'll work out our abstraction muscle by studying effects in general, extending the toolbox we started to fill in Chapter 6, *Exploring Built-In Effects*, with new concepts.

Questions

1. Why is the property of associativity that is essential for the monoid useful in a distributed setup?
2. Implement a monoid for a `Boolean` under `OR`.
3. Implement a monoid for a `Boolean` under `AND`.
4. Given a `Monoid[A]`, implement `Monoid[Option[A]]`.
5. Given a `Monoid[R]`, implement `Monoid[Either[L, R]]`.
6. Generalize two previous implementations for any effect parameterized by `A`, or describe why this is not possible.

Further reading

Atul S. Khot, *Scala Functional Programming Patterns*: Grok and performing effective functional programming in Scala

Ivan Nikolov, *Scala Design Patterns* - Second Edition: Learn how to write efficient, clean, and reusable code with Scala

8
Dealing with Effects

In the previous two chapters, we had quite a shift in perspective. In Chapter 6, *Exploring Built-In Effects*, we looked at a handful of implementations of the concrete effects available in the standard library. In Chapter 7, *Understanding Algebraic Structures* we jumped from the real to the theoretical and played with abstract algebraic structures.

Now that we are familiar with the process of working with abstractions defined by laws, we can finally deliver on the promise we gave in Chapter 6, *Exploring Built-In Effects*, and identify abstractions lying beneath the standard implementations we touched on there.

We'll define and implement a functor, an abstract concept that's useful in relation to any effect. Moreover, we'll have three different flavors of them, so stay tuned!

By the end of this chapter, you'll be able to identify and implement or use the existing implementation of one of the following structures:

- Functor
- Applicative functor
- Traversable functor

Technical requirements

- JDK 1.8+
- SBT 1.2+

The source code for this chapter is available in our GitHub repository at https://github.com/PacktPublishing/Learn-Scala-Programming/tree/master/Chapter08.

Functor

In the previous chapter, we discussed the situation in which we wanted to combine elements inside of a container. We found out that abstractions such as `Reducible` and `Foldable` can help with that by taking a function of two arguments and bringing it *into* the container so that it can be applied on pairs of elements inside of it. As an example, we showed you how this approach makes it possible to implement different survival strategies for a bucket of fish.

What we haven't covered is a case where we don't want to *combine* elements in the container but *do* something with all of them, a single element at a time. This is the bread and butter of functional programming—applying pure functions to arguments and getting the results back, then repeating this process with the result. Usually, the functions applied to the argument in succession can be combined into a single function, which in a sense is *fusing* all of the intermediate steps into one step.

Back to our fish example. Let's imagine that we have a fish and that we'd like to eat it. We'd first check that the fish is healthy and still fresh, then we would cook it somehow, and finally, we'd consume it. We might represent this sequence with the following model, extending the original `Fish` definition from the previous chapter:

```
final case class Fish(volume: Int, weight: Int, teeth: Int, poisonousness:
Int)

sealed trait Eatable

final case class FreshFish(fish: Fish)
final case class FriedFish(weight: Int) extends Eatable
final case class CookedFish(goodTaste: Boolean) extends Eatable
final case class Sushi(freshness: Int) extends Eatable
```

And our possible actions would naturally be represented as functions:

```
import ch08.Model._
import ch08.ModelCheck._
val check: Fish => FreshFish = f => FreshFish(f)
val prepare: FreshFish => FriedFish = f => FriedFish(f.fish.weight)
val eat: Eatable => Unit = _ => println("Yum yum...")
```

Then, we might want to combine our actions so that they represent the whole process from fresh to eaten fish:

```
def prepareAndEat: Fish => Unit = check andThen prepare andThen eat
```

Now, we can act on the fish as desired by applying the combined function to the fish:

```
val fish: Fish = fishGen.sample.get
val freshFish = check(fish)
```

In this example, we're using the `Gen[Fish]` function we defined in the previous chapter. Please consult the GitHub repository if you need to refresh your understanding on how this was done.

So far so good—we're satisfied and happy. But the situation will change if we have a bucket of fish. Suddenly, all of the functions we've defined are useless because we don't know how to apply them to the fish inside of the bucket! What do we do now?

 The requirement to work "inside" of the bucket might sound strange, but it is only because our example is disconnected from the implementation. In programming, most of the time, working with collections implies that we have the same collection (though with changed elements) after applying the operation. Moreover, if the *structure* of the collection is preserved, then the category theory we mentioned previously can provide some guarantees in regard to combining the operations as long as these obey a required set of laws. We've seen how this works with abstract algebraic structures, and the principle is the same for all abstractions derived from category theory. In practice, the requirement to preserve the structure of the collection means that the operation cannot change the type of the collection or the number of elements in it or throw an exception.

It turns out that there is an abstraction that can help us in this situation.

The `Functor` has a `map` method which takes a container and a function and applies this function to all of the elements in the container, and finally returning the container with the same structure but filled with new elements. This is how we can specify this in Scala:

```
import scala.language.higherKinds
trait Functor[F[_]] {
  def map[A,B](in: F[A])(f: A => B): F[B]
}
```

`F[_]` is a type constructor for the container. The `map` itself takes a container and a function to apply and returns a container with new elements. We could also define the `map` slightly differently, in a curried form:

```
def mapC[A,B](f: A => B): F[A] => F[B]
```

Here, `mapC` takes a function called `A => B` and returns a function called `F[A] => F[B]`, which can then be applied to the container.

As this is an abstract definition, we would naturally expect some laws to be defined and satisfied—exactly like in the previous chapter. For functors, there are two of them:

- The *identity* law states that mapping over an identity function should not change the original collection
- The *distributive* law requires that successive mapping over two functions should always produce the same result as mapping over the combination of these functions

We will capture these requirements as properties in the same that way we did in the previous chapter.

First, let's take a look at the identity law:

```
def id[A, F[_]](implicit F: Functor[F], arbFA: Arbitrary[F[A]]): Prop =
    forAll { as: F[A] => F.map(as)(identity) == as }
```

In this property, we're using the `identity` function from Chapter 3, *Deep Dive into Functions*, which just returns its argument.

The associativity law is a bit more involved because we need to test it with random functions. This requires that a lot of implicits are available:

```
import org.scalacheck._
import org.scalacheck.Prop._

def associativity[A, B, C, F[_]](implicit F: Functor[F],
                            arbFA: Arbitrary[F[A]],
                            arbB: Arbitrary[B],
                            arbC: Arbitrary[C],
                            cogenA: Cogen[A],
                            cogenB: Cogen[B]): Prop = {
  forAll((as: F[A], f: A => B, g: B => C) => {
    F.map(F.map(as)(f))(g) == F.map(as)(f andThen g)
  })
}
```

Here, we're creating the arbitrary functions `f: A => B` and `g: B => C` and checking that the combined function has the same effect as applying both functions in succession.

Now, we need some functors to apply our checks. We can implement a `Functor[Option]` by delegating to the map function defined on `Option`:

```
implicit val optionFunctor: Functor[Option] = new Functor[Option] {
  override def map[A, B](in: Option[A])(f: A => B): Option[B] = in.map(f)
  def mapC[A, B](f: A => B): Option[A] => Option[B] = (_: Option[A]).map(f)
}
```

The instance is defined as `implicit`, the same way as in the previous chapter, so that represents a type class.

Does this implementation obeys the necessary laws? Let's see. The properties in this chapter are defined in the test scope and can be run in SBT using the `test` command. They cannot be pasted into the REPL standalone, but only as a part of the `Properties` definition:

```
property("Functor[Option] and Int => String, String => Long") = {
  import Functor.optionFunctor
  functor[Int, String, Long, Option]
}
+ Functor.Functor[Option] and Int => String, String => Long: OK, passed 100
tests.

property("Functor[Option] and String => Int, Int => Boolean") = {
  import Functor.optionFunctor
  functor[String, Int, Boolean, Option]
}
+ Functor.Functor[Option] and String => Int, Int => Boolean: OK, passed 100
tests.
```

We can see that we need to specify types of the functor and functions to check the laws that make it impossible—in our case—to formulate the functor properties *in general*. The functional programming library, cats, solves this problem by also defining type classes for the types of arguments. We'll stick to the explicit definition—this is sufficient for our learning purposes.

We can also implement functors for the other effects we saw in Chapter 6, *Exploring Built-In Effects* in the same way we did for `Option`. The functor for `Try` is identical with respect to the type of effect. We'll leave this implementation as an exercise for the reader.

The case of `Either` is a bit more complicated, because we need to convert the two type arguments it takes to one type argument that's expected by a `Functor` type constructor. We do this by fixing a type of the left side to `L` and using the type lambda in the definition of the functor:

```
implicit def eitherFunctor[L] = new Functor[({ type T[A] = Either[L, A]
})#T] {
   override def map[A, B](in: Either[L, A])(f: A => B): Either[L, B] =
in.map(f)
   def mapC[A, B](f: A => B): Either[L, A] => Either[L, B] = (_: Either[L,
A]).map(f)
}
```

Interestingly, the implementation itself is the same again. It turns out that this is the abstraction we were looking for at the end of Chapter 6, *Exploring Built-In Effects*. All of the standard effects we discussed in Chapter 6, *Exploring Built-In Effects* are functors! The visible difference in the definition of the `map` method comes from the fact that, for the standard effects, it is defined using object-oriented polymorphism, and in our functor code, we're doing this by using ad-hoc polymorphism with type classes.

Let's get back to our fish. As we have a bucket of them, which is represented by the `List` type, we'll need a `Functor[Bucket]` as well:

```
implicit val bucketFunctor: Functor[List] = new Functor[List] {
   override def map[A, B](in: List[A])(f: A => B): List[B] = in.map(f)
   def mapC[A, B](f: A => B): List[A] => List[B] = (_: List[A]).map(f)
}
```

The definition is once again the same as before. However, we can perform actions on the fish in the bucket as desired now, reusing the `bucketOfFishGen`:

```
type Bucket[S] = List[S]
val bucketOfFishGen: Gen[List[Fish]] = Gen.listOf(fishGen)

val bucketOfFriedFish: Bucket[FriedFish] =
ch08.Functor.bucketFunctor.map(bucketOfFishGen.sample.get)(check andThen
prepare)
```

Here, we're using our freshly defined functor to check and prepare the fish inside of the bucket. The nice thing about our implementation is that the bucket can be any type that has a functor. To demonstrate this, we need a helper function that will allow us to pass a functor as a third parameter, along with the two we have in the definition of the `Functor.map`:

```
def mapFunc[A, B, F[_]](as: F[A])(f: A => B)(implicit functor:
ch08.Functor[F]): F[B] = functor.map(as)(f)
```

This function takes an effect and a function and implicitly resolves the appropriate functor. The calling code does not make this distinction any more since we're mapping over three different types of effects in the same way by using different functions:

```
import ch08.Functor._
import ch08.ModelCheck._
{
  type Bucket[S] = Option[S]
  mapFunc(optionOfFishGen.sample.get)(check)
}
{
  type Bucket[S] = Either[Exception, S]
  mapFunc(eitherFishGen.sample.get)(check andThen prepare)
}
{
  type Bucket[S] = List[S]
  mapFunc(listOfFishGen.sample.get)(prepareAndEat)
}
```

Now, it is starting to look like a useful abstraction—well, as long as our desires are limited to the functions of one argument. We'll see why in the next section.

Applicative

With functor, we now have a convenient way to apply functions to the contents of an effect, regardless of the type of the effect itself. We were able to check the fish and cook it by applying the same logic we had for an effect-free fish. To get even more comfortable with functors, we will now make a fish pie with our new tool.

First, we'll define a function to make a pie from a single fish:

```
final case class FishPie(weight: Int)
import ch08.Model._
def bakePie(fish: FreshFish, potatoes: Int, milk: Float): FishPie =
FishPie(fish.fish.weight)
```

That was easy—one fish, one pie, with the size of the fish. Now, we are ready to bake every fish in the bucket:

```
mapFunc(listOfFishGen.sample.get)(bakePie)
```

Oops! This won't compile because the functor only accepts the function of one argument, and we have three.

What can we do? One of the possibilities would be to refactor and partially apply our function. We could also create a function that uses `mapC` to convert the bucket of fish in to a fresh fish bucket so that we can simplify further actions:

```
val freshFishMaker: List[Fish] => List[FreshFish] =
ch08.Functor.bucketFunctor.mapC(check)
```

And then we can implement the rest of the logic with the partially applied function:

```
def bucketOfFish: Bucket[Fish] = listOfFishGen.sample.get

def bakeFishAtOnce(potatoes: Int, milk: Float): FreshFish => FishPie =
  bakePie(_: FreshFish, potatoes, milk)

val pie: Seq[FishPie] =
mapFunc(freshFishMaker(bucketOfFish))(bakeFishAtOnce(20, 0.5f))
```

This is a valid approach and would work, but this will use the same amount of ingredients for each and every fish. Some of the pies won't taste very good if this strategy. Can we do better?

Well, we can make our original function curried. This will give us a function that accepts a single fish and then other arguments on top:

```
def bakeFish: FreshFish => Int => Float => FishPie = (bakePie _).curried
val pieInProgress: List[Int => Float => FishPie] =
  mapFunc(freshFishMaker(bucketOfFish))(bakeFish)
```

Now, we would like to use the ingredients from another bucket so that we can add to the `pieInProgress`. Unfortunately, this is something that a functor can't help us with. If we try and nest, the map calls for a bucket of potatoes and a bucket of milk, so we would come up with something like the following:

```
mapFunc(pieInProgress) { (pieFactory: Int => Float => FishPie) =>
  mapFunc(bucketOfPotatoes) { potato =>
    mapFunc(bucketOfMilk) { milk =>
      pieFactory(potato)(milk)
    }
  }
}
```

Unfortunately, each nested call will leave the result in the nested bucked so that even if this were able to compile at the end, we'd have three nested buckets. Our functors do not know how to extract nested buckets from each other.

What can help us is the *Applicative Functor*. Sometimes just known as *Applicative*, this structure extends the original functor with two more methods:

```
trait Applicative[F[_]] extends Functor[F] {
  def apply[A,B](a: F[A])(f: F[A => B]): F[B]
  def unit[A](a: => A): F[A]
}
```

The apply method takes an effect, `a`, and a function, `f`, defined in the context of the same effect and applies `f` to `a`, thus returning the result that's wrapped in the very same effect.

The `unit` method allows us to wrap a plain value, `a`, into the effect. This is often called *lifting*, especially if `a` is a function, as it "lifts" the original value (or function) into the context of the effect, `F`.

An astute reader will expect some laws to pop up for the aforementioned functions. And you would be absolutely right! There are a few of them:

1. Identity law states that an application of an identity function should return the argument unchanged, the same way the identity function does. This is similar to the identity law for the functor, but this time defined for the `apply` function.
2. Homomorphism law states that applying a function to a value and then lifting the result is the same as first lifting this function and value and then applying them in the context of the applicative.
3. Interchange law states that changing the order of the parameters for the apply method should not change the result.
4. Composition law states that function composition should be preserved.

Now, this might start to sound abstract. Let's make these points clear by capturing them as properties.

The identity property is the simplest one. The only caveat is that we can't use the `identity` function—we have to be explicit about the type of the argument for the `unit` method because there is no possibility for the compiler to infer it for us:

```
def identityProp[A, F[_]](implicit A: Applicative[F],
                          arbFA: Arbitrary[F[A]]): Prop =
  forAll { as: F[A] =>
    A(as)(A.unit((a: A) => a)) == as
  }
```

Homomorphism is also not very spectacular—it literally encodes the rules we stated in prose. Similar to the case of `identityProp`, we're taking advantage of the `apply` syntax:

```
def homomorphism[A, B, F[_]](implicit A: Applicative[F],
                             arbA: Arbitrary[A],
                             arbB: Arbitrary[B],
                             cogenA: Cogen[A]): Prop = {
  forAll((f: A => B, a: A) => {
    A(A.unit(a))(A.unit(f)) == A.unit(f(a))
  })
}
```

The interchange law is where it starts to become interesting. We'll define left and right sides separately to simplify the definition:

```
def interchange[A, B, F[_]](implicit A: Applicative[F],
                            arbFA: Arbitrary[F[A]],
                            arbA: Arbitrary[A],
                            arbB: Arbitrary[B],
                            cogenA: Cogen[A]): Prop = {
  forAll((f: A => B, a: A) => {
    val leftSide = A(A.unit(a))(A.unit(f))
    val func = (ff: A => B) => ff(a)
    val rightSide = A(A.unit(f))(A.unit(func))
    leftSide == rightSide
  })
}
```

The left side is identical to the homomorphism definition—we're lifting some random function and a value into the applicative. Now, we need to change the order of f and a. The f is a first-class value, so we're fine on this side, but a is not a function. Therefore, we're defining a helper func which takes something with the same type as f and returns type B. Given a, we have only one way to implement this. With this helper, the types will align. Finally, we are defining the rightSide with the changed order of arguments and finish with the property comparing them.

The composition property is the most lengthy one because we have to define the functions that we are about to compose. First, let's define function composition as a function:

```
def composeF[A, B, C]: (B => C) => (A => B) => (A => C) = _.compose
```

Given two functions with matching types, composeF will return a function composition by delegating to the compose method of the first argument.

We'll again define left and right sides of the property separately:

```
def composition[A, B, C, F[_]](implicit A: Applicative[F],
                        arbFA: Arbitrary[F[A]],
                        arbB: Arbitrary[B],
                        arbC: Arbitrary[C],
                        cogenA: Cogen[A],
                        cogenB: Cogen[B]): Prop = {
  forAll((as: F[A], f: A => B, g: B => C) => {
    val af: F[A => B] = A.unit(f)
    val ag: F[B => C] = A.unit(g)
    val ac: F[(B => C) => (A => B) => (A => C)] = A.unit(composeF)
    val leftSide = A(as)(A(af)(A(ag)(ac)))
    val rightSide = A(A(as)(af))(ag)

    leftSide == rightSide
  })
}
```

The right side is straightforward—we're applying lifted functions f and g in succession on some effect, as. As the composition law states, this must be preserved if we apply composition inside of an applicative. This is what the left side does. It is better to read it from right to left: we're lifting our function which composes functions into the applicative and than applying lifted f and g in succession, but this time inside of the A. This gives us a compose function that's built inside of the applicative, which we finally apply to as.

For a valid applicative, all of these properties must hold, as well as the functor properties we defined earlier, as shown in the following snippet (not showing the implicit parameters):

```
identityProp[A, F] && homomorphism[A, B, F] && interchange[A, B, F] &&
composition[A, B, C, F] && FunctorSpecification.functor[A, B, C, F]
```

Secured with properties, we can define a few instances of applicative for the standard effects, just like we did for functor. The Option is arguably the easiest one to implement. Unfortunately, we can't just delegate to the instance method as we did with map, so we have to get our hands dirty:

```
implicit val optionApplicative: Applicative[Option] = new
Applicative[Option] {
  ... // map and mapC are the same as in Functor
  override def apply[A, B](a: Option[A])(f: Option[A => B]): Option[B] =
(a,f) match {
    case (Some(a), Some(f)) => Some(f(a))
    case _ => None
  }
  override def unit[A](a: => A): Option[A] = Some(a)
}
```

The type signatures dictate the implementation. We can't return Option[B] in any other way but by applying f to a. Similarly, we can't return Option[A] from the unit method. Please pay attention, though, to how we're using the Some constructor in both cases instead of the Option constructor. This is done in order to preserve structure in the case of null parameters or returned values.

The implementation for Either and Try is very similar with respect to the effect type. Remarkably, our Bucket type, which is represented by List, is quite different:

```
implicit val bucketApplicative: Applicative[List] = new Applicative[List] {
  ... // map and mapC are the same as in Functor
  override def apply[A, B](a: List[A])(f: List[A => B]): List[B] = (a, f)
match {
    case (Nil, _) => Nil
    case (_, Nil) => Nil
    case (aa :: as, ff :: fs) =>
      val fab: (A => B) => B = f => f(aa)
      ff(aa) :: as.map(ff) ::: fs.map(fab) ::: apply(as)(fs)
  }
  override def unit[A](a: => A): List[A] = List(a)
}
```

Because we need to apply all functions to all arguments, we're doing this in a recursive way in our example (notice that it is not tail-recursive!) by splitting the process into four parts—dealing with both first elements, the first element and all of its functions, all of the elements and the first function, and the recursive call for all but the first elements from both lists.

With `bucketApplicative` at hand, we can finally finish our curried `pieInProgress` function by first applying it to `potato` and then to `milk`:

```
def bakeFish: FreshFish => Int => Float => FishPie = (bakePie _).curried

val pieInProgress: List[Int => Float => FishPie] =
  mapFunc(freshFishMaker(bucketOfFish))(bakeFish)

def pie(potato: Bucket[Int], milk: Bucket[Float]) =
  bucketApplicative(milk)(bucketApplicative(potato)(pieInProgress))

scala> pie(List(10), List(2f))
res0: List[ch08.Model.FishPie] = List(FishPie(21), FishPie(11),
FishPie(78))
```

This definition works and produces the expected result—nice. But the implementation does not show the intent to mix three ingredients, which is not so nice. Let's improve this.

In fact, there are three different valid ways to define an applicative in terms of its basic functions:

1. The one we just implemented, with `apply` and `unit`.
2. To define it with the `unit` and `map2` methods so that `map2[A, B, C](fa: F[A], fb: F[B])(f: (A, B) => C): F[C]`.
3. To define it with the `unit`, `map`, and `product` functions so that `product[A, B](fa: F[A], fb: F[B]): F[(A, B)]`.

The `apply` and `map2` methods are equally powerful in the sense that it is possible to implement one in terms of another. The same applies to `product`, though it is weaker as it needs a `map` function to be defined.

As these functions are equally powerful, we can implement them directly in the type class definition so that they are available on all type class instances. The `map2` method looks good to start with:

```
trait Applicative[F[_]] extends Functor[F] {
  // ...
  def map2[A,B,C](fa: F[A], fb: F[B])(f: (A, B) => C): F[C] =
```

```
            apply(fb)(map(fa)(f.curried))
    }
```

The implementation almost looks disappointing in its simplicity—we just apply `fa` and `fb` in succession to the given `f` we converted to the curried form so that we are able to apply them in two steps.

It is interesting how the `map2` method is implemented in terms of `map`, which in a sense is a map of *lower power*. The curious readers out there could be asking if it is possible to implement a `map` with yet another function of *lower power*. It turns out we can do this! Here is the implementation:

```
override def map[A,B](fa: F[A])(f: A => B): F[B] = apply(fa)(unit(f))
```

All we need to do is lift the given function `f` into the context of applicative and use the `apply` function we already have.

This way of defining functions in terms of other functions is common in functional programming. All the way down in the abstraction, there are methods that provide the basis for all other definitions and cannot be defined as a combination of other methods. These are called *primitive*. The tree flavors of applicative we are talking about are different by their choice of primitive functions. As it turns out, our initial choice was the first of them, that is, the `unit` and `apply` methods. Using these primitive functions, we were able to define the `Functor` in terms of `Applicative`! It makes sense to do the same and define a `Functor.mapC` in terms of `map`:

```
def mapC[A,B](f: A => B): F[A] => F[B] = fa => map(fa)(f)
```

The nice side-effect of deriving implementations this way is that as soon as primitive functions are implemented properly and obey the applicative (or functor) laws, the derived implementations should be lawful as well.

Back to the flavors of applicative—we still need to implement the `product` method which creates an applicative of a product from two applicatives:

```
def product[G[_]](G: Applicative[G]): Applicative[({type f[x] = (F[x],
G[x])})#f] = {
  val F = this
  new Applicative[({type f[x] = (F[x], G[x])})#f] {
    def unit[A](a: => A) = (F.unit(a), G.unit(a))
    override def apply[A,B](p: (F[A], G[A]))(fs: (F[A => B], G[A => B])) =
      (F.apply(p._1)(fs._1), G.apply(p._2)(fs._2))
  }
}
```

This time, we had to use a type lambda again to represent a product of two types, F and G, as a single type. We also needed to store the reference to the current instance of the applicative as F so that we're able to call its methods later. The implementation itself is naturally expressed in terms of the unit and apply primitives. For the resulting applicative, the unit is defined as a product of units for F and G, and the apply is just a product of using an apply method on the given arguments.

Unfortunately, we still can't define our pie function in a very readable way. If only we had map3, we could implement it as follows:

```
def pie3[F[_]: Applicative](fish: F[FreshFish], potato: F[Int], milk:
F[Float]): F[FishPie] =
    implicitly[Applicative[F]].map3(fish, potato, milk)(bakePie)
```

Obviously, this implementation expresses a very clear intent: take three containers full of ingredients, apply a function on these ingredients, and get a container with pies back. This works for any container for which an instance of an Applicative type class is available.

Well, we already know how to derive functions from primitives defined for an abstraction. Why don't we do this again? Here goes:

```
def map3[A,B,C,D](fa: F[A],
                  fb: F[B],
                  fc: F[C])(f: (A, B, C) => D): F[D] =
    apply(fc)(apply(fb)(apply(fa)(unit(f.curried))))
```

Hmm, it turned out to be a definition for the map2 function, just extended with one more call for an apply for a third parameter! Needless to say, it is possible to implement the mapN method for any arity like this. We can also define it in an inductive way by calling a map of smaller arity:

```
def map4[A,B,C,D,E](fa: F[A],
                    fb: F[B],
                    fc: F[C],
                    fd: F[D])(f: (A, B, C, D) => E): F[E] = {
    val ff: (A, B, C) => D => E = (a,b,c) => d => f(a,b,c,d)
    apply(fd)(map3(fa, fb, fc)(ff))
}
```

We just needed to convert the provided function to the form where we can feed it with all but the last parameters and the last parameter separately.

Now, as we have our `pie3` implementation, we must stop for a moment. We need to tell you something. Yes, we need to admit that we cheated a bit as we defined the `check` function. Surely, we can't just return `FreshFish` every time we have `Fish` as we did before:

```
lazy val check: Fish => FreshFish = f => FreshFish(f)
```

We did this on purpose so that we're able to focus on `Applicative`. Now, we are ready to improve on this. We are already familiar with the notion of optionality, so we could change this function to return an `Option`:

```
lazy val check: Fish => Option[FreshFish]
```

But let's decide which kind of effect it should be later. Let's call it `F` for now. We need two possibilities:

- To return an empty `F` in the case that the fish is not fresh
- To return an `F` with a fresh fish otherwise

In terms of abstractions, we have a way to lift a fish into `F` as soon as we have an applicative for it—the applicative gives this as a `unit`. All we need is an empty `F[FreshFish]`, which we'll provide as an argument to the function.

Hence, our new definition for the check will look as follows:

```
def checkHonestly[F[_] : Applicative](noFish: F[FreshFish])(fish: Fish):
F[FreshFish] =
  if (scala.util.Random.nextInt(3) == 0) noFish else
implicitly[Applicative[F]].unit(FreshFish(fish))
```

Having empty `F` as a separate argument list will allow us to partially apply this function later. The preceding implementation returns an empty `F` in approximately 30% of cases. We're asking the compiler to check that the implicit `Applicative` is available for `F`, as discussed. If this is the case, our implementation will delegate to it to create a proper result.

OK, we now have a way to separate fresh fish from the rest, but there is another problem. Our `pie3` function expects all of the ingredients to be wrapped in the same type of applicative. This is common in functional programming, and we'll deal with this impediment by lifting other parameters into the same container. We could introduce checks for freshness for potatoes and milk in the same way that we did for fish, but for simplicity, we'll assume they are always fresh (sorry, critical reader):

```
def freshPotato(count: Int) = List(Some(count))
def freshMilk(gallons: Float) = List(Some(gallons))
```

```
val trueFreshFish: List[Option[FreshFish]] =
  bucketOfFish.map(checkHonestly(Option.empty[FreshFish]))
```

With all of the ingredients checked for freshness, we can use our existing pie3 function, almost like we did before:

```
import ch08.Applicative._
def freshPie = pie3[({ type T[x] = Bucket[Option[x]]})#T](trueFreshFish,
freshPotato(10), freshMilk(0.2f))
```

The difference is that we need to help the compiler to recognize the proper type parameter. We do this by using the type lambda to define the type of the container explicitly. There is one missing piece of the puzzle, though. If we try to compile the preceding code, it will fail because we don't have an instance of Applicative[Bucket[Option]] yet.

Ready to roll up your sleeves and implement it? Well, although there is nothing wrong with getting our hands dirty, we don't want to implement a new applicative each time we'd like to have a composition of them. What we'll do instead is define a generic combination of applicatives, which is itself an applicative. The fact that applicatives *compose* is their most admirable property. Let's see how this works. This is how we can implement it for our Applicative[F]:

```
    def compose[G[_]](G: Applicative[G]): Applicative[({type f[x] =
F[G[x]]})#f] = {
      val F = this

      def fab[A, B]: G[A => B] => G[A] => G[B] = (gf: G[A => B]) => (ga:
G[A]) => G.apply(ga)(gf)

      def fg[B, A](f: F[G[A => B]]): F[G[A] => G[B]] = F.map(f)(fab)

      new Applicative[({type f[x] = F[G[x]]})#f] {
        def unit[A](a: => A) = F.unit(G.unit(a))
        override def apply[A, B](a: F[G[A]])(f: F[G[A => B]]): F[G[B]] =
          F.apply(a)(fg(f))
      }
    }
```

Again, we had to use the type lambda to tell the compiler that this is actually just a single type parameter and not two. The implementation of the unit method is just wrapping one applicative into another. The apply method is more complex and we implemented it as a local function to make it clearer what is happening. The first thing we're doing is converting the internal function of type G[A => B] to the type G[A] => G[B]. We're doing this by applying the applicative G on the "internal" function wrapped inside of f. Now that we have this function, we can call the map function of the outer applicative to wrap the result into F. The last thing we're doing is applying this wrapped composed function on the original function and the resulting function, that is, to the original argument of the apply method.

Now, we can compose these applicatives as we wish:

```
implicit val bucketOfFresh: ch08.Applicative[({ type T[x] =
Bucket[Option[x]]})#T] =
  bucketApplicative.compose(optionApplicative)
```

And use this combination to call our original pie-making logic:

```
scala> println(freshPie)
List(Some(FishPie(40)), None, Some(FishPie(36)))
```

The beauty of this approach is that it allows us to reuse existing logic with arbitrarily nested applicatives, just like in the following artificial example:

```
import scala.util._
import ch08.Applicative
def deep[X](x: X) = Success(Right(x))
type DEEP[x] = Bucket[Try[Either[Unit, Option[x]]]]

implicit val deepBucket: Applicative[DEEP] =
bucketApplicative.compose(tryApplicative.compose(eitherApplicative[Unit].co
mpose(optionApplicative)))

val deeplyPackaged =
  pie3[DEEP](trueFreshFish.map(deep), freshPotato(10).map(deep),
freshMilk(0.2f).map(deep))
```

All that we need in the case that the structure of containers changes is to define a new composite applicative (and a few syntactic helpers like the type alias as a constructor, but these aren't essential). Then, we are able to use the existing logic as we did previously. This is what the result looks like in REPL:

```
scala> println(deeplyPackaged)
List(Success(Right(Some(FishPie(46)))), Success(Right(Some(FishPie(54)))),
Success(Right(None)))
```

We can easily change the structure of the result by rewiring the composite applicative:

```
type DEEP[x] = Try[Either[Unit, Bucket[Option[x]]]]

implicit val deepBucket: Applicative[DEEP] =
tryApplicative.compose(eitherApplicative[Unit].compose(bucketApplicative.co
mpose(optionApplicative)))

val deeplyPackaged =
  pie3[DEEP](deep(trueFreshFish), deep(freshPotato(10)),
deep(freshMilk(0.2f)))
```

We changed the composition order and now the result looks different:

```
scala> println(deeplyPackaged)
Success(Right(List(Some(FishPie(45)), Some(FishPie(66)), None)))
```

Does it feel like combining applicatives leaves no desires unfulfilled? Well, in a sense, it is, except for the case that we want to change the structure of the result at hand. To give you an example, let's recall the result of our baking endeavor for the fresh fish: `List(Some(FishPie(45)), Some(FishPie(66)), None)`. It is a bucket containing either a pie, if the fish was fresh, or nothing if it was not. But what if we hired a new cook and now every single fish in the bucket has to be fresh or the whole bucket is discarded? Our return type would be `Option[Bucket[FishPie]]` in this case—the bucket is full of pies if we have a bucket of fresh fish, or nothing. We want to keep our kitchen processes, though! This is the time for the `Traversable` functor to enter the scene.

Traversable

The `Traversable` functor is similar to `Reducible` and `Foldable`, which we talked about in the previous chapter. The difference is that methods defined on `Traversable` preserve the underlying structure while going over it, as opposed to the other abstractions which collapse it into the single result. The `Traversable` defines two methods:

```
import scala.{ Traversable => _ }

trait Traversable[F[_]] extends Functor[F] {
  def sequence[A,G[_]: Applicative](a: F[G[A]]): G[F[A]]
  def traverse[A,B,G[_]: Applicative](a: F[A])(f: A => G[B]): G[F[B]]
}
```

Unfortunately, Scala has a deprecated `Traversable` definition left over from previous versions, so we are getting rid of it by using import renaming. Our `Traversable` defines the `sequence` and `traverse` methods, which loosely correspond to the `reduce` and `fold` methods defined on monoids. Starting with the `sequence` method, we can see that it turns its argument *inside out*. This is exactly what we needed to make our new cook happy. Let's skip the implementation part for a moment and see how it works in practice:

```
scala> println(freshPie)
List(None, None, Some(FishPie(38)))

scala>println(ch08.Traversable.bucketTraversable.sequence(freshPie))
None
```

As soon as we have `None` in the list, we're getting `None` back as the result. Let's give it another try:

```
scala> println(freshPie)
List(Some(FishPie(40)), Some(FishPie(27)), Some(FishPie(62)))

scala> println(ch08.Traversable.bucketTraversable.sequence(freshPie))
Some(List(FishPie(40), FishPie(27), FishPie(62)))
```

If all of the fish are fresh, we get `Some` bucket of pies, as expected. But we're still not 100% satisfied with this approach. The reason for this is that we first bake all of the fresh pies we possibly can and then discard them in the case that not all of the fish was fresh. Instead, we would like to stop as soon as we encounter the first rotten fish. This is what the `traverse` method is for. Using it, we can implement our baking process like so:

```
ch08.Traversable.bucketTraversable.traverse(bucketOfFish) { a: Fish =>
  checkHonestly(Option.empty[FreshFish])(a).map(f => bakePie(f, 10, 0.2f))
}
```

Here, we're traversing over the `bucketOfFish`. We're using `bucketTraversable` for this. It expects a function called `Fish => G[?]` so that `G` is applicative. We can satisfy this requirement by providing a function called `Fish => Option[FishPie]`. We're using `checkHonestly` to lift a `Fish` into the `Option[FreshFish]`, and then we need to `map` over it with our original `bakePie` method.

How is `traverse` implemented? Unfortunately, the implementation for this requires knowing the structure of the effect so that it can be preserved. Because of this, it needs to be implemented for each instance of the type class or delegated to another abstraction where this knowledge is preserved, like `Foldable`.

This is how the `traverse` method can be implemented for `Traversable[List]`:

```
override def traverse[A, B, G[_] : Applicative](a: Bucket[A])(f: A =>
G[B]): G[Bucket[B]] = {
  val G = implicitly[Applicative[G]]
  a.foldRight(G.unit(List[B]()))((aa, fbs) => G.map2(f(aa), fbs)(_ :: _))
}
```

To preserve the structure of the list, we `foldRight` over it, starting by lifting an empty list into the context of G. We're using `map2` in each fold iteration to call the provided function on the next element of the original list, lift it into G, and append it to the result.

For the `Option`, we could use an approach similar to what we used for `fold`, but as we only need to handle two cases, a pattern matching implementation reveals the intent much better:

```
implicit val optionTraversable = new Traversable[Option] {
  override def map[A, B](in: Option[A])(f: A => B): Option[B] =
  Functor.optionFunctor.map(in)(f)
  override def traverse[A, B, G[_] : Applicative](a: Option[A])(f: A =>
G[B]): G[Option[B]] = {
    val G = implicitly[Applicative[G]]
    a match {
      case Some(s) => G.map(f(s))(Some.apply)
      case None => G.unit(None)
    }
  }
}
```

We're just lifting the `Option` into the context of G by using the appropriate methods for different states of an `Option`. It is worth noting that we're using `Some.apply` directly in the case of the non-empty `Option` to preserve the structure as required.

The good news is that the second method, `sequence`, is less powerful than traverse. Because of this, it can be defined directly on `Traversable` in terms of `traverse`:

```
def sequence[A,G[_]: Applicative](a: F[G[A]]): G[F[A]] =
traverse(a)(identity)
```

It just uses the `identity` function to return a proper value of `G[A]`, as expected by `traverse`.

Being a functor, `Traversables` also compose. The `compose` function will have the following signature:

```
trait Traversable[F[_]] extends Functor[F] {
  // ...
  def compose[H[_]](implicit H: Traversable[H]): Traversable[({type f[x] =
F[H[x]]})#f]
}
```

We'll leave the task of implementing this to the reader.

This is how composing `Traversables` can make life easier. Remember our controversial `deeplyPackaged` example? This is, once again, what the type of the container looks like:

```
type DEEP[x] = scala.util.Try[Either[Unit, Bucket[Option[x]]]]
```

Can you imagine iterating over it and applying some logic to the elements of it? With a composed `Traversable`, this is absolutely straightforward:

```
import ch08.Traversable._
val deepTraverse =
tryTraversable.compose(eitherTraversable[Unit].compose(bucketTraversable))

val deepYummi = deepTraverse.traverse(deeplyPackaged) { pie:
Option[FishPie] =>
  pie.foreach(p => println(s"Yummi $p"))
  pie
}
println(deepYummi)
```

We first compose the `Traversable` to match our nested types. Then, we traverse over it, as we did previously. Please note how we omitted the bottom `Option` type and have it as a wrapper type for the function parameter for traverse. This is the output of the preceding snippet:

```
Yummi FishPie(71)
Yummi FishPie(5)
Yummi FishPie(82)
Some(Success(Right(List(FishPie(82), FishPie(5), FishPie(71)))))
```

Does it feel like you have superpowers yet? If you're still not feeling it, we have something more to offer in the next chapter!

Summary

This was an intense chapter. We learned about the concept of working with effects in a way that the knowledge of the effects' structure is *outsourced* to another abstraction. We looked at three such abstractions.

The `Functor` allows us to apply a function of one argument to each element stored in the container.

The `Applicative` (or applicative functor) extends the `Functor` in a way that it is possible to apply a function of two arguments (and by induction, functions of any number of arguments). We've seen that it is possible to choose one of three equally valid sets of primitives that define applicative and derive all of the other methods from these primitives.

We said that this approach of defining a minimal set of primitive functions and the rest of functionality in terms of these primitives is a common approach in functional programming.

The last abstraction we saw was the `Traversable` (or traversable functor), which allows us to iterate over effects, thus changing their content, but preserving the underlying structure.

We paid special attention to combining applications and later to combining traversable. Having implemented the general methods that allow us to build stacks of arbitrary functors and use these stacks to go straight to the *heart*, we were able to reuse existing functions that were defined in terms of plain effect-free types.

What we haven't demonstrated, though, is the way that data from one applicative can influence functions that are called deeper in the stack—we just used constant parameters in our examples. The reason we did this is that applications do not support sequencing computations.

In the next chapter, we'll learn about another abstraction that is capable of truly chaining computations—a monad.

Questions

1. Implement `Functor[Try]`. Check that your implementation passes the property check, just like it did in this chapter.
2. Implement `Applicative[Try]`. Check that your implementation passes the property check, just like it did in this chapter.
3. Implement `Applicative[Either]`. Check that your implementation passes the property check, just like it did in this chapter.
4. Implement `Traversable[Try]`.
5. Implement `Traversable[Either]`.
6. Implement `Traversable.compose`, in the same way, that we discussed at the end of this chapter.

Further reading

- Atul S. Khot, *Scala Functional Programming Patterns*: Grok and performing effective functional programming in Scala
- Ivan Nikolov, *Scala Design Patterns* - Second Edition: Learn how to write efficient, clean, and reusable code with Scala

9
Familiarizing Yourself with Basic Monads

In the previous chapter, we got to know Functors, an abstraction that gives the `map` method the effects defined in the standard library. Looking back at Chapter 6, *Exploring Built-In Effects*, there is still something missing here—the source of the `flatMap` method, which all standard effects also have.

In this chapter, we will finally meet the concept of a monad, the structure that defines `flatMap`. To learn about this function inside and out, we'll implement four different monads.

By the end of this chapter, you'll be familiar with the following topics:

- Abstracting a monad and its properties
- Implementing monads for standard effects
- The implementation and applicability of the following basic monads:
    - Id
    - State
    - Reader
    - Writer

Technical requirements

Before we begin, make sure you have the following installed:

- JDK 1.8+
- SBT 1.2+

The source code for this chapter is available in our GitHub repository at `https://github.com/PacktPublishing/Learn-Scala-Programming/tree/master/Chapter09`.

Introduction to monads

It took us three chapters to get to the moment where we're ready to discuss the origins of the `flatMap` method in regards to the effects we looked at in Chapter 6, *Exploring Built-In Effects*. The reason for this is not the complexity of the topic, but the richness of the family of abstractions related to it.

After this introduction, a suspicious reader will think with disappointment—OK, now they are going to use their usual trick and say that there is an abstraction for `flatMap`, `flattener` or `flatMapative`, pull some laws out of thin air, and consider themselves done. What cheaters!

Well, technically we're not cheating because we're not pulling things out of anywhere. Instead, we're taking them from category theory, the branch of mathematics we mentioned previously. The rules our abstractions must obey are defined by mathematicians. There is an advantage to this approach, though—as soon as we can prove that our implementation obeys the required laws, we can use everything that has been proved by category theory to our advantage. One example of this is the possibility of combining two applicatives into one, just like in the example we discussed in the previous chapter.

Going back to our `flatMap` method, there is still some intrigue there. The abstraction name is `Monad`, and it is defined by two methods, `flatMap`, and `unit`:

```scala
import scala.language.higherKinds
trait Monad[F[_]] {
  def unit[A](a: => A): F[A]
  def flatMap[A, B](a: F[A])(f: A => F[B]): F[B]
}
```

The monad is defined for a container of type `F`. The `unit` method *lifts* its parameter into the context of `F`; the `flatMap` is similar to the plain `map` method in a sense that it applies `f` to `a`. What is different in `flatMap` and what makes it special is its ability to *collapse* or *flatten* two layers of `F` into one. This is easy to see from the type signatures of `a` and `f`.

This possibility to flatten F[F[A]] into F[A] is the reason why monads are often expressed with a different set of methods; that is, map and flatten:

```
trait Monad[F[_]] {
  def unit[A](a: => A): F[A]
  def map[A, B](a: F[A])(f: A => B): F[B]
  def flatten[A](fa: F[F[A]]): F[A]
}
```

The flatten method does exactly what we just said—it allows us to reduce the stack of Fs into a single F. Sometimes, the flatten method is also called a join. We will see in a moment why this name makes sense.

Clearly, we have the same situation with monads that we had with applicatives—we can choose the set of primitive functions and implement the rest of functionality in terms of primitives. For instance, the flatMap is equally powerful as a combination of map and flatten, and we can choose one of these combinations.

Let's stick to the initial definition and implement other methods in terms of flatMap. This is what map will look like:

```
def map[A, B](a: F[A])(f: A => B): F[B] =
  flatMap(a)(a => unit(f(a)))
```

What we're doing here is basically mapping with the function f and lifting the result in context of F as the types require.

Can you remember the name of the abstraction that is characterized by having a map method? Right, this is the functor. Our ability to define a map solely in terms of flatMap for every Monad proves that every Monad is a Functor. Because of this, we can state that Monad extends Functor.

The definition of the flatten method is similarly straightforward:

```
def flatten[A](a: F[F[A]]): F[A] = flatMap(a)(identity)
```

With the identity function, we are using part of the flatMap power to convert two layers of F into one without actually doing anything with a.

Can we go further and apply a function that is already in the context of F to the a? It turns out that we can, and we know the method that does this—this is the apply defined in Applicative:

```
def apply[A, B](a: F[A])(f: F[A => B]): F[B] =
  flatMap(f) { fab: (A => B) => map(a) { a: A => fab(a) }}
```

Here, we're pretending that f is a value, so we just need to represent a as a function that can be applied to this value. The fab function takes a function called A => B that we use to map over the original a, returning B, which becomes an F[B] because of the application of map.

The apply function is also defined in terms of flatMap (and map, which is derived from flatMap) for every monad. This provides evidence that every Monad is an Applicative. Thus, our definition of Monad can be changed into the following form:

```
trait Monad[F[_]] extends ch08.Applicative[F] {
  def flatMap[A, B](a: F[A])(f: A => F[B]): F[B]

  def flatten[A](a: F[F[A]]): F[A] = flatMap(a)(identity)

  override def unit[A](a: => A): F[A]
  override def map[A, B](a: F[A])(f: A => B): F[B] =
    flatMap(a)(a => unit(f(a)))

  override def apply[A, B](a: F[A])(f: F[A => B]): F[B] =
    flatMap(f) { fab: (A => B) => map(a) { a: A => fab(a) }}
}
```

We can see that the flatMap method is only available for the Monad, not for an Applicative. This leads to interesting consequences, which we will look at later in this chapter.

Now, before switching gears and starting to implement the instances of specific monads, let's discuss the monadic laws first.

Fortunately, there are only two of them, and both are very similar to the functor laws we discussed in the previous chapter; that is, the *identity* and *associativity* laws.

The identity law states that applying flatMap and unit should return the original argument. Depending on the order of application, there are left and right identities. We'll represent them formally as usual with ScalaCheck properties (the following snippet does not show the implicit parameters; please consult the accompanying code for the full definition):

```
val leftIdentity = forAll { as: M[A] =>
  M.flatMap(as)(M.unit(_)) == as
}
```

The left identity stipulates that the result of using flatMap over the argument by lifting it into the context of the monad should be equal to the original argument.

The right identity is a bit more complex:

```
val rightIdentity = forAll { (a: A, f: A => M[B]) =>
  M.flatMap(M.unit(a))(f) == f(a)
}
```

Basically, the rule is that lifting a into the context and then flatmapping it with some function, f, should produce the same result as applying this function to a directly.

Now, all we need to do is combine both of these properties into a single identity property. We'll need quite a bit of different implicit Arbitrary arguments in order to generate input data, including A, M[A] and A => M[B], but the property itself should be anything but surprising:

```
import org.scalacheck._
import org.scalacheck.Prop._

def id[A, B, M[_]](implicit M: Monad[M],
                   arbFA: Arbitrary[M[A]],
                   arbFB: Arbitrary[M[B]],
                   arbA: Arbitrary[A],
                   cogenA: Cogen[A]): Prop = {
  val leftIdentity = forAll { as: M[A] =>
    M.flatMap(as)(M.unit(_)) == as
  }
  val rightIdentity = forAll { (a: A, f: A => M[B]) =>
    M.flatMap(M.unit(a))(f) == f(a)
  }
  leftIdentity && rightIdentity
}
```

The associativity property says that flatmapping using functions in succession should be the same as applying functions in the context of the monad:

```
forAll((a: M[A], f: A => M[B], g: B => M[C]) => {
  val leftSide = M.flatMap(M.flatMap(a)(f))(g)
  val rightSide = M.flatMap(a)(a => M.flatMap(f(a))(g))
  leftSide == rightSide
})
```

We'll omit the definition of the implicit parameters for this and a combination rule:

```
def monad[A, B, C, M[_]](implicit M: Monad[M], ...): Prop = {
  id[A, B, M] && associativity[A, B, C, M]
}
```

 Please look up the source code in GitHub to see the full signature of these properties.

Now that we have an understanding of what methods we need to define and how they should behave, let's implement some monads! We'll need to know the internals of the respective containers in order to implement the `flatMap`. In the previous chapter, we implemented the `map` method by delegating to the underlying container. Now, we'll use a low-level approach to show that the knowledge of the structure is indeed necessary.

As usual, we will start with the simplest of the standard effects, `Option`. This is how we implement `Monad[Option]`:

```
implicit val optionMonad = new Monad[Option] {
  override def unit[A](a: => A): Option[A] = Some(a)

  override def flatMap[A, B](a: Option[A])(f: A => Option[B]): Option[B] =
a match {
    case Some(value) => f(value)
    case _ => None
  }
}
```

The implementation of `unit` should be apparent—the only way to turn A into `Option[A]` is by wrapping it. Like we did previously, we're using the case class constructor directly to preserve the structure in the case that a is `null`.

The `flatMap` implementation is also very transparent—we can't apply a given function to `None`, and hence we return `None` as is. In the case that we have provided a is defined, we unwrap the value and apply `f` to it. This *unwrapping* is exactly the moment where we're using our knowledge of the internals of `Option` to flatten the potentially nested result.

We can check that our implementation obeys monadic laws by defining a couple of properties for different types of a and f:. These properties need to be placed in a class extending `org.scalacheck.Properties`, as usual:

```
property("Monad[Option] and Int => String, String => Long") = {
  monad[Int, String, Long, Option]
```

```
  }
  property("Monad[Option] and String => Int, Int => Boolean") = {
    monad[String, Int, Boolean, Option]
  }
+ Monad.Monad[Option] and Int => String, String => Long: OK, passed 100
tests.
+ Monad.Monad[Option] and String => Int, Int => Boolean: OK, passed 100
tests.
```

Given that our properties hold for two different types of a and two different types of functions, we can be pretty sure that our code is correct and proceed with other containers.

For `Either`, we have a small complication, exactly like we had when we defined a Functor for it - two type parameters instead of one required by the `Monad`. Are you ready to deal with it the same way as before—by fixing the second type parameter and using the type lambda to define the final type of the monad? The good news is that we won't need to do this! The type lambda is such a common thing that's used in type class programming that many people craved an easier way to do this. This is the projector that plugin was created for. It allows us to use simplified syntax for type lambdas in Scala.

All we need to do so that we can start using the plugin is add the dependency to our project configuration in the `build.sbt` file:

```
addCompilerPlugin("org.spire-math" %% "kind-projector" % "0.9.8")
```

Now that we have this, we can simplify the type lambda syntax from our usual (`{type T[A] = Either[L, A]}`)`#T` to just `Either[L, ?]`. The plugin is feature-rich, and we will not go into further details here; visiting the documentation page at `https://index. scala-lang.org/non/kind-projector/kind-projector/0.9.7` is highly recommended.

With our new tool, the definition of `eitherMonad` is easy to read:

```
implicit def eitherMonad[L] = new Monad[Either[L, ?]] {
  override def unit[A](a: => A): Either[L, A] = Right(a)

  override def flatMap[A, B](a: Either[L, A])(f: A => Either[L, B]):
Either[L, B] = a match {
    case Right(r) => f(r)
    case Left(l) => Left(l)
  }
}
```

The type class constructor takes a type parameter, L, for the left side of Either. The rest of the implementation should be very familiar by now. It's worth reminding yourself that Either is right-biased—this it the reason we're returning Right from the unit method. It's also worth mentioning the last case in the flatMap pattern match where we repacked l from Left[L, A] into Left[L, B]. This is done to help the compiler infer the correct return type.

For the property definition, we also have to fix a type of the left side. We can do this by defining a type alias, which will improve readability:

```
type UnitEither[R] = Either[Unit, R]

property("Monad[UnitEither[Int]] and Int => String, String => Long") = {
  monad[Int, String, Long, UnitEither]
}

property("Monad[UnitEither[String]] and String => Int, Int => Boolean") = {
  monad[String, Int, Boolean, UnitEither]
}
```

Except for the type alias, the definition of properties is the same as we had for Option.

The definition of Monad[Try] is done by analogy, and we'll leave it as an exercise for the reader.

In contrast, Monad[List] (or Monad[Bucket], if we're to use terms from the previous chapter) is quite different as the List can contain more than one element:

```
implicit val listMonad = new Monad[List] {
  def unit[A](a: => A) = List(a)

  def flatMap[A,B](as: List[A])(f: A => List[B]): List[B] = as match {
    case Nil => Nil
    case a :: as => f(a) ::: flatMap(as)(f)
  }
}
```

The unit is implemented in the same way as the other effects were—just by wrapping its argument. The flatMap is defined in a recursive manner. For Nil, we return Nil. This case is analogous to the case of None in Monad[Option]. In the case of a non-empty list, we have to apply the given function to all of the elements of the list and flatten the result at the same time. This is done in the second matching case.

```
property("Monad[List] and Int => String, String => Long") = {
  monad[Int, String, Long, List]
}
property("Monad[List] and String => Int, Int => Boolean") = {
  monad[String, Int, Boolean, List]
}
+ Monad.Monad[List] and Int => String, String => Long: OK, passed 100
tests.
+ Monad.Monad[List] and String => Int, Int => Boolean: OK, passed 100
tests.
```

It looks like it is, but the only reason for this is that the list generator in ScalaCheck does not generate input lists of a significant size. If it did, our property would fail with StackOverflowError because it is not tail-recursive!

Let's fix this by using the techniques that we discussed in Chapter 3, *Deep Dive into Functions*:

```
override def flatMap[A,B](as: List[A])(f: A => List[B]): List[B] = {
  @tailrec
  def fMap(as: List[A], acc: List[B])(f: A => List[B]): List[B] = as match
{
    case Nil => acc
    case a :: aas => fMap(aas, acc ::: f(a))(f)
  }
  fMap(as, Nil)(f)
}
```

Now that we have made our implementation tail-recursive by introducing the accumulator, we can safely use it with lists of an arbitrary length. But this approach is still quite direct and slow because of that. On my laptop, this implementation consumed approximately five times more time than the "native" optimized implementation of List's flatMap method. It turns out that this is exactly the case where delegating makes sense:

```
override def flatMap[A,B](as: List[A])(f: A => List[B]): List[B] =
as.flatMap(f)
```

OK, so we have ignored Future, but have implemented type class instances for all of the containers we discussed in Chapter 6, *Exploring Built-In Effects*. Are we done with monads? It turns out that we're not—not by a long shot. Just like it's possible to define an indefinite number of applicatives for different types constructors as long as the applicative properties hold, it is possible to do the same with monads.

In the following section, we'll put some widely used monads such as Id, State, Reader, and Writer into code and discuss what are they good for.

Id Monad

The same way `Option` encodes optionality, the `Id` represents *nothing special*. It wraps a value but does nothing with it. Why would we need something that's *not a thing*? The `Id` is kind of a *meta-lifting*, which can represent anything as an effect without changing it. How can this be done? Well, first of all, we have to say to the compiler that an `Id[A]` is the same thing as an `A`. This is easily done with a type alias:

```
type Id[A] = A
```

This type definition will dictate the details of the monad's implementation:

```
implicit val idMonad = new Monad[Id] {
  override def unit[A](a: => A): Id[A] = a
  override def flatMap[A, B](a: Id[A])(f: A => Id[B]): Id[B] = f(a)
}
```

Obviously, `unit(a)` is just a, and by having the type alias we just defined, we're making the compiler believe that it is not of type A, but an `Id[A]`. Similarly, with the `flatMap`, we can't do anything fancy, so we're just applying the given function f to a, utilizing the fact that `Id[A]` is actually just A.

Obviously, as we're doing nothing, the monadic laws should hold. But just to be 100% sure, we'll encode them as properties:

```
property("Monad[Id] and Int => String, String => Long") = {
  monad[Int, String, Long, Id]
}
property("Monad[Id] and String => Int, Int => Boolean") = {
  monad[String, Int, Boolean, Id]
}
+ Monad.Monad[Id] and Int => String, String => Long: OK, passed 100 tests.
+ Monad.Monad[Id] and String => Int, Int => Boolean: OK, passed 100 tests.
```

The property holds—what else would you expect from something that does nothing? But why do we need this something in the first place?

This question has multiple answers. From an abstract perspective, the Id monad carries the function of (surprise!) an identity element in the space of monads in the same way that zero or one are the identity elements in the space of numbers under addition or multiplication. Because of this, it can be used as a placeholder for monad transformers (we'll learn about them in the next chapter). It can also be useful in a situation where in existing code expects a monad but we don't need one. We will see how this approach works later in this chapter.

Now that we have got our feet wet with the simplest monad, it is time to do something more involving—implementing the State monad.

State monad

In imperative programming, we have the concept of global variables—variables that are available anywhere in the program. This approach is considered to be a bad practice, but is still used quite often. The concept of global state extends global variables by including system resources. As there is only one filesystem or system clock, it totally makes sense to make them globally and universally accessible from anywhere in the program code, right?

In JVM, some of these global resources are available via the java.lang.System class. It contains, for instance, references to "standard" input, output, and error streams, the system timer, environment variables, and properties. The global state should definitely be a good idea, then, if Java exposes it on a language level!

The problem with global state is that it breaks the *referential transparency* of the code. In essence, referential transparency means that it should always be possible to replace a part of the code, for example, a function call, with the result of the evaluation of this call everywhere in the program, and this change should not cause observable changes in program behaviour.

The concept of referential transparency is closely related to the concept of a pure function—a function is pure if it is referentially transparent for all its referentially transparent arguments.

We will see how this works in a moment, but for starters, please consider the following example:

```
var globalState = 0

def incGlobal(count: Int): Int = {
  globalState += count
  globalState
}
```

```
val g1 = incGlobal(10) // g1 == 10
val g2 = incGlobal(10) // g1 == 20
```

In the case of `incGlobal`, the function is not pure because it is not referentially transparent (because we cannot replace a call of it with the result of evaluation since these results are different each time the function is called). This makes it impossible to reason about the possible outcomes of the program without knowing the global state at every moment it is accessed or modified.

In contrast, the following function is referentially transparent and pure:

```
def incLocal(count: Int, global: Int): Int = global + count

val l1 = incLocal(10, 0) // l1 = 10
val l2 = incLocal(10, 0) // l2 = 10
```

In functional programming, we are expected to use only pure functions. This makes global state as a concept unsuitable for functional programming.

But there are still many cases where it is necessary to accumulate and modify state, but how should we deal with that?

This is where the `State` monad comes into play. The state monad is build around a function that takes a relevant part of the *global state* as an argument and returns a result and modified state (of course, without changing anything in a *global* sense). The signature of such a function looks like this: `type StatefulFunction[S, A] = S => (A, S)`.

We can wrap this definition into a case class to simplify the definition of helper methods on it. This `State` class will denote our effect:

```
final case class State[S, A](run: S => (A, S))
```

We can also define a few constructors in the companion object so that we're able to create a state in three different situations (to do this in REPL you need to use `:paste` command and paste *both* the case class and a companion object, then press *Ctrl + D*:

```
object State {
  def apply[S, A](a: => A): State[S, A] = State(s => (a, s))
  def get[S]: State[S, S] = State(s => (s, s))
  def set[S](s: => S): State[S, Unit] = State(_ => ((), s))
}
```

The default constructor lifts some value, `a: A`, into the context of `State` by returning the given argument as a result and propagating the existing state without changes. The getter creates a `State` that wraps some function, returning the given argument both as the state and as a result. The setter wraps the `State` over the function, which takes a state to be wrapped and produces no result. The semantics of these are similar to reading the global state (hence the result is the equal state) and setting it (hence the result is `Unit`), but applied to `s: S`.

For now, the `State` is nothing but a thin wrapper around some computation which involves pushing through (and potentially changing) a bit of state. What we would like to be able to do is compose this computation with the next one. We'd like to do this similarly to how we compose functions, but instead of `(A => B) compose (B => C)`, we now have `State[S, A] compose State[S, B]`. How can we do this?

By definition, our second computation accepts the result of the first one as its argument, hence we start with `(a: A) =>`. We also stated that, as a result (because of the possible state change and return type of the second state), we'll have a `State[S, B]` which gives us a full signature for the computation to compose with the first one: `f: A => State[S, B]`.

We can implement this composition as a method on `State`:

```
final case class State[S, A](run: S => (A, S)) {
  def compose[B](f: A => State[S, B]): State[S, B] = {
    val composedRuns = (s: S) => {
      val (a, nextState) = run(s)
      f(a).run(nextState)
    }
    State(composedRuns)
  }
}
```

We define our composed computation as a combination of two runs. The first is done with the input provided to the first state, which we decompose into the result and a next state. We then call the provided transformation `f` on the result and `run` it with the next state. These two successive runs might seem strange at first glance, but they just represent the fact that we're fusing two `run` functions from different states into one function defined on the composed state.

Now, we have an effect and can create a monad for it. You should have noticed by now that the signature of the `compose` method we just defined is the same as that of the monadic `flatMap`.

The `compose` in this and the following cases does not refer to the function composition we learned about in `Chapter 3`, *Deep Dive into Functions*, but to the concept of Kleisli composition. It is often called Kleisli arrow, and in essence is just a wrapper over the `A => F[B]` function, which allows for the composition of functions returning monadic values. It is frequently named `>>=`, but we'll stick to `compose` here.

This allows us to delegate monadic behavior to the logic we already have in the `State`, the same way as we could do for standard effects:

```
import ch09._
implicit def stateMonad[S] = new Monad[State[S, ?]] {
  override def unit[A](a: => A): State[S, A] = State(a)
  override def flatMap[A, B](a: State[S, A])(f: A => State[S, B]): State[S,
B] = a.compose(f)
}
```

Luckily, we can also delegate the lifting done by the `unit` to the default constructor! This means that we're done with the definition of the monad and can continue with our rigorous testing approach by specifying a property check for it.

Except in this case, we won't.

The rationale behind this is the fact that the `State` is quite different from the other effects we looked at until now in regard to the value it incorporates. The `State` is the first effect which is built *exclusively* around some function. Technically, because functions are first-class values in Scala, other effects such as `Option` could also contain a function and not a value, but this is an exception.

This brings complications to our testing attempts. Earlier, we modified the value contained in the effect in different ways and checked that the results we equal, as required by the monadic laws, by comparing them. With the requirement to have a function as a value of the effect, we face the challenge of comparing two functions for equality. At the time of writing this book, this is a topic of active academic research. For our practical purposes, there is currently no other way to prove that two functions are equal other than testing them for each possible input parameter(s) and checking whether they return same results—which we obviously cannot afford to do in our properties.

Instead, we will *prove* that our implementation is correct. We will use a method called the *substitution model* for this. The essence of the method is in using referential transparency in order to substitute all of the variables and function calls with values they return repeatedly until the resulting code can't be simplified anymore—very much like solving an algebraic equation.

Let's see how this works.

To get us prepared before proving the monadic laws, we'll prove a useful lemma first.

The lemma is stated as follows: having `as: M[A]`, `f: A => M[B]` and `M = State` so that `as.run = s => (a, s1)` (the run method returns a pair of `a` and `s1` for some input `s` and `f(b) = (b: A) => State(s1 => (b, s2))`, `M.flatMap(as)(f)` will always yield `State(s => (b, s2))`.

This is how we're getting this formula:

1. By definition, `as.run = s => (a, s1)`, which gives us `as = State(s => (a, s1))`
2. The `flatMap` delegates to the `compose` method defined on `State`, and therefore `M.flatMap(a)(f)` for `M = State` becomes `a.compose(f)`
3. In terms of `as` and `f`, `as.compose(f)` can be formulated as `State(s => (a, s1)).compose(f)`

Now, we're going to substitute the call of the `compose` method with its definition:

```
State(s => (a, s1)).compose(f) = State(s => {
  f(a).run(s1) // substituting f(a) with the result of the call
}) = State(s => {
  State(s1 => (b, s2)).run(s1)
}) = State(s => (b, s2))
```

Here, we have proved our assumption that `Monad[State].flatMap(as)(f) = State(s => (b, s2))` for `as = State(s => (a, s1))` and `f(a) = (b: A) => State(s1 => (b, s2))`.

Now, we can use this lemma while proving the monadic laws for `State`.

We'll start with the identity laws, and more specifically, with the left identity. This is how we formulated it in our `ScalaCheck` property:

```
val leftIdentity = forAll { as: M[A] =>
  M.flatMap(as)(M.unit(_)) == as
}
```

Thus, we want to prove that if we let `M = State`, then every `as: M[A]` following it is always true:

```
M.flatMap(as)(M.unit(_)) == as
```

Let's simplify the left side of the equation first. By definition, we can replace `as` with `State` implementation:

```
M.flatMap(State(s => (a, s1)))(M.unit(_))
```

The next step that we must do is substitute the call of the `unit` method with its implementation. We're just delegating to the default constructor of the `State`, which is defined as follows:

```
def apply[S, A](a: => A): State[S, A] = State(s => (a, s))
```

Hence, our definition becomes the following:

```
M.flatMap(State(s => (a, s1)))(b => State(s1 => (b, s1)))
```

To substitute the `flatMap` call, we have to recall that all it does is just delegate to the `compose` method defined on `State`:

```
State(s => (a, s1)).compose(b => State(s1 => (b, s1)))
```

Now, we can use our lemma for state composition, which gives us the following simplified form:

```
State(s => (a, s1))
```

This can't be simplified further, so we will now take a look at the right side of equation, `as`. Again, by definition, `as` can be represented as `State(s => (a, s1))`. This gives us final proof that `State(s => (a, s1)) == State(s => (a, s1))`, which always holds for any `a: A`.

The right side identity is proved similarly to the left side, and we leave this as an exercise to the reader.

The second law we need to prove is the associative law. Let's recall how it is described in ScalaCheck terms:

```
forAll((as: M[A], f: A => M[B], g: B => M[C]) => {
  val leftSide = M.flatMap(M.flatMap(as)(f))(g)
  val rightSide = M.flatMap(as)(a => M.flatMap(f(a))(g))
  leftSide == rightSide
})
```

Let's see what we can do with that, starting with the `leftSide`, `M.flatMap(M.flatMap(as)(f))(g)`.

By substituting M with State in the internal part, M.flatMap(as)(f) becomes State(s => (a, s1)).compose(f), which by the application of our lemma transforms it into State(s => (b, s2)).

Now, we can substitute the outer flatMap:

M.flatMap(State(s => (b, s2)))(g) is the same as State(s => (b, s2)).compose(g) **(1)**

Let's leave it in this form and look at the rightSide: M.flatMap(as)(a => M.flatMap(f(a))(g)).

First we substitute the internal flatMap with the compose, before turning a => M.flatMap(f(a))(g) into (a: A) => f(a).compose(g).

Now, by the definition of f we used for the left side, we have f(a) = a => State(s1 => (b, s2)) and thus the internal flatMap becomes a => State(b, s2).compose(g).

Replacing the outer flatMap with compose gives us—in combination with the previous definition—State(s => (a, s1)).compose(a => State(s1 => (b, s2)).compose(g)).

We'll use our lemma again to substitute the first application of compose, which will have State(s => (b, s2)).compose(g) as the outcome. **(2)**

(1) and **(2)** are identical, which means that the leftSide and rightRide of our property are always equal; we just proved the associativity law.

Great, we have an implementation of the State and the corresponding monad, which has been proven to be correct. It's time to look at them in action. As an example, let's imagine that we're going fishing by boat. The boat has a position and direction, and can go forward for some time or change direction:

```
final case class Boat(direction: Double, position: (Double, Double)) {
  def go(speed: Float, time: Float): Boat = ??? // please see the
accompanying code
  def turn(angle: Double): Boat = ??? // please see the accompanying code
}
```

We could go around with this boat by calling its methods:

```
scala> import ch09._
import ch09._
scala> val boat = Boat(0, (0d, 0d))
boat: Boat = Boat(0.0,(0.0,0.0))
scala> boat.go(10, 5).turn(0.5).go(20, 20).turn(-0.1).go(1,1)
res1: Boat = Boat(0.4,(401.95408575015193,192.15963378398988))
```

There is a problem with this approach, though—it does not include fuel consumption. Unfortunately, this aspect was not envisioned at the time the boat's navigation was developed, and has been added later as a global state. We will now refactor the old style with the state monad. If the quantity of fuel is modelled as a number of litres, the most straightforward way to define the state is as follows:

```
type FuelState = State[Float, Boat]
```

Now, we can define our boat moving logic that takes fuel consumption into account. But before doing that, we are going to simplify the syntax of our monadic calls a bit. Currently, the flatMap and map methods of our Monad take two parameters—the container and the function to apply to the container.

We would like to create a wrapper that will incorporate both the effect and a monad so that we have an instance of the effect and only need to pass the transforming function to the mapping methods. This is how we can express this approach:

```
object lowPriorityImplicits {
  implicit class MonadF[A, F[_] : Monad](val value: F[A]) {
    private val M = implicitly[Monad[F]]
    def unit(a: A) = M.unit(a)
    def flatMap[B](fab: A => F[B]): F[B] = M.flatMap(value)(fab)
    def map[B](fab: A => B): F[B] = M.map(value)(fab)
  }
}
```

The implicit conversion MonadF will wrap any effect, F[A], as soon as there is an implicit monad definition available for F. Having value, we can use it as a first parameter for the flatMap and map methods defined on monad—thus, in the case of MonadF, they are reduced to higher-order functions taking single parameters. By importing this implicit conversion, we now can call flatMap and map directly on State:

```
State[Float, Boat](boat).flatMap((boat: Boat) => State[Float, Boat](???))
```

We also need to create pure functions that will take fuel consumption into account while moving the boat. Assuming that we can't change the original definition of `Boat`, we have to pass the `boat` as a parameter to these functions:

```
lazy val consumption = 1f
def consume(speed: Float, time: Float) = consumption * time * speed
def turn(angle: Double)(boat: Boat): FuelState =
  State(boat.turn(angle))
def go(speed: Float, time: Float)(boat: Boat): FuelState =
  new State(fuel => {
    val newFuel = fuel - consume(speed, time)
    (boat.go(speed, time), newFuel)
  })
```

The `consume` function calculates fuel consumption based on `speed` and `time`. In the `turn` function, we're taking a `boat`, turning it by the specified `angle` (by delegating to the default implementation), and returning the result as an instance of `FuelState`.

A similar approach is used in the `go` method—to compute the boat's position, we are delegating to the boat logic. To sum the new volume of fuel available, we reduce the initial fuel quantity (which is passed as a parameter) and return the result as a part of the state.

We can finally create the same chain of actions we had defined initially, but this time by tracking fuel consumption:

```
import Monad.lowPriorityImplicits._
def move(boat: Boat) = State[Float, Boat](boat).
  flatMap(go(10, 5)).
  flatMap(turn(0.5)).
  flatMap(go(20,20)).
  flatMap(turn(-0.1)).
  flatMap{b: Boat => go(1,1)(b)}
```

If you compare this snippet with the original definition, you'll see that the path of the boat is the same. However, much more is happening behind the scenes. Each call of the `flatMap` passes the state over—this is how it is defined in the code of the monad. In our case, the definition is the `compose` method defined on the `State`. The function given as a parameter to the `flatMap` method describes what should happen with the result and possibly with the passed state. In a sense, using monads gives us a responsibility separation—*the monad describes what should happen between computation steps* as the result of one step being passed to the next step, and *our logic describes what should happen with the result before it is passed over to the next computation*.

We defined our logic with partially applied functions, which obscure what is really happening a bit—to make this obvious, the last step is defined using explicit syntax. We could also make the process of passing results between steps more explicit by using for-comprehension:

```
def move(boat: Boat) = for {
  a <- State[Float, Boat](boat)
  b <- go(10,5)(a)
  c <- turn(0.5)(b)
  d <- go(20, 20)(c)
  e <- turn(-0.1)(d)
  f <- go(1,1)(e)
} yield f
```

The approach is the same as before, but just the syntax has changed—Now, passing the boat between steps is done explicitly, but the state passing had visually disappeared—The for-comprehension makes monadic code look like it's imperative. This is the result of executing both of these approaches:

```
scala> println(move(boat).value.run(1000f))
(Boat(0.4,(401.95408575015193,192.15963378398988)),549.0)
```

How can we be sure that the state has been passed correctly? Well, this is what monad law guarantees. For those of you that are curious, we can even manipulate the state using methods we've defined in the state's companion object:

```
def logFuelState(f: Float) = println(s"Current fuel level is $f")

def loggingMove(boat: Boat) = for {
  a <- State[Float, Boat](boat)
  f1 <- State.get[Float]
  _ = logFuelState(f1)
  _ <- State.set(Math.min(700, f1))
  b <- go(10,5)(a)
  f2 <- State.get[Float]; _ = logFuelState(f2)
  c <- turn(0.5)(b)
  f3 <- State.get[Float]; _ = logFuelState(f3)
  d <- go(20, 20)(c)
  f3 <- State.get[Float]; _ = logFuelState(f3)
  e <- turn(-0.1)(d)
  f3 <- State.get[Float]; _ = logFuelState(f3)
  f <- go(1,1)(e)
} yield f
```

We augmented our previous for-comprehension with logging statements to output the current state after each step—These are the statements of the form:

```
f1 <- State.get[Float]
_ = logFuelState(f1)
```

Does it feel like we're really reading some global state? Well, in reality, what is happening is that we're getting the current State as a result (this is how we defined State.get earlier), which is passed then over to the next computation—the logging statement. Further computations just use the results of the previous steps explicitly, just like they had before.

Using this technique, we're also modifying the state:

```
_ <- State.set(Math.min(700, f1))
```

Here, we're simulating that our boat has a fuel tank of a maximal capacity equal to 700. We're doing this by first reading the current state and then setting back whatever is smaller—the state passed by the caller of the run method or our tank capacity. The State.set method returns Unit—this is why we ignore it.

The output of the definition augmented with the logging looks like this:

```
scala> println(loggingMove(boat).value.run(1000f))
Current fuel level is 1000.0
Current fuel level is 650.0
Current fuel level is 650.0
Current fuel level is 250.0
Current fuel level is 250.0
```

As we can see, the limit of 700 was applied before the first movements of the boat.

There is still an issue with our implementation of move—it uses hardcoded go and turn functions as if we would only be able to navigate one specific boat. However, this is not the case—we should be able to do this with any boat which has go and turn functionality, even if they are implemented slightly differently. We could model this by passing the go and turn functions as parameters to the move method:

```
def move(
  go: (Float, Float) => Boat => FuelState,
  turn: Double => Boat => FuelState
)(boat: Boat): FuelState
```

This definition will allow us to have different implementations for the go and turn functions in different situations, but still, steer the boat along the given hardcoded path.

If we look carefully, we'll see that after creating the initial wrapper over the provided boat parameter, the definition of the move method has no further notion of the State—we need it to be a monad to be able to use for-comprehension, but this requirement is much more generic than the State we currently have.

We can make the definition of the move function generic by improving on these two aspects—by passing the effect instead of creating it and making the method polymorphic:

```
def move[A, M[_]: Monad](
  go: (Float, Float) => A => M[A],
  turn: Double => A => M[A]
)(boat: M[A]): M[A] = for {
  a <- boat
  b <- go(10,5)(a)
  // the rest of the definition is exactly like before
} yield f
```

Now, we can follow the given path with any type which has a monad and the go and turn functions with specified signatures. Given the fact that this functionality is now generic, we can also move it into the Boat companion object along with the definition of the default boat.

Let's see how this approach works together with the state monad. It turns out that our definition of the go and turn methods does not need to change at all. All we need to do is call the new generic move method:

```
import Boat.{move, boat}
println(move(go, turn)(State(boat)).run(1000f))
```

It looks much nicer, but still there is some room for improvement. Specifically, the turn method does nothing but propagate the call to the default implementation. We can make it generic in the same way as we did for the move method:

```
def turn[M[_]: Monad]: Double => Boat => M[Boat] =
  angle => boat => Monad[M].unit(boat.turn(angle))
```

We can't make it polymorphic in regard to the Boat because we need to propagate a call to the specific type, but we still have the generic monad type. This specific code uses the implicit definition of Monad.apply to summon the monad of a specific type.

Actually, we can also do the same for the `go` method—provide a default facade implementation—and place them both into the companion object of the `Boat`:

```
object Boat {
  val boat = Boat(0, (0d, 0d))
  import Monad.lowPriorityImplicits._
  def go[M[_]: Monad]: (Float, Float) => Boat => M[Boat] =
    (speed, time) => boat => Monad[M].unit(boat.go(speed, time))
  def turn[M[_]: Monad]: Double => Boat => M[Boat] =
    angle => boat => Monad[M].unit(boat.turn(angle))
  def move[A, M[_]: Monad](go: (Float, Float) => A => M[A], turn: Double =>
A => M[A])(boat: M[A]): M[A] = // definition as above
}
```

Again, to put this definition into the REPL you need to use the `:paste` command, followed by both the definition of `boat` case class and a companion object, and a combination of *Ctrl + D*.

Now, we can use the default implementations for the cases where we don't need to override the default behavior. For instance, we can get rid of the default `turn` implementation for the case of State and call `move` with the default one:

```
import ch09._
import Boat.{move => moveB, turn => turnB, boat}
import StateExample._
type FuelState[B] = State[Float, B]
println(moveBoat(go, turnB[FuelState])(State(boat)).run(1000f))
```

We have to help the compiler to infer the correct type of monad to use by providing the type parameter, but now our definition of stateful behavior is reduced to the overriden definition of the `go` method—the rest of the code is generic.

As an illustration, we can reuse everything we have used so far with the `Id` monad—the result should be the same as executing the chain of calls directly on `Boat`. This is the complete implementation that's done with the `Id` monad:

```
import Monad.Id
import Boat._
println(move(go[Id], turn[Id])(boat))
```

Again, we're providing the type of monad to use, but this is pretty much it. Since `Id[Boat]` = `Boat`, we even can pass the `boat` directly without wrapping it into the `Id`.

Isn't that nice? We could use any monad we've defined so far to pass different effects to the main logic formulated in monadic terms. We'll leave the easy part—using existing definitions—as an exercise for the reader, and will now implement two other monads representing the read and write side of the State, that is, the Reader and Writer monads.

Reader monad

The State monad represents an external (to the definition of the logic) state, which needs to be taken into account and possibly modified. The Reader monad is similar in the taking into account part—it accepts an external context and passes it over unchanged to every computation down the queue. In terms of the global state we discussed during the examination of the state monad, the Reader will have access to read-only system properties. Because of this, the reader monad is often known as a mechanism for dependency injection—because it takes some outside configuration (not necessarily basic things like strings or numbers, but also possibly other complex components, database access mechanisms, network sockets, or other resources) and makes it available for the function it wraps.

Let's see how Reader is defined. We have already compared State and Reader, and the definition is also quite similar—with the only difference that we don't need to return the changed context (it is read-only, after all). In code, it looks like this:

```
final case class Reader[R, A](run: R => A) {
  def compose[B](f: A => Reader[R, B]): Reader[R, B] =
    Reader { r: R =>
      f(run(r)).run(r)
    }
}
```

The Reader type is just a wrapper over a function which takes a context of type R and returns some result of type A. The flatMap combines two run functions together—we're doing this by calling run with a given context, applying the given transformation to the result, and then calling the run for the result. The first call of the run is basically for this, while the second is for the Reader we're getting by applying f.

We can also define a constructor for some value that ignores any given context:

```
object Reader {
  def apply[R, A](a: => A): Reader[R, A] = Reader(_ => a)
}
```

Now that we have this model, we can have a monad for it, just like we did with the state monad—by using the kind-projector syntax:

```
implicit def readerMonad[R] = new Monad[Reader[R, ?]] {
  override def unit[A](a: => A): Reader[R, A] = Reader(a)
  override def flatMap[A, B](a: Reader[R, A])(f: A => Reader[R, B]):
Reader[R, B] = a.compose(f)
}
```

Unsurprisingly, the monad just delegates to both the constructor and the `compose` method we just defined. Surprisingly, now that we've done this, we're done defining the reader monad and can use it with our definition of the move function!

Let's imagine that we have a regulation that defines a speed limit for boats and the maximal angle they are allowed to turn at once (sounds strange, but in the place, we're fishing we have case law, so this is what we've got).

As this is external regulation, we have to model it with a case class:

```
final case class Limits(speed: Float, angle: Double)
type ReaderLimits[A] = ch09.Reader[Limits, A]
```

We'll also define an alias fixes the type of context for a `Reader` to be `Limits`.

Now, we can redefine our `go` and `turn` methods by applying these limits, like so:

```
def go(speed: Float, time: Float)(boat: Boat): ReaderLimits[Boat] =
  ch09.Reader(limits => {
    val lowSpeed = Math.min(speed, limits.speed)
    boat.go(lowSpeed, time)
  })

def turn(angle: Double)(boat: Boat): ReaderLimits[Boat] =
  ch09.Reader(limits => {
    val smallAngle = Math.min(angle, limits.angle)
    boat.turn(smallAngle)
  })
```

There is nothing special about the implementation itself. The type signature of functions are predefined by the `move` method. After each action, we return `Reader[Limits, Boat]`. To calculate the new state of the boat, we delegate to its methods after figuring out the maximal speed or angle we can apply.

As we designed the rest of the code in a generic way, this is all we need to do—Let's `move`:

```
import Monad.readerMonad
import Boat._
println(move(go, turn)(ch09.Reader(boat)).run(Limits(10f, 0.1)))
Boat(0.0,(250.00083305560517,19.96668332936563))
```

To run this example, please use the SBT `run` command.

We're passing the `go` and `turn` functions we just defined to the generic `move` method, along with the properly wrapped `boat`, and `run` it afterward. By looking at the result, we can say that the speed limits were properly applied.

After scrutinizing the state monad, there is not much left to discuss the reader, so we're good to proceed to the Writer monad.

Writer monad

The `Writer` monad is a sibling of the state and the reader, oriented on modifying the state. Its main purpose is to provide a facility to write into some kind of log by passing this log between computations. The type of the log is not specified, but usually, some structure with a possibly low overhead of the append operation is chosen. To name a few suitable possibilities, you could use a `Vector` from the standard library or a `List`. In the case of the List, we need to prepend the log entries and revert the resulting log at the very end.

Before we get too deep into the discussion about the type of log, it is good to realize that we can defer the decision until later. All we need to know is how to append an entry to the existing log. Or, in other words, how to combine two logs, one of which contains just a single entry, together. We already know about the structure with such a functionality—it is a `Semigroup`. Actually, we also need to be able to represent an empty log, and so our end decision will be to have a `Monoid`.

Let's bring this together. The Writer takes two type arguments, one for the log entry, and one for the result. We also need to be able to have a `Monoid` for the log. The logic itself does not take anything from outside; it just returns the result and updated log:

```
import ch07._
final case class Writer[W: Monoid, A](run: (A, W))
```

Next, we want to compose our writer with another monadic function, just like we did before:

```
final case class Writer[W: Monoid, A](run: (A, W)) {
  def compose[B](f: A => Writer[W, B]): Writer[W, B] = Writer {
    val (a, w) = run
    val (b, ww) = f(a).run
    val www = implicitly[Monoid[W]].op(w, ww)
    (b, www)
  }
}
```

The signature of the method is very similar to other monads we had in this chapter. Inside, we are decomposing the state of our current `Writer` into the result `a` and log `w`. Then, we apply the given function to the result and collect the next result and the log entries. Finally, we combine the log entries by utilizing the monoid operation and returning the result and the combined log.

We can also define the default constructor, which just returns a given argument with an empty log:

```
object Writer {
  def apply[W: Monoid, A](a: => A): Writer[W, A] = Writer((a,
implicitly[Monoid[W]].identity))
}
```

The monad definition is now a mechanical delegation to these methods. The only small difference is the requirement for the `Monoid[W]` to be available:

```
implicit def writerMonad[W : Monoid] = new Monad[Writer[W, ?]] {
  override def unit[A](a: => A): Writer[W, A] = Writer(a)
  override def flatMap[A, B](a: Writer[W, A])(f: A => Writer[W, B]):
Writer[W, B] = a.compose(f)
}
```

Yet again, we are done, and we can start to use our new abstraction. Let's suppose that now regulations require us to write every bot movement into the journal. We are happy to comply. As long as it is only about movements, we don't need to touch the `turn` function—we'll only need to extend the `go` definition:

```
type WriterTracking[A] = Writer[Vector[(Double, Double)], A]

def go(speed: Float, time: Float)(boat: Boat): WriterTracking[Boat] = new
WriterTracking((boat.go(speed, time), Vector(boat.position)))
```

We are writing the position of the boat in the journal represented by a `Vector`. In the definition, we merely propagate the call to the boat again and return the position of the boat before the move as the log entry. We also need to satisfy the monoid requirement. The monoid is defined in a similar fashion to the one we had in Chapter 7, *Understanding Algebraic Structures*:

```
implicit def vectorMonoid[A]: Monoid[Vector[A]] =
  new Monoid[Vector[A]] {
    override def identity: Vector[A] = Vector.empty[A]
    override def op(l: Vector[A], r: Vector[A]): Vector[A] = l ++ r
  }
```

With these preparations, we are ready to move our boat once again in SBT session using the `run` command:

```
import Monad.writerMonad
import Boat.{move, boat, turn}
println(move(go, turn[WriterTracking])(Writer(boat)).run)

(Boat(0.4,(401.95408575015193,192.15963378398988)),Vector((0.0,0.0),
(50.0,0.0), (401.0330247561491,191.77021544168122)))
```

We are passing the augmented `go` function and the original `turn` function (though typed with the `WriterTracking`) as a first parameter list and a `boat` wrapped in the `Writer` as a second parameter list. The output speaks for itself—it is the original result and vector containing positions of our boat before each move—all without touching the definition of the steering logic!

The `Writer` monad concludes our tour of the land of monads. In the next chapter, we'll take a look at combining them. If your intuition tells you that it can be a bit more involving than combining applicatives—after all, there is a whole chapter dedicated to that topic—then you're right. It is more complex, but also more interesting. Let's take a look!

Summary

In this chapter, we looked at monads as a way of sequencing computations. We studied how the meaning of this sequencing changes among the different monads we've implemented. The `Id` just composes computations as is. The `Option` adds a possibility to stop with no result if one of the steps returns no result. `Try` and `Either` have semantics similar to `Option` but allow you to specify the meaning of *no result* in terms of an `Exception` or as a `Left` side of `Either`. The `Writer` makes an append-only log available for computation in the chain. The `Reader` provides some configuration to every computation step. The `State` carries a *mutable* state between actions.

We discussed how the two primitive methods defining a monad, `unit` and `flatMap`, allow you to implement other useful methods such as `map`, `map2`, and `apply`, thus proving that every monad is a functor and an applicative.

In terms of `map` and `flatMap`—as for-comprehensions—we defined some small business logic to steer a boat. We then demonstrated how this logic can be reused without changes, even if the implementation of the underlying monad was reshaped.

Questions

1. Implement `Monad[Try]`.
2. Prove the right identity law for the `State` monad.
3. Pick one of the monads we defined in this chapter and implement the `go` function, which will encode the notion of sinking the boat with a probability of 1%.
4. Please do the same as question 3, but encode the notion of motor breaking in 1% of the moves, leaving the boat immobilized.
5. Describe the essence of the monads we defined in this chapter by using the (loosely) following template—The state monad passes state between chained computations. The computation itself accepts the outcome of the previous calculation and returns the result, along with the new state.

6. Define a `go` method that both tracks the position of the boat and takes the possibility of sinking the boat by using the structure with the following type:

```
type WriterOption[B] = Writer[Vector[(Double, Double)], Option[Boat]]
```

7. Compare the answer to the 6th question and the way we combined `Applicatives` in the previous chapter.

Further reading

- Atul S. Khot, *Scala Functional Programming Patterns: Grok and performing effective functional programming in Scala*
- Ivan Nikolov, *Scala Design Patterns - Second Edition: Learn how to write efficient, clean, and reusable code with Scala*

10
A Look at Monad Transformers and Free Monad

In *Chapter 6*, *Exploring Built-In Effects*, we looked at standard effects and promised to reveal the truth about the concepts underlying them; we also discussed the topic of combining them. Since then, we have discussed algebraic structures, such as monoids and groups, functors, applicatives, and monads, delivering on our first promise. But the composition topic has remained uncovered all this time.

In *Chapter 8*, *Dealing with Effects*, we implemented a general way to compose applicatives—which is very useful on its own, but can't help us with combining the standard effects of a monadic nature.

In this chapter, we will finally take on and keep our second promise by discussing some ways to bring different monadic effects together. We will look at the complications related to that and some of the solutions used in the Scala community to deal with these obstacles, including:

- Monad transformers
- Monad transformer stacks
- Free monads

Technical requirements

Before we begin, make sure you have the following installed:

- JDK 1.8+
- SBT 1.2+

The source code for this chapter is available at https://github.com/PacktPublishing/Learn-Scala-Programming/tree/master/Chapter10.

Combining monads

In Chapter 6, *Exploring Built-In Effects*, we talked about standard effects such as Option, Try, Either, and Future. In Chapter 9, *Familiarizing Yourself with Basic Monads*, we moved on and implemented monads for all of them. In our examples, we demonstrated how Scala provides nice syntax for the code formulated in monadic terms by having for-comprehension, which is a syntactic sugar for the combination of map, flatMap, and possibly filter methods. In all our examples, we used for-comprehension to define a sequence of steps which constitute some process where the result of the previous computation is consumed by the next step.

For an instance, this is the way we defined the process of fishing in terms of Option in Chapter 6, *Exploring Built-In Effects*:

```
val buyBait: String => Option[Bait]
val makeBait: String => Option[Bait]
val castLine: Bait => Option[Line]
val hookFish: Line => Option[Fish]

def goFishing(bestBaitForFish: Option[String]): Option[Fish] =
  for {
    baitName <- bestBaitForFish
    bait <- buyBait(baitName).orElse(makeBait(baitName))
    line <- castLine(bait)
    fish <- hookFish(line)
  } yield fish
```

With our new obtained knowledge about monads, we could make this implementation effect-agnostic:

```
def goFishing[M[_]: Monad](bestBaitForFish: M[String]): M[Fish] = {

  val buyBait: String => M[Bait] = ???
```

```
val castLine: Bait => M[Line] = ???
val hookFish: Line => M[Fish] = ???

import Monad.lowPriorityImplicits._

for {
  baitName <- bestBaitForFish
  bait <- buyBait(baitName)
  line <- castLine(bait)
  fish <- hookFish(line)
} yield fish
}
Ch10.goFishing(Option("Crankbait"))
```

One thing we can't do with this approach is to use the `orElse` method specific to `Option` to define the unhappy path for bait-acquiring.

Another simplification we're making here is pretending that all our actions can be described by the same effect. In reality, this will almost definitely not be the case. To be more specific, obtaining the bait and waiting to hook the fish will probably take much longer than casting the line. Thus, we probably would like to represent these actions with `Future` instead of `Option`:

```
val buyBait: String => Future[Bait]
val hookFish: Line => Future[Fish]
```

Or, in generic terms, we would have the type of effect `N` instead of `M`:

```
def goFishing[M[_]: Monad, N[_]: Monad](bestBaitForFish: M[String]):
N[Fish] = {

  val buyBait: String => N[Bait] = ???
  val castLine: Bait => M[Line] = ???
  val hookFish: Line => N[Fish] = ???
  // ... the rest goes as before
}
import scala.concurrent.ExecutionContext.Implicits.global
Ch10.goFishing[Option, Future](Option("Crankbait"))
```

But, unfortunately, this won't compile anymore. Let's consider a simpler example to understand why:

```
import scala.concurrent.ExecutionContext.Implicits.global
import scala.concurrent.Future

scala> for {
     |   o <- Option("str")
```

```
        | c <- Future.successful(o)
        | } yield c
              c <- Future.successful(o)
              ^
On line 3: error: type mismatch;
        found : scala.concurrent.Future[String]
        required: Option[?]
```

The compiler ceases to accept `Future` instead of the `Option`. Let's desugar our for-comprehension to see what is going on:

```
Option("str").flatMap { o: String =>
  val f: Future[String] = Future(o).map { c: String => c }
  f
}
```

Now the problem lies on the surface—the `Option.flatMap` expects some function returning an `Option` as an effect (this is using the definition of `Option.flatMap[B](f: A => Option[B]): Option[B]` in particular, and `Monad.flatMap` in general). But the value we return is wrapped in `Future`, as a result of applying the `map` function of the `Future`.

Generalising this reasoning, we can conclude that it is only possible to use effects of the same type in the single for-comprehension.

Because of this, it looks like we have two possibilities to combine desired effects:

- Put them in separate for-comprehensions
- Lift different effects to some kind of common denominator type

We can compare both approaches using our fishing example as the playground. The variation of separate for-comprehensions would look like the following:

```
for {
  baitName <- bestBaitForFish
} yield for {
  bait <- buyBait(baitName)
} yield for {
  line <- castLine(bait)
} yield for {
  fish <- hookFish(line)
} yield fish
```

This looks slightly worse than the original version but is still quite nice, apart from the fact that the type of the result has changed from N[Fish] to the M[N[M[N[Fish]]]]. In the specific cases of Future and Option, it would be Option[Future[Option[Future[Fish]]]] and there is no easy way to extract the result other than going through all of the layers one by one. This is not a very nice thing to do and we'll leave it as an exercise for the scrupulous reader.

Another option would be to abandon the generosity of our implementation and make it nonpolymorphic as follows:

```
def goFishing(bestBaitForFish: Option[String]): Future[Fish] =
  bestBaitForFish match {
    case None => Future.failed(new NoSuchElementException)
    case Some(name) => buyBait(name).flatMap { bait: Bait =>
      castLine(bait) match {
        case None => Future.failed(new IllegalStateException)
        case Some(line) => hookFish(line)
      }
    }
  }
```

Besides losing general applicability, this implementation has the obvious disadvantage of being much less readable.

Let's hope that the second approach, the common denominator for the effect type, will bear more fruit than the first one.

First, we need to decide how we want to compose the two effects we currently have. There are two choices: Future[Option[?]] and Option[Future[?]]. Semantically, having an optional result at some point later feels better than optionally having an operation which will complete in the future, hence we will continue with the first alternative.

With this fixed new type, the functions we have became invalid—they all now have the wrong type of result. Conversion to the proper type just involves juggling the types and we can do this on the spot:

```
val buyBaitFO: String => Future[Option[Bait]] = (name: String) =>
buyBait(name).map(Option.apply)
val castLineFO: Bait => Future[Option[Line]] =
castLine.andThen(Future.successful)
val hookFishFO: Line => Future[Option[Fish]] = (line: Line) =>
hookFish(line).map(Option.apply)
```

All we need to do is to wrap `Option` into the `Future` or `Future` into the `Option`, depending on the return type of the original function.

To keep everything consistent, we'll also change the type of the argument and return type of the `goFishing` function in the same way:

```
def goFishing(bestBaitForFish: Future[Option[String]]):
Future[Option[Fish]] = ???
```

As we strive to formulate the logic itself as a for-comprehension, it is reasonable to try to draw it up it in terms of the `flatMap`:

```
bestBaitForFish.flatMap { /* takes Option[?] and returns Future[Option[?]]
*/ }
```

As an argument to `flatMap`, we have to provide some function which takes an `Option[String]` and returns `Future[Option[Fish]]`. But our functions expect "real" input, not optional. We can't `flatMap` over the `Option` as discussed before and we can't just use `Option.map` because it will wrap our result type in an additional layer of optionality. What we can use is a pattern match to extract the value:

```
case None => Future.successful(Option.empty[Fish])
case Some(name) => buyBaitFO(name) /* now what ? */
```

In the case of `None`, we just shortcut the process and return the result. In that case, we indeed have a `name`; we can call a corresponding function, passing this `name` as an argument. The question is, how do we proceed further? If we look carefully at the return type of `buyBaitFO(name)`, we will see that this is the same as we had for the initial argument—`Future[Option[?]]`. Hence, we can try to reuse the approach with flatmapping and pattern matching again, which after all its iterations gives us the following implementation:

```
def goFishingA(bestBaitForFish: Future[Option[String]]):
Future[Option[Fish]] =
  bestBaitForFish.flatMap {
    case None => Future.successful(Option.empty[Fish])
    case Some(name) => buyBaitFO(name).flatMap {
      case None => Future.successful(Option.empty[Fish])
      case Some(bait) => castLineFO(bait).flatMap {
        case None => Future.successful(Option.empty[Fish])
        case Some(line) => hookFishFO(line)
      }
    }
  }
```

There is a lot of duplication in this snippet, but it already looks somehow structured. It is possible to improve its readability by extracting the repetitive code fragments. First, we can make the case of *no result* polymorphic as shown below:

```
def noResult[T]: Future[Option[T]] = Future.successful(Option.empty[T])
```

Second, we might capture our reasoning about `flatMap` and pattern match as a standalone polymorphic function:

```
def continue[A, B](arg: Future[Option[A]])(f: A => Future[Option[B]]):
Future[Option[B]] =
  arg.flatMap {
    case None => noResult[B]
    case Some(a) => f(a)
  }
```

With these changes, our last attempt starts to look more concise:

```
def goFishing(bestBaitForFish: Future[Option[String]]):
Future[Option[Fish]] =
  continue(bestBaitForFish) { name =>
    continue(buyBaitFO(name)) { bait =>
      continue(castLineFO(bait)) { line =>
        hookFishFO(line)
      }
    }
  }
```

This is arguably something that is already quite good, and we could stop at this moment, but there is one aspect we might improve further on. The `continue` function calls are nested. This makes it nontrivial to formulate the business logic flow. It might be beneficial if we could have a kind of fluent interface instead and we would be able to chain the `continue` calls.

It is easily achieved by capturing the first argument of `continue` as a value of some class. This will change our implementation to the following form:

```
final case class FutureOption[A](value: Future[Option[A]]) {
  def continue[B](f: A => FutureOption[B]): FutureOption[B] = new
FutureOption(value.flatMap {
    case None => noResult[B]
    case Some(a) => f(a).value
  })
}
```

There are two ways to improve this further. First, the signature of `continue` reveals that it is a Kleisli arrow, which we introduced in the previous chapter. Second, in this form, we will need to wrap the `value` in `FutureOption` manually each time we need to call the `continue` method. This will make the code unnecessarily verbose and we can enhance our implementation by making it an `implicit` class:

```
implicit class FutureOption[A](value: Future[Option[A]]) {
  def compose[B](f: A => FutureOption[B]): FutureOption[B] = new
FutureOption(value.flatMap {
    case None => noResult[B]
    case Some(a) => f(a).value
  })
}
```

Let's take a look at what our main flow looks like with these changes incorporated:

```
def goFishing(bestBaitForFish: Future[Option[String]]):
Future[Option[Fish]] = {
  val result = bestBaitForFish.compose { name =>
    buyBaitFO(name).compose { bait =>
      castLineFO(bait).compose { line =>
        hookFishFO(line)
      }
    }
  }
  result.value
}
```

Wonderful! Can you spot further possibility for improvement? If we scrutinise the type signature of the `FutureOption`, we'll see that everything we're doing with the wrapped `value` is calling a `flatMap` method which is defined on `Future`. But we already know the proper abstraction for that—this is a monad. Utilizing this knowledge will allow us to make our class polymorphic and possibly reuse it for other types of effects, if needed:

```
implicit class FOption[F[_]: Monad, A](val value: F[Option[A]]) {
  def compose[B](f: A => FOption[F, B]): FOption[F, B] = {
    val result = value.flatMap {
      case None => noResultF[F, B]
      case Some(a) => f(a).value
    }
    new FOption(result)
  }
  def isEmpty: F[Boolean] = Monad[F].map(value)(_.isEmpty)
}
```

To demonstrate that the polymorphic nature of the new implementation won't harm our flexibility to define helper functions as needed, we've also added a method to check that the composition of monads we have is empty.

Unfortunately, if we'll try to make this implementation polymorphic in the type of the second effect, we'll see that it is impossible—we need to decompose it as explained previously, and for this we need to know the specifics of the effect's implementation.

At this point, an astute reader will remember that all monads we developed in the previous chapter were implemented in terms of `compose` function, which had the same signature. Could we try to do the same trick again and implement a monad for the `FutureOption` type? Readers familiar with the previous chapter will know that this is almost a mechanical task of delegating to the implementation we just came up with:

```
implicit def fOptionMonad[F[_] : Monad] = new Monad[FOption[F, ?]] {
  override def unit[A](a: => A): FOption[F, A] =
Monad[F].unit(Monad[Option].unit(a))
  override def flatMap[A, B](a: FOption[F, A])(f: A => FOption[F, B]):
FOption[F, B] =
    a.compose(f)
}
```

Now, we also need to change the return type of the original functions to be a `FOption[Future, ?]` to match the type signature of our new monad. We don't need to touch the implementation—the compiler will wrap `implicit` `FOption` around the result automatically:

```
val buyBaitFO: String => FOption[Future, Bait] = // as before
val castLineFO: Bait => FOption[Future, Line] = // as before
val hookFishFO: Line => FOption[Future, Fish] = // as before
```

Now we can formulate our logic once again, this time in terms of for-comprehension:

```
def goFishing(bestBaitForFish: FOption[Future, String]): FOption[Future,
Fish] = for {
  name <- bestBaitForFish
  bait <- buyBaitFO(name)
  line <- castLineFO(bait)
  fish <- hookFishFO(line)
} yield fish
```

Finally, this is nice and clean! The final touch would be to do something with the adhoc name of `FOption`. What the type does is *transform* an `Option` into something monadic of higher order, by wrapping an `Option` into a monadic effect of our choice. We could rename it into `OptionTransformer` or `OptionT` for short.

Congratulations! We just implemented a monad transformer.

Monad transformers

Let's hold on for a second and recap what we just did.

We made a small sacrifice and increased the complexity of the return type of our original functions to some "common denominator" type. This sacrifice is rather small because in our example, as well as in real life, this is usually done by just lifting the original functions into their proper context.

The signatures we came up with look a little awkward, but this is partly because we started to develop them as concrete implementations. In fact, the user-facing API of our fishing component should be similar to the following snippet straight from the beginning, if implemented in a more abstract way:

```
abstract class FishingApi[F[_]: Monad] {

  val buyBait: String => F[Bait]
  val castLine: Bait => F[Line]
  val hookFish: Line => F[Fish]

  def goFishing(bestBaitForFish: F[String]): F[Fish] = for {
    name <- bestBaitForFish
    bait <- buyBait(name)
    line <- castLine(bait)
    fish <- hookFish(line)
  } yield fish
}
```

This approach abstracts over the type of effect, giving more flexibility to us as library authors and more structure to the user of our API.

This API can be used with any effect with a monad. This is an example of how it can be implemented utilizing functions we currently have—returning mixed Future and Optional results:

```
import Transformers.OptionTMonad
import ch09.Monad.futureMonad
import scala.concurrent.ExecutionContext.Implicits.global

// we need to fix the types first to be able to implement concrete
fucntions
object Ch10 {
```

```
    type Bait = String
    type Line = String
    type Fish = String
}

object Ch10FutureFishing extends FishingApi[OptionT[Future, ?]] with App {

    val buyBaitImpl: String => Future[Bait] = Future.successful
    val castLineImpl: Bait => Option[Line] = Option.apply
    val hookFishImpl: Line => Future[Fish] = Future.successful

    override val buyBait: String => OptionT[Future, Bait] =
        (name: String) => buyBaitImpl(name).map(Option.apply)
    override val castLine: Bait => OptionT[Future, Line] =
        castLineImpl.andThen(Future.successful(_))
    override val hookFish: Line => OptionT[Future, Fish] =
        (line: Line) => hookFishImpl(line).map(Option.apply)

    goFishing(Transformers.optionTunit[Future, String]("Crankbait"))
}
```

Exactly as before, we implemented facades for our original functions, doing nothing more than routine lifting of them into the appropriate effect. And the goFishing method can be used as is—the compiler takes only a monad for the OptoinT[Future] available to make it happen.

For instance, at some point the implementor of the underlying functions can decide that they should return Try instead of the future now. This is OK because requirements change and we can incorporate this change in our logic quite easily:

```
import scala.util._
object Ch10OptionTTryFishing extends FishingApi[OptionT[Try, ?]] with App {

    val buyBaitImpl: String => Try[Bait] = Success.apply
    val castLineImpl: Bait => Option[Line] = Option.apply
    val hookFishImpl: Line => Try[Fish] = Success.apply

    override val buyBait: String => OptionT[Try, Bait] =
        (name: String) => buyBaitImpl(name).map(Option.apply)
    override val castLine: Bait => OptionT[Try, Line] =
        castLineImpl.andThen(Try.apply(_))
    override val hookFish: Line => OptionT[Try, Fish] =
        (line: Line) => hookFishImpl(line).map(Option.apply)

    goFishingM(Transformers.optionTunit[Try, String]("Crankbait"))

}
```

Assuming that the change in the library is given, the only things we need to alter on our side are:

- The lifting approach for the `castLine` function; it changes from `Future.success` to `Try.apply`
- The type parameter we're passing over for the wrapper for the initial argument of the `goFishing` function

And we're done. We don't need to touch our fishing "business" logic at all!

The monad transformer in a sense "flattens" both monads, such that it is possible to cut through all layers at once when calling the `map` and `flatMap` methods—and thus also in for-comprehension.

Currently, it is not possible to change the type of the "inner" effect though— we only have an `OptionT` monad transformer available. But this is just a matter of implementing another transformer once, entirely like we did with monads. To be more specific, let's see the effect of altering the return type of the basic functions to `Either` instead of `Option`. Supposing it is expected that the new version uses `String` as a description of the unhappy case; we would have the following code:

```
object Ch10EitherTFutureFishing extends FishingApi[EitherT[Future, String,
?]] with App {

  val buyBaitImpl: String => Future[Bait] = Future.successful
  val castLineImpl: Bait => Either[String, Line] = Right.apply
  val hookFishImpl: Line => Future[Fish] = Future.successful

  override val buyBait: String => EitherT[Future, String, Bait] =
    (name: String) => buyBaitImpl(name).map(l => Right(l): Either[String,
Bait])
  override val castLine: Bait => EitherT[Future, String, Line] =
    castLineImpl.andThen(Future.successful(_))
  override val hookFish: Line => EitherT[Future, String, Fish] =
    (line: Line) => hookFishImpl(line).map(l => Right(l): Either[String,
Fish])

  goFishing(Transformers.eitherTunit[Future, String,
String]("Crankbait")).value

}
```

The return type of `castLineImpl` is now `Either[String, Line]` as new requirements dictate. The lifting we are doing is slightly convoluted, just because we need to convey the types of both the left and right side of `Either` to the compiler. The rest of the implementation is the same as before.

And it relies on the fact that we have an instance of `EitherT` and a corresponding monad available. We already know how to implement monad transformers and can come up with the code in no time. First, the `EitherT` class, which resembles an `OptionT` almost identically, with respect to the need to carry the type of the left side of `Either` around as follows:

```
implicit class EitherT[F[_]: Monad, L, A](val value: F[Either[L, A]]) {
  def compose[B](f: A => EitherT[F, L, B]): EitherT[F, L, B] = {
    val result: F[Either[L, B]] = value.flatMap {
      case Left(l) => Monad[F].unit(Left[L, B](l))
      case Right(a) => f(a).value
    }
    new EitherT(result)
  }
  def isRight: F[Boolean] = Monad[F].map(value)(_.isRight)
}
```

Instead of pattern matching on `None` and `Some`, we pattern-match on the `Left` and `Right` sides of `Either`. We also replace the helper method `isEmpty` with the more suitable `isRight`.

The lifting function and the implementation of the monad are also considerably similar—just boilerplate, if you will:

```
def eitherTunit[F[_]: Monad, L, A](a: => A) = new EitherT[F, L,
A](Monad[F].unit(Right(a)))

implicit def EitherTMonad[F[_] : Monad, L]: Monad[EitherT[F, L, ?]] =
  new Monad[EitherT[F, L, ?]] {
    override def unit[A](a: => A): EitherT[F, L, A] =
      Monad[F].unit(ch09.Monad.eitherMonad[L].unit(a))
    override def flatMap[A, B](a: EitherT[F, L, A])(f: A => EitherT[F, L,
B]): EitherT[F, L, B] =
      a.compose(f)
  }
```

Incredible! We now have two monad transformers in our toolbox and the previously broken definition of `Ch10EitherTFutureFishing` has started to compile and run!

Eager to implement `TryT` to cement this newly gained knowledge? We're happy to leave this as an exercise for you.

Monad transformers stacks

In the meantime, we'll entertain ourselves with the following ideas:

- Monad transformers require an instance of a monad for the outer layer
- A monad transformer itself has a monad
- Will something bad happen if we use a monad transformer as an instance of a monad for another monad transformer?

Let's try it out. We've already implemented two monad transformers so let's bring them together. To start, we'll define the type of stack. It will be `EitherT` wrapped in `OptionT`. This will give us an unwrapped type of the following code:

```
Future[Either[String, Option[Fish]]]
```

This can be interpreted as an operation which takes time and might return an error in the case of nontechnical failure and needs to have an explanation (technical failures are denoted by failed `Futures`). An `Option` represents an operation which can return no result in a natural way that requires no further explanation.

With type aliases, we can represent the type of the inner transformer, fixing `String` as the type of the left side, as follows:

```
type Inner[A] = EitherT[Future, String, A]
```

The outer transformer in the stack is even simpler. In contrast to the inner type, where we fixed the type of effect to be `Future`, it takes a type constructor for an effect as the type parameter, as follows:

```
type Outer[F[_], A] = OptionT[F, A]
```

We can now use these aliases to define the whole stack as follows:

```
type Stack[A] = Outer[Inner, A]
```

To make the situation realistic, we'll just take the last version of our original fishing functions—the one with `castLineImpl` returns `Either[String, Line]`. We need to decorate all original functions so that the result type matches the type of the stack we now have. This is where it starts to become unwieldy. The compiler is not allowed to apply two implicit conversions in a row, so therefore we have to apply one of them by hand. For the two functions returning `Future[?]`, we also need to envelop the bottom layer into the `Option`:

```
override val buyBait: String => Stack[Bait] =
  (name: String) => new EitherT(buyBaitImpl(name).map(l =>
Right(Option(l)): Either[String, Option[Bait]]))

override val hookFish: Line => Stack[Fish] =
  (line: Line) => new EitherT(hookFishImpl(line).map(l => Right(Option(l)):
Either[String, Option[Fish]]))
```

Now the compiler will be able to apply implicit conversion to the `OptionT`.

Likewise, the function returning `Either[String, Line]` needs to be converted to `EitherT` on the outer side as follows:

```
override val castLine: Bait => Stack[Line] =
  (bait: Bait) => new
EitherT(Future.successful(castLineImpl(bait).map(Option.apply)))
```

Internally, we have to `map` the contents of `Either` into an `Option` and apply `Future` to the whole result.

The compiler can help us to create an input of the proper type by applying implicit conversions as required—we won't see a lot of changes on this side, as follows:

```
val input = optionTunit[Inner, String]("Crankbait")
```

A small tweak is needed at the moment as we're calling our business logic with this transformer stack—now we have two layers of transformation, so we need to call `value` two times to extract the result, as follows:

```
val outerResult: Inner[Option[Fish]] = goFishing(input).value
val innerResult: Future[Either[String, Option[Fish]]] = outerResult.value
```

It can become tedious quite quickly to turn to the `value` method repeatedly on each of the monad transformers that constitute the stack. Why do we need to? Because returning the result with the type of specific transformer can pollute the client's code quite quickly. Hence, there are usually a couple of suggestions related to the monad transformers and monad transformer stacks worth considering, as follows:

- Stacking monads and especially monad transformers adds performance and garbage collection overhead. It is essential to carefully consider the necessity of adding every additional layer of effects to the existing type.
- It is also arguable that more layers in the stack add mental overhead and clutter the code. The approach is the same as with the first suggestion—don't do this unless absolutely needed.
- Clients usually do not operate in terms of monad transformers, therefore they (transformers) should be considered to be an implementation detail. The API should be defined in generic terms. If it needs to be specific, prefer effect types over transformer types. In our example, it is better to return the result of the type `Future[Option[?]]` compared to `OptionT[Future, ?]`.

Given all these considerations, are monad transformers really useful in real life? Surely they are! Nevertheless, as always there are alternatives, for example the free monad.

Free monads

In this chapter and the previous chapters, we represented sequenced computations with monads. The `flatMap` method of the monad describes how the computation steps should be joined and the function given to it as an argument—the computation step itself. The free monad elevates the concept of sequenced computations to the next level.

First, we start to represent the computation steps as instances of some **ADT** (**algebraic data type**) of our choice. Second, we represent the monadic concept with instances of another ADT.

To substantiate this approach, we can turn to the fishing example once again. Earlier, we had three actions we encoded as functions. These actions will be represented as value classes now. We also need to give specific meaning to the type aliases we've used before to be able to run examples later.

Here is the definition of the fishing model and corresponding ADT as follows:

```
case class Bait(name: String) extends AnyVal
case class Line(length: Int) extends AnyVal
```

```
case class Fish(name: String) extends AnyVal

sealed trait Action[A]
final case class BuyBait[A](name: String, f: Bait => A) extends Action[A]
final case class CastLine[A](bait: Bait, f: Line => A) extends Action[A]
final case class HookFish[A](line: Line, f: Fish => A) extends Action[A]
```

In the model, we represent some properties of the bait, line, and a fish so that we can make use of them later.

The Action type has a few aspects worth discussing. First of all, the instances of Action reflect that the functions we had before take a single parameter by declaring this parameter as a field of the class. Second, all actions are typed by the *type of the next action* and this next action is captured as another field of the class, in the form of a function which expects the result of the wrapping action to be an argument. This second field is how we encode the sequencing of actions.

Now we need to represent the monadic methods as classes.

Done assembles an instance of Free from a value the same way as Monad.unit does:

```
final case class Done[F[_]: Functor, A](a: A) extends Free[F, A]
```

The F[_] refers to the type of actions to wrap and A is the type of the result. F needs to have a Functor; we will see why in a moment.

The Join constructs a representation of flatMap—it should do so by applying the F to the previous instance of Free. This gives us the following type of action parameter as follows:

```
final case class Suspend[F[_]: Functor, A](action: F[Free[F, A]]) extends
Free[F, A]
```

Now, as we said, this is a monad, so we need to provide an implementation of flatMap. We'll do this on the Free so that it is possible to use both instances of Done and Join in for-comprehensions as follows:

```
class Free[F[_]: Functor, A] {
  def flatMap[B](f: A => Free[F, B]): Free[F, B] = this match {
    case Done(a)  => f(a)
    case Join(a)  => Join(implicitly[Functor[F]].map(a)(_.flatMap(f)))
  }
}
```

The `flatMap` naturally takes the Kleisli arrow as an argument. Similar to the definitions of `flatMap` on other monads, for example, an `Option`, we distinguish between shortcutting and exiting and continuing the computation chain. In the former case, we can just apply the given function; in the latter case we have to build up the sequence. This is where we're using the `Functor[F]` to get inside the `F` and apply the `flatMap` on the wrapped `Free[F, A]`, basically doing the sequencing in a good, old monadic way.

The fact that the functor is here to give us the possibility to succeed in computations dictates how the functor for our actions should be implemented —the given function should be called on the result of the next action. Our actions might have quite a different structure, hence the easiest way to describe this approach is pattern matching, as follows:

```
implicit val actionFunctor: Functor[Action] = new Functor[Action] {
  override def map[A, B](in: Action[A])(f: A => B): Action[B] = in match {
    case BuyBait(name, a) => BuyBait(name, x => f(a(x)))
    case CastLine(bait, a) => CastLine(bait, x => f(a(x)))
    case HookFish(line, a) => HookFish(line, x => f(a(x)))
  }
}
```

Values of our ADT are structured similarly and this is the reason why the tranformations look alike for all actions.

The last preparation step we need is to have a user-friendly way to create instances of the free monad for each of the actions. Let's create helper methods for that in the following manner:

```
def buyBait(name: String): Free[Action, Bait] = Join(BuyBait(name, bait =>
Done(bait)))
def castLine(bait: Bait): Free[Action, Line] = Join(CastLine(bait, line =>
Done(line)))
def hookFish(line: Line): Free[Action, Fish] = Join(HookFish(line, fish =>
Done(fish)))
```

Each of these methods creates a free monad instance which describes a computation consisting of a single action; the `Done(...)` encodes the fact that we are, well, done, and have some result.

Now we can use these helper functions to build a computation chain like we did before. But this time the computation won't be something callable—it is just a sequence of instances of the free monad captured as a single instance of `Free`, as follows:

```
def catchFish(baitName: String): Free[Action, Fish] = for {
  bait <- buyBait(baitName)
  line <- castLine(bait)
```

```
        fish <- hookFish(line)
    } yield fish
```

This single instance we have incorporates all of the steps in the form of `Free` containing actions. Represented as pseudo-code, the result of calling this method would look like a nested structure, as given below:

```
Join(BuyBait("Crankbait", Join(CastLine(bait, Join(HookFish(line,
Done(fish))))))))
```

At this moment, we have created the computation sequence, but this sequence is useless because it's just a data structure. We need a way to make it useful—we have to create an interpreter for it. And this is where the free monad really starts to shine—it is up to us how we will render this data. We can create as many interpreters as we wish, for example, one for testing purposes and another for production use. For instance, for testing, it might be useful just to collect all of the actions which should happen in some journal—in an event-sourced way (we'll look at event sourcing in detail later in this book). As we're just testing, our journal does not need to be persistent—hence, we can just use some kind of collection; for example, a `List` would do, as follows:

```
@tailrec
def goFishingAcc[A](actions: Free[Action, A], log: List[AnyVal]):
List[AnyVal] = actions match {
  case Join(BuyBait(name, f)) =>
    val bait = Bait(name)
    goFishingAcc(f(bait), bait :: log)
  case Join(CastLine(bait, f)) =>
    val line = Line(bait.name.length)
    goFishingAcc(f(line), line :: log)
  case Join(HookFish(line, f)) =>
    val fish = Fish(s"CatFish from ($line)")
    goFishingAcc(f(fish), fish :: log)
  case Done(_) => log.reverse
}
```

The preceding snippet is indeed an interpreter for the program which is built in terms of the actions wrapped in `Free`. The logic is repetitive—we're producing the result of the action and calling this action recursively, passing the log with the added entry as a parameter. In the case of `Done`, we're ignoring the result; our goal is the log, and we return it in reversed form by calling `.reverse` to compensate for building it up in the opposite direction.

The result of the execution looks like the following:

```
scala> import ch10.FreeMonad._
import ch10.FreeMonad._
scala> println(goFishingAcc(catchFish("Crankbait"), Nil))
List(Bait(Crankbait), Line(9), Fish(CatFish from (Line(9))))
```

For production, we can do something else, such as collecting the executed actions. We will model this side-effecting by writing to the console, as follows:

```
def log[A](a: A): Unit = println(a)

@scala.annotation.tailrec
def goFishingLogging[A](actions: Free[Action, A], unit: Unit): A = actions
match {
  case Join(BuyBait(name, f)) =>
    goFishingLogging(f(Bait(name)), log(s"Buying bait $name"))
  case Join(CastLine(bait, f)) =>
    goFishingLogging(f(Line(bait.name.length)), log(s"Casting line with
${bait.name}"))
  case Join(HookFish(line, f)) =>
    goFishingLogging(f(Fish("CatFish")), log(s"Hooking fish from
${line.length} feet"))
  case Done(fish) => fish
}
```

The structure of this interpreter is naturally the same as before. The result type of the computation is `Unit`—everything we do is side-effecting, so there is no need to pass anything around. Instead of accumulating actions into the log we are just writing a report directly to the console. The case of `Done` is also little different—we're returning the `fish`, the result of the performed combined action.

The result of the execution changes as expected, as follows:

```
scala> println(goFishingLogging(catchFish("Crankbait"), ()))
Buying bait Crankbait
Casting line with Crankbait
Hooking fish from 9 feet
Fish(CatFish)
```

We managed to implement a very basic version of the free monad along with a small fishing language and two different interpreters. It is quite a bit of code so it's time to answer an obvious question: for what purpose do we invest this additional effort?

The free monad has obvious advantages; we touched upon these, and they are as as follows:

- Gluing the computations together as classes happens in a heap and saves stack memory.
- It is possible to pass the computation over to different parts of the code and the side-effects will be deferred until it is explicitly run.
- Having multiple interpreters allows for different behaviour in different circumstances.
- This chapter's scope has not allowed us to show how different "languages" (ADTs) can be composed into one algebraic structure, which then can be used to define the logic using both languages at the same time. This possibility offers an alternative to the monad transformers and monad transformer stacks, for example, a language that combines business terms and persistence terms.

The disadvantages lie in the same plane as they do for monads. These include additional initial implementation effort, runtime overhead for the garbage collector, and processing additional instructions and mental overhead for developers new to the concept.

Summary

Monads are arguably the most ubiquitous abstraction in functional programming. Unfortunately they cannot be composed in general—in contrast to functions and applicatives.

Monad transformers provide a way to work around this limitation by specifying a set of overarching structures to represent combinations of monads, each combination being specific to a single internal effect type. Monad transformers compose monads in a way that it is possible to cross both effects with a single call of the `flatMap` or `map`.

Monad transformer stacks lift the concept of monad transformers one level higher, utilizing the fact that each monad transformer is also a monad. By stacking monad transformers, it is possible to work with virtually any number of effects combined together in a single pile the same way we would do with a single monad.

Monad transformers are not without disadvantages. The list includes increased garbage collection footprint and processor utilization because of the need to unpack and repack effects in the stack. The same reasoning applies to the mental model developers needed to build and maintain in their head while working with the code.

The free monad provides a reasonable alternative by clearly separating structure and interpretation of the computations. It does so by representing business logic as a sequence of steps encoded as data by some ADT and executing these steps with suitable interpreter(s).

This chapter concludes the second part of the book. In this part and the first part, we refrained from using third-party libraries and focused on giving readers a deep understanding of the language features and underlying theoretical concepts.

Needless to say, the code examples in this part were decidedly simplistic and only suitable for learning purposes.

Specifically to the functional programming aspects, there are two exceptionally good libraries, worth mentioning one more time and available for Scala: Cats (`https://typelevel.org/cats/`) and Scalaz (`https://github.com/scalaz/scalaz`). If we managed to ignite your interest in programming Scala using the functional style shown in this part of the book, we highly recommend taking a look at both of them. Besides offering production-ready implementation for the concepts we studied, they also contain lots of abstractions we weren't able to discuss.

In the third part of the book we will relax our self-imposed constraint about third-party dependencies and dedicate it to the topic of reactive programming in Scala using different Akka libraries.

Questions

1. Why does the type of monad transformer reflect the type of the stack "upside-down" with its name referring to the type of innermost monad?
2. Why is it possible to reuse existing monads for the top layer of the stack?
3. Why is it impossible to reuse existing monads for the bottom layer of the stack?
4. Implement a `TryT` monad transformer.
5. Use the `TryT` monad transformer instead of `EitherT` with the example functions from the chapter.
6. Implement another take on the monad transformer stack, this time with the layers placed upside-down: `EitherT[OptionT[Future, A], String, A]`.
7. Add an action to release the caught fish in the free monad example we developed in the chapter.

Further reading

Anatolii Kmetiuk, *Mastering Functional Programming*: Learn how functional programming can help you in deploying web servers and working with databases in a declarative and pure way

Atul S. Khot, *Scala Functional Programming Patterns*: Grok and perform effective functional programming in Scala

Ivan Nikolov, *Scala Design Patterns* - Second Edition: Learn how to write efficient, clean, and reusable code with Scala

An Introduction to the Akka and Actor Models

11

In this chapter, we'll learn about the actor model and how it is implemented in Akka. We'll make ourselves familiar with Akka by building a simple yet complete actor system. We will then learn how to create an actor system and actors, pass messages between them, make use of location transparency and remoting, properly structure the system for effective supervision, and look at how **finite-state machine** (**FSM**) actors work. Finally, we'll show you how to test actor-based applications.

The following topics will be covered in this chapter:

- The actor model
- The basics of Akka
- Akka FSM
- Akka remoting
- Testing

Technical requirements

Before we begin, make sure you have the following installed:

- Java 1.8+
- SBT 1.2+

Please refer to the installation instructions in `Appendix A`, *Preparing the Environment and Running Code Samples*, if you need to perform a first-time setup of Java or SBT.

The source code is available on our GitHub repository at: `https://github.com/PacktPublishing/Learn-Scala-Programming/tree/master/Chapter11`.

Introduction to the actor model

From the first days of computing applications of all kinds, they have faced growing demands for processing increasing volumes of data within diminishing processing times. Up until recently, these challenges were addressed by scaling applications vertically, by adding more memory and higher speed processors. This approach was possible because of growing processor speed, which is described by Moore's law as the following:

> *"Moore's law is the observation that the number of transistors in a dense integrated circuit doubles about every two years. ... Moore's prediction proved accurate for several decades, and has been used in the semiconductor industry to guide long-term planning and to set targets for research and development. .... Moore's law is an observation and projection of a historical trend and not a physical or natural law."*

But the pace of advancement in hardware started to slow down, as stated by Intel in 2015. This trend made it obvious that the only way to scale applications from now on was via horizontal scalability—by increasing the number of processing cores and machines which are to process data in parallel by using multiple application threads. Two obvious challenges in this situation are as follows:

- To prevent concurrent modification and, as a result, corruption of data
- To provide access to the data for processes running on different cores or machines

The first challenge is traditionally solved by using shared memory and different locking approaches. Unfortunately, this approach effectively makes the parts of the application that are synchronizing with each other pseudo-sequential, which in turn limits possible speedup in accordance with Amdahl's law:

> *"Amdahl's law is a formula that gives theoretical speedup in terms of latency in the execution of a task at the fixed workload that can be expected of a system whose resources have been improved. ... Amdahl's law is often used in parallel computing to predict the theoretical speedup when using multiple processors."*

 The most important corollary is that the speedup is limited by the serial part of the program.

Fortunately, there are other solutions that make it possible for different parts of the program to work together toward the same goal in parallel. One of these approaches is the actor model. Fortunately, the actor model also addresses the second challenge with a concept known as **location transparency**.

The concept of actors was first introduced in 1973 by *Carl Hewitt*, *Peter Bishop*, and *Richard Steiger*.

 Carl Hewitt, Peter Bishop, and Richard Steiger: A Universal Modular Actor Formalism for Artificial Intelligence. In: Proceeding IJCAI'73 Proceedings of the 3rd International Joint Conference on Artificial Intelligence. 1973, S. 235–245 (`https://dl.acm.org/citation.cfm?id=1624804`).

The idea is that everything is represented as an actor, which is a basic computational entity. Actors communicate with each other using messages. In response to a message, an actor can undertake any of the following actions:

- Send a finite number of messages to other actor(s)
- Create a finite number of other actors
- Change its behavior for the next message to be processed

This definition is quite abstract, but already allows you to recognize a couple of constraints that the implementation must satisfy:

- Actors communicate using messages and are not allowed to expose or inspect the internal states of each other.
- A shared mutable state has no place in the actor model.
- Side-effects are not mentioned in this definition, but they are obviously the end goal of any system. Therefore, an actor's response to the message might be any combination of the following:
    1. Changing internal state
    2. Modifying behavior
    3. Producing side-effects
- Actors need to be able to address each other. Consequently, a naming system is expected to exist. Having an appropriate naming system is a prerequisite for location transparency, meaning that every actor can be addressed by some canonical name regarding its actual location.

The preceding definition also leaves the following questions unanswered, among others:

- What would be an effect of the limitations of the underlying hardware, operating system, and runtime environment?
- Where do actors coexist and how is the first actor created?
- How are messages delivered from one actor to another?
- Are actors mortal, and if yes, how do they die?

The most prominent languages that use the actor model are Erlang, Io, D, Pony, and Scala.

We will take a closer look at the Scala implementation—Akka—by building an enterprise bakery application. Our bakery will be crowded by different actors, each with their own responsibilities, producing cookies as a result of their teamwork.

Akka basics

We will start by adding an Akka dependency into the `build.sbt` file of an empty Scala SBT project:

```
libraryDependencies += "com.typesafe.akka" %% "akka-actor" % akkaVersion
```

The `akkaVersion` could be looked upon the Akka website. At the time of writing this book, it was 2.5.13, so we would prepend `val akkaVersion = "2.5.13"` to the preceding snippet.

> The SBT can create a minimal Akka project for you via a giter8 template: `sbt new https://github.com/akka/akka-quickstart-scala.g8`.

Now, we can instantiate an `ActorSystem`, which is the place where Akka's actors live:

```
import akka.actor._
val bakery = ActorSystem("Bakery")
```

Avoid defining multiple actor systems in the same JVM or even on the same machine. An actor system is not very lightweight and is usually configured to closely reflect the hardware configuration it is running on. Thus, multiple actor systems will not only consume more resources than needed but, in the worst case, they will compete for these resources.

It is also possible to create a default actor system without providing a name, but it would be best if you don't do this. Naming the actor system and actors will make your life easier while you reason about it and debug existing code.

As a next step, let's define an actor.

Defining actors

An actor in Akka must extend traits of the same name and implement the `receive` method:

```
class Cook extends Actor {
  override def receive = {
    case _ =>
  }
}
```

The type of the `receive` action is defined as `type Receive = PartialFunction[Any, Unit]`, which closely resembles the abstract definition of an actor model. In Akka, actors can receive any message, and any of the actor's activities are manifested as a change in its state or as a side-effect.

Our defined actor accepts any message and does nothing. This is probably the simplest and laziest actor possible.

In order to make it useful, let's define its behavior and vocabulary.

As we're building an enterprise bakery, our actors will have a single responsibility, which is also a good idea in any kind of system, not just one that's actor-based. Our cook actor will take a ready-made dough and make raw cookies out of it. First, we must define the messages:

```
object Cook {
  final case class Dough(weight: Int)
  final case class RawCookies(number: Int)
}
```

And then the behavior of the actor:

```
class Cook extends Actor {
  override def receive = {
    case Dough(weight) =>
      val numberOfCookies = makeCookies(weight)
      sender() ! RawCookies(numberOfCookies)
```

```
    }

    private val cookieWeight = 30
    private def makeCookies(weight: Int):Int = weight / cookieWeight
  }
```

There are a couple of things going on in this definition:

1. Our actor understands only one message type, `Dough`
2. It *makes* raw cookies out of dough by calculating their number
3. We're using `sender()` to obtain a reference to the actor from which the received message is originating and send the response to this reference

Also, some more subtle details are worth mentioning:

- If, by coincidence, our `Cook` will get any other message except `Dough`, this message won't be handled by the actor and will be lost. Akka has a special mechanism for such messages called *dead message queue.*
- We defined case classes for each message type to make understanding the code less complicated.
- The actor's logic is decoupled from the protocol and can be extracted into the companion object. This is done to make testing easier.

Now that we have a definition of the actor, it is time to instantiate it and send some messages to it. In Akka, we have to use a special `Prop` constructor:

```
val cookProps: ActorRef = Props[Cook]
```

We don't need to pass any constructor parameters to the actor in this case and therefore we can benefit from using the `Props` form, which takes a sole type of an actor as its parameter.

 Don't construct actors directly using a class constructor. It is possible to do so and then obtain the *ActorRef* from the actor, but this will result in an error at runtime.

Now, we can bring everything together and send out our first message:

```
object Bakery extends App {
  val bakery = ActorSystem("Bakery")
  val cook: ActorRef = bakery.actorOf(Props[Cook], "Cook")
  cook ! Dough(1000)
}
```

Here, we have created a named actor using an actor system and sent one message to it.

Let's define a couple of other actors to make our bakery lively. We will separate the responsibilities, as follows:

- A boy will visit the groceries store and get the necessary ingredients.
- He will hand them over to the bakery manager so that they can check the amount and quality.
- The ingredients are then given to the chef, who prepares a dough out of them.
- The chef uses one or more mixers depending on the volume of the dough.
- The ready dough is given to the cook, who prepares the raw cookies.
- The raw cookies are baked by the baker.
- The baker uses the oven for baking. It might take a couple of rounds to bake all of the cookies because of the oven's limited size.
- The cookies are returned to the manager as soon as they are ready.

Then, we need to figure out the relationships between actors, like so:

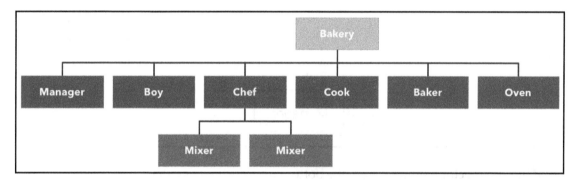

And then we need to build and show the message flow among them:

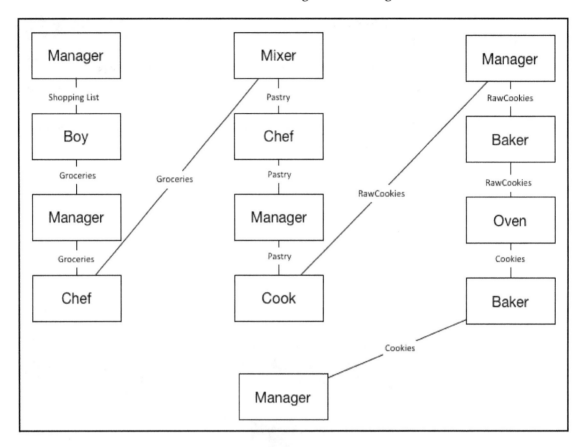

We'll build our actor hierarchy from the bottom up, starting from the oven:

```
object Oven {
  final case object Extract
  final case class Cookies(count: Int)
  def props(size: Int) = Props(classOf[Oven], size)
}

class Oven(size: Int) extends Actor {
  private var cookiesInside = 0
  override def receive = LoggingReceive {
    case RawCookies(count) => insert(count).foreach(sender().!)
    case Extract => sender() ! Cookies(extract())
  }

  def insert(count: Int): Option[RawCookies] =
```

```
      if (cookiesInside > 0) {
        Some(RawCookies(count))
      } else {
        val tooMany = math.max(0, count - size)
        cookiesInside = math.min(size, count)
        Some(tooMany).filter(_ > 0).map(RawCookies)
      }

    def extract(): Int = {
      val cookies = cookiesInside
      cookiesInside = 0
      cookies
    }
  }
}
```

We introduced a number of new features here.

First, we defined two new message types that will be used to command an oven to return cookies and make a container for the ready cookies. In the actor itself, we're using a constructor parameter to specify how many cookies will fit inside it. We're also using Akka's `LoggingReceive`, which writes incoming messages into the log. In the `receive` method itself, we stick to the principle of separating Akka semantics from the business logic.

The `insert` method checks whether the oven is empty and places as many raw cookies as possible into it, optionally returning these which don't fit inside back, so that we can forward them to the sender.

In the `extract` method, we modify the number of cookies inside the oven and return them to the sender.

Having `var` inside of an actor is absolutely safe and illustrates one of the core features of Akka features—messages are processed by actors one-by-one in the order they are received. Even in a highly concurrent environment, Akka shields actor code from any concurrency-related matters.

 Always use deeply immutable messages. Using mutable structures will allow two different actors to access the same data from different threads, which can lead to concurrent modifications and corrupt data.

To instantiate an oven, we'll use another flavor of the `Prop` constructor, which allows us to define constructor parameters:

```
val prop = Props(classOf[Oven], size)
```

By convention, it is placed into the companion object of an actor. The `size` of the oven is defined here as well.

As shown in the following code, we'll describe the user of the oven, that is, the `Baker` actor:

```scala
object Baker {
  import scala.concurrent.duration._
  private val defaultBakingTime = 2.seconds
  def props(oven: ActorRef) = Props(new Baker(oven))
}
class Baker(oven: ActorRef,
            bakingTime: FiniteDuration = Baker.defaultBakingTime)
    extends Actor {
  private var queue = 0
  private var timer: Option[Cancellable] = None
  override def receive: Receive = {
    case RawCookies(count) =>
      queue += count
      if (sender() != oven && timer.isEmpty) timer = sendToOven()
    case c: Cookies =>
      context.actorSelection("../Manager") ! c
      assert(timer.isEmpty)
      if (queue > 0) timer = sendToOven() else timer = None
  }
  private def sendToOven() = {
    oven ! RawCookies(queue)
    queue = 0
    import context.dispatcher
    Option(context.system.scheduler.scheduleOnce(bakingTime, oven,
Extract))
  }
  override def postStop(): Unit = {
    timer.foreach(_.cancel())
    super.postStop()
  }
}
```

Let's take a closer look at what is going on here. First, we need to use yet another kind of `Props` constructor because Akka does not support constructors with default parameters.

 `Props`, along with the instance, is a very powerful construct that allows you to create anonymous actors which in turn can close over the internal state of another actor. Try to avoid using it, if possible.

The `Baker` actor receives an `ActorRef` of the `Oven` as a parameter. This reference is used by the baker to send cookies to the `Oven` and extract them.

After receiving the baked cookies from the `Oven`, the `Baker` looks up the `Manager` actor and sends the `Cookies` to it. After that, it puts another batch of raw cookies into the `Oven`, if needed. We will discuss the intrinsics of `context.actorSelection` later in this chapter.

The `Baker` maintains an internal queue of raw cookies and periodically puts them into the oven. This is an old oven, and to use it, we need set up a kitchen timer in order to extract the baked cookies at the proper time. Finally, we include a `postStop` life cycle hook for the timer in order to cancel it if our actor stops. We have done this because, if the actor is no longer there, there will be no one around to listen out for the timer signal.

The life cycle of an actor

Actors in Akka define a number of methods which are called at different moments during their lifetime, specifically:

- `preStart`: Called after the actor is started or during restart
- `preRestart`: Called on the actor which is about to be destroyed because of the restart
- `postRestart`: Called on the actor who was just created after the restart
- `postStop`: Called after the actor is stopped

The order of execution, given two instances of the same actor—one that has failed and another one that has been created as a replacement—is shown as follows:

- Actor A, stopping: `constructor` | `preStart` | `preRestart` | `postStop`
- Actor B, starting: `constructor` | `postRestart` | `preStart` | `postStop`

Now, we can implement a `Chef` actor.

This actor will combine ingredients to produce dough. It will use its magical powers to create a `Mixer` and will use this `Mixer` to do the actual blending work. One `Mixer` has limited capacity, and so the `Chef` will need to create multiple mixers for bigger shopping lists and use them in parallel in order to speed up the preparation process.

We'll start by defining a mixer:

```
object Mixer {
  final case class Groceries(eggs: Int, flour: Int, sugar: Int, chocolate:
Int)
  def props: Props = Props[Mixer].withDispatcher("mixers-dispatcher")
}

class Mixer extends Actor {
  override def receive: Receive = {
    case Groceries(eggs, flour, sugar, chocolate) =>
      Thread.sleep(3000)
      sender() ! Dough(eggs * 50 + flour + sugar + chocolate)
  }
}
```

The `Mixer` only understands a single type of message, `Groceries`. After getting this type of message, it produces a certain amount of `Dough` by mixing all of the ingredients together and returns it to the sender. `Thread.sleep` represents blocking—waiting for the hardware to complete its operation.

 Try to avoid blocking. Blocking in the actor consumes a thread, and if many actors have blocked, other actors will be starved for threads and won't be able to process messages.

Unfortunately, in our case, blocking is unavoidable during the mixing operation because of hardware limitations. Akka offers a solution to this problem in the form of dispatchers.

Dispatchers

Dispatchers are the machinery that makes actors work. They are responsible for assigning CPU to the actors, managing actor's mailboxes, and passing over messages from the mailbox to an actor. There are four commonly used types of dispatchers:

- **Default dispatcher:** This dispatcher creates one mailbox per actor and may be shared by any number of actors. It uses `java.util.concurrent.ExecutorService` for this process. It is designed to be used in combination with actors having a nonblocking code. The dispatcher selects an idle thread and assigns it to an actor of its choice. The actor then processes a certain number of messages before releasing the thread.

- **Balanced dispatcher:** This dispatcher creates a single mailbox that can be shared by multiple actors of the same kind. Messages from the mailbox are distributed among actors sharing the dispatcher.

- **Pinned dispatcher:** This dispatcher uses a thread pool with a single thread. This thread is assigned to a single actor. Thus, each actor has its own thread and mailbox, and can perform blocking or long-running activities without starving other actors.

- **CallingThread dispatcher:** This dispatcher assigns one thread per actor. This is mainly used for testing.

In our case, the `Mixer` has a blocking call in its implementation. Because of this, we are better off with the pinned dispatcher. First, we'll add a dispatcher configuration to `application.conf`:

```
mixers-dispatcher {
   executor = "thread-pool-executor"
   type = PinnedDispatcher
}
```

The name of the dispatcher is defined at the root level of the configuration and isn't nested into the `akka` namespace.

> Akka uses Typesafe Config as a configuration library. It is a very powerful and useful configuration facility that's absolutely worth checking out. You can find it at `https://github.com/lightbend/config`.

And then we can use the configured dispatcher at the moment we create an actor:

```
def props: Props = Props[Mixer].withDispatcher("mixer-dispatcher")
```

This way, each of the mixers will have its own thread, and blocking will not affect its siblings and other actors in the system.

After waiting, the mixer returns the produced dough to the `sender()` and sends itself a `PoisonPill` so that it can terminate.

Terminating actors

There are a couple of ways to stop an actor in Akka. The most direct approach involves calling the `stop` method of the context, like so:

```
context stop child
context.stop(self)
```

The actor terminates asynchronously after it finishes processing its current message, but not after other messages in the inbox. This contrasts to sending an actor a `PoisonPill` or `Kill` message, which is enqueued into the mailbox and processed in an orderly fashion.

The `Kill` message will cause an actor to throw an `ActorKilledException`, which in turn will involve its supervision chain (more on that topic later in this chapter) to decide how this actor's *failure* should be handled.

Stopping an actor using a `context` or `PoisonPill` in contrast to `Kill` is done gracefully. The actor will stop all of its children, execute life cycle hooks, and inform its supervisor appropriately.

 The actor's termination is propagated top-down, but the actual stopping occurs bottom-up. One slow actor that takes a long (or infinite) time to stop can prevent the whole chain of actors from being terminated.

Now that we have our blocking `Mixer`, it is time to define a `Chef`:

The ask pattern

With the `Chef`, we will introduce another popular pattern in Akka—the ask pattern:

```
class Chef extends Actor with ActorLogging with Stash {
  import scala.concurrent.duration._
  private implicit val timeout = Timeout(5 seconds)

  override def receive = {
    case Groceries(eggs, flour, sugar, chocolate) =>
      for (i <- 1 to eggs) {
        val mixer = context.watch(context.actorOf(Mixer.props,
s"Mixer_$i"))
        val message = Groceries(1, flour / eggs, sugar / eggs, chocolate /
eggs)
        import akka.pattern.ask
        val job = (mixer ? message).mapTo[Dough]
```

```
        import context.dispatcher
        import akka.pattern.pipe
        job.pipeTo(sender())
      }
      log.info("Sent jobs to {} mixers", eggs)
      context.become(waitingForResults, discardOld = false)
  }
  def waitingForResults: Receive = {
    case g: Groceries => stash()
    case Terminated(child) =>
      if (context.children.isEmpty) {
        unstashAll()
        context.unbecome()
        log.info("Ready to accept new mixing jobs")
      }
  }
}
```

There are lots of things happening here, so let's go over the code line by line and describe what's going on.

```
    class Chef extends Actor with ActorLogging with Stash
```

Our `Chef` actor is not only an `Actor`—but it also extends `ActorLogging` and `Stash`. The `ActorLogging` trait gives an actor a predefined `logger`. It is also possible to define the `Logger` directly, for example, as shown in the following code:

```
    val log = akka.event.Logging(this)
```

Akka uses a special message-based logging facility internally to minimize blocking inside of an actor.

Akka logging supports SLF4J as a backend. The official documentation (https://doc.akka.io/docs/akka/2.5/logging.html) has a detailed explanation on how to extend the configuration to enable SLF4J logging into an Akka application:

```
        import scala.concurrent.duration._
        private implicit val timeout = Timeout(5 seconds)
```

Here, we have defined a timeout of 5 seconds, which will be necessary the moment we start working with mixers:

```
    override def receive = {
      case Groceries(eggs, flour, sugar, chocolate) =>
```

In the `receive` method, our actor only accepts `Groceries` messages and uses pattern matching to extract field values:

```
for (i <- 1 to eggs) {
    val message = Groceries(1, flour / eggs, sugar / eggs, chocolate / eggs)
```

Our mixers are small, so we need to split the groceries at hand into portions of one egg so that the portion fits into the mixer:

```
val mixer = context.watch(context.actorOf(Mixer.props, s"Mixer_$i"))
```

Here, we created a `Mixer` actor using the `props` defined earlier (which in turn assigns the proper dispatcher to it) and named it appropriately.

In the following two lines of code, we can see implicit `ask` magic at work:

```
import akka.pattern.ask
val job: Future[Dough] = mixer ? message
```

Having to `ask` in scope allows us implicitly to convert an `ActorRef` into `AskableActorRef`, which is then used as a target for the message. The `actor ? message` syntax represents the ask pattern. Akka sends a message to the target actor and creates an expectation of the response as a `Future[Any]`. This `Future` can be worked with like any other `Future`. For convenience, Akka provides a `mapTo[T]` method, which allows you to convert it into the `Future[T]`.

The final piece of code in the `for` comprehension uses another implicit conversion provided by Akka, this time acting on the `Future`:

```
import akka.pattern.pipe
import context.dispatcher
job.pipeTo(sender())
```

Here, we're bringing in scope a `pipe` which transforms the normal `Future` into the `PipeableFuture`. The latter can be piped into one or multiple actors, as shown in the third line of the preceding code, by using an implicit execution context that was imported in the second line.

The third line of code pipes the result of the `Future` execution to the sender in the case of it being a success.

 We could use `job.recoverWith` to resend the job to the mixer if the first attempt fails. This is a simple way to implement "at least once" semantics using the ask pattern.

Having created all of the mixers and sent them work packages, the `Chef` actor writes a log entry and starts to wait for the results:

```
log.info("Sent jobs to {} mixers", eggs)
context.become(waitingForResults, discardOld = false)
```

There is a special syntax in Akka logging. The first argument is a `String` that incorporates `{}` placeholders to denote other arguments. The substitution is done in a separate thread, but only if the respective log level is enabled. This is done to minimize the logging work done by the actor's thread.

Changing an actor's behavior using context

In the last line of code, the actor changes its behavior by using the `context.become` construct.

`become` and `unbecome` is an Akka way of changing the behavior of the actor in response to a message. `become` takes a `Receive` argument (which is a type alias for `PartialFunction[Any, Unit]`, which is also just a normal sign of the `receive` method) which becomes a new actor's behavior starting from the next message (this change in behavior is not preserved across actor restarts). The `discardOld` parameter controls whether this new behavior should replace an old one or whether it should just push it down to the stack of behaviors that actors maintain internally. We'll see how this stack works in a minute.

Let's go over the `waitingForResults` method, which became a new behavior of the actor a moment ago. The first line puts any `Groceries` messages on hold because we are already waiting for jobs to be finished. This is done by using the `stash()` method of the `Stash` trait, which puts the current message into an internal stash of the actor:

```
case g: Groceries => stash()
```

The `Chef` actor watches over the `Mixer` actors it has created. In this case, if a child actor dies, the watching actor will receive a `Terminated` message with an actor reference of the victim:

```
case Terminated(child) =>
```

The actor checks whether all of the children are terminated by using `context.children`, and if this is the case, it prepends all of the stashed messages to the message box by using `unstashAll()` and returns to its previous behavior by using `context.unbecome()`.

Unbalanced `context.become()` and `context.unbecome()` operations might introduce the source of a memory leak in long-running applications.

Now that our `Chef` is ready, let's move on and implement a `Manager`.

Advanced topics

Up until now, we have implemented our bakery by relying on basic Akka concepts. It is time to deepen our knowledge and start to use higher level concepts.

Akka FSM

The `Manager` pushes the cookie-making process forward by coordinating all other inhabitants of the bakery. It does so by taking the messages representing job results from one actor and passing them further along to an appropriate successor. It is important that this process is consequent, that is, it should be impossible to make raw cookies at the moment since we only have a shopping list and no dough. We'll represent this behavior as a state machine.

An FSM is an abstraction defined by a set of states the machine can be in. For each state, it also defines which message types can be accepted in this state and the possible reaction of the machine, including its new state.

Let's dive into the code and see how this approach is implemented with Akka FSM.

The actor is defined by extending the `FSM` trait:

```
class Manager(chef: ActorRef, cook: ActorRef, baker: ActorRef) extends
FSM[State, Data]
```

The type parameter, `State`, represents the type of states the actor can be in, and the `Data` represents the possible associated internal state.

There is an obvious confusion between the term *State*, referring to the state of the FSM our actor represents, and a *State* referring to the data which is associated with each of the steps in the process. To avoid ambiguity, we'll further refer to the state of the actor as *Data* and the state of the FSM as *State*.

States of the actor reflect the processes that occur in the bakery: the goods moving from the shop boy over to the chef and cook, which then move over to the baker and back to the manager (note that because of the sequential art of work-passing done by the manager, there will be only one worker actor active in our bakery at the moment, even if they could work in parallel with a more sophisticated manager).

The following messages represent the state of the managed bakery:

```
trait State
case object Idle extends State
case object Shopping extends State
case object Mixing extends State
case object Forming extends State
case object Baking extends State
```

The messages we defined previously also need to be extended to represent the possible types of data:

```
sealed trait Data
case object Uninitialized extends Data
final case class ShoppingList(...) extends Data
final case class Groceries(...) extends Data
final case class Dough(weight: Int) extends Data
final case class RawCookies(count: Int) extends Data
```

The FSM itself is defined by describing three primary aspects of the state machine:

- States
- State transitions
- An initial state

Let's take a look at the actor's code to see how this is done. The states are defined within the when block, which accepts a state name and a state function:

```
when(Idle) {
  case Event(s: ShoppingList, Uninitialized) ⇒
    goto(Shopping) forMax (5 seconds) using s
  case _ =>
    stay replying "Get back to work!"
}
```

When there are multiple when blocks for the same states, the state functions that constitute them are concatenated.

The state function is a `PartialFunction[Event, State]`, and describes a new state for each event type received in a particular state. Akka FSM provides a nice domain specific language (DLS) for this. For example, in the preceding code, the actor reacts to the `ShoppingList` event by transitioning to the `Shopping` state with a timeout of 5 seconds. The shopping list is used as new state data.

In the case of any other message, the actor stays in the same state and replies to the sender with a friendly remark.

In the `Shopping` state, the `Manager` reacts differently depending upon whether the groceries conform to the shopping list or not:

```
when (Shopping) {
    case Event (g: Groceries, s: ShoppingList)
          if g.productIterator sameElements s.productIterator ⇒
        goto (Mixing) using g
    case Event (_: Groceries, _: ShoppingList) ⇒
        goto (Idle) using Uninitialized
}
```

In the first case, it uses `Groceries` as a new state and goes to the next state. In the second case, it goes back to the `Idle` state and sets its state to `Uninitialized`.

Other states are described in a similar fashion:

```
when (Mixing) {
    case Event (p: Dough, _) ⇒
        goto (Forming) using p
}

when (Forming) {
    case Event (c: RawCookies, _) ⇒
        goto (Baking) using c
}

when (Baking, stateTimeout = idleTimeout * 20) {
    case Event (c: Cookies, _) ⇒
        log.info ("Cookies are ready: {}", c)
        stay () replying "Thank you!"
    case Event (StateTimeout, _) =>
        goto (Idle) using Uninitialized
}
```

We're just moving on to the next state and updating the state data in the process. The most obvious observation at the moment would be that `This actor does nothing but enjoying himself`, and we're going to fix this by using the `onTransition` block, which describes the behavior of the actor at the moment state transition occurs:

```
onTransition {
  case Idle -> Shopping ⇒
    val boy = sendBoy
    boy ! stateData
  case Shopping -> Idle =>
    self ! stateData
  case Shopping -> Mixing ⇒
    chef ! nextStateData
  case Mixing -> Forming =>
    cook ! nextStateData
  case Forming -> Baking =>
    baker ! nextStateData
}
```

The `Manager` already knows its subordinates, so it only needs to look up a `Boy`. Then, for each of the state transitions, it obtains the necessary state by using either `stateData` or `nextStateData`, which references the actor's state data before and after the respective state transition. This data is sent to the appropriate subordinate.

Now, all that's missing is an optional `whenUnhandled` block, which is executed in all states. The timer setting and a mandatory `initiate()` call sets up the defined timer and performs a state transition to the initial state.

 Akka FSM forces you to mix business logic with actor-related code, which makes it hard to test and support it. It also locks you into the provided implementation and makes it impossible to bring in another state machine realization. Always consider another possibility before fixing upon Akka FSM.

At the same time, by separating the definition of states separately from behavior, Akka FSM allows for clean structuring of the business logic.

Akka remoting

Now, we can implement the final piece of the puzzle—the shop boy and the `sendBoy` function that we left uncovered until now. The `Boy` does not belong to the `Bakery`. The `Manager` will need to send the `Boy` to the grocery `Store`, which is represented by another actor system.

In order to do so, we'll rely on Akka's location transparency and remote capabilities. First, the manager will deploy a boy actor to the remote system. The deployed actor will get a reference to the `Seller` actor in the store so that it can get groceries as and when required.

There are two ways to use remoting in Akka—either by using actor lookup or actor creation. Both are used in the same way that we did locally until now, that is, by calling `actorSelection` and `actorOf`, respectively.

Here, we will demonstrate both ways that the manager will look up a seller from whom the boy should get groceries (imagine this seller is working with the bakery on a prepaid basis) and then require the boy to interact with this specific actor.

Before we dive into the code, we need to augment the setup of our application. Remoting is a separate dependency in Akka which we will put into the `build.sbt`:

```
libraryDependencies += "com.typesafe.akka" %% "akka-remote" % akkaVersion
```

Then, we need to replace the local actor provider with the remote one and configure the network settings in `application.conf`:

```
akka {
  actor.provider = remote
  remote {
    enabled-transports = ["akka.remote.netty.tcp"]
    netty.tcp {
      hostname = "127.0.0.1"
      port = 2552
    }
  }
}
```

The same configuration, but with a necessarily different port, is provided for the second actor system that's representing the grocery store. This is done by reusing the `application.conf` via inclusion and redefining the TCP port:

```
include "application"
akka.remote.netty.tcp.port = 2553
```

Then, we need to define the grocery store:

```
import akka.actor._
import com.example.Manager.ShoppingList
import com.example.Mixer.Groceries
import com.typesafe.config.ConfigFactory

object Store extends App {
  val store = ActorSystem("Store", ConfigFactory.load("grocery.conf"))

  val seller = store.actorOf(Props(new Actor {
    override def receive: Receive = {
      case s: ShoppingList =>
        ShoppingList.unapply(s).map(Groceries.tupled).foreach(sender() ! _)
    }
  }), "Seller")
}
```

We can't use the default configuration as it is already taken by the bakery system, so we need to load a custom `grocery.conf` by using `ConfigFactory.load`. Next, we need to create an anonymous (but named!) actor whose sole responsibility is to return groceries, as described by the `ShoppingList`, to the sender.

Finally, we're ready to implement the `sendBoy` function in the `Manager`:

```
private def sendBoy: ActorRef = {
  val store = "akka.tcp://Store@127.0.0.1:2553"
  val seller = context.actorSelection(s"$store/user/Seller")
  context.actorOf(Boy.props(seller))
}
```

First, we must define the address of the grocery store. Then, we need to look up a seller by using its address on the remote system. Akka's documentation specifies the following pattern for remote actor lookup:

```
akka.<protocol>://<actor system name>@<hostname>:<port>/<actor path>
```

We'll take a look at this template and especially the actor path in a moment.

Then, we need to create a boy by using our usual `actorOf` method. To tell Akka to deploy this actor remotely, we need to put the following configuration into `application.conf`:

```
akka.actor.deployment {
  /Manager/Boy {
    remote = "akka.tcp://Store@127.0.0.1:2553"
  }
}
```

This instructs Akka not to instantiate a local actor but to contact the remote daemon running in the actor system with the name `Store` with a network address of `127.0.0.1:2553` and to tell this daemon to create a remote actor.

We could achieve the same result without extending configuration by providing deployment configuration directly in the code:

```
val storeAddress = AddressFromURIString(s"$store")
val boyProps = Boy.props(seller).withDeploy(Deploy(scope =
RemoteScope(storeAddress)))
context.actorOf(boyProps)
```

This snippet creates a store address from the string we defined earlier and explicitly tells Akka to use it while creating the actor.

The implementation of `Boy` is trivial now:

```
object Boy {
  def props(seller: ActorSelection): Props = Props(classOf[Boy], seller)
}

class Boy(seller: ActorSelection) extends Actor {
  override def receive = {
    case s: ShoppingList =>
      seller forward s
      self ! PoisonPill
  }
}
```

The `Boy` constructor's takes a parameter of type `ActorSelection`, which is the result of the remote lookup that was done by the `Manager` previously. By receiving a `ShoppingList`, our implementation uses `forward` to, well, forward the message directly to the seller. Because of this forwarding, the seller will receive a message with the original actor (who is a manager) as a sender.

Finally, we will take into the account that the boy was created by the manager just for the purpose of going shopping once, and we need to clean up the resources. This can be done by the manager actor, but we prefer self-cleanup here. The `Boy` sends himself a `PoisonPill` immediately after forwarding the original message and terminates.

Now that we're done defining all of the inhabitants of our bakery, we can wire them together and bake some cookies:

```
object Bakery extends App {
  val bakery = ActorSystem("Bakery")
  val cook: ActorRef = bakery.actorOf(Props[Cook], "Cook")
```

```
    val chef: ActorRef = bakery.actorOf(Props[Chef], "Chef")
    val oven: ActorRef = bakery.actorOf(Oven.props(12), "Oven")
    val baker: ActorRef = bakery.actorOf(Baker.props(oven), "Baker")
    val manager: ActorRef = bakery.actorOf(Manager.props(chef, cook, baker),
"Manager")
}
```

Before we run our app and enjoy some cookies, let's take a break from coding and look at the actor path we saw in the remote actor lookup pattern.

The actor path

In accordance with the actor model, Akka actors are hierarchical.

The actor path is built by taking the names of each actor in the hierarchy up to the root actor and concatenating them right-to-left using slashes. In the beginning of the path, there is an address part identifying the protocol and location of the actor system. This address part is called the **anchor** and its representation is different for local and remote systems.

In our example, the whole path for the `Boy` which is described by the local path `/Manager/Boy` in the deployment configuration will be `akka://user/Bakery/Manager/Boy` (purely local path) for the `Boy` actor and an `akka.tcp://Store@127.0.0.1:2553/user/Seller` (remote path) for the `Seller` actor in the remote `Store` actor system, as shown from the `Bakery` side.

As you can see, remoting introduces the necessary differences in the way the actor path is built and used.

The main purpose of the actor path is to address an actor we are about to send messages to. On a technical level, we have an abstraction for sending messages to an actor, which is `ActorRef`. For each actor, its `ActorRef` provides access to its local reference through the `self` field and to the sender of the current message via the `context.sender()`. Each `ActorRef` references exactly one actor. `ActorRef` also incorporates a dispatcher and a mailbox for the actor. The dispatcher is responsible for queueing messages in the actor's mailbox and dequeueing them at a certain time before passing them to the actors' `receive` method.

We've already seen both ways to create an `ActorRef`:

1. By creating an actor using `context.actorOf`
2. By looking up one or multiple actors using `context.actorSelection`

There are different ways to provide an actor path for the lookup in the second case:

- **Absolute path**: `context.actorSelection("/user/Manager/Boy")` returns a single actor with a path specified or empty selection
- **Relative path**: `context.actorSelection("../sibling")` goes up to the parent in the hierarchy and then down to the "sibling" in the case that it exists.
- **Wildcards**: `context.actorSelection("../*")` goes up in the hierarchy and selects all of the children of the actor's parent, including the current actor

Actor supervision

Now, let's explain another strangeness in the actor path that you are probably wondering about—the leading `/user` part in the actors paths we've seen before. The existence of this part is Akka's answer to the question we stated at the beginning of this chapter—*How is the very first actor created?*

In Akka, the very first actor is created by the library itself. It represents a root actor and is called the root guardian accordingly (we'll explain the *guardian* part in a moment).

In fact, Akka creates three guardian actors for each actor system, as shown in the following diagram.

The / root guardian is a parent for two other guardians and thus an ancestor of any other actor in the system.

The `/user` guardian is a root actor for all user-created actors in the system. Thus, every actor created by any user of the Akka library has two parents in the hierarchy and therefore has `/user/` as a prefix in its path.

The `/system` is a root actor for internal actors that have been created by the system.

Let's extend our actor diagram with the guardian actors we just learned about:

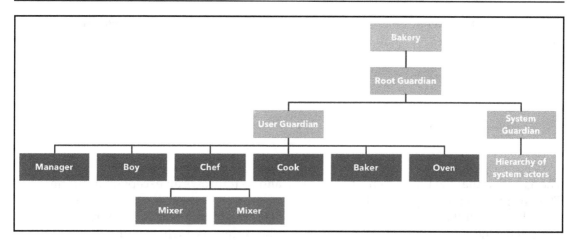

We instantiate all of our actors except mixers by using `system.context`. Because of this, they are created as children of the user guardian. The root guardian is on the top of the hierarchy and has a user guardian and a system guardian as its children.

The guardians are a part of another important feature of Akka—supervision. To understand what supervision is and why it is important, let's finally run our application.

The following is the sanitized output in the console:

```
. . .
[INFO] Remoting now listens on addresses:
[akka.tcp://Bakery@127.0.0.1:2552]
[INFO] [akka.tcp://Bakery@127.0.0.1:2552/user/Chef] Sent jobs to 24 mixers
[INFO] [akka.tcp://Bakery@127.0.0.1:2552/user/Chef] Ready to accept new
mixing jobs
[INFO] [akka.tcp://Bakery@127.0.0.1:2552/user/Manager] Cookies are ready:
Cookies(12)
[ERROR] [akka.actor.LocalActorRefProvider(akka://Bakery)] guardian failed,
shutting down system
java.lang.AssertionError: assertion failed
 at scala.Predef$.assert(Predef.scala:204)
  . . .
. . .
[akka.tcp://Bakery@127.0.0.1:2552/system/remoting-terminator] Remoting shut
down.
```

What happened? The actor system has started and communication between actors begun, but then an `AssertionError` was thrown and the whole system terminated!

The reason for this exception is a trivial programming error in the `Baker` actor we described previously:

```
override def receive: Receive = {
  ...
  case c: Cookies =>
    context.actorSelection("../Manager") ! c
    assert(timer.isEmpty)
    if (queue > 0) timer = sendToOven() else timer = None
}
```

The assertion that the timer is empty is wrong, and so it throws an exception at runtime. The exception is not caught and leads to termination of the program. Obviously, in this case, the rules of the actor model (as described at the beginning of this chapter) are not respected. One actor affects all other actors and the system as a whole without sending any messages.

In fact, this is not some deficiency of Akka. The reason our application behaves as it does is that we ignored the very important aspect of actor-based systems—supervision.

Supervision in Akka means that any actor creating a child is responsible for its management in case problems occur.

An actor detecting erroneous conditions is expected to suspend all of its descendants and itself and report a failure to its parent. This failure reporting has a form of exception throwing.

By convention, expected erroneous conditions, for example, an absence of a record in the database, are modelled on the protocol level via messages and errors of a technical nature, such as unavailable database connections modelled with exceptions. To better differentiate between erroneous conditions, developers are encouraged to define a rich set of exception classes, similar to that of normal message classes.

Exceptions thrown by the child actor are delivered to the parent, who then needs to handle the situation in one of four possible ways:

- Resume the child and let it process messages in the message box, starting from the next one. The message that caused the actor to fail is lost.
- Restart the child. This will clean up its internal state and recursively stop all of its descendants.
- Stop the child completely. This is also recursively propagated to the descendants.
- Propagate the failure to its own parent. By doing this, the supervisor is failing itself with the same cause as the subordinate.

Before delving into the technical aspects of defining a supervision strategy, let's revisit our actor's structure. Currently, all of our actors (with the exception of dynamic mixers) are created as direct children of the user guardian. This leads to the necessity to define the supervision strategy in one place for the whole actor hierarchy. This is a clear violation of the principle of separation of concerns, and is known in Akka as a *Flat Actor Hierarchy* anti-pattern. What we should aim for instead is creating a structure where failure handling happens close to the place the error occurred by the actor that is most capable of handling such errors.

With this goal in mind, let's restructure our application so that the `Baker` actor is responsible for the supervision of the `Oven` and the `Manager` is responsible for all of the actors in the system. This structure is represented in the following diagram:

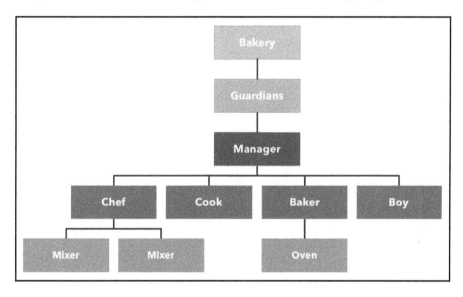

Now, we have a sane hierarchical structure where each supervisor has the best knowledge about possible failures of its children and how to deal with them.

On a technical level, the supervision strategy is defined by overriding the `supervisorStrategy` field of the corresponding actor. To demonstrate how this is done, let's extend our `Mixer` actor with the capability to report different hardware failures. First, we must define a rich set of exceptions in the companion object:

```
class MotorOverheatException extends Exception
class SlowRotationSpeedException extends Exception
class StrongVibrationException extends Exception
```

And then we need to throw them randomly during message processing:

```scala
class Mixer extends Actor with ActorLogging {
  override def receive: Receive = {
    case Groceries(eggs, flour, sugar, chocolate) =>
      val rnd = Random.nextInt(10)
      if (rnd == 0) {
        log.info("Motor Overheat")
        throw new MotorOverheatException
      }
      if (rnd < 3) {
        log.info("Slow Speed")
        throw new SlowRotationSpeedException
      }
      ...
  }
}
```

Now, we'll override a supervision strategy in the `Chef` actor:

```scala
override val supervisorStrategy: OneForOneStrategy =
  OneForOneStrategy(maxNrOfRetries = 10, withinTimeRange = 1 minute) {
    case _: MotorOverheatException =>
      self ! Dough(0)
      Stop
    case _: SlowRotationSpeedException =>
      sender() ! message
      Restart
    case _: StrongVibrationException =>
      sender() ! message
      Resume
    case _: Exception => Escalate
  }
```

The `OneForOneStrategy` instructs the `Chef` to deal with any children's failures on an individual basis.

For `MotorOverheatException`, we decide to stop the failing `Mixer`. The `Chef` sends an empty `Dough` message to itself which is counted as the response from the broken child.

The `SlowRotationSpeedException` means that something went wrong during the placement of groceries into the `Mixer`. The original message was lost by the `Mixer` at the moment it threw an `Exception`, so we're resending this message and restarting the `Mixer`.

We can tolerate `StrongVibrationException`, so we just compensate for the lost message by resending it and resuming the child.

In the case of any other exception, the `Chef` has no knowledge of how to handle it and just propagates failure to the `Manager`. The `Manager` does not have any `supervisorStrategy` defined and the exception is ultimately propagated to the user guardian.

The user guardian handles exceptions as specified by the default strategy. The default strategy is the same for all actors in the userspace if not overridden, and is defined as follows:

- `ActorInitializationException`: Stops the failing child actor
- `ActorKilledException`: Stops the failing child actor
- `DeathPactException`: Stops the failing child actor
- `Exception`: Restarts the failing child actor
- `Throwable`: Escalates to the parent actor

The root guardian is configured with `SupervisorStrategy.stoppingStrategy`, which differentiates between the `Exception` and other throwables. The former leads to the termination of the failing actor (which effectively means all of the actors in the `/user` or `/system` space), while the latter is propagated further and leads to the termination of the actor system. This is what happened when our earlier implementation threw an `AssertionError`.

The supervision strategy for the user guardian can be overridden by using its configuration property. Let's demonstrate how to use it to handle the occasional `LazinessException`, which could be thrown by any actor in the system. First, we augment `application.conf`:

```
akka {
 actor {
  guardian-supervisor-strategy =
ch11.GuardianSupervisorStrategyConfigurator
 }
}
```

And then we implement the configured strategy, as follows:

```
class GuardianSupervisorStrategyConfigurator
    extends SupervisorStrategyConfigurator {
  override def create(): SupervisorStrategy = AllForOneStrategy() {
    case _: LazyWorkerException ⇒
      println("Lazy workers. Let's try again with another crew!")
      Restart
  }
}
```

Laziness is contagious, so we use `AllForOneStrategy` to replace the whole team by restarting all of the children of the user guardian.

Testing actors

Actor-based systems are different from systems that are built using a traditional approach. Naturally, testing actors is different from regular testing. Actors send and receive messages in an asynchronous manner and are usually examined via message flow analysis. A typical setup will include three parts:

1. The source of the messages
2. The actor under test
3. The receiver of the actor's responses

Luckily, Akka includes a testing module that abstracts a lot of setup logic and provides useful helpers for common testing activities. The name of the module is Akka `TestKit` and it is contained in a separate module that needs to be added to the project's test scope:

```
libraryDependencies += "com.typesafe.akka" %% "akka-testkit" % akkaVersion
% Test
```

Having this dependency allows us to extend a `TestKit` class. The `TestKit` implements a special testing environment that mimics the internals of a normal actor system but provides access to some of the details that are hidden in a production implementation.

Here is an example of the `ScalaTest` specification that extends `TestKit`:

```
class BakerySpec(_system: ActorSystem) extends TestKit(_system)
    with Matchers with WordSpecLike with BeforeAndAfterAll
    with ImplicitSender {

  def this() = this(ActorSystem("BakerySpec"))

  override def afterAll: Unit = shutdown(system)
```

Here, we extend a `TestKit` with usual the `ScalaTest` matchers and `WordSpec`, but also mix a `BeforeAndAfterAll` and an `ImplicitSender` in. Then, we implement the default constructor by instantiating a `BakerySpec` actor system. Lastly, we override an `afterAll` method to make sure that our test actor system is properly terminated after the test.

In SBT, tests are usually run in parallel. In this case, it is important to name an actor system properly and in this case, remoting is also used to override the default port to avoid conflicts between simultaneously executing tests. Also, we should not forget to shut down the actor system gracefully to ensure that our resources are cleaned up properly.

The `TestKit` implements and brings into scope a `testActor` field, which we can use to send messages from the test code. Usually, we'd like these messages to be sent from a well-known actor. The `ImplicitSender` trait implements a reference to the `testActor` that is attached to the message at the moment it is sent.

The `TestKit` also maintains an internal queue of the messages sent to the `testActor` and defines a host of useful methods to inspect this queue.

This is how some of these predefined methods can be used to test our `Boy` actor:

```
"The boy should" should {
  val boyProps = Boy.props(system.actorSelection(testActor.path))
  val boy = system.actorOf(boyProps)

  "forward given ShoppingList to the seller" in {
    val list = ShoppingList(0, 0, 0, 0)
    boy ! list
    within(3 millis, 20 millis) {
      expectMsg(list)
      lastSender shouldBe testActor
    }
  }
  "ignore other message types" in {
    boy ! 'GoHome
    expectNoMessage(500 millis)
  }
}
```

Recapping the logic of the `Boy` actor, all it is doing is forwarding `ShoppingList` to another actor provided as a constructor parameter. In order to test this behaviour, we first create an `ActorSelection` as required by the boy's constructor, use our default `testActor` as a target, and create a boy actor as a child of the test actor system that the `TestKit` provides us with.

In the first test, we send a `ShoppingList` to the `Boy` and expect it to forward the list to the `testActor` within a predefined time interval between 3 and 30 milliseconds. We verify that the message is indeed a `ShoppingList` and that the sender is a `testActor`.

In the second test, we verify that the `Boy` ignores other messages. To check this, we send it a message with a `Symbol` type and expect our `testActor` to receive nothing within 500 milliseconds. As normal forwarding is expected to take no more than 20 milliseconds by our first test, we can be sure that the message has been ignored by the `Boy`.

`testActor`, `lastSender`, `within`, `expectMsg`, and `expectNoMsg` are implemented by the `TestKit` and save us from writing boilerplate code.

There are lots of other helpful methods in the `TestKit` that we will take a look at shortly. Most of them exist in two forms: one takes a timeout as a parameter and another uses a default timeout. The timeout defines how long `TestKit` will wait for the condition to happen. The default timeout can be overridden by using the `within` wrapper, as shown previously, by changing the configuration or by using a `timescale` parameter that will affect all durations within the scope.

We are already familiar with the `expectMsg` and `expectNoMessage` assertions. Let's take a look at some of the other available helpers:

- `def expectMsgClass[C](c: Class[C]):C` expects and returns a single message of type C.
- `def expectMsgType[T](implicit t: ClassTag[T]):T` does the same as the previous helper, but uses implicit to construct the type parameter.
- `def expectMsgAnyOf[T](obj: T*): T` This expects one message and verifies that it is equal to one of the constructor parameters.
- `def expectMsgAnyClassOf[C](obj: Class[_ <: C]*):C` does the same as before, but verifies the type of the message instead of the actual message.
- `def expectMsgAllOf[T](obj: T*):Seq[T]` expects the number of messages and verifies that all of them are equal to the constructor parameters.
- `def expectMsgAllClassOf[T](obj: Class[_ <: T]*):Seq[T]` does the same as before, but verifies types of messages.
- `def expectMsgAllConformingOf[T](obj: Class[_ <: T]*):Seq[T]` does the same as `expectMsgAllClassOf`, but checks conformity (instanceOf) instead of class equality.
- `def expectNoMessage():Unit` verifies that no message is received during the specified or default timeout.
- `def receiveN(n: Int):Seq[AnyRef]` receives N messages and returns them to the caller for further verification.
- `def expectMsgPF[T](max: Duration = Duration.Undefined, hint: String = "")(f: PartialFunction[Any, T]):T` expects a single message and verifies that a given partial function is defined.

- `def expectTerminated(target: ActorRef, max: Duration = Duration.Undefined): Terminated` expects a single `Terminated` message from a specified `target`.
- `def fishForMessage(max: Duration = Duration.Undefined, hint: String = "")(f: PartialFunction[Any, Boolean]): Any` expects multiple messages for which given partial function is defined. It returns the first message for which `f` returns true.

Our `Baker` actor is designed in such a way that it sends messages to its parent, which means that we will be unable to receive responses from the `Baker` if we create it using the test actor system. Let's take a look at how `TestKit` can help us in this situation:

```
"The baker should" should {
  val parent = TestProbe()
  val baker = parent.childActorOf(Props(classOf[Baker], 0 millis))
  "bake cookies in batches" in {
    val count = Random.nextInt(100)
    baker ! RawCookies(Oven.size * count)
    parent.expectMsgAllOf(List.fill(count)(Cookies(Oven.size)):_*)
  }
}
```

Here, we're constructing a test actor using `TestProbe()`. The `TestProbe` is another nice feature provided by the `TestKit` that allows you to send, receive, and reply to messages, and is useful in testing scenarios when multiple test actors are required. In our case, we're using its ability to create child actors to create a `Baker` actor as a child.

Then, we need to generate a number of `RawCookies` so that it requires a number of turns to bake them. We expect this number of messages to be sent to the `parent` in the next line.

Up until now, we have tested actors in isolation. Our grocery `Store` is built in a way that it instantiates an anonymous actor. This makes the approach of testing an actor in isolation impossible. Let's demonstrate how we can verify that the `Seller` actor returns the expected `Groceries` if given a `ShoppingList`:

```
class StoreSpec(store: Store) extends TestKit(store.store)
    with Matchers with WordSpecLike with BeforeAndAfterAll {

  def this() = this(new Store {})

  override def afterAll: Unit = shutdown(system)

  "A seller in store" should {
    "do nothing for all unexpected message types" in {
```

```
          store.seller ! 'UnexpectedMessage
          expectNoMessage()
       }
       "return groceries if given a shopping list" in {
          store.seller.tell(ShoppingList(1, 1, 1, 1), testActor)
          expectMsg(Groceries(1,1,1,1))
       }
     }
  }
```

We will construct our test class like we did previously, but with one subtle difference. The `Seller` actor is defined anonymously and therefore is only constructed as a part of the whole actor system. Because of this, we instantiate the `Store` in the default constructor and use the underlying actor system that's accessible via the `store` field as a constructor parameter for the `TestKit` instance.

In the test itself, we're sending test inputs directly to the `seller ActorRef` using the `store` that we constructed previously. We have not extended `ImplicitSender` and need to provide a `testActor` as a sender reference explicitly.

Now that we have our application implemented and tested, let's run it!

Running the application

Please refer to `Appendix A`, *Preparing the Environment and Running Code Samples*, if you don't have Java and SBT installed yet.

We will run our application in the terminal by using two separate terminal sessions for `Shop` and `Bakery`. It is possible to run both by issuing one of the two following commands in the corresponding shell:

- `sbt "runMain ch11.Store"`
- `sbt "runMain ch11.Bakery"`

In our code, we do not handle the `StateTimeout` for the `Shopping/ShoppingList` state. Therefore, it is mandatory to start the store session first and after it loads and starts to accept connections stating that the bakery session can be started.

It is also possible to use an approach documented in `Appendix A`, *Preparing the Environment and Running Code Samples,* to run the code from within the SBT session and choose the appropriate main class after that. This approach is represented in the following screenshot:

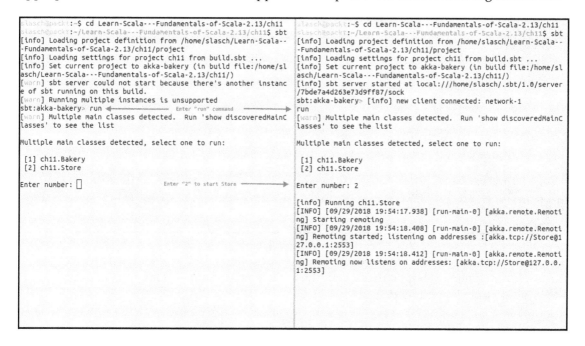

Here, we can see how two SBT sessions are initiated in the `ch11` folder. On the right-hand side of the screen, the main class for the store was already selected and run by SBT. The logs show that the `Store` is listening for connections, so it is safe to start the main `Bakery` session.

This happens after we enter 1 in the left Terminal window:

```
slasch@packt:~$ cd Learn-Scala---Fundamentals-of-Scala-2.13/ch11        slasch@packt:~/Learn-Scala---Fundamentals-of-Scala-2.13/ch11$ sbt
slasch@packt:~/Learn-Scala---Fundamentals-of-Scala-2.13/ch11$ sbt       [info] Loading project definition from /home/slasch/Learn-Scala--
[info] Loading project definition from /home/slasch/Learn-Scala--       -Fundamentals-of-Scala-2.13/ch11/project
-Fundamentals-of-Scala-2.13/ch11/project                                [info] Loading settings for project ch11 from build.sbt ...
[info] Loading settings for project ch11 from build.sbt ...             [info] Set current project to akka-bakery (in build file:/home/sl
[info] Set current project to akka-bakery (in build file:/home/sl       asch/Learn-Scala---Fundamentals-of-Scala-2.13/ch11/)
asch/Learn-Scala---Fundamentals-of-Scala-2.13/ch11/)                    [info] sbt server started at local:///home/slasch/.sbt/1.0/server
[warn] sbt server could not start because there's another instanc       /7bde7a4d263e73d9ff87/sock
e of sbt running on this build.                                         sbt:akka-bakery> [info] new client connected: network-1
[warn] Running multiple instances is unsupported                        run
sbt:akka-bakery> run                                                    [warn] Multiple main classes detected.  Run 'show discoveredMainC
[warn] Multiple main classes detected.  Run 'show discoveredMainC       lasses' to see the list
lasses' to see the list
                                                                        Multiple main classes detected, select one to run:
Multiple main classes detected, select one to run:
                                                                           [1] ch11.Bakery
   [1] ch11.Bakery                                                         [2] ch11.Store
   [2] ch11.Store
                                                                        Enter number: 2
Enter number: 1  ◄──────── Enter "1" to start Shop
                                                                        [info] Running ch11.Store
[info] Running ch11.Bakery                                              [INFO] [09/29/2018 19:54:17.938] [run-main-0] [akka.remote.Remoti
[INFO] [09/29/2018 19:54:31.443] [run-main-0] [akka.remote.Remoti       ng] Starting remoting
ng] Starting remoting                                                   [INFO] [09/29/2018 19:54:18.408] [run-main-0] [akka.remote.Remoti
[INFO] [09/29/2018 19:54:31.921] [run-main-0] [akka.remote.Remoti       ng] Remoting started; listening on addresses :[akka.tcp://Store@1
ng] Remoting started; listening on addresses :[akka.tcp://Bakery@       27.0.0.1:2553]
127.0.0.1:2552]                                                         [INFO] [09/29/2018 19:54:18.412] [run-main-0] [akka.remote.Remoti
[INFO] [09/29/2018 19:54:31.922] [run-main-0] [akka.remote.Remoti       ng] Remoting now listens on addresses: [akka.tcp://Store@127.0.0.
ng] Remoting now listens on addresses: [akka.tcp://Bakery@127.0.0       1:2553]
.1:2552]                                                                [WARN] [SECURITY][09/29/2018 19:54:34.080] [Store-akka.remote.def
[WARN] [SECURITY][09/29/2018 19:54:33.850] [Bakery-akka.remote.de       ault-remote-dispatcher-6] [akka.serialization.Serialization(akka:
fault-remote-dispatcher-6] [akka.serialization.Serialization(akka       //Store)] Using the default Java serializer for class [ch11.Mixer
://Bakery)] Using the default Java serializer for class [ch11.Man       SGroceries] which is not recommended because of performance impli
ager$ShoppingList] which is not recommended because of performanc       cations. Use another serializer or disable this warning using the
e implications. Use another serializer or disable this warning us       setting 'akka.actor.warn-about-java-serializer-usage'
ing the setting 'akka.actor.warn-about-java-serializer-usage'           ]
```

The store side reflects that the connection was established and the bakery side starts to output log statements about current activities. It keeps running and logging what is happening until stopped by pressing *Ctrl + C*.

Summary

Let's recap what we've learned in this chapter.

Current scaling demands are hard to meet using traditional approaches. The actor model with its shared nothing paradigm offers a solution to this problem. Akka is a library for building actor-based applications on the JVM.

Actors communicate by sending and receiving messages and change their internal state and produce side-effects in response. Each actor has an address in the form of an `ActorRef`, which also encapsulates ab actor's mailbox and a dispatcher. Actors are organized into hierarchies where parent actors are responsible for the supervision of their children.

Actors have a well-defined life cycle and implement a number of methods, which are called at appropriate moments during their lifetimes.

Akka provides additional modules that extend provided functionality even further.

We also looked at Akka FSM, which gives us the possibility to represent an actor as an FSM by encoding its possible states and state transitions.

Akka remoting implements the location transparency principle in practice and allows you to access remote Akka systems easily.

Testing actors is different from testing regular code. Akka `TestKit` is a library that's provided by the Akka team, which simplifies and streamlines the testing process. It does so by placing a tested actor in a controlled—but close to the real—environment.

In the next chapter, we will rebuild our bakery using different actor-based approach and different Akka library—Akka Typed.

Questions

- Name two ways in which an actor can change itself in response to the received message.
- What is the purpose of `ActorRef`?
- Lookup is in the official documentation description of the system guardian. What is the main purpose of it?
- What are the advantages and disadvantages of using Akka FSM?
- In how many ways can an actor in another actor system be accessed? Describe them.
- Why does testing actors require a special toolkit?

Further reading

- Christian Baxter, *Mastering Akka*: Master the art of creating scalable, concurrent, and reactive applications using Akka.
- Héctor Veiga Ortiz and Piyush Mishra, *Akka Cookbook*: Learn how to use the Akka framework to build effective applications in Scala.

12
Building Reactive Applications with Akka Typed

This chapter reveals another way to build reactive applications with Akka. We will introduce Akka Typed, an Akka module which implements the actor model in a slightly different way compared to untyped Akka. We will contrast *classical* and typed approaches and show how the latter reduces the developer's choices but increases type safety and simplifies reasoning about actor-based programs during the maintenance phase.

The following topics will be covered in this chapter:

- Differences between typed and untyped approaches
- Creating, stopping, and discovering actors
- The life cycle of an actor and supervision
- Schedulers
- Stashing
- Combining behaviors
- Testing

Technical requirements

Before we begin, make sure you have the following installed:

- Java 1.8+
- SBT 1.2+

The source code for this chapter is available on our GitHub repository at: `https://github.com/PacktPublishing/Learn-Scala-Programming/tree/master/Chapter12`.

The code snippets in this chapter have been simplified a bit to omit unnecessary technical details. Please refer to the GitHub repository for fully functioning examples.

Introduction

In `Chapter 11`, *An Introduction to the Akka and Actor Models*, we discovered the actor model and how Akka implements it.

The original actor paper states three possible actions that actors can perform as computational units:

- They can send messages to other known actors
- They can create new actors
- They can designate behavior for future message processing

Because of the universality of this model, the specifics of how these points are to be implemented depends on the hardware, operating system, programming language, existing libraries, and ultimately on the design choices of the implementer. Akka Typed offers a slightly different programming model compared to untyped Akka.

 Furthermore, in this chapter, we'll refer to normal Akka as Akka untyped to be specific about which library is being mentioned, even though *untyped* Akka was always named just *Akka* in the previous chapter.

Let's take a closer look at the differences and similarities between the two implementations.

The typed approach and the differences between Akka untyped

Compared to the untyped version, Akka Typed takes a slightly different approach to define what an actor is.

In Akka untyped, an actor is any object that is a subclass of an abstract `Actor` and overrides a `def receive: PartialFunction[Any, Unit]` method. This allows the developer to do anything in the implementation except return a meaningful result, which makes it hard to reason about the code and impossible to combine actor logic.

Akka Typed declares that any well-defined behavior is a computation entity and thus can be declared to be an actor. The *well-defined* in terms of Akka Typed means anything that defines a statically typed `Behavior`. The type of `Behavior` limits actors to receiving messages of this specific type only. The return type of the actor's behavior is required to be the next `Behavior` of the same type with respect to inheritance. This way, it is possible to ensure at compile time that the actor will receive only messages of the type it declares to handle.

In order to achieve this, actor addresses also need to be typed, and the type of address needs to be known at compile time. Hence, features of untyped Akka such as implicit access to the sender of the present message and general actor lookup are not available in typed Akka. By contrast, actor's addresses need to be defined as part of the protocol or need to be managed by an external (to the actor) facility.

Another notable change is the introduction of `Signal` message types, which represent events in the life cycle of an actor and replace dedicated callback methods that were exposed by the `Actor` class in untyped Akka. Although this is not a very big spot in a whole picture of changes, it is a good move to make the implementation of Akka's actor model closer to the abstract actor model.

In short, Akka Typed restricts actor communication and behavior to the model, which can then be type checked at compile time. This limits the developer's choices and possibilities for the implementation, but at the same time makes the result easier to reason about and test. The unavailability of some untyped features makes it impossible to write code in a way that represents an Akka anti-pattern and leads to solutions resembling what are considered to be the best practices in *normal* Akka.

This module is currently marked as **may change** (https://doc.akka.io/ docs/akka/2.5/common/may-change.html). This reflects the fact that the topic itself is the subject of active research and there might be some changes in the API. However, the current implementation is solid and changes in the API are minimal among recent version updates. Therefore, the Akka team considers Akka Typed to be production-ready.

Let's take a look at what these differences look like in practice.

Example actor system

To illustrate features of Akka Typed, we'll reimplement an example we built in `Chapter 11`, *An Introduction to the Akka and Actor Models*, but this time with typed actors.

For those readers who are familiar with the content of the previous chapter, this approach will allow you to compare two different styles. For those who just joined, let's quickly recap the structure of this example.

We're building a small cookie bakery which is populated by a number of actors, each with their own set of responsibilities:

- The Manager drives the process and passes over materials from one worker to another.
- The Boy takes a ShoppingList and returns to the Manager the respective Groceries from the Store.
- The Chef takes the Groceries and makes them into Dough. It does so by using a number of Mixers with the exact mixer count depending on the amount of stuff to mix.
- The Cook takes Dough and makes RawCookies.
- The Baker bakes the RawCookies in batches using a single Oven of a limited capacity.

The structure of the actor system we're going to build is represented in the following diagram:

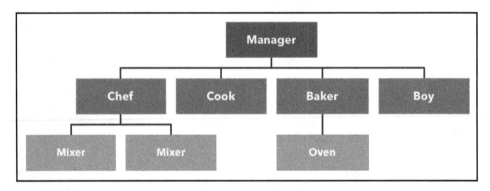

Let's start with an implementation of the simplest actor in our system – the **Oven**. Here and later on in this chapter, we'll refer to the previous implementation, meaning the implementation we came up with in regards to untyped actors in Chapter 11, *An Introduction to the Akka and Actor Models*. The differences are very illustrative, so we advise the reader to refer to the code in the previous chapter, even if you haven't read it because you are already familiar with untyped Akka.

To be able to use Akka `Typed` in our code, we need to put the following dependency in
`build.sbt`:

```
lazy val akkaVersion = "2.5.13"
libraryDependencies += "com.typesafe.akka" %% "akka-actor-typed" %
akkaVersion
```

Defining `akkaVersion` separately as a `val` has the advantage that it can be reused for other
modules and changed in a single place at the moment a new version becomes available.

To keep our examples clean and short, we'll assume that the following inputs are present in
every code snippet:

```
import akka.actor.typed._
import akka.actor.typed.scaladsl._
```

The first input brings lower level actor system abstractions into scope, and the second
allows us to use higher level DSL for an actor's behavior definition.

First example

First, we need to define the protocol that our `Oven` will speak. In contrast to the untyped
implementation, we can't reuse messages that are defined by another actor. The reason for
this is that the `Oven` (and other actors at later stages) defines the type of messages it is
supposed to handle. This type should not be too general in order to avoid making the
whole implementation less typed than desirable.

The domain model is common for all actors, so we'll define it on the `Bakery` app level:

```
final case class Groceries(eggs: Int, flour: Int, sugar: Int, chocolate:
Int)
final case class Dough(weight: Int)
final case class RawCookies(count: Int)
final case class ReadyCookies(count: Int)
```

And this is the small language our `Oven` speaks:

```
sealed trait Command
case class Put(rawCookies: Int, sender: ActorRef[Baker.Command]) extends
Command
case class Extract(sender: ActorRef[Baker.Command]) extends Command
```

The Oven can return ReadyCookies (a cookie is considered to be ready as soon as it has been put into the oven) and RawCookies in the case where there are more cookies in the Put command than can fit inside the oven. The Command is a type of behavior for our actor. We can see that it includes the sender field so that the oven knows who is the receiver of the extracted cookies.

Now, we need to define the actor's behavior. If you followed the previous chapter, you will remember that we used the internal mutable field to store the contents of the oven in the current moment. By using this field, we can differentiate its reaction on incoming messages. Akka Typed urges us to exercise a different approach and use separate behaviors for different states of the actor. First, we define what should happen in the case that there is nothing inside:

```
def empty: Behaviors.Receive[Command] = Behaviors.receiveMessage[Command] {
  case Put(rawCookies, sender) =>
    val (inside, overflow: Option[RawCookies]) = insert(rawCookies)
    overflow.foreach(sender.tell)
    full(inside)
}
```

Here, we define a behavior of the empty Oven using the Behaviors factory. In our case, this is a receiveMessage method with a type parameter called Command. This designates the type of messages our actor can handle.

Next, we define a course of action in the case of the incoming Put command. The insert method returns a number of cookies that we can put inside the Oven and an optional overflow. In this case, if there is an overflow, we return it to the sender by using the tell method of its ActorRef[Cookies]. The type of reference allows us to send RawCookies back. Because of the type-safe nature of the actor definition, this binds the behavior of the Baker actor (that we'll implement soon) to be Behaviors.Receive[Cookies].

Now, we need to define what should happen in the case that the Oven is not empty:

```
def full(count: Int): Behaviors.Receive[Command] =
Behaviors.receiveMessage[Command] {
  case Extract(sender) =>
    sender ! ReadyCookies(count)
    empty
}
```

This Behavior is even simpler, but still has the same type—Behaviors.Receive[Command]. We just return all of the cookies that were inside to the sender and change the future behavior to the empty behavior we defined earlier.

Now, if we compile this implementation, we'll get complaints from the compiler:

```
Warning: (18, 77) match may not be exhaustive.
 It would fail on the following input: Extract(_)
 def empty: Behaviors.Receive[Command] = Behaviors.receiveMessage[Command]
{
 Warning: (25, 88) match may not be exhaustive.
 It would fail on the following input: Put(_, _)
 def full(count: Int): Behaviors.Receive[Command] =
Behaviors.receiveMessage[Command] {
```

The compiler has helped us to identify our first two bugs already! The reason it is unhappy with the current implementation is that we forgot to define a reaction to the messages that are *inappropriate* in specific states. This will be an attempt to extract cookies from the empty oven and to put something into the full one. From the type perspective, this is possible, and the compiler informed us of this.

Let's fix this by implementing our states properly:

This is the augmented definition of an `empty` state:

```
def empty: Behaviors.Receive[Command] = Behaviors.receiveMessage[Command] {
  case Put(rawCookies, sender) =>
    val (inside, tooMuch) = insert(rawCookies)
    tooMuch.foreach(sender.tell)
    full(inside)
  case Extract(sender) =>
    sender ! ReadyCookies(0)
    Behaviors.same
}
```

The sender will be sent zero cookies, and we keep current behavior by using
`Behavior.same`.

The principle stays the same for the `full` case:

```
def full(count: Int): Behaviors.Receive[Command] =
Behaviors.receiveMessage[Command] {
  case Extract(sender) =>
    sender ! ReadyCookies(count)
    empty
  case Put(rawCookies, sender) =>
    sender ! RawCookies(rawCookies)
    Behaviors.same
}
```

Again, we just returned to the sender everything we've got and kept the current behavior exactly like we did in the empty case.

Akka Typed basics

Now that we've made the compiler happy and got our first impression about how typed actors tick, let's take a more principled approach and look in detail at how they can be created, discovered, and stopped, and what possibilities there are to change an actor's behavior.

Creating an actor

In accordance to the actor model definition, there is exactly one way that an actor can be created—it can be spawned by another actor. Akka gives you two slightly different possibilities to do this by using `ActorContext`. Both methods are not thread safe and should only be used directly within the actor's thread.

The first variant allows you to instantiate an anonymous actor from a behavior and returns an `ActorRef[T]`:

```
def spawnAnonymous[T](behavior: Behavior[T], props: Props = Props.empty):
ActorRef[T]
```

This implementation provides a default empty value for the props parameter so that the actual call can be reduced to `spawnAnonymous(behavior)`.

Not naming actors might be useful in specific situations, but it is considered to be a bad practice in general. This is because it makes debugging harder and looking up children by name impossible without relying on the current implementation details of the library.

Thus, another realization should be preferred whenever it makes sense to use one:

```
def spawn[T](behavior: Behavior[T], name: String, props: Props =
Props.empty): ActorRef[T]
```

Here, we're required to provide a behavior and a name for an actor, which is about to be instantiated.

Both `spawn` and `spawnAnonymous` accept a `props` parameter, which can be used to further configure an actor instance. As of now, it is only possible to configure an actor's dispatcher.

Dispatchers make up the machinery that runs behaviors. Dispatchers use `ExecutorServices` to assign threads to actors and can be configured as described in `Chapter 11`, *An Introduction to the Akka and Actor Models*. Currently, Akka Typed only supports the dispatchers definition from the configuration. Properties of the default dispatcher can be changed by overriding the settings under `akka.actor.default-dispatcher`.

In our example system, the `Chef` actor should instantiate `Mixers` as being required to work with big chunks of work in parallel. In addition, mixers use blocking code because of the limitations of hardware and therefore need separate dispatchers in order to avoid thread starvation for the rest of the system. Let's look at how this behavior can be implemented.

First, by using `application.conf`, we configure a dispatcher that will be used for blocking mixers:

```
mixers-dispatcher {
   executor = "thread-pool-executor"
   type = PinnedDispatcher
}
```

Then, we instantiate the required number of child actors:

```
object Chef {
   sealed trait Command
   final case class Mix(g: Groceries, manager: ActorRef[Manager.Command])
extends Command
   def idle = Behaviors.receive[Command] {
      case (context, mix@Mix(Groceries(eggs, flour, sugar, chocolate),
manager)) =>
      val props = DispatcherSelector.fromConfig("mixers-dispatcher")
      val mixers = for (i <- 1 to eggs) yield
         context.spawn(Mixer.mix, s"Mixer_$i", props)
      mixing
   }
   def mixing = Behaviors.unhandled[Command]i
}
```

The `Chef` actor has its own hierarchy of commands which we, for now, limit to `Mix`. We need a separate `Mixer` for each egg, so we instantiate them by using `spawn`. `spawn` returns an actor reference and we collect them in the `mixers val`. Finally, we return the next actor's `Behavior`, which for now is `unhandled`.

OK, so it's possible to create new actors from an actor's context. This brings us to a **Zeno's paradox** kind of situation with Achilles and the tortoise. Naturally, to create a new actor, we need to have an actor already. Akka solves this paradox by requiring the developer to provide a definition of a root actor at the moment an actor system is created:

```
def apply[T](guardian: Behavior[T],name: String): ActorSystem[T]
```

This leaves the developer with no choice but to design a proper actor hierarchy top-down. Following this typed approach automatically leads to avoidance of the *flat actor hierarchy* anti-pattern!

There is another possibility for instantiating an actor. This can be done by using the `ActorSystem`'s `systemActorOf` method, which creates an actor in the `/system` space. It is arguable that this feature shouldn't normally be used, and therefore it is not covered here.

Now, since our `Chef` spawned enough `Mixers` to do the job, we need a way to get rid of them after our work is complete.

Stopping an actor

An actor can be stopped in one of the following ways:

- By designating its next behavior to be `Behaviors.stopped`.
- By applying the `stop` method of the `ActorContext` to the immediate child. The child will finish processing the current message but leave other messages that are still in the mailbox unprocessed.
- By the actor system as it stops its ancestor. The actual shutdown happens recursively, bottom-up, following the hierarchy.

The most natural approach in our mixers example would be to pick the first option. We implement it in the following example:

```
object Mixer {
  final case class Mix(groceries: Groceries, sender: ActorRef[Collect])
  def mix = Behaviors.receiveMessage[Mix] {
    case Mix(Groceries(eggs, flour, sugar, chocolate), sender) =>
      Thread.sleep(3000)
      sender ! Collect(Dough(eggs * 50 + flour + sugar + chocolate))
      Behaviors.stopped
  }
}
```

The `Mixer` behavior is very simple, so we don't need to define an ADT for that and use the single `Mix` command directly. The `Chef` actor expects `Collect(Dough)` back. This obliges us to define it as a type parameter for the sender reference. The behavior itself simulates the hardware delay for the mixing to be finished, sends the prepared dough to the `Chef`, and returns `Behaviors.stopped` as the next behavior. This leads to the graceful termination of the `Mixer` actor.

Now that we've sent the dough back to the `Chef`, let's see how it is supposed to be handled. The `Chef` needs to collect the results from all of the mixers it has created. To do so, we could pass references to the child actors we've created in the idle state to the mixing behavior, but let's imagine we lost the references we collected for some reason. In this case, `Chef` could look up its children.

Discovering an actor

Actor discovery is an alternative way to obtain an actor reference. The preferred way is still to incorporate actor references into the message protocol.

Akka provides the possibility to look up a single child actor by name (only exact match) with the following method:

```
def child(name: String): Option[ActorRef[Nothing]]
```

This returns a reference to a child actor if a child with such a name exists and is alive. Please note that because of the return type of this method, the result needs to be coerced to the proper type by the use of the `narrow` method of `ActorRef`.

Another method that allows us to look up all of the children of an actor that are alive is as follows:

```
def children: Iterable[ActorRef[Nothing]]
```

The type of result is, again, a collection of `ActorRef`s with no particular type.

It is arguable that the lookup methods we have described here are of little use because of their basically untyped nature. Akka Typed offers a better alternative in the form of the `receptionist`.

The `receptionist` is a (cluster) singleton actor that is available on the actor system level and can be obtained from the `ActorContext` using the following call chain:

```
val receptionist: ActorRef[Receptionist.Command] =
context.system.receptionist
```

The receptionist is just an actor of type [Receptionist.Command], so let's investigate the Receptionist.Command type to understand what it is capable of.

There are three concrete implementations of the abstract Command class: Register, Find, and Subscribe.

Register is used for associating the given ActorRef with the provided ServiceKey. It is possible to register multiple references for the same key. The registration is automatically removed from the receptionist if the registered actor is stopped.

By providing an optional reference, it is possible to provide another actor, who should be notified if the service was successfully registered.

Find is a mechanism for asking the receptionist about all currently known registered actors for the given ServiceKey. The receptionist responds with a Set of known actor references (which are called **services**) that are registered to the given key, and a key itself wrapped in a Listing. Find can be used to implement one-time queries to the receptionist.

Subscribe is a way to implement push behavior for the receptionist. An actor can use subscribe to receive notifications about all added or removed services for some predefined key.

In our example, the Manager actor is used to provide a Boy with a reference to the seller actor. The Boy is supposed to communicate with the provided reference. In the previous chapter, we used untyped Akka's remote lookup to get this reference. In the typed environment, we will utilize the receptionist for this purpose.

This is how it is done.

First, the seller behavior needs to register itself with the receptionist at the moment it is initialized:

```
import akka.actor.typed.receptionist.Receptionist._

val SellerKey = ServiceKey[SellByList]("GrocerySeller")

val seller = Behaviors.setup { ctx ⇒
    ctx.system.receptionist ! Register(SellerKey, ctx.self)
    Behaviors.receiveMessage[SellByList] {
        case SellByList(list, toWhom) ⇒
          import list._
          toWhom ! Groceries(eggs, flour, sugar, chocolate)
          Behaviors.same
    }
}
```

The Shop defines the SellerKey that will be used by the actor to register as a service and by the service clients to look up the seller's reference.

Next, we introduce a new type of behavior constructor—Behaviors.setup. setup is a behavior factory. It takes the behavior constructor as a by-name parameter and creates the behavior at the moment the actor is started (as opposed to the moment the behavior is constructed). We need to use this factory for two reasons:

- We need our actor to be instantiated so that we can access its context
- We want our Seller to register itself exactly once

After registering the Seller with the receptionist, the real behavior is constructed. The behavior itself is just accepting the SellByList messages and responding with the Groceries that are to be provided to the toWhom reference.

On the opposite side of the receptionist, the Manager actor needs to look up the Seller and use its reference to guide the Boy:

```
def idle: Behavior[Command] = Behaviors.setup { context =>
  implicit val lookupTimeout: Timeout = 1.second
  context.ask(context.system.receptionist)(Find(Shop.SellerKey)) {
    case Success(listing: Listing) =>
      listing
        .serviceInstances(Shop.SellerKey)
        .headOption
        .map { seller =>
          LookupSeller(seller)
        }
        .getOrElse {
          NoSeller
        }
    case Failure(_) =>
      NoSeller
  }
}
```

There is quite a bit going on here. Once again, we're using setup to define the behavior.

Looking up actors is an asynchronous operation, and in this case, we utilize the ask pattern to keep the code concise. Ask needs to know how long it is allowed to wait for the answer, so, in the second line, we define a lookupTimeout.

Then, we call the `ask` method that's available in the actor context and provide a reference of a `receptionist` as an actor to be asked. The second parameter is the receptionist's `Find` command, which is given a seller key. Normally, the `Find` command takes a second parameter that defines a receiver for the response, but as it is used quite often together with `ask`, there is a special constructor that allows for the nice syntax we are using in this snippet.

The case literal, which comes next, defines a transformation that must be applied to the response before actually sending it back to the asking actor. It deconstructs and converts the receptionist's response so that it is either a `NoSeller` or just one `OneSeller`.

Next, we have to deal with the converted response by defining a behavior which is returned as a result of this lengthy factory method:

```
Behaviors.receiveMessagePartial {
  case OneSeller(seller) =>
    val boy = context.spawn(Boy.goShopping, "Boy")
    boy ! GoShopping(shoppingList, seller, context.self)
    waitingForGroceries
  case NoSeller =>
    context.log.error("Seller could not be found")
    idle
}
```

In the current manager's behavior, we only expect a small subset of all of the possible messages to arrive. We're using `receiveMessagePartial` to avoid compiler warnings for unhandled message types.

In this case, if there is no seller, we can use the `log` that's available in the actor's `context` to report this condition and return the current behavior.

In this case, if there is a `Seller` available, we instantiate a `Boy` and use it to transfer a `shoppingList` to this seller. Note how we used `context.self` as a second parameter for the `GoShopping` message. By doing this, we're making it possible to use the provided manager's reference to persuade the `Seller` to send groceries directly to the `Manager`, and then the `Boy` can immediately stop itself after sending the message:

```
object Boy {
  final case class GoShopping(shoppingList: ShoppingList,
                              seller: ActorRef[SellByList],
                              manager: ActorRef[Manager.Command])

  val goShopping = Behaviors.receiveMessage[GoShopping] {
    case GoShopping(shoppingList, seller, manager) =>
      seller ! SellByList(shoppingList, manager)
```

```
        Behaviors.stopped
    }
}
```

Here, we have seen how the `GoShopping` command prohibits us from interchanging actor references for the seller and manager, as this could easily happen in the case of untyped Akka.

Akka Typed – beyond the basics

We've defined the behavior of the `Chef` actor to distribute work across mixers but left the waiting part uncovered, so let's look at that now.

We left the `Chef` definition for the `mixing` behavior as follows:

```
def mixing = Behaviors.unhandled[Command]
```

Actually, the `Chef` needs to know about the mixers that were created by its `idle` behavior. Though technically it is possible to do a children lookup, as described earlier, doing so will introduce an implicit assumption that, at the moment, we'll get the listing stating that all of the mixers are still processing jobs. This assumption might be wrong in a highly concurrent environment or in the case of failed mixers.

Therefore, we need to refactor the behavior constructor a bit:

```
def mixing(mixers: Set[ActorRef[Mixer.Mix]],
           collected: Int,
           manager: ActorRef[Manager.Command]): Behavior[Command]
```

Now, we have a builder that captures all of the parts of the Chef's state. Let's see how these parts are used in the definition of its behavior:

```
Behaviors.receivePartial {
  case (context, Collect(dough, mixer)) =>
    val mixersToGo = mixers - mixer
    val pastryBuf = collected + dough.weight
    context.stop(mixer)
    if (mixersToGo.isEmpty) {
      manager ! ReceivePastry(Dough(pastryBuf))
      idle
    } else {
      mixing(mixersToGo, pastryBuf, manager)
    }
}
```

We're already familiar with the constructor. In the behavior itself, we count every `Dough` message received from the mixer and recreate the behavior with the new state. In this case, if all of the mixers have delivered their parts, we return the result to the manager and go to the `idle` state.

Life cycle of an actor

Our implementation of the `Mixer` is quite naive and does not take into account that hardware occasionally breaks.

Conventionally, in Akka, we distinguish between expected and unexpected failures. An expected failure of some operation, for example, a validation error is usually represented on the protocol level with the appropriate message types. Exceptional conditions of an unexpected nature such as hardware errors, are communicated by throwing exceptions. This allows you to separate handler definitions for successful and erroneous paths, which leads to the separation of business logic from the technical details of the underlying platform. Thus, having a rich set of exceptions is a prerequisite for proper error-handling definitions.

Let's take this aspect into account. We'll represent unreliable hardware by defining a set of exceptions, one for every possible failure. We'll do this the same way as we did in `Chapter 11`, *An Introduction to the Actor Model and Akka*:

```
class MotorOverheatException extends Exception
class SlowRotationSpeedException extends Exception
class StrongVibrationException extends Exception
```

Now, in order to simulate the hardware failure, we'll add some code with the purpose of throwing defined exceptions to the logic of the `Mixer`. To keep the example simple, let's just throw one of them:

```
case (_, Mix(Groceries(eggs, flour, sugar, chocolate), sender)) =>
  if (Random.nextBoolean()) throw new MotorOverheatException
  ...
```

It looks like it is very warm in our bakery. The mixer motors are overheating roughly every second time the `Chef` tries to mix the `Groceries`.

Actors can watch themselves by calling the `receiveSignal` method on the actor's context and providing a `PartialFunction[(ActorContext[T], Signal), Behavior[T]]` as a parameter. The provided partial function will be called, with a life cycle message as a parameter, if the actor terminates or restarts.

This possibility for self-watching can be useful to change the behavior of the actor in appropriate cases. The following code snippet shows how mixers can monitor themselves:

```
val monitoring: PartialFunction[(ActorContext[Mix], Signal), Behavior[Mix]]
= {
  case (ctx, PostStop) =>
    ctx.log.info("PostStop {}", context.self)
    Behaviors.same
  case (context, PreRestart) =>
    ctx.log.info("PreRestart {}", context.self)
    Behaviors.same
  case (context, t: Terminated) =>
    ctx.log.info("Terminated {} while {}", context.self, t.failure)
    Behaviors.same
}
```

In our case, mixers just write into the log what kind of life-changing event had happened and keep the same behavior. To take a look at the situations in which `PostStop`, `PreRestart`, and `Terminated` events happen, we first need to become familiar with the concept of supervision.

Supervision

In essence, supervision in Akka Typed refers to the fact that all exceptions thrown from a behavior are caught and acted upon. An action can have one of three forms: resume, restart, and stop.

Let's see how supervision can be defined and which effect it has.

First, let's run our system as it is and observe its output:

```
...
[INFO] Opening Bakery
[INFO] Go shopping to Actor[akka://Typed-Bakery/user/Seller#1376187311]
[INFO] Mixing Groceries(13,650,130,65)
[ERROR] [akka://Typed-Bakery/user/Chef/Mixer_5] null
  ch12.Mixer$MotorOverheatException
  at ch12.Mixer$.$anonfun$mix$1(Mixer.scala:19)
  at
akka.actor.typed.internal.BehaviorImpl$ReceiveBehavior.receive(BehaviorImpl
.scala:73)
  ...
  at java.lang.Thread.run(Thread.java:745)
[INFO] PostStop Actor[akka://Typed-Bakery/user/Chef/Mixer_5#-1604172140]
  ...
```

We can see how our actors start processing messages up to the point where an exception is thrown by the `Mixer`. This exception is handled using the default supervision strategy that is stopping the actor. The mixer logs the `PostStop` event via the monitoring function we defined earlier and attaches it to the actor's behavior, like so:

```
def mix: Behavior[Mix] = Behaviors.receive[Mix] {
  ...
}.receiveSignal(monitoring)
```

Let's see what will happen if we override the default supervision strategy. To change the behavior, we just wrap it into the supervising behavior by using the standard constructor. Let's restart the mixer instead of stopping it in the case of the motor overheating:

```
val controlledMix: Behavior[Mix] =
  Behaviors
    .supervise(mix)
    .onFailure[MotorOverheatException](SupervisorStrategy.restart)
```

If we use this behavior by using the `Chef` actor to create mixers, running the app will produce a slightly different output:

```
  ...
  [INFO] Mixing Groceries(6,300,60,30)
  [ERROR] Supervisor [restart] saw failure: null
      ch12.Mixer$MotorOverheatException
      at ch12.Mixer$.$anonfun$mix$1(Mixer.scala:29)
  ...
[INFO] PreRestart Actor[akka://Typed-Bakery/user/Chef/Mixer_2#-1626989026]
[INFO] PreRestart Actor[akka://Typed-Bakery/user/Chef/Mixer_4#-668414694]
[INFO] PreRestart Actor[akka://Typed-Bakery/user/Chef/Mixer_4#-668414694]
```

Now, the exception has been reported by the supervisor and the mixers have been restarted, as we can conclude by observing the `PreRestart` events that have been logged by the mixers. There is no `PostStop` event here.

There is still one more supervision strategy to look at, so let's check it out:

```
val controlledMix: Behavior[Mix] =
  Behaviors
    .supervise(mix)
    .onFailure[MotorOverheatException](SupervisorStrategy.resume)
```

With this strategy, we'll still see a log output from the supervisor, but actors won't log any life cycle events:

```
  ...
  [INFO] Mixing Groceries(5,250,50,25)
```

```
[ERROR] Supervisor [resume] saw failure: null
    ch12.Mixer$MotorOverheatException
    at ch12.Mixer$.$anonfun$mix$1(Mixer.scala:29)
...
```

It is possible to define different supervision strategies for different types of exceptions that are thrown by the same behavior by nesting supervisor constructors:

```
val controlledMix: Behavior[Mix] =
  Behaviors.supervise(
  Behaviors.supervise(
  Behaviors.supervise(
        mix)
.onFailure[MotorOverheatException(SupervisorStrategy.stop))
.onFailure[SlowRotationSpeedException(SupervisorStrategy.restart))
.onFailure[StrongVibrationException](SupervisorStrategy.resume)
```

The definition is obviously a bit verbose.

The supervision strategies are sticky. They are recursively applied to new behaviors that are returned by the supervised behavior.

Sometimes, it might be useful to try and restart an actor a few times, and if the situation is not improving, then finally stop it. A special constructor is available for this:

```
Behaviors.supervise(mix).onFailure[SlowRotationSpeedException](
  SupervisorStrategy.restartWithLimit(
    maxNrOfRetries = 4,
    withinTimeRange = 2.seconds))
```

In an unlucky case, the mixer actor would throw an exception from the `Behavior.setup` constructor every time it was constructed, and we would see the following output:

```
...
  [INFO] Mixing Groceries(6,300,60,30)
  [ERROR] Supervisor [restartWithLimit(4, 2.000 s)] saw failure: null
  ch12.Mixer$MotorOverheatException
  at ch12.Mixer$.$anonfun$mix$1(Mixer.scala:26)
  ...
  [ERROR] Supervisor [restartWithLimit(4, 2.000 s)] saw failure: null
  ...
  [ERROR] Supervisor [restartWithLimit(4, 2.000 s)] saw failure: null
  ...
  [ERROR] Supervisor [restartWithLimit(4, 2.000 s)] saw failure: null
  ...
  [ERROR] [akka://Typed-Bakery/user/Chef/Mixer_1] null
  akka.actor.ActorInitializationException: akka://Typed-
  Bakery/user/Chef/Mixer_1: exception during creation at
```

```
akka.actor.ActorInitializationException$.apply(Actor.scala:193)
  . . .
 Caused by: ch12.Mixer$MotorOverheatException at
ch12.Mixer$.$anonfun$mix$1(Mixer.scala:26)
  . . .
 [INFO] Message [ch12.Mixer$Mix] without sender to Actor[akka://Typed-
Bakery/user/Chef/Mixer_1#-263229034] was not delivered.
```

The supervisor tried to restart the actor four times, but then gave up and stopped it. Because of the fact that the failure happened in the setup block, the actor was able to receive neither the `Mix` command nor life cycle event notifications.

Watching an actor

If we look back to the `Chef` actor's implementation, we'll be able to see that our system is now stuck. This happened because, if mixers fail, they are stopped by an external supervising force. However, the `Chef` actor is still waiting for this mixer's part to work. It turns out that we need a way to inform the `Chef` about terminated mixers.

Akka Typed offers a watching mechanism for this. To watch for mixers that were stopped, we'll add the following code to the `Chef`:

```
val mixers = for (i <- 1 to eggs)
  yield context.spawn(Mixer.controlledMix, s"Mixer_$i")
mixers.foreach(mixer => context.watchWith(mixer, BrokenMixer(mixer)))
```

Here, for each spawned `Mixer`, we're calling `context.watchWith`. The first parameter is an actor to watch and the second parameter is a message adapter. The need for the message adapter comes from the fact that the *proper* message type for the terminated actor would be `akka.actor.typed.Terminated`. We could use a watch, taking just a single actor reference, to subscribe to this message type—`def watch[T](other: ActorRef[T]): Unit`.

But, the fact is that our `Chef` can't handle this message type because it does not belong to its `Command` type. Therefore, we would need to define a separate actor type to watch for mixer terminations. Instead, we need to use the *extended* version of the watch method, which takes a message to be sent as a second parameter. The `BrokenMixer` message is defined and handled as follows:

```
case class BrokenMixer(mixer: ActorRef[Mixer.Mix]) extends Command

def mixing(...): Behavior[Command] = Behaviors.receivePartial {
  . . .
```

```
      case (context, BrokenMixer(m)) =>
        context.log.warning("Broken mixer detected {}", m)
        context.self ! Collect(Dough(0), m)
        Behaviors.same
  }
```

In this case, if we detect a terminated child actor, the Chef writes a log entry and sends itself a message to compensate for the lost part of the work.

Now, we have the Dough ready and need a Cook to form cookies and a Baker to bake them in the Oven. The implementation of the Cook is trivial—it just converts Dough into a number of RawCookies and sends them back to the manager. Please refer to the code in the GitHub repository if you're interested in the implementation details.

Timers

The Baker is more interesting. First of all, it needs a single Oven. We'll implement this by using a special behavior that we'll execute only once:

```
def turnOvenOn: Behavior[Command] = Behaviors.setup { context =>
  val oven = context.spawn(Oven.empty, "Oven")
  idle(oven)
}
```

Now, let's define the idle behavior that's just waiting for work:

```
def idle(oven: ActorRef[Oven.Command]): Behavior[Command] =
  Behaviors.receivePartial {
    case (context, BakeCookies(rawCookies, manager)) =>
      oven ! Put(rawCookies.count, context.self)
      Behaviors.withTimers { timers =>
        timers.startSingleTimer(TimerKey, CheckOven, DefaultBakingTime)
        baking(oven, manager)
      }
  }
```

Here, we expect a message from the manager telling us to bake cookies. Then, we use a new behavior constructor, withTimers, which gives us access to the TimerScheduler. With the scheduler, it is possible to define periodic and single timers that have been identified by some key. The definition of a new timer with the same key cancels the previously defined timer and also removes messages that have been sent by it, if they are still in the message box of the actor.

Here, we're using the timer as a kitchen clock to set up a single reminder to check the `Oven` after baking time passes.

Stashing

Another challenge is that the `Baker` needs to accept `RawCookies` from the `Manager` as required, but needs to bake them in batches because of the oven's limited capacity. Basically, it needs to manage a queue of the `RawCookies`.

We'll implement this by using a stash. By using stashing, our actor will buffer messages that cannot be handled by the current behavior and replay them before switching to the alternative behavior in which buffered messages are supposed to be handled.

Let's see how this approach is reflected in the baking behavior of the actor:

```
def baking(oven: ActorRef[Oven.Command],
           manager: ActorRef[Manager.Command]): Behavior[Command] =
  Behaviors.setup[Command] { context =>
    val buffer = StashBuffer[Command](capacity = 100)
    Behaviors.receiveMessage {
      case CheckOven =>
        oven ! Extract(context.self)
        Behaviors.same
      case c: TooManyCookies=>
        buffer.stash(BakeCookies(c.raw, manager))
        Behaviors.same
      case c : BakeCookies =>
        buffer.stash(c)
        Behaviors.same
      case CookiesReady(cookies) =>
        manager ! ReceiveReadyCookies(cookies)
        buffer.unstashAll(context, idle(oven))
    }
  }
```

First, we define a buffer that will contain our stashed messages.

 The stash is keeping messages in memory. By stashing too many messages, it is possible to crash the system with an `OutOfMemory` error. The capacity parameter helps to avoid this situation. But, in the case that the specified capacity is too low, the `StashOverflowException` will be thrown after an attempt to stash a message into the full buffer.

Then, we handle four types of messages. `CheckOven` is a reminder that is sent to the `Baker` by the timer so that it does not forget to extract cookies from the `Oven`.

In the case of `TooManyCookies` (which is a message from the `Oven` returning cookies that did not fit into it) or `BakeCookies` being received from the manager, the `Baker` stashes them until it becomes idle again and is able to process baking work.

`CookiesReady` indicates that the `Oven` is now empty, so we forward the cookies to the `Manager`, unstash all of the messages, and go to the `idle` state.

Combining behaviors

Now that we have defined every worker in the bakery, it is time to finally get us a `Manager`. In `Chapter 11`, *An Introduction to the Akka and Actor Models*, we implemented a `Manager` using the FSM library. In Akka Typed, we can achieve the same effect without any libraries just by defining atomic behaviors for each state and then returning the appropriate behavior as required:

```
def waitingForGroceries = receiveMessagePartial[Command] {
  case ReceiveGroceries(g) =>
    context.log.info("Mixing {}", g)
    chef ! Chef.Mix(g, context.self)
    waitingForPastry
}
def waitingForPastry = receiveMessagePartial[Command] {
  case ReceivePastry(p) =>
    context.log.info("Forming {}", p)
    cook ! Cook.FormCookies(p, context.self)
    waitingForRawCookies
}
...
```

Here, we have defined two behaviors, and each of them expects a specific message type, performs the required message passing to the managed actors, and returns the next behavior in the chain. This way, it is possible to model the serial behavior we implemented with untyped Akka.

However, we can do better. Akka Typed allows us to combine behaviors so that we can implement a parallel version of the `Manager` by chaining behaviors together and returning the combined behavior from every atomic behavior we define:

```
def manage(chef: ActorRef[Chef.Command],
           cook: ActorRef[Cook.FormCookies],
           baker: ActorRef[Baker.Command]): Behavior[Command] =
```

```
  ...
  def sendBoyShopping = receiveMessagePartial ...
  def waitingForGroceries = receivePartial[Command] {
   ...
   manage(chef, cook, baker)
  }
  def waitingForPastry = receiveMessagePartial[Command] {
   ...
    manage(chef, cook, baker)
  }
  def waitingForRawCookies = receiveMessagePartial[Command] {
    case ReceiveRawCookies(c) =>
      baker ! Baker.BakeCookies(c, context.self)
      manage(chef, cook, baker)
  }
  def waitingForReadyCookies = receiveMessagePartial[Command] {
    case ReceiveReadyCookies(c) =>
      context.log.info("Done baking cookies: {}", c)
      manage(chef, cook, baker)
  }

  lookupSeller orElse
    sendBoyShopping orElse
    waitingForGroceries orElse
    waitingForPastry orElse
    waitingForRawCookies orElse
    waitingForReadyCookies
}
```

Here, the `manage` constructor is used to define atomic behaviors for each message type the `Manager` is supposed to be able to handle. Then, the existing behaviors are combined into one. This makes our `Manager` capable of processing every message in any processing state.

Cluster

The `Bakery` is now in place, but we would still like the grocery store to run as a separate actor system, just like we had it in the previous chapter. With untyped Akka, we implemented this communication with the help of remoting, but remoting is not available in the typed setup. With Akka Typed, we can achieve this with the help of clustering.

Akka clustering is a group of Akka systems working as a dynamic whole. This is the main difference from Akka remote, on top of which clustering is built. A single system represents one node from the cluster. An actor can exist anywhere in the cluster. Some of the features of clustering include load balancing (routing messages to specific nodes in the cluster), node partitioning (assigning specific roles to nodes), and cluster management (fault-tolerant node membership), to name a few. In our example, we don't use any advanced clustering features, and instead just throw it in an order so that we have the possibility to communicate with a remote actor system.

To be able to use clustering in our project, we need to add the following dependency to `build.sbt`:

```
"com.typesafe.akka" %% "akka-cluster-typed" % akkaVersion,
```

Clustering also requires that a few configuration parameters are defined. We can provide them by putting the following additional lines into `application.conf`. This will be the default configuration used by the `Bakery`:

```
akka {
  actor.provider = "cluster"
  remote {
    netty.tcp {
      hostname = "127.0.0.1"
      port = 2552
    }
  }
  cluster.seed-nodes = [
    "akka.tcp://Typed-Bakery@127.0.0.1:2553",
    "akka.tcp://Typed-Bakery@127.0.0.1:2552"
  ]
}
```

The configuration for the `Store` is defined by importing the default configuration and overriding the port definition:

```
include "application"
akka.remote.netty.tcp.port = 2553
```

Now, we need to instantiate an actor system for `Store`:

```
object Store extends App {
  val config = ConfigFactory.load("grocery.conf")
  val system = ActorSystem(seller, "Typed-Bakery", config)
}
```

And we need another one for the `Bakery` itself:

```
object Bakery extends App {
  ...
  val system = ActorSystem(Manager.openBakery, "Typed-Bakery")
}
```

Both of these defined actor systems can now be started and will simulate baking cookies by acquiring the required resources from the remote system via clustering.

We just demonstrated Akka's location transparency by turning a local actor system into clustered one just by changing the configuration.

Testing

Currently, we have a working `Bakery` implementation, but we cannot be sure that our actors are doing what we expect them to do. Let's fix this by testing their behavior.

Testing actors is notoriously difficult because of their concurrent nature and message orientation. Luckily, in Akka Typed, an actor's behavior is just a function and thus can generally be tested in isolation. There are cases where we might want to test the interaction between actors, and in this case, it is inevitable to resort to asynchronous testing.

In synchronous setup, we create a behavior under test, send events that it should be able to react on, and verify that the behavior produces the expected effects (for example, spawning or stopping child actors) and sends further required messages.

The asynchronous scenario brings this approach into the context of a test actor system, which is close to a real one. We will see how this is done in practice in a moment.

Dependencies and setup

To automate repetitive tasks such as setting up testing environments for actors, Akka Typed provides a test kit in the same way Akka untyped does. We need the following dependencies to be present in `build.sbt` so that we can use it within our project:

```
"com.typesafe.akka" %% "akka-actor-testkit-typed" % akkaVersion % Test,
"org.scalatest" %% "scalatest" % "3.0.5" % Test
```

Having both of them in scope will allow us to create `ScalaTest` specifications and use the Akka Typed test kit functionality.

As mentioned previously, in regards to synchronous actor testing, we do not need to have an `ActorSystem`. The only dependency, in this case, is an actor context. Akka provides a factory for building special testing actor contexts in the form of the `BehaviorTestKit`. A skeleton of the `ScalaTest` specification, in this case, could look as follows:

```
import akka.actor.testkit.typed.scaladsl.BehaviorTestKit
import org.scalatest.WordSpec

class SynchronousSpec extends WordSpec {

  "TestScenario" should {
    "have test conditions" in {
      val testKit = BehaviorTestKit(behaviorToTest)
      // ... testing logic
    }
  }
}
```

In the case of asynchronous testing, we have to extend the `ActorTestKit` to have a test actor system in the scope of the specification. This actor system needs to be shut down after all tests are finished running in order to prevent resource leakage. Because of this, the minimal specification in the case of asynchronous testing will look a bit more involved:

```
class AsyncronousSpec extends WordSpec with ActorTestKit with
BeforeAndAfterAll {

  override def afterAll: Unit = shutdownTestKit()
  // actual testing code
}
```

Now, it is time to look at the different features Akka `TestKit` has to offer to simplify checking the correctness of the actor-based system.

Synchronous testing

The `BehaviorTestKit` provides the possibility to verify the reaction of an actor behavior to specific messages. The reaction can be in the form of an `Effect` (different ways of spawning and stopping children actors), sending and receiving messages, and changes in behavior. Let's illustrate this testing process with an example:

```
"The boy should" should {
  "forward given ShoppingList to the seller" in {
    val testKit = BehaviorTestKit(Boy.goShopping)
    val seller = TestInbox[Shop.SellByList]()
    val manager = TestInbox[Manager.Command]()
```

```
            val list = ShoppingList(1, 1, 1, 1)
            testKit.run(GoShopping(list, seller.ref, manager.ref))
            seller.expectMessage(SellByList(list, manager.ref))
            assert(!testKit.isAlive)
            testKit.expectEffect(NoEffects)
        }
    }
```

Here, we have wrapped a `goShopping` behavior into the `BehaviorTestKit` so that we can test it synchronously. The two `TestInbox` references represent actors that the `Boy` is supposed to communicate with. They are basically `ActorRefs`, but they allow us to express expectations regarding incoming messages. To trigger the test, we can create a message and run the `testKit` using this message as an input.

In the next line, we expect the `seller` actor to receive the same message, with the `manager` reference being propagated as a sender. This is how our boy's logic is supposed to work. Then, we verify that the `Boy` stopped itself by checking that it is not alive. Finally, we don't expect any effects on children as the `Boy` actor is not supposed to have or create any children.

In the same way that we tested that the `Boy` has no effects on children, we can test that the `Chef` has such effects:

```
    "The chef should" should {
      "create and destroy mixers as required" in {
        val mixerFactory = Mixer.mix(0 seconds)
        val chef = BehaviorTestKit(Chef.idle(mixerFactory))
        val manager = TestInbox[Manager.Command]()
        val message = Mix(Groceries(1, 1, 1, 1), manager.ref)
        val dispatcher = DispatcherSelector.fromConfig("mixers-dispatcher")
        chef.run(message)
        chef.expectEffect(Spawned(mixerFactory, "Mixer_1", dispatcher))
        val expectedByMixer = Mixer.Mix(Groceries(1, 1, 1, 1), chef.ref)
        chef.childInbox("Mixer_1").expectMessage(expectedByMixer)
      }
    }
```

In this test, we create a behavior under test in the same way we just did with the `Boy` actor. We create a message and run it with the testing behavior wrapper. As a result, we expect a `chef` to have the effect of spawning a single `Mixer` actor with an appropriate name and dispatcher. Finally, we're looking up the mailbox of the spawned child actor by using the `childInbox` method and expect it to have a message that's been sent by the `chef` to be present in it.

Unfortunately, at the time of writing this book, the Akka `TestKist` still has some rough edges that require us, in this specific case, to refactor our `Chef` behavior to accept the mixer factory as a parameter. The reason for this is that behaviors are compared by reference, which requires us to have the same instance of the behavior for the test to pass.

Another limitation of the `BehaviorTestKit` is its lack of support for extensions like cluster, cluster singleton, distributed data, and receptionist. This makes it impossible to test the `Seller` actor in a synchronous setup because this actor registers itself with the receptionist:

```
context.system.receptionist ! Register(SellerKey, context.self)
```

We could use the synchronous approach or we could refactor the seller to take a constructor function for the receptionist and provide a mock receptionist in the test. This is an example of how this can be done in the code of the `Seller`:

```
type ReceptionistFactory = ActorContext[SellByList] =>
ActorRef[Receptionist.Command]
val systemReceptionist: ReceptionistFactory = _.system.receptionist
def seller(receptionist: ReceptionistFactory) = setup { ctx =>
    receptionist(ctx) ! Register(SellerKey, ctx.self)
. . .
```

The factory is just a function from `ActorContext` to the `ActorRef` with the appropriate types.

With this change, we can implement our test, as follows:

```
"A seller in the shop" should {
  "return groceries if given a shopping list" in {
    val receptionist = TestInbox[Receptionist.Command]()
    val mockReceptionist: Shop.ReceptionistFactory = _ => receptionist.ref
    val seller = BehaviorTestKit(Shop.seller(mockReceptionist))
    val inbox = TestInbox[Manager.Command]()
    val message = ShoppingList(1,1,1,1)
    seller.run(SellByList(message, inbox.ref))
    inbox.expectMessage(ReceiveGroceries(Groceries(1, 1, 1, 1)))
    receptionist.expectMessage(Register(Shop.SellerKey, seller.ref))
    seller.expectEffect(NoEffects)
  }
}
```

We provide a mock receptionist which is just a `TestInbox[Receptionist.Command]` and use it as the result of the factory, ignoring the actual actor context. Then, we execute the test as we did previously and expect the messages to be sent to the `manager` and `receptionist` appropriately.

Asynchronous testing

Synchronous testing is a good and deterministic way to test actor logic, but sometimes it is just not enough, for example, when testing specific aspects of communication between actors. Another example is having asynchronous code in the actor's behavior, for example, `Feature` or scheduler, which needs to be finished before test assertions can be executed.

One example of such a situation is the `Baker` actor. We expect it to check the `Oven` after some predefined time interval. Unfortunately, this interval is hardcoded, so there is no possibility of being able to override it in the test and we need to wait for the timer to trigger.

As part of the asynchronous testing toolkit, Akka provides a `ManualTimer`, which can be used to advance time in tests in a flexible manner. We'll use it to reliably test our `Baker` actor.

First, we need to provide an appropriate configuration for the manual timer. We do this by overriding the `config` method of the actor system which is represented by the `ActorTestKit` and define an instance of the time we'll use in our test:

```
override def config: Config = ManualTime.config
val manualTime: ManualTime = ManualTime()
```

Now, we can specify the testing logic:

```
"The baker should" should {
  "bake cookies in batches" in {
    val oven = TestProbe[Oven.Command]()
    val manager = TestInbox[Manager.Command]()
    val baker = spawn(Baker.idle(oven.ref))
    baker ! BakeCookies(RawCookies(1), manager.ref)
    oven.expectMessage(Oven.Put(1, baker))
    val justBeforeDone = DefaultBakingTime - 1.millisecond
    manualTime.expectNoMessageFor(justBeforeDone, oven)
    manualTime.timePasses(DefaultBakingTime)
    oven.expectMessage(Extract(baker))
  }
}
```

In this scenario, we create an `oven` and a `manager` using `TestProbe` (as opposed to the `TestInbox` we used before) and also a `baker` behavior using the `spawn` method of the `ActorTestKit`. We send a request to the `baker` and expect it to react appropriately by putting a single cookie into the oven.

Next, we can see that the `baker` waits for the cookies to be ready by checking that no messages are sent during this period of time. We're using the annual time here, and because of this, the check itself is done instantly. Finally, we manually advance the timer so that the `baker` needs to extract the cookies from the oven and verify that this has indeed happened, and that the `oven` received the `Extract` message as expected.

The application has been successfully tested; let's wait no more and run it!

Running the application

Please refer to `Appendix A`, *Preparing the Environment and Running Code Samples*, if you don't have Java and SBT installed yet.

We will run our application in the Terminal in the same way as we did in the previous chapter by using two separate terminal sessions for `Store` and `Bakery`. It is possible to run both in interactive mode, or by issuing one of the two following commands in the corresponding shell:

```
sbt "runMain ch12.Store"
sbt "runMain ch12.Bakery"
```

Because we're using clustering instead of remoting for our example, we don't need to start them in a particular order as we had to in the previous chapter. The following screenshot shows two Terminal windows ready to run the application with the aforementioned commands typed in:

As both parts of the application start, they will establish a connection and start to work together to produce cookies. The following screenshot shows us that the bakery part of the application is already running and waiting for the store to start on the right-hand side of the screen:

```
slasch@packt:~$ cd Learn-Scala---Fundamentals-of-Scala-2.13/ch12        slasch@packt:~$ cd Learn-Scala---Fundamentals-of-Scala-2.13/ch12
slasch@packt:~/Learn-Scala---Fundamentals-of-Scala-2.13/ch12$ sbt       slasch@packt:~/Learn-Scala---Fundamentals-of-Scala-2.13/ch12$ sbt
"runMain ch12.Bakery"                                                   "runMain ch12.Store"
[info] Loading project definition from /home/slasch/Learn-Scala--       [info] Loading project definition from /home/slasch/Learn-Scala--
-Fundamentals-of-Scala-2.13/ch12/project                                -Fundamentals-of-Scala-2.13/ch12/project
[info] Loading settings for project ch12 from build.sbt ...             [info] Loading settings for project ch12 from build.sbt ...
[info] Set current project to akka-typed-bakery (in build file:/h       [info] Set current project to akka-typed-bakery (in build file:/h
ome/slasch/Learn-Scala---Fundamentals-of-Scala-2.13/ch12/)              ome/slasch/Learn-Scala---Fundamentals-of-Scala-2.13/ch12/)
[warn] Multiple main classes detected.  Run 'show discoveredMainC
lasses' to see the list
[info] Packaging /home/slasch/Learn-Scala---Fundamentals-of-Scala
-2.13/ch12/target/scala-2.12/akka-typed-bakery_2.12-1.0.jar ...
[info] Done packaging.
[info] Running ch12.Bakery
[INFO] [09/30/2018 14:01:25.137] [run-main-0] [akka.remote.Remoti
ng] Starting remoting
[INFO] [09/30/2018 14:01:25.790] [run-main-0] [akka.remote.Remoti
ng] Remoting started; listening on addresses :[akka.tcp://Typed-B
akery@127.0.0.1:2552]
[INFO] [09/30/2018 14:01:25.798] [run-main-0] [akka.remote.Remoti
ng] Remoting now listens on addresses: [akka.tcp://Typed-Bakery@1
27.0.0.1:2552]
[INFO] [09/30/2018 14:01:25.904] [run-main-0] [akka.cluster.Clust
er(akka://Typed-Bakery)] Cluster Node [akka.tcp://Typed-Bakery@12
7.0.0.1:2552] - Starting up, Akka version [2.5.17] ...
[INFO] [09/30/2018 14:01:26.072] [run-main-0] [akka.cluster.Clust
er(akka://Typed-Bakery)] Cluster Node [akka.tcp://Typed-Bakery@12
7.0.0.1:2552] - Registered cluster JMX MBean [akka:type=Cluster]
[INFO] [09/30/2018 14:01:26.072] [run-main-0] [akka.cluster.Clust
er(akka://Typed-Bakery)] Cluster Node [akka.tcp://Typed-Bakery@12
7.0.0.1:2552] - Started up successfully
[WARN] [09/30/2018 14:01:26.690] [New I/O boss #3] [NettyTranspor
t(akka://Typed-Bakery)] Remote connection to [null] failed with j
ava.net.ConnectException: Connection refused: /127.0.0.1:2553
[WARN] [09/30/2018 14:01:26.696] [Typed-Bakery-akka.remote.defaul
```

If you'd like to start the demo in interactive mode from the SBT shell, please refer to Chapter 11, *An Introduction to the Akka and Actor Models*, where we explained how to do this in detail.

Summary

Akka Typed allows you to implement an actor system in a type-safe way. It represents actor logic as a well-typed behavior with the types of both input and output channels determined at compile time. Behaviors can be combined together, allowing for a higher degree of code reuse.

Typed actors are not only supposed to receive and send messages but are also required to explicitly define a new behavior after processing every message. Interactions with other actors are limited to creating, stopping, looking up, and watching children, and getting typed references to explicitly registered services.

Actor context provides useful functionality, such as timers and stashing.

Typed supervision is defined directly on behavior, and the failure propagation to the parent actor must be implemented explicitly if needed. The Akka team took a holistic approach by promoting an actor's life cycle hooks, from methods to events.

Actors in typed Akka are basically just functions. Because of this, testing is not limited to asynchronous communication as it was before. This can be done synchronously, thus allowing for deterministic and stable test code that executes quickly.

Akka Typed offers a set of useful extensions like cluster, cluster singleton, persistence, and distributed data. We touched briefly upon how the cluster module allows us to utilize the existing code in a distributed scenario by solely changing the configuration of the system. Please refer to the Akka Typed official documentation online (`https://doc.akka.io/docs/akka/current/typed/index.html`) to explore further capabilities provided by the typed actor's toolkit.

In the next chapter, we're going to implement the bakery once again, this time using yet another Akka library—Akka Streams.

13
Basics of Akka Streams

In this chapter, we'll take a closer look at Akka Streams. We will start with a basic description of streams in general, and Reactive Streams in particular. We'll touch on the concept of back pressure and provide some motivation for you to use Akka Streams as a concrete implementation of the Reactive Streams standard. We'll reimplement our bakery yet again, this time using streams as a design abstraction. This will allow us to examine in detail the basics of Akka Streams, such as flows and graphs, error handling, and testing.

The following topics will be covered in this chapter:

- Reactive Streams
- Back pressure
- Akka Streams philosophy
- Akka Streams essential concepts
- Sources and sinks
- Flows
- Graphs
- Logging
- Materialization
- Failure handling
- Testing

Technical requirements

- Installed Scala
- Installed SBT

Source code for this chapter is available on GitHub: `https://github.com/ PacktPublishing/Learn-Scala-Programming/tree/master/Chapter13`.

Introduction to Akka Streams

The word *stream* is vastly overloaded in meaning in modern computing. It carries many different meanings depending on the context. For instance, in Java, in different times streaming meant an abstraction over blocking IO, non-blocking IO, and later, a way to express data processing queries.

In essence, a stream in computing is just a flow of data or instructions. Usually, the content of a stream is not loaded into memory fully. This possibility to process basically unlimited amounts of information on devices with limited memory capacity is a motivating factor for the rise of streams, popularity that has been happening recently.

The definition of the stream as a flow implies that it should have some source and a destination of data elements. In computing, these concepts are naturally expressed in the code in a way that on one side of the flow the code emits data and on another side other code consumes this data. The emitting side is usually called the **producer** and the receiving side is respectively a **consumer**. Usually, there will be a portion of data in the memory which was already issued by the producer but not yet ingested by the consumer.

This aspect of the stream brings up the next idea: it should be possible to manipulate data in-flight by code in-between, the same way a water heater is plugged in between the inlet and a water tap and *changes* cold water into hot water. Interestingly, the presence of a water heater in this scenario is not known to the producer or to the consumer. If the scenario is that the water flow increases in intensity, we could easily imagine having another heater plugged in or replacing the existing one with a more powerful model. The water heater becomes the property of the flow in the sense that the quantity of the water received by the consumer depends on the amounts emitted by the producer, but the temperature depends on properties of the pipe system, or in essence, of the flow.

This is the basic idea behind using streams: a stream is usually seen as a combination of producer, consumer, and transformation steps in between. In a streaming scenario, the producer and consumer become less interesting and the main focus shifts to the transformation steps in the middle. For the sake of modularity and code reuse, defining many tiny transformations is usually considered to be a preferable approach.

Depending on the art of transferring data between the parts of the stream, we distinguish between pushing and pulling elements of the stream.

With the push, it is the producer who controls the process. The data is pushed to the stream as soon as it becomes available and the rest of the stream is supposed to be able to absorb it. Naturally, it is not always possible to consume data which is produced at an unpredictable rate. In the case of streaming, it is dealt with by dropping data or using buffers. Dropping data is sometimes appropriate but more often is undesired. Buffers have limited size and thus can become full if data is produced faster than it is consumed for a long period of time. A full buffer yet again leads to memory overflow or the need to drop data. Visibly, with the push model, a combination of a fast producer and a slow consumer is a problem.

With the pull model, it is the consumer who drives the process. It tries to read the data from the stream as soon as it needs it. If there is some data, it is taken. If there is no data, the consumer has a choice between waiting for it or trying again at a later moment. Usually, both possibilities are less than ideal. Waiting for the data is usually done by blocking and polling data, which means excessive consumption of resources and delays between the moment the data becomes available and its consumption. Evidently, the pull model is not optimal in the case of a slow producer and fast consumer.

This dichotomy led to the creation of the dynamic pull-push concept named Reactive Streams and an initiative of the same name in 2013 by engineers at Lightbend, Netflix, and Pivotal.

Reactive Streams and backpressure

Reactive Streams (`http://www.reactive-streams.org`) is an initiative to provide a standard for asynchronous stream processing with non-blocking backpressure.

The non-blocking back pressure is a mechanism to deal with deficiencies of both pull and push semantics in the streaming environment. It is better explained by an example.

Imagine a building site with a foreman responsible for timely delivery of building materials among other duties. The site can only accommodate as much as 100 tons of materials. The foreman can order materials from another company but the orders are taken by one of the truck drivers as soon as one is in the company's office and not bringing materials to the customer.

The pull behavior for the foreman would be to call a contractor and wait until a truck driver is in the office and answers the call (blocking pull) or make calls periodically with the hope that this time somebody will pick up the phone (polling). In our case, the foreman sends a voice message to the contractor asking for 100 tons of materials and returns to his daily work instead. This is a non-blocking pull.

The contractor accepts the order as soon as they have the capacity to do so. They are about to send a couple of trucks with the capacity of 32 tons each but realize they cannot send more than 100 tons because the building site won't be able to receive such volume. Therefore, only three trucks and 96 tons of materials are sent.

After 30 tons of materials are consumed, the foreman realizes that they can order more from the contractor to avoid the building site becoming idle later if the rest of materials are quickly consumed. They order another 30 tons. But the contractor remembers that there are still another 4 tons remaining from the previous order so it is safe to send another full truck with 32 tons which can fit in the single truck. We reflect the fact that some demand in the first request was satisfied later by consecutive delivery and saying that requests are additive.

And this is basically how the backpressure concept of Reactive Streams works. It is arguable that in reality the approach would be better reflected by the name *forward ease* but probably this name wouldn't take off as *back-pressure* did.

The Reactive Stream specification strives to define a low-level API which can be implemented by different libraries in order to achieve interoperability between implementation. The standard defines the API and the **Technology Compatibility Kit (TCK)** which is a standard test suite for the API implementations.

 TCK purpose is to help library authors to validate that their implementations adhere to the standard.

The API contains the following components:

- Publisher
- Subscriber
- Subscription
- Processor

The `Publisher` represents the source, the `Subscriber` relates to the consumer, the Processor is a processing stage of the stream, and the `Subscription` is a representation of the back-pressure.

All of the methods defined in the API return `void` which means they are intended to be executed without the caller waiting for the result, hence the *asynchronous stream processing* in the definition of the Reactive Streams standard.

Reactive Streams is a library standard and defines how libraries are expected to communicate with each other in order to be able to interoperate. It is expected that libraries will offer different, higher-level APIs to the user, likely reflecting some aspects of the implementation details.

Akka Streams is one of such libraries built using Akka actors as the underlying technology. It implements the Reactive Streams standard and has a rich, high-level API which allows you to describe streams using high-level DSL and also exhibits the underlying Akka machinery.

Akka Streams

The purpose of Akka Streams (`https://doc.akka.io/docs/akka/2.5.13/stream/stream-introduction.html`) is to offer an intuitive and safe way to formulate stream processing setups such that we can execute them efficiently and with bounded resource usage.

Akka Streams fully implements a Reactive Stream standard in order to interoperate with another compliant Reactive Streams library, but this fact is usually considered to be an implementation detail.

The initial motivation for Akka Streams was the fact that all Akka actor systems share the same sets of technical problems, which adds accidental complexity and needs to be solved for almost every single project separately over and over again. For example, Akka does not have any general flow control mechanism, and in order to prevent an actor's mailboxes from overflowing, it needs to be implemented as a home-grown solution within every application. Another common pain point is the at-most-once messaging semantics, which is less than ideal in most cases, but also dealt with on an individual basis. Yet another inconvenience Akka is criticized for is its untyped nature. The absence of types makes it impossible to check the soundness of possible interactions between actors at the compile time.

Akka Streams aim to solve this problem by placing a streaming layer on top of the actor system. This layer adheres to the small set of architectural principles to provide a consistent user experience. These principles are a comprehensive domain model for stream processing and compositionally. The focus of the library lies in modular data transformation. In this sense, Reactive Streams are just an implementation detail for how data is passed between steps of the flow and Akka actors are the implementation detail for individual steps.

The principle of the completeness of the domain model for distributed bounded stream processing means that Akka Streams has a rich DSL that allows you to express all aspects of the domain, such as single processing and transformation steps and their interconnections, streams with complex graph topologies, back-pressure, error and failure handling, buffering and so on.

The modularity principle means that the definition of single transformations, multiple transformations connected in specific ways, or even whole graphs must be freely shareable. This principle leads to the design decision to make the description of the stream separate from the execution of the stream. Therefore, a user of Akka Streams has to go over the following three steps to execute a stream:

1. Describe the stream in the form of building blocks and connections between them. The result of this step is usually called a *blueprint* in Akka documentation.
2. Materialize the blueprint which creates an instance of the flow. The materialization is done by providing a materializer which in Akka takes the form of using an actor system or an actor context to create actors for each processing stage.
3. Execute a materialized stream using one of the run methods.

In practice, usually the last two steps are combined and the materializer is provided as an implicit parameter.

With this theory in mind, let's take a look at what building and executing streams with Akka Streams looks like in practice.

Setup and dependency

In order to make Akka Streams available in our project, we need to put the following dependency into the `build.sbt` file:

```
lazy val akkaVersion = "2.5.14"
libraryDependencies += "com.typesafe.akka" %% "akka-stream" % akkaVersion
```

This gives us the possibility to import related classes in our examples using the following import statements:

```
import akka.stream._
import akka.stream.scaladsl._
```

These import statements are assumed to be present in every example later in this chapter.

We will also need a wrapper which would provide an actor system in order for us to be able to create materializers for our streams. The wrapper will need to terminate the actor system as soon as stream processing is finished:

```
package ch13

import akka.actor.ActorSystem
import akka.stream._

object Bakery extends App {
  implicit val bakery: ActorSystem = ActorSystem("Bakery")
  implicit val materializer: Materializer = ActorMaterializer()

  // stream processing happens here

  private def afterAll = bakery.terminate()
}
```

Now, before we dive into the code, we need some vocabulary to be able to describe what we are doing in our examples.

Essential concepts

Let's take a look at the vocabulary Akka Streams uses to describe streams and their elements.

As described earlier, every stream has producer, consumer, and transformation steps. In Akka Streams they are named `Source`, `Sink`, and `Flow` respectively.

More formally, in Akka Streams any building block of a stream is named a **processing stage**. A processing stage with a single output is a `Source`, a single input is a `Sink` and with one input, and one output is a `Flow`. By connecting a source and a sink to the flow we build a *Runnable Graph* which can be executed.

There are also special processing stages:

- Fan-in with two or more inputs and one output
- Fan-out with one input and two or more outputs
- Bidiflow with two inputs and two outputs pointing in opposite directions

We made up the following diagram with all processing stages interconnected to simplify grasping the concept. The dotted lines represent the backpressure we mentioned earlier:

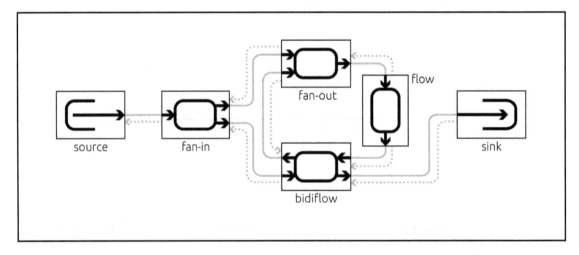

Figure 1. Different processing stages interconnected in runnable graph

Structure of the example

Let's see how the streaming implementation changes the shape of our bakery app we've built Chapter 11, *An Introduction to the Akka and Actor Models*, and Chapter 12, *Building Reactive Applications with Akka Typed*. To recap, this is the design of the bakery represented with actors:

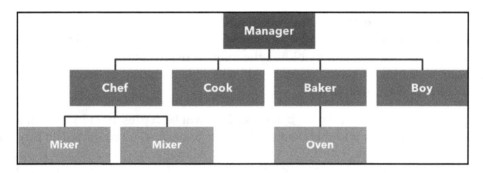

Actors in this hierarchy had the following responsibilities:

- The **Manager** initiated new baking rounds and performed the transfer of work packages between subordinates and supervised them.
- The **Boy** was given a shopping list and acquired groceries from the remote system.
- The **Chef** created and used a number of mixers of limited capacity in order to convert given groceries into dough.
- The **Cook** formed a number of raw cookies from the given dough.
- The **Baker** baked raw cookies in the **Oven** of fixed size. It maintained an internal queue of raw cookies in case the rest of the bakery was making them quicker than the **Oven** was able to bake them.
- The **Oven** and **Mixers** represent hardware resources. They convert raw cookies into edible cookies and groceries into dough respectively but do so after some delay and with possible failures.

Now we have the possibility of defining relationships between participants in a more static way, so we will only keep initiating the behavior of the **Manager** and organize the work transfer at the flow level by connecting involved transformation steps directly together.

This is what the structure of our bakery will look like, represented in processing stages:

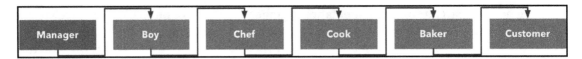

The hierarchical structure of the actor system has transformed into the flat data flow. Obviously, there are no `Mixers` and `Oven` anymore in this diagram. What happened to them? Well, we're cheating a bit by hiding the internal details of transformation steps here. In reality, some of these steps are composite blocks constructed from smaller components. Let's describe how it looks in detail.

The **Manager** only kept his initiating behavior. This will be represented by a timer source which will tick every now and then and push others to bake some cookies. The **Boy** can't work with just the **Manager**'s desire so we need the **Manager** to give a proper shopping list to it. Thus we'll have to convert the ticking urge into the **Shopping List** as represented in the next diagram:

This composite block has exactly one output and no inputs and therefore it is clearly a `Source[ShoppingList]`.

 The real type of the source is `Source[+Out, +Mat]` as it is also taken into the account the materialization aspect. The materialization is non-essential for us for now so we'll talk about simplified pseudo-types as we describe the structure of the flow.

The `Boy` and the `Cook` are simple steps; both of them can be seen as a transformation of input into the output, and we'll look at the details of this transformation in a moment. From this description, we can conclude that the `Boy` is a `Flow[ShoppingList, Groceries]` and a `Cook` is just a `Flow[Dough, RawCookies]`.

The `Chef` is clearly not as simple as his siblings. It needs to create a number of **Mixer** corresponding to the amount of groceries, use them in parallel to mix the dough, and combine the results together before sending them further. We'll represent this with the following structure:

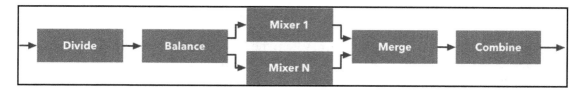

There is more going on in this diagram than we described before. This is because we combine the flow from building blocks with a single responsibility and we need to do transformations:

1. We need to divide incoming groceries into portions suitable for a single mixer; this is the **Divide** step.
2. Next, we need to be sure that work is evenly distributed among the mixers to avoid the situation where we need to wait for one of the mixers because it got multiple work packages. This is where **Balance** comes in play.
3. The involvement of multiple mixers is obvious.
4. The **Merge** step's responsibility is to be a fan-in block; it merges multiple streams of small portions of dough into a single stream of the same pieces.
5. Finally we **Combine** small pieces into one big bowl before we give it further to process.

The kinds of internal sub-flows are as following the **Divide**, **Combine** and all of the **Mixer**s are just Flows, the **Balance** is fan-out and the **Merge** is fan-in. The resulting type is the `Flow[Groceries, Dough]`.

The Baker is also not as simple as it appears in the previous diagram because it hides an oven and the interactions with it:

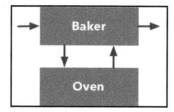

The **Oven** in this diagram has one input and one output so this is just a `Flow[RawCookies,ReadyCookies]`. The **Baker** has two inputs and two outputs and its shape is a `BidiFlow[RawCookies, RawCookies, ReadyCookies, ReadyCookies]`.

The resulting type of combination is `Flow[RawCookies,ReadyCookies]`.

In the example built earlier, with an actor system the **Baker** maintained an internal queue of raw cookies as they arrived if the oven was not empty. This has a disadvantage that in the case of a really eager `Manager` the baking process could be initiated quite often and the raw cookies could arrive at the baker at much quicker pace than the oven can possibly bake them. The queue of the raw cookies can thus grow indefinitely large until it occupies all available space, and we'll need to either throw away raw cookies to free some space or close the bakery because there is no place for other actors to work.

In this version of the bakery we decided not to implement any queue but rely on the back pressure instead. We would expect the `Oven` to communicate with the `Baker` if it can't accept more work. The `Baker` will do the same, all the way back to the `Manger`, so that it won't be possible to even express the desire to have more cookies baked until there is more oven capacity available. With different buffering strategies, it is possible to manage how much work in progress there is at the bakery at any moment. For the purpose of the example, we'll set this limit low to demonstrate back pressure in action.

The last step of our flow is a `Customer`, which is of type `Sink[ReadyCookies]`.

Now let's switch gears and set in the code the structure we came up with.

Basics of Akka Streams

Elements of the Akka Streams flow are usually defined using constructors of the appropriate type. We'll implement building blocks which constitute our diagram one by one, starting with the simplest and moving on to the increasingly complex as we go over them.

Sources and sinks

The simplest component of our flow is possibly the `Consumer`. It is just a sink which is supposed to print out information about incoming data. To construct it, we'll use the `Sink` factory, as follows:

```
val consumer: Sink[ReadyCookies, Future[Done]] =
  Sink.foreach(cookie => println(s"$cookie, yummi..."))
```

The `Sink` factory offers more than two dozens different constructors to define a sink. We're utilizing one of the simplest, which invokes a provided function for each element of the stream.

Here we see that the real type of it is the `Sink[ReadyCookies, Future[Done]]`. This reflects the type `ReadyCookies` elements and the type the `Sink` is materialized to. In this case, it is materialized into `Success` if stream ends by reaching its end and to the `Failure` if there is a failure in the stream.

Now we'll take a look at the opposite end of the stream and define a source. The `Source` factory similarly provides almost three dozens of different methods to create a source. We don't want to overwhelm our bakery's team with work so we decided to use a timed source of data:

```
private val delay = 1 second
private val interval = 1 second

val manager1: Source[NotUsed, Cancellable] =
  Source.tick(delay, interval, NotUsed)
```

This represents the first block in our composite `Source` and its type is no-fit for our `Boy`, so we need to implement the second block of the diagram, the generator, and connect both together. This is more easily done than explained:

```
val manager: Source[ShoppingList, Cancellable] =
  Source.tick(delay, interval, NotUsed).map { _ =>
    shoppingList
  }
```

We basically just map over the input but ignore it and return a `shoppingList` instead. Now our `Source` has a proper type so that we can connect a `Boy` to it later.

There is a subtle aspect of this implementation which we didn't take into the account. We have a predefined interval with the intention that the rest of the flow is not overwhelmed with requests. But at the same time, we're about to rely on the back pressure from the `Oven` for the same purpose. This is not optimal because if we pick too big an interval, our bakery will be under-utilized and if we pick too small an interval, this will be the back pressure which will manage the flow. We can simplify our source to the form that will just produce shopping lists and put them into the pipeline as soon as there is some downstream capacity available:

```
val manager: Source[ShoppingList, NotUsed] =
  Source.repeat(NotUsed).map(_ => shoppingList)
```

Here, we just repeat the `NotUsed` element (which provides a nice syntax) and then replace it with the random shopping list as before. The difference is that the manager will generate a shopping list every time there is a demand for that without potentially waiting too long because of the timer settings.

Flows

Now that we have the source and the sink, let's implement the flow itself. Again, we will start with the simplest parts and switch to the more complex as we progress.

The easiest flow building block is surely the `Cook`. It could be implemented as a map function called on the preceding flow definition but for composing reasons, we'd like to define it separately.

The approach of the flow definition is consistent with the previous two—the `Flow` constructor is the way to go. The flow is defined in terms of operations on the input but the definition itself is decoupled from this input. Again there are lots of methods to choose from; for our purposes, we pick the simple `map`:

```
object Cook {
  def formFlow: Flow[Dough, RawCookies, NotUsed] =
    Flow[Dough].map { dough =>
      print(s"Forming $dough - ")
      val result = RawCookies(makeCookies(dough.weight))
      println(result)
      result
    }
  private val cookieWeight = 50
  private def makeCookies(weight: Int): Int = weight / cookieWeight
}
```

The `cook`'s flow is just mapping over the input dough and converting it to the output, raw cookies, as it represented by the type annotation.

The Boy is quite similar to the `Cook` in the sense that it is a simple building block which transforms its input into the output. There is one caveat though—our `Boy` needs to communicate with the remote actor in order to do this.

Akka Streams is built upon Akka and thus offers some possibilities to utilize and communicate with actors at different stages; for instance, it is possible to use an `ActorRef` as a source or sink. The remoting aspect in this situation turns out to be just an implementation and configuration detail because of Akka's location transparency.

In our use case, the most appropriate way to communicate with a Seller deployed in the remote shop system will be an ask pattern. Let's do this step by step. First, we'll look up a remote actor in order to be able to communicate with it:

```
def lookupSeller(implicit as: ActorSystem): Future[ActorRef] = {
  val store = "akka.tcp://Store@127.0.0.1:2553"
  val seller = as.actorSelection(s"$store/user/Seller")
  seller.resolveOne()
}
```

Given an `ActorSystem`, we look up an actor using an address of the remote system and an actor path. We know there should be exactly one actor, therefore we resolve one reference. Depending on the result of the lookup it will return either `Success` with the reference we need or a `Failure[ActorNotFound]`. The failure will be propagated via the error flow and will lead to the termination of the stream because we don't define how to handle it. Let's call this the desired behavior because without a seller we won't be able to convert a shopping list into groceries.

We can use a `Future[ActorRef]` to talk to the actor:

```
def goShopping(implicit as: ActorSystem, ec: ExecutionContext):
  Future[Flow[ShoppingList, Groceries, NotUsed]] =
  lookupSeller.map { ref =>
    Flow[ShoppingList].ask[Groceries](ref)
}
```

Here, we not only need an `ActorSystem` but also an `ExecutionContext` in order to be able to map over the `Future` we acquire from the `lookupSeller`. We're using the actor reference (if there is one) as a parameter to call `Flow.ask`. The type of the `Flow` corresponds to the expected input type and the type of the `ask`—to the expected output type.

Now we can use another `Flow` constructor to convert a `Future[Flow]` to the `Flow`:

```
def shopFlow(implicit as: ActorSystem, ec: ExecutionContext):
Flow[ShoppingList, Groceries, Future[Option[NotUsed]]] =
  Flow.lazyInitAsync { () => goShopping }
```

The `lazyInitAsync` translates an internal `Flow` of the `Future` into the normal `Flow`. This sub-flow has a proper type of input and output and thus we can plug it into our flow definition later.

It is important to extend the configuration in the `application.conf` with properties, needed for the Akka remoting as described in `Chapter 11`, *An Introduction to the Akka and Actor Models*.

The next composite step we're going to implement is a `Baker`, including its constituent `Oven`.

The `Oven` needs to spend some time turning raw cookies into edible cookies and we could implement this by introducing a bit of blocking behavior. But doing so will affect the rest of the system by needlessly consuming available threads. Because of this, we'll use another feature of Akka Streams, `Flow.delay`, which allows us to shift the emission of elements in time:

```
def bakeFlow: Flow[RawCookies, ReadyCookies, NotUsed] =
  Flow[RawCookies]
    .delay(bakingTime, DelayOverflowStrategy.backpressure)
    .addAttributes(Attributes.inputBuffer(1, 1))
    .map(bake)
```

As we only have one `Oven`, we define a buffer size to be of the initial and maximum size of 1. We also don't want to drop arriving raw cookies or release cookies which are not ready yet, therefore we define an overflow strategy to be a back pressure.

The `bake` method is a trivial conversion once again:

```
private def bake(c: RawCookies): ReadyCookies = {
  assert(c.count == ovenSize)
  ReadyCookies(c.count)
}
```

Now, with this `Oven` we can define a `Baker` which we planned to give a type of `BidiFlow`:

```
def bakeFlow = BidiFlow.fromFlows(inFlow, outFlow)
```

In order to do this, we need to separately define the `inFlow` and `outFlow` for both flow directions.

The `outFlow` is just passing cookies that are ready to the consumer and we already know how to do that:

```
private def outFlow = Flow[ReadyCookies]
```

The `inFlow` is a bit more involving because we need to regroup incoming raw cookies from groups of some random quantity to groups with the size of the oven. We'll do this by defining a sub-source of single cookies and then grouping them as desired. Here is the first step:

```
def extractFromBox(c: RawCookies) =
  Source(List.fill(c.count)(RawCookies(1)))
```

We're creating a source: the number of single cookies. The regrouping logic looks like this:

```
val inFlow = Flow[RawCookies]
  .flatMapConcat(extractFromBox)
  .grouped(Oven.ovenSize)
  .map(_.reduce(_ + _))
```

The `flatMapConcat` consumes one source after another and concatenates the results. We then group the stream of single cookies to the stream of `List[RawCookie]` of `ovenSize`. Lastly, we reduce this list of single cookies into `RawCookie(ovenSize)` as `Oven` expects it.

Now we can combine a baker's `BidiFlow` and oven's `Flow` into the composite `Flow` by joining them:

```
val bakerFlow: Flow[RawCookies, ReadyCookies, NotUsed] =
  Baker.bakeFlow.join(Oven.bakeFlow)
```

The `join` method adds a given `Flow` as a final transformation to the stack of `BidiFlows`. In our case, the size of the stack is one and the type of the resulting flow is `Flow[RawCookies, ReadyCookies, NotUsed]`. The resulting sub-flow hides all of the details of regrouping the cookies and waiting for their readiness, leaving us with a nice definition.

Graphs

The final piece of our flow is a `Chef`. It incorporates work management across Mixers. Let's implement `Mixers` first.

The mixing behavior itself is straightforward but to mimic real hardware we include a block for the time of mixing:

```
def mix(g: Groceries) = {
  Thread.sleep(mixTime.toMillis)
  import g._
  Dough(eggs * 50 + flour + sugar + chocolate)
}
```

Because of the mixing behavior, we need to use a special async flow constructor to start a separate thread for every mixer. In order to better control how threads are assigned, we'll put into the configuration a definition of the separate pinned thread dispatcher which assigns one thread per sub-flow:

```
mixers-dispatcher {
  executor = "thread-pool-executor"
  type = PinnedDispatcher
}
```

With this definition in place, we are now able to define the blocking mixing behavior:

```
private def subMixFlow: Flow[Groceries, Dough, NotUsed] =
  Flow[Groceries].async("mixers-dispatcher", 1).map(mix)
```

The `async` constructor takes a buffer size as a parameter and we want our mixers not to have any large buffers assigned to them.

The work management can be implemented as a separate concept which closely resembles one of the recipes from the Akka Streams documentation cookbook—the Balancer. It takes a worker `subFlow` and a count of workers and constructs a graph with the given number of workers:

```
import akka.stream.scaladsl.GraphDSL
import GraphDSL.Implicits._

def createGraph[Out, In](subFlow: Flow[In, Out, Any], count: Int) = {
  val balanceBlock  = Balance[In](count, waitForAllDownstreams = false)
  val mergeBlock = Merge[Out](count, eagerComplete = false)
  GraphDSL.create() { implicit builder =>
    val balancer = builder.add(balanceBlock)
    val merge = builder.add(mergeBlock)

    for (_ <- 1 to count) balancer ~> subFlow ~> merge

    FlowShape(balancer.in, merge.out)
  }
}
```

The `Balance` block is a fan-out flow with several outputs. It distributes stream elements evenly between the workers. With `waitForAllDownstreams = false` we specify that the distribution can start as soon as at least one of the workers demands a job. With `false` we change the behavior to wait for all of the workers to demand a job before it will be distributed. The `Merge` is a fan-in block with a specified number of inputs. By specifying `eagerComplete = false` we tell it to wait for all down streams to complete as compared to completing as soon as one of the workers is done.

Then we construct a graph using `GraphDSL.create()` and provide actual graph building logic as a parameter. First, we convert `balanceBlock` and `mergeBlock` into Shapes by adding them to the `builder`. Then we connect as many sub-flows as needed to the balancer and merge using the `~>` syntax provided by the `import GraphDSL.Implicits._`. The `for` comprehension for five workers would be equivalent to the following plain definition:

```
balancer ~> subFlow ~> merge
balancer ~> subFlow ~> merge
balancer ~> subFlow ~> merge
balancer ~> subFlow ~> merge
```

Having this graph defined, we can specify the rest of the `Balancer` flow using another `Flow` constructor:

```
def apply[In, Out](subFlow: Flow[In, Out, Any],
                   count: Int): Flow[In, Out, NotUsed] =
  Flow.fromGraph(createGraph(subFlow, count))
```

We can use it to construct our `Chef` sub-flow:

```
def mixFlow: Flow[Groceries, Dough, NotUsed] =
  Flow[Groceries]
    .map(splitByMixer)
    .flatMapConcat(mixInParallel)

def splitByMixer(g: Groceries) = {
  import g._
  val single = Groceries(1, flour / eggs, sugar / eggs, chocolate / eggs)
  List.fill(g.eggs)(single)
}

def mixInParallel(list: List[Groceries]) =
  Source(list)
    .via(Balancer(subMixFlow, list.size))
    .grouped(list.size)
    .map(_.reduce(_ + _))
```

Here, again we split `Groceries` into a stream of smaller portions, mix each of these portions using a dedicated mixer in parallel, and combine them using the same technique we used before with the `Baker` and `Oven`.

Logging

In `Cook`'s flow, we used two `print` statements in order to see how the `Cook` was doing. It's OK for our example but we would be better off with proper logging. Let's improve on that.

Akka provides a `log` method which takes a logger name as a parameter and can be called on any processing stage in the flow. Let's use it instead of our `print` statements:

```
def formFlow: Flow[Dough, RawCookies, NotUsed] =
  Flow[Dough]
    .log("Cook[Before Map]")
    .map { dough =>
      RawCookies(makeCookies(dough.weight))
    }
    .log("Cook[After Map]")
    .withAttributes(
      Attributes.logLevels(
        onElement = Logging.InfoLevel,
        onFinish = Logging.DebugLevel,
        onFailure = Logging.WarningLevel
      )
    )
```

Here, we're writing into the log elements of the flow before and after transformation and also providing an optional logging configuration in order to specify log levels for different types of events.

To see the effect of these changes we need to extend the `application.conf`:

```
akka {
  loggers = ["akka.event.Logging$DefaultLogger"]
  # Options: OFF, ERROR, WARNING, INFO, DEBUG
  loglevel = "INFO"
}
```

Now, after starting our example, we'll see the following entries in the log:

```
[INFO] [Bakery-akka.actor.default-dispatcher-14]
[akka.stream.Log(akka://Bakery/system/StreamSupervisor-0)] [Cook[Before
Map]] Element: Dough(575)
  . . .
  [INFO] [Bakery-akka.actor.default-dispatcher-14]
[akka.stream.Log(akka://Bakery/system/StreamSupervisor-0)] [Cook[After
Map]] Element: RawCookies(11)
  . . .
  [INFO] [Bakery-akka.actor.default-dispatcher-14]
[akka.stream.Log(akka://Bakery/system/StreamSupervisor-0)] [Cook[Before
```

```
Map]] Element: Dough(1380)
  [INFO] [Bakery-akka.actor.default-dispatcher-14]
[akka.stream.Log(akka://Bakery/system/StreamSupervisor-0)] [Cook[After
Map]] Element: RawCookies(27)
```

With logging in place, we have finished defining all of the parts of our flow and can try to bring them together.

Materialization

Now we can specify the whole flow for our bakery:

```
val flow = Boy.shopFlow
  .via(Chef.mixFlow)
  .via(Cook.formFlow)
  .via(bakerFlow)

val graph: RunnableGraph[Future[Done]] =
manager.via(flow).toMat(consumer)(Keep.right)

implicit val materializer: Materializer = ActorMaterializer()

graph.run().onComplete(_ => afterAll)
```

Here, we first construct the full flow by combining sub-flows we defined before. Then we convert the flow to runnable graph by attaching the `manager` Source and the `consumer` Sink.

We also specify that we want to keep the right materialized value. The left materialized value would be the result of the stream, which is `NotUsed` in our case because we just writing produced cookies to the console. The right value is a future which is completed when the flow has finished running and we want to use it to shut down our actor system as soon is it happens.

Finally, we run the graph by bringing an `ActorMaterializer` in scope and calling the corresponding `run` method.

Our system runs and bakes tasty cookies, but unfortunately, we forgot to take an important aspect into account: Mixers in our setup are liable to hardware failure.

Handling failure

In order to make the mixing step more realistic we'll add a couple of exceptions and throw them in randomly at the mixing stage. This will simulate hardware failures appearing at unpredicted times. The mixer can throw one of the three exceptions the same way it did before in the actor-based examples in the previous two chapters:

```
object MotorOverheatException extends Exception
object SlowRotationSpeedException extends Exception
object StrongVibrationException extends Exception

val exceptions = Seq(MotorOverheatException,
                     SlowRotationSpeedException,
                     StrongVibrationException)
```

The realistic `mix` method could look like this:

```
private def mix(g: Groceries) = {
  if (Random.nextBoolean()) throw
exceptions(Random.nextInt(exceptions.size))
  Thread.sleep(mixTime.toMillis)
  import g._
  Dough(eggs * 50 + flour + sugar + chocolate)
}
```

There are a couple of different ways the exceptions can be dealt with. The most straightforward approach would be to catch them directly in the logic:

```
private def mix(g: Groceries) = try {
  if (Random.nextBoolean()) throw
exceptions(Random.nextInt(exceptions.size))
  Thread.sleep(mixTime.toMillis)
  import g._
  Dough(eggs * 50 + flour + sugar + chocolate)
} catch {
  case SlowRotationSpeedException =>
    Thread.sleep(mixTime.toMillis * 2)
    import g._
    Dough(eggs * 50 + flour + sugar + chocolate)
}
```

In the case of slow rotation, we decide to ignore the issue, keep the mixed stuff, and just give the mixer double the time to finish the mixing.

This works but it has an obvious disadvantage that we tangle our business and error-handling implementations. More often then not this is undesirable because the code for both aspects usually have different natures. The happy path contains business-related code and error handling is of a technical essence. Therefore it is usually preferred to separate these code paths. In our case, it is justified to handle the failure at the stage level because we don't want to drop the element of the stream.

Akka offers alternative ways to specify failure handling. One of them is recovery logic which can be defined for the stage so that failure is converted into the final element of the stream:

```
def subMixFlow: Flow[Groceries, Dough, NotUsed] =
  Flow[Groceries].async("mixers-dispatcher", 1).map(mix).recover {
    case MotorOverheatException => Dough(0)
  }
```

Here we decide to return an empty bowl of dough in the case of motor failure. The stream is then completed but this is fine in our case because our mixers are one-off sub-flows anyway.

The `recover` method is a special case of the `recoverWithRetries`. The latter accepts not only a partial function for decision-making but also a number of retries in the case multiple failures happen in the same processing stage.

Now we are only missing a decision as to how to handle the `StrongVibrationException`. If we decide not to handle it, the default behavior will be able to stop the whole stream. If that happens, the downstream stages will get informed about the failure and upstream stages will be cancelled.

We definitely don't want to close our bakery in case one of our mixers vibrates too much. Quite the opposite; we'd like to ignore this completely. Some stages support a defining supervision strategy the same way actors do. We can use this possibility to define a common error-handling behavior. First, we need to define a decision strategy:

```
val strategy: Supervision.Decider = {
  case StrongVibrationException   => Supervision.resume
  case _ => Supervision.Stop
}
```

There are three strategies available—stop, restart, and resume:

- The stopping strategy is the default one and it will stop the processing stage and propagate the failure of up and downstream stages.
- The resuming strategy just drops the current element and the stream continues.
- Restart is similar to resume—it drops current element and the stream continues but before that the stage is restarted and so any internal state is cleared.

In our decider, we just want the stream to continue in the case of strong vibrations, but stop in the case of any other failure. We handle both other types of exceptions in addition to a supervision strategy and therefore we're safe with this decision.

This is how we apply our supervision strategy to the definition of the processing stage:

```
private def subMixFlow: Flow[Groceries, Dough, NotUsed] =
  Flow[Groceries].async("mixers-dispatcher", 1).map(mix).recover {
    case MotorOverheatException => Dough(0)
  }.withAttributes(ActorAttributes.supervisionStrategy(strategy))
```

Now, if we start our example, it will run and deal with hardware failures as expected.

It looks good but we're not done because we haven't tested our bakery yet.

Testing

Testing stream-based code might look complex because of the interconnectedness of all of the parts of the system. But more often than not testing streams boils down to unit-testing processing stages in isolation and relying on the Akka Streams that data flow between this stages will happen as expected.

Frequently, no special testing library is needed. Let's demonstrate this by testing our source:

```
"manager source" should {
  "emit shopping lists as needed" in {
    val future: Future[Seq[ShoppingList]] =
Manager.manager.take(100).runWith(Sink.seq)
    val result: Seq[ShoppingList] = Await.result(future, 1.seconds)
    assert(result.size == 100)
  }
}
```

In order to run this test snippet we need an implicit materializer to be in scope:

```
implicit val as: ActorSystem = ActorSystem("test")
implicit val mat: Materializer = ActorMaterializer()
```

The general approach is that in order to test a `Sink` it can be attached to the special `Source`, and for a `Source` under test, we'll need a special `Sink`.

In both cases, sequence-based `Sources` and `Sinks` are probably the most useful ones. In our example, we're testing that our source emits at least one hundred shopping lists and does this in a timely manner. The results are available as a `Seq[ShoppingList]` and can be inspected if needed.

In order to test a flow, we need to provide both a test `Source` and `Sink`:

```
"cook flow" should {
  "convert flow elements one-to-one" in {
    val source = Source.repeat(Dough(100)).take(1000)
    val sink = Sink.seq[RawCookies]
    val future: Future[Seq[RawCookies]] =
source.via(Cook.formFlow).runWith(sink)
    val result: Seq[RawCookies] = Await.result(future, 1.seconds)
    assert(result.size == 1000)
    assert(result.forall(_.count == 2))
  }
}
```

Here, we see the same approach. After defining the test input and output we drive the flow under test and verify that the output has expected properties.

There is an undesirable call to `Await.result` in both cases which relates to the fact that running the Akka Streams flow produces a `Future`. We can improve on that by using testing techniques as described in Chapter 5, *Property-Based Testing in Scala*.

Alternatively, it is also possible to use test toolkits provided by other Akka libraries.

Akka TestKit

Akka Streams offers integration with Akka actors via the `actorRef` method. It is available as a Sink constructor so we can use an actor to receive elements of the flow which are then represented as messages received by the actor. It is convenient to use `TestProbe` from the Akka `TestKit` to verify assumptions about the flow. First, we need to add a dependency to the Akka `TestKit` in `build.sbt`:

```
libraryDependencies += com.typesafe.akka" %% "akka-testkit" % akkaVersion %
Test
```

Here is an example of how the `TestProbe` can be employed:

```
"the boy flow" should {
  "lookup a remote seller and communicate with it" in {
    val probe = TestProbe()
    val source = Manager.manager.take(1)
    val sink = Sink.actorRef[Groceries](probe.ref, NotUsed)
    source.via(Boy.shopFlow).runWith(sink)
    probe.expectMsgType[Groceries]
  }
}
```

We test that there will be one message coming from the flow if one message goes into it. This time we're not waiting for the future to complete but formulate our assumptions with the syntax the `TestProbe` supports.

By now, you should have recognized the pattern we're using. First, set up the source and/or the sink, then wait for the flow to complete, and finally verify assumptions about the output of the flow. Surely enough, the Akka team abstracted this in a special test kit provided for Akka Streams.

Streams TestKit

In order to use the Akka Streams `TestKit`, we need to add another dependency to our project configuration to `build.sbt`:

```
libraryDependencies ++= "com.typesafe.akka" %% "akka-stream-testkit" %
akkaVersion % Test
```

Let's see how the `TestSink` and `TestSource` provided by this module can simplify the way we formulate our testing logic. Now we'll test the whole flow from the `Boy` to the `Baker`:

```
"the whole flow" should {
  "produce cookies" in {
    val testSink = TestSink.probe[ReadyCookies]
    val source = TestSource.probe[ShoppingList]
    val (publisher: TestPublisher.Probe[ShoppingList],
        subscriber: TestSubscriber.Probe[ReadyCookies]) =
      source.via(Bakery.flow).toMat(testSink)(Keep.both).run()
    subscriber.request(10)
    publisher.sendNext(ShoppingList(30, 1000, 100, 100))
    subscriber.expectNext(40.seconds, ReadyCookies(12))
  subscriber.expectNext(40.seconds, ReadyCookies(12))
  }
}
```

In this scenario, we first create `TestSink` and `TestSource` probes using constructors provided by the testing toolkit. Then we materialize them to `publisher` and `subscriber` in order to be able to drive the flow. Here, we're using the `toMat` syntax again. Until now, we implicitly used the default value (`Keep.left`) but now we want to keep both materialized results of the flow and of the sink. Running the flow returns its materialized instance which is a pair: `TestPublisher` and `TestSubscriber`.

We then use `subscriber` to request 10 messages from the flow. In Reactive Streams, the producer is not supposed to send anything downstream until there is demand, and we express the demand with this call. We expect the flow to output elements representing `RawCookies(12)`. Thus, our `subscriber.request` translates to 120 cookies to be produced.

Having this demand, we then initiate the flow by sending the next shopping list from the source.

Finally, we expect at least two batches of cookies to arrive at the sink. We provide sufficient time for the stream to push messages through all of the stages, accounting for delays in the mixing and baking stage.

We also cannot reliably predict how many cookies will be made because of the way we drop messages at the mixing stage in the case of `MotorOverheatException` and `SlowRotationSpeedException`.

In this example, we barely scratched the surface of all of the possibilities provided by the Akka Streams `TestKit`. As you develop Akka Streams-based systems it is worth revisiting both the documentation and the source code of the library and keeping in mind the different testing approaches they offer.

Running the application

Please refer to `Appendix A`, *Preparing the Environment and Running Code Samples*, if you still have to install Java and/or SBT.

We will run our application in the terminal the same way we did in `Chapter 11`, *An Introduction to the Akka and Actor Models* and `Chapter 12`, *Building Reactive Applications with Akka Typed*, using two separate terminal sessions for `Store` and `BakeryApp` using the following commands:

- `sbt "runMain ch13.BakeryApp"`
- `sbt "runMain ch13.Store"`

We prefer this method because of its conciseness. If you're about to run the app in interactive mode, please consult `Chapter 11`, *An Introduction to the Akka and Actor Models*, for a detailed explanation of this approach.

In our examples, we expect the remote `Store` app to be available at the moment we start the main `Bakery` stream. Because of this, we have to start the `Store` first or the `BakeryApp` will exit with an exception at the moment it fails to connect to the store. The next screenshot shows two terminal windows with commands to run the `Store` entered in the left window and the `BakeryApp` started in the right window. In the following screenshot, we can see that the `Store` has already been running for some time and the BakeryApp has just started to execute:

```
slasch@packt:~$ cd Learn-Scala---Fundamentals-of-Scala-2.13/ch13
slasch@packt:~/Learn-Scala---Fundamentals-of-Scala-2.13/ch13$ sbt
"runMain ch13.BakeryApp"
[info] Loading project definition from /home/slasch/Learn-Scala--
-Fundamentals-of-Scala-2.13/ch13/project
[info] Loading settings for project ch13 from build.sbt ...
[info] Set current project to akka-streams-bakery (in build file:
/home/slasch/Learn-Scala---Fundamentals-of-Scala-2.13/ch13/)
[warn] Multiple main classes detected.  Run 'show discoveredMainC
lasses' to see the list
[info] Running ch13.BakeryApp
[INFO] [09/30/2018 19:04:03.522] [run-main-0] [akka.remote.Remoti
ng] Starting remoting
[INFO] [09/30/2018 19:04:04.014] [run-main-0] [akka.remote.Remoti
ng] Remoting started; listening on addresses :[akka.tcp://Bakery@
127.0.0.1:2552]
[INFO] [09/30/2018 19:04:04.016] [run-main-0] [akka.remote.Remoti
ng] Remoting now listens on addresses: [akka.tcp://Bakery@127.0.0
.1:2552]
Shopping list ShoppingList(8,400,80,40)
Shopping list ShoppingList(10,500,100,50)
[WARN] [SECURITY][09/30/2018 19:04:05.439] [Bakery-akka.remote.de
fault-remote-dispatcher-8] [akka.serialization.Serialization(akka
://Bakery)] Using the default Java serializer for class [ch13.Sto
re$ShoppingList] which is not recommended because of performance
implications. Use another serializer or disable this warning usin
g the setting 'akka.actor.warn-about-java-serializer-usage'
Shopping list ShoppingList(11,550,110,55)
resuming
```

```
slasch@packt:~$ cd Learn-Scala---Fundamentals-of-Scala-2.13/ch13
slasch@packt:~/Learn-Scala---Fundamentals-of-Scala-2.13/ch13$ sbt
"runMain ch13.Store"
[info] Loading project definition from /home/slasch/Learn-Scala--
-Fundamentals-of-Scala-2.13/ch13/project
[info] Updating ProjectRef(uri("file:/home/slasch/Learn-Scala---F
undamentals-of-Scala-2.13/ch13/project/"), "ch13-build")...
[info] Done updating.
[info] Loading settings for project ch13 from build.sbt ...
[info] Set current project to akka-streams-bakery (in build file:
/home/slasch/Learn-Scala---Fundamentals-of-Scala-2.13/ch13/)
[info] Updating ...
[info] downloading https://repo1.maven.org/maven2/com/typesafe/ak
ka/akka-stream-testkit_2.12/2.5.14/akka-stream-testkit_2.12-2.5.1
4.jar ...
[info]   [SUCCESSFUL ] com.typesafe.akka#akka-stream-testkit_2.12;
2.5.14!akka-stream-testkit_2.12.jar (263ms)
[info] Done updating.
[warn] There may be incompatibilities among your library dependen
cies.
[warn] Run 'evicted' to see detailed eviction warnings
[info] Compiling 3 Scala sources to /home/slasch/Learn-Scala---Fu
ndamentals-of-Scala-2.13/ch13/target/scala-2.12/classes ...
[info] Done compiling.
WARNING: An illegal reflective access operation has occurred
WARNING: Illegal reflective access by com.google.protobuf.UnsafeU
til (file:/home/slasch/.sbt/boot/scala-2.12.6/org.scala-sbt/sbt/1
.2.3/protobuf-java-3.3.1.jar) to field java.nio.Buffer.address
WARNING: Please consider reporting this to the maintainers of com
.google.protobuf.UnsafeUtil
WARNING: Use --illegal-access=warn to enable warnings of further
illegal reflective access operations
WARNING: All illegal access operations will be denied in a future
 release
[warn] Multiple main classes detected.  Run 'show discoveredMainC
lasses' to see the list
```

The `Bakery` in the right terminal will now run until stopped with the *Ctrl* + *C* shortcut or the terminal window is closed.

Summary

Traditional streaming solutions suffer from one of two issues. In the case of pulling, there is a need for locking or extensive use of resources on the side of the quick consumer. In the case of pushing, there is a possibility that a number of messages to process will grow bigger than the available memory, requiring a slow consumer to drop messages or terminate because of the memory overflow. Reactive Streams solves this problem by defining dynamic asynchronous pull-push with back pressure. Akka Streams implements the Reactive Streams standard using Akka which allows for seamless integration with both technologies.

Streams in Akka are built from blocks called stages or flows. These blocks can be nested and connected to each other, forming graphs. Graphs with single input and single output can be made runnable by connecting them to the source and sink. Graph definitions can be freely shared and reused.

Running a graph requires a materializer and produces a materialized value depending on the graph and sink definition.

Error handling in Akka Streams can be done in different ways including catching errors directly in the flow definition, defining a recovery method with optional retries and/or overriding a supervision strategy for processing stages which support it.

The modular nature of the flow definition allows for straightforward testing of single stages and their combinations. In order to reduce boilerplate for recurring test setup and expectation definitions, Akka Streams offers special test toolkit.

The reader is encouraged to take a look at the official Akka documentation at `https://doc.akka.io/docs/akka/current/stream/index.html` to explore the possibilities offered by Akka Streams in more detail.

Questions

1. Name two different modes associated with "classic" streams. What is problematic with them?
2. Why are Reactive Streams considered as workable in dynamic pull-push mode?
3. What are the typical building blocks of Akka Stream's graph?
4. How do we convert a graph into a runnable graph?
5. What is the main goal of having materialization as a separate explicit step?
6. Describe the effects of applying different supervision strategies.
7. Which main abstractions provide an Akka Streams `TestKit`? Why are they useful?

Further reading

- Christian Baxter, *Mastering Akka: Master the art of creating scalable, concurrent, and reactive applications using Akka*
- Héctor Veiga Ortiz, Piyush Mishra, *Akka Cookbook: Learn how to use the Akka framework to build effective applications in Scala*
- Rambabu Posa, *Scala Reactive Programming: Build fault-tolerant, robust, and distributed applications in Scala*

14
Project 1 - Building Microservices with Scala

During this book, we have gradually increased the scope of our interests. In the first part, we started with language constructs and small building blocks, such as types and functions. The second part was dedicated to the patterns of functional programming. In the third part, we looked at even bigger abstractions—the actor model and streaming.

In this section, we'll zoom out once again, this time moving from design aspects up to the architectural level. We will use what we've learned so far to build two fully-scoped projects.

Nowadays, it goes without saying that all server-side software should provide an API, specifically an HTTP RESTful API. Software providing an API is called a **service** and if it conforms to a set of principles, it is often called a **microservice**. We will follow the crowd and design our projects as microservices.

In this chapter, we'll cover two topics. First, we'll discuss the concept of microservices and describe their advantages and building principles. We'll also take a look at few technical and organizational challenges related to the microservice-based approach.

Second, we'll use the knowledge gained from the rest of the book to build two real projects from scratch. Both represent simple microservices implementing stateful REST APIs, which represent the grocery shop you're familiar with from the third section of the book. This time, we'll provide not only an opportunity to place orders, but also to create and delete articles, and to replenish items in stock and get the current status of the stock.

The first project will be built on principles covered in the second section of this book. We will build it using open source functional programming libraries—http4s and circe for the client API, and doobie for database access.

The second project will be built using reactive programming libraries and techniques covered in the third section of this book. We'll use Akka-HTTP to construct an API layer, and Akka Persistence to implement the stateful part of it.

The following topics will be covered in this chapter:

- Essentials of microservices
- Purely functional HTTP APIs with http4s
- Purely functional database access with doobie
- API integration testing with Http1Client
- Reactive HTTP API with Akka-HTTP
- Event-sourced persistent state with Akka Persistence

Technical requirements

Before we begin, make sure you have the following installed:

- SBT 1.2+
- Java 1.8+

The source code for this chapter is available on GitHub at `https://github.com/PacktPublishing/Learn-Scala-Programming/tree/master/Chapter14`.

Essentials of microservices

When discussing microservices, it is better to start with the question of size. Evidently, software systems are growing in size in response to increasing demands from users. The number of features, their complexity and sophistication grow and so do the lines of code in software projects. Even in well-structured living systems, the size of components and their number is getting bigger over time. Given limited human mental capabilities, the proportion of the system that is understood by a single programmer shrinks, which leads to the increased number for developers in the team. Bigger team size leads to the growth of the communication overhead and so less time for writing code, leading to the need for additional developers, which introduces a self-reinforced cycle.

The *traditional* monolithic way to build systems as a single project with a single deployment module or executable and a single database is therefore becoming less and less efficient, and ultimately just makes it impossible to deliver working software in a timely manner. An alternative approach is to split the monolith into separate projects, called microservices, that can be developed independently.

Microservices look like the only feasible alternative to the monolithic approach, and are therefore becoming more and more popular. But, what are they precisely? According to `http://microservices.io`, microservices—also known as the microservice architecture—is an architectural style that structures an application as a collection of loosely-coupled services, which implement business capabilities.

What does it mean? In essence, this is what would happen to the well-structured application if one would tear it apart and make an autonomous application from each module responsible for single business feature.

The *autonomy* in this definition applies on multiple levels:

- **Codebase and technological stack**: The code of the service should not be shared with other services.
- **Deployment:** The service is deployed independently of other services both in terms of time and underlying infrastructure.
- **State:** The service has its own persistent store and the only way for other services to access the data is by calling the owning service.
- **Failure-handling:** Microservices are expected to be resilient. In the case of failures of downstream services, the one in question is expected to isolate failure.

These aspects of autonomy allow us to reap a number of benefits from a microservice-based architecture:

- Continuous delivery even for very complex applications
- The complexity of each service is low because it is limited to a single business capability
- Independent deployment implies independent scalability for services with different loads
- Code-independence enables polyglot environments and makes the adoption of new technologies easier
- Teams can be scaled down in size, which reduces communication overhead and speeds up decision-making

Of course, there are downsides to this approach as well. The most obvious drawbacks are related to the fact that microservices need to communicate with each other. To name a few important difficulties:

- Unavailability of habitual transactions
- Debugging, testing, and tracing calls involving multiple microservices

- The complexity shifts from the individual service into the space between them
- Service location and protocol discovery require lots of effort

But don't be scared! In the reminder of this chapter, we'll build just a single microservice so we won't be affected by these weaknesses.

Building a microservice with http4s and doobie

Let's take a look at how a microservice with a RESTful interface will look if implemented with open source libraries based on the principles we've learned in first two sections of the book.

We will start with the discussion of the building blocks that constitute the application and how they connect together. Speaking of blocks, we'll need to briefly talk about the FS2 library, which is a foundation of other libraries we will use and thus shapes the ways we join them together. After that, we'll go over database migrations, project configurations, the implementation of the database logic, and the service layer. Naturally we conclude our discourse with the implementation of integration testing for the service we've built.

Project structure

Our project will include the following components:

- Database repository represents an abstraction layer over the database
- Database migrator contains initialization logic for the database table
- The REST API defines available HTTP calls and associated business logic
- The configuration consolidates application parameters, such as server binding and database properties
- The server wires all other components together, and spawns and binds an HTTP server to the configured address

We'll start by adding following dependencies to `build.sbt` (the exact versions can be found in the GitHub repository):

```
libraryDependencies ++= Seq(
  "org.http4s" %% "http4s-blaze-server" % http4sVersion,
  "org.http4s" %% "http4s-circe" % http4sVersion,
  "org.http4s" %% "http4s-dsl" % http4sVersion,
```

```
    "org.tpolecat" %% "doobie-core" % doobieVersion,
    "org.tpolecat" %% "doobie-h2" % doobieVersion,
    "org.tpolecat" %% "doobie-hikari" % doobieVersion,
    "com.h2database" % "h2" % h2Version,
    "org.flywaydb" % "flyway-core" % flywayVersion,
    "io.circe" %% "circe-generic" % circeVersion,
    "com.github.pureconfig" %% "pureconfig" % pureConfigVersion,
    "ch.qos.logback" % "logback-classic" % logbackVersion,
    "org.typelevel" %% "cats-core" % catsVersion,

    "org.http4s" %% "http4s-blaze-client" % http4sVersion % "it,test",
    "io.circe" %% "circe-literal" % circeVersion % "it,test",
    "org.scalatest" %% "scalatest" % scalaTestVersion % "it,test",
    "org.scalamock" %% "scalamock" % scalaMockVersion % Test
)
```

This list definitely looks longer than what you would expect for an example project. Let's inspect carefully why we need each of the dependencies we've put into it:

- http4s is the library we will be using for the HTTP layer
- doobie is a functional JDBC (Java DataBase Connectivity) decorator
- H2 is an embedded database which we will use to avoid installing a standalone instance
- Flyway is for database migrations (versioned SQL statements used to change the database structure)
- Circe is a JSON Swiss Army knife
- PureConfig is a typed configuration wrapper
- Cats is a library containing general functional programming abstractions

FS2 – functional streams

You may be wondering why we have a section about the FS2 library if we're not using it as a component for our application. Well, in fact, we are. It is an underlying building block for the database and HTTP libraries we're using, and therefore it is important to briefly discuss it to give you an understanding of how the other building blocks are connected.

FS2 is a streaming library that allows us to construct and transform complex streams. The streams in FS2 do not only contain elements, but also can embody effects such as IO. This feature makes it possible to describe almost everything as an FS2 stream. Libraries such as http4s and doobie are built upon this and give a higher-level API to the user. But this API is still a streaming one.

The stream is represented as `Stream[F,O]`, where `F` describes a possible effect of the stream and `O` is a type of its elements or output. This definition needs to be given two type parameters in order to fully specify it. If the stream has no effects, it will be pure: `Stream[Pure, O]`.

Let's construct a stream of `chars`:

```
val chars: fs2.Stream[fs2.Pure,Char] = Stream.emits(List('a','b','c'))
```

Pure streams can be converted to the `List` or `Vector` without evaluation: `chars.toList`

Streams with effects can't be converted the same way because of the presence of effects. The effects first need to be *reduced* to a single effect. At the same time, we need to define how the output of the stream should be dealt with. Finally, we can execute the effect and get the output of the stream. This process is similar to the definition and materialization of the Akka streams we looked at in Chapter 13, *Basics of Akka Streams*. Because we have quite a number of things to define, the syntax is a bit cumbersome, but it reflects the logic we described:

```
object Test extends App {
  import fs2.Stream
  import cats.effect.IO // 1
  val io: IO[String] = IO { println("IO effect"); "a" * 2 } // 2
  val as: Stream[IO, String] = Stream.eval(io) // 3
  val c: Stream.ToEffect[IO, String] = as.compile // 4
  val v: IO[Vector[String]] = c.toVector // 5
  val l: IO[List[String]] = c.to[List] // 6
  val d: IO[Unit] = c.drain // 7
  val e: IO[Option[String]] = c.last // 8
  println(v.unsafeRunSync()) // 9
  println(e.unsafeRunSync()) // 10
  Stream.eval(IO { 42 }).compile.toList.unsafeRunSync() // 11
}
```

Let's go over this snippet line by line and look at what is happening. The numbers in the code will correspond to the numbers in the following explanation:

1. We are using the cats `IO` as type of our effect.
2. We define an `IO` as a by-name parameter to write to the console and return `aa`.
3. We `eval` our `IO`. This creates a single-element stream.
4. By compiling the stream, we create its projection to a single effect.

5. By converting a `ToEffect` projection to `Vector` it is compiled to the expected effect type. The process can be thought of as executing a stream of effects and logging emitted results into the desired structure.

6. We demonstrate another way to define conversion to collection.

7. `drain` is used to discard any emitted values and is useful if we are only interested in executing effects.

8. There are also other possibilities to define what should happen with output elements of the stream, for example, just collecting the `last` one.

9. `unsafeRunSync()` runs the definition, synchronously producing effects and emitting output. This is the first moment anything appears in the console because so far we've just created and modified the definition of the stream.

10. The definition is immutable and can be shared. Because of this, we can run the same stream description multiple times (with respect to the kind effects).

11. All of this is usually defined as a one-liner: eval the effect, compile the stream to the single effect, define the type of the output for the elements, run the stream later.

Now let's see how FS2 are utilized by `http4s` and `doobie`. We'll start with the database layer as its implementation will guide the structure of other layers.

Database migrations

In order for the database to be used in the application, it needs to contain all required tables, indexes, and other definitions.

We'll represent our store as a simple table with the name of the item serving as a primary key and a non-negative count of each item:

```
CREATE TABLE article (
  name   VARCHAR PRIMARY KEY,
  count INTEGER NOT NULL CHECK (count >= 0)
);
```

We'll place this definition into `db_migrations/V1__inventory_table.sql` and use Flyway to check that our database is in the correct state during startup time.

 Flyway provides a mechanism to define and change database schema in well-defined steps by adhering to specific naming conventions while placing schema migrations SQL in the project folder. You can learn more about it at `https://flywaydb.org`.

The Flyway code for migrations is straightforward:

```
def initialize(transactor: HikariTransactor[IO]): IO[Unit] = {
  transactor.configure { dataSource =>
    IO {
      val flyWay = new Flyway()
      flyWay.setLocations("classpath:db_migrations")
      flyWay.setDataSource(dataSource)
      flyWay.migrate()
    }
  }
}
```

Given a `transactor` (which we'll describe a bit later, at the moment we'll talk about `doobie`), we use the datasource it provides to create an instance of `Flyway`, configure it to use proper migrations location, and perform the migration. Please note that the initialization logic is wrapped into the `IO` effect and thus delayed until the effect is evaluated.

The transactor is created using the utility provided by doobie from the configuration:

```
def transactor(c: DBConfig): IO[HikariTransactor[IO]] = {
  HikariTransactor
    .newHikariTransactor[IO](c.driver, c.url, c.user, c.password)
}
```

Again it is wrapped in `IO` so no effects will be evaluated until we run the result of this function.

Before going over to the definition of the database repository, let's have a quick look at the configuration abstraction we've used in the `transactor` method.

Configuration with PureConfig

We're already familiar with the Typesafe Config library, which we actively used in our bakery examples. It is a very useful and flexible library. Unfortunately, because of this flexibility, it has one shortcoming: each configuration bit needs to be read and converted to the appropriate type individually. Ideally, we'd like our configuration to be represented as case classes and rely on naming conventions to map the structure of the configuration file to the structure of the (typed) configuration we have in the application. Ideally, we'd like to fail fast at startup time if the configuration file can't be mapped to the case classes that describe the configuration at the code level.

The `pureconfig` library makes this possible. This library can be found at `https://github.com/pureconfig/pureconfig`.

Using it, we can define the configuration structure in Scala like the following:

```
case class ServerConfig(host: String, port: Int)
case class DBConfig(driver: String, url: String, user: String, password:
String)
case class Config(server: ServerConfig, database: DBConfig)
```

This definition reflects the structure of the configuration in HOCON format:

```
server {
  host = "0.0.0.0"
  port = 8080
}
database {
  driver = "org.h2.Driver"
  url = "jdbc:h2:mem:ch14;DB_CLOSE_DELAY=-1"
  user = "sa"
  password = ""
}
```

Now we can load and map it to the case classes directly using `pureconfig`:

```
object Config {
  def load(fileName: String): IO[Config] = {
    IO {
      val config = ConfigFactory.load(fileName)
      pureconfig.loadConfig[Config](config)
    }.flatMap {
      case Left(e) =>
        IO.raiseError[Config](new ConfigReaderException[Config](e))
      case Right(config) =>
        IO.pure(config)
    }
  }
}
```

Again, wrapped in `IO` and thus delayed, we're trying to load and map the configuration and raise an appropriate error in the context of an `IO` in the case this attempt has failed.

The configuration bit concludes the infrastructural part of the example and we can finally turn to the core—the database repository.

Doobie – functional database access

The database layer in our example is implemented with the Doobie library. Its official website describes it as *a pure functional JDBC layer for Scala and Cats*. It allows us to abstract existing JDBC functionality in a nice functional way. Let's show how this is done. The library can be found at `https://tpolecat.github.io/doobie/`. In the following examples, please assume the following imports to be in scope:

```
import cats.effect.IO
import fs2.Stream
import doobie._
import doobie.implicits._
import doobie.util.transactor.Transactor
import cats.implicits._
```

We also need some model classes to persist, and for the purpose of the example, we'll keep the ADT as small as possible:

```
object Model {
  type Inventory = Map[String, Int]
  abstract sealed class Operation(val inventory: Inventory)

  final case class Purchase(order: Inventory)
      extends Operation(order.mapValues(_ * -1))

  final case class Restock(override val inventory: Inventory)
      extends Operation(inventory)
}
```

This model will allow us to represent the inventory of our shop as a map with keys referring to the article name and a values denoting number of the respective items in stock. We'll also have two operations that can be applied to the inventory—the Purchase operation will reduce the number of corresponding items and the Restock operation will increase number of respective items by combining our existing stocks together.

Now we can define our repository for this model. We'll do this in the same pure functional way we did before:

```
class Repository(transactor: Transactor[IO]) { ... }
```

The repository is given `Transactor[IO]` as a constructor parameter. The `IO` in this example is `cats.effect.IO`. The transactor knows how to work with database connections. It can manage connections in the same logical way a connection pool does. In our implementation, `Transactor` is used to convert an FS2 `Stream[IO, ?]` into the `IO`, which will connect to the database and execute SQL statements if run. Let's see in detail how this is done for article-creation:

```
def createArticle(name: String): IO[Boolean] = {
  val sql: Fragment = sql"INSERT INTO article (name, count) VALUES ($name,
0)"   // 1
  val update: Update0 = sql.update  // 2
  val conn: ConnectionIO[Int] = update.run //3
  val att: ConnectionIO[Either[Throwable, Int]] = conn.attempt //4
  val transact: IO[Either[Throwable, Int]] = att.transact(transactor) // 5
  transact.map { // 6
    case Right(affectedRows) => affectedRows == 1
    case Left(_)             => false
  }
}
```

Let's go over this definition line by line to see what is going on here:

1. We define a `Fragment`, which is an SQL statement that can include interpolated values. Fragments can be combined together.

2. From `Fragment`, we construct an `Update`. `Update` can be used to construct a `ConnectionIO` later.

3. We construct a `ConnectionIO` by calling the `run` method on `update`. `ConnectionIO` is basically an abstraction over the possible operations available on the JDBC connection.

4. By calling an `attempt` method, we're adding error-handling to our `ConnectionIO`. This is the reason the type parameter of `ConnectionIO` has changed from `Int` to `Either[Throwable, Int]`.

5. By providing a `transactor` to the `transact` method, we convert `ConnectionIO` into `IO`, which represents a runnable doobie program.

6. We coerce different sides of `Either` to a single Boolean value. We expect the number of created rows to be exactly one, in which case the call was a success. If we failed to create a row or if there was an exception thrown, it is a failure.

> It would be more appropriate in the erroneous case to differentiate between the *unique index or primary key violation* and other cases but unfortunately different database drivers have different encoding for that, so it is not possible to provide concise generic implementation.

Other methods in our repository will follow the same pattern. `deleteArticle` is a one-liner and we don't bother to handle errors in this case (exceptions will bubble up to the upper layers and be propagated to the client if they will be thrown), so we can just check whether the number of affected rows was exactly one:

```
def deleteArticle(name: String): IO[Boolean] =
sql"DELETE FROM article WHERE name = $name"
.update.run.transact(transactor).map { _ == 1 }
```

`getInventory` is a bit different because it needs to return the results of the query:

```
def getInventory: Stream[IO, Inventory] = {
  val query: doobie.Query0[(String, Int)] =
      sql"SELECT name, count FROM article".query[(String, Int)]
  val stream: Stream[IO, (String, Int)] =
      query.stream.transact(transactor)
  stream.fold(Map.empty[String, Int])(_ + _)
}
```

Here, we see that the query is of the `doobie.Query0[(String, Int)]` type with the type parameter representing the column types of the result. We convert the query to `Stream[ConnectionIO, (String, Int)]` (an FS2 stream with the `ConnectionIO` effect type and the tuple as a type of elements) by calling a `stream` method and then convert `ConnectionIO` to `IO` by providing a transactor. At last, we fold elements of the stream into `Map`, thus constructing the inventory state at the present moment from individual rows.

Updating the inventory has another caveat. We would like to update multiple articles at once so that if there is insufficient supply for some of the articles, we discard the whole purchase.

This is a design decision. We could decide to return a partially-fulfilled order to the client.

The count of every article needs to be updated separately, therefore we need to have multiple update statements running in a single transaction. This is how it is done:

```
def updateStock(inventory: Inventory): Stream[IO, Either[Throwable, Unit]]
= {
  val updates = inventory.map { case (name, count) =>
      sql"UPDATE article SET count = count + $count WHERE name =
```

```
$name".update.run
  }.reduce(_ *> _)
  Stream
    .eval(
      FC.setAutoCommit(false) *> updates *> FC.setAutoCommit(true)
    )
    .attempt.transact(transactor)
}
```

We're given a map of `name -> count` pairs as a parameter. The first thing we do is to convert each of these pairs into an update operation by mapping over them. This leaves us with a collection of `CollectionIO[Int]`. We then combine these updates together by using the cats `Apply` operator, which produces a single `CollectionIO[Int]`.

JDBC by default has auto-commit enabled, which will lead to the effect that our updates in the batch will be executed and committed one by one. This can lead to partially-fulfilled orders. In order to avoid that, we wrap the updates into the stream, which will disable auto-commits before the updates and enable auto-commits again after all of them are executed. We then lift the error-handling of the result and convert it into the runnable `IO` as before.

The result of the method is the `Stream[IO, Either[Throwable, Unit]]` type. The type of the elements of the stream encodes the possibilities to have both updates that weren't possible because there were insufficient articles in the inventory as `Left` and a successful update as `Right`.

With these four methods, we actually have all the required basic functionality and can start to use it in the API layer.

http4s – streaming HTTP

The implementation of the HTTP interface in our project is based on the http4s (https://http4s.org) library. http4s is built on top of the FS2 and Cats IO and therefore we have a nice interplay with the persistence layer implemented with doobie. With http4s, it is possible to build functional server-side services using high-level DSL, as well as use it on the client-side to call HTTP APIs. We will use the client functionality to build an integration test for our API later in this chapter.

The server side is represented by `HttpService[F]`, which is essentially just a mapping from `Request` to `F[Response]` and `F` is a cats `IO` in our case. http4s DSL helps to construct such RESTful services by using pattern-matching.

This is how it looks in practice. First we need to have following imports for `fs2` and `IO`, and http4s DSL and circe in scope:

```
import cats.effect.IO
import fs2.Stream
import org.http4s._
import org.http4s.dsl.Http4sDsl
import org.http4s.circe._
import org.http4s.headers.`Content-Type`
import io.circe.generic.auto._
import io.circe.syntax._
```

With these imports in place, we can start to build up our service definition:

```
class Service(repo: Repository) extends Http4sDsl[IO] { ... }
```

The service is given a database repository as a parameter.

The routes are defined separately for each HTTP verb and a URL template. We start with the definition of the service method, which takes a partial function from request to response:

```
val service: HttpService[IO] = HttpService[IO] {
```

Then we follow with the simple route for article deletion:

```
case DELETE -> Root / "articles" / name if name.nonEmpty =>
  val repoResult: IO[Boolean] = repo.deleteArticle(name)
  val toResponse: Boolean => IO[Response[IO]] = if (_) NoContent() else
NotFound()
  val response: IO[Response[IO]] = repoResult.flatMap(toResponse)
  response
```

Here we are using `http4s` DSL in order to deconstruct `Request` into parts and pattern-match against these parts. The `->` object extracts the path from the request and the `/` class allows us to represent the concatenation of subpaths of the request URL (there is also `/:`, which matches the URL from the point of application and to the end of the url). The pattern-match itself is just a normal Scala case, hence we can use its full power. In this case, we're mapping the last part of the URL to `name` and have a guardian to make sure the path only matches if `name` is not empty (because we don't want to have anonymous articles in our shop!).

The expected result of the function is the `IO[Response[IO]]` type. Luckily, the return type of the `deleteArticle` method of our repository is `IO[Boolean]`, so we can just `flatMap` the returned boolean value into the response body *inside* of an `IO`. In this case, we don't want to respond with the body, but just inform the caller about the success of the operation, which is represented with the respective response codes: `204 No Content` and `404 Not Found`. http4s provides a nice constructors for this with a bit of a verbose type: `IO[Response[IO]]`. In our case, we define a function from `Boolean` to this type and use this function to `flatMap` the result of the repository call, which leaves us with `IO[Response[IO]]` as an end result, which is exactly the type expected to be returned.

Of course, all of this logic can be written in a succinct manner. Here is an example for the API call to create an article:

```
case POST -> Root / "articles" / name if name.nonEmpty =>
    repo.createArticle(name).flatMap { if (_) NoContent() else Conflict() }
```

The approach is absolutely the same as the one we had for article deletion.

The API we're building is not a principle RESTful API. For this example to be a valid, level two API, we need to also implement a GET call that retrieves a representation for the individual articles. This can be done by adding a corresponding method to the repository and a `case` to the service. The implementation is left to the reader as an exercise.

Now that we have created a few articles in the repository, we would like to be able to retrieve the current state of it. We can implement it as follows:

```
case GET -> Root / "inventory" =>
  val inventory: Stream[IO, Inventory] = repo.getInventory
  renderInventory(inventory)
```

The above pattern-match is straightforward and so is the call to the `getInventory` method of the repository. But it returns the result of the `Stream[IO, Inventory]` type and we need to convert it to the matching type for `HttpService[IO]`. http4s has a concept of `EntityEncoder` for this.

Here is the corresponding implementation:

```
private def renderInventory(inventory: Stream[IO, Inventory]):
IO[Response[IO]] = {
  val json: Stream[IO, String] = inventory.map(_.asJson.noSpaces)
  val response: IO[Response[IO]] =
          Ok(json, `Content-Type`(MediaType.`application/json`))
```

```
    response
}
```

Here, we prepare the inventory to be represented as an HTTP response by converting the returned `Map[String, Int]` to JSON. We rely on circe (`https://github.com/circe/circe`) to perform automatic conversion. Next, the stream is converted to the appropriate response type by the `Ok` status constructor and an implicit `EntityEncoder[IO, String]`. We explicitly force the content type of the response to be `application/json` in order to have it correctly represented in the response.

Finally, we want to provide a way to modify the state of the inventory like we did with the repository. We'll implement two API calls, one for replenishing the inventory and another for purchases. They are implemented similarly, so we'll cover only one of them; the other can be found in the `GitHub` repository. Here is the implementation for the restock call:

```
case req @ POST -> Root / "restock" =>
  val newState = for {
    purchase <- Stream.eval(req.decodeJson[Restock])
    _ <- repo.updateStock(purchase.inventory)
    inventory <- repo.getInventory
  } yield inventory
  renderInventory(newState)
```

We need a request to read its body, therefore we bind it to the `req` variable in the pattern match. Next, we decode the JSON body of the request and map it to our model. Here we rely on circe to do the heavy lifting again. The `updateStock` repository method returns the stream, so we need to bring our parameter in the same context in order to be able to use it nicely in the `for` comprehension. We're doing this by wrapping the result of the decoding into `Stream.eval`.

Then we call the repository and provide the required changes in the form of `Inventory`. This method returns `Stream[IO, Either[Throwable, Unit]]`, so we ignore the result (it will shortcut the for comprehension in the case of an error). Finally, we read the new state of the repository and render it for the caller as before.

 The read-after-write is a known database anti-pattern. We used this approach to illustrate how streaming calls can be nicely chained in a for comprehension. In a real project, it might be better to formulate SQL statements in a way that the new state is returned immediately after the update.

The service layer is implemented now. We can wire our application together and see how it works.

Bringing it all together

The server code will require a few new imports in addition to our usual set:

```
import org.http4s.server.blaze.BlazeBuilder
import scala.concurrent.ExecutionContext.Implicits.global
```

`BlazeBuilder` is a server factory, and `ExecutionContext` will be needed at the moment we start the server. The server is defined as follows:

```
object Server extends StreamApp[IO] { ... }
```

`StreamApp` requires us to implement a `stream` method, with the solely purpose to produce side-effects and provides cleanup hooks for this stream. This is our implementation:

```
override def stream(args: List[String],
          requestShutdown: IO[Unit]): Stream[IO, ExitCode] = {
  val config: IO[Config] = Config.load("application.conf")
  new ServerInstance(config).create().flatMap(_.serve)
}
```

We just read the configuration and delegate the actual server creation to `ServerInstance`. Let's have a look at it:

```
class ServerInstance(config: IO[Config]) {
  def create(): Stream[IO, BlazeBuilder[IO]] = {
    for {
      config <- Stream.eval(config)
      transactor <- Stream.eval(DB.transactor(config.database))
      _ <- Stream.eval(DB.initialize(transactor))
    } yield BlazeBuilder[IO]
      .bindHttp(config.server.port, config.server.host)
      .mountService(new Service(new Repository(transactor)).service, "/")
  }
}
```

Here again we see the same approach: we lift `config` into the context of `Stream`, create a transactor, initialize the database, build the repository from the transactor and the service from the repository, and finally mount the service by using the `BlazeBuilder` factory.

The caller method will then execute the serve method of the server, starting the whole IO program we've built so far.

We were following a pattern for providing dependencies as we've build up this example—we gave them as constructor parameters at the moment we constructed class instances. The approach of passing dependencies as constructor parameters is called constructor-based dependency-injection in Scala.

Now our application can be started and played with. But we want to be sure that it behaves correctly by testing it.

Testing

This example is quite simple and basically just an HTTP facade over the database, so we won't test components in isolation. Instead, we'll use integration-testing to check the system as a whole.

In order to have SBT properly recognize our integration tests, we need to add the proper configurations to `build.sbt`. Please refer to the chapter code on GitHub (https://github.com/PacktPublishing/Learn-Scala-Programming) to see how this is done.

In our integration test, we will let our system run normally (but with the test database) and use an HTTP client to call the API and inspect the responses it will return.

First, we need to prepare our HTTP client and server:

```
class ServerSpec extends WordSpec with Matchers with BeforeAndAfterAll {
  private lazy val client = Http1Client[IO]().unsafeRunSync()
  private lazy val configIO = Config.load("test.conf")
  private lazy val config = configIO.unsafeRunSync()
  private val server: Option[Http4sServer[IO]] = (for {
    builder <- new ServerInstance(configIO).create()
  } yield builder.start.unsafeRunSync()).compile.last.unsafeRunSync()
```

Here we create the client we'll be using to query our API by instantiating the `Http1Client` provided by the `http4s` library. We also read a test config that overrides database settings so that we can freely modify the data. We're using an in-memory H2 database, which is destroyed after our test finishes so that we don't need to clean up the state after the test. Then we're building a server by re-using `ServerInstance`. In contrast to the production code, we're starting it with the `start` method, which returns a server instance. We'll use this instance after the test to shut down the server.

Please note how we use `unsafeRunSync()` in multiple places to evaluate the contents of `IO`. For the server, we're even doing this twice, once for `IO` and once for `Stream[IO,`
`...]`. This is okay to do in the test code as it helps to keep the testing logic concise.

We need to shut down the client and the server after the test:

```
override def afterAll(): Unit = {
  client.shutdown.unsafeRunSync()
  server.foreach(_.shutdown.unsafeRunSync())
}
```

Again, we're running an IO here because we want the have the shutdown happen right now.

Now, let's take a look at one of the test methods:

```
"create articles" in {
  val eggs = Request[IO](method = Method.POST, uri =
Uri.unsafeFromString(s"$rootUrl/articles/eggs"))
  client.status(eggs).unsafeRunSync() shouldBe Status.NoContent
  val chocolate = Request[IO](method = Method.POST, uri =
Uri.unsafeFromString(s"$rootUrl/articles/chocolate"))
  client.status(chocolate).unsafeRunSync() shouldBe Status.NoContent
  val json = client.expect[Json](s"$rootUrl/inventory").unsafeRunSync()
  json shouldBe json"""{"eggs" : 0,"chocolate" : 0}"""
}
```

Here we first create a test request using a factory provided by http4s. We then check that the API returns the correct `NoContent` status if we send this request with the client we created earlier in this section. We then create the second article by using the same approach.

Finally, we're using the client to call the URL directly and let it parse the response to the JSON form. Finally, we check that the inventory has a correct state by comparing the JSON response with circe's JSON literal.

For testing other API calls, we could also provide a request body using circe JSON literals. Please refer to the chapter's source code placed on GitHub to see how this is done.

It is absolutely possible to implement the same testing logic using other HTTP clients or even command-line tools. The `Http1Client` provided by `http4s` allows for nice syntax and concise expectation definitions.

Running the application

The easiest way to run our API is in the SBT shell by issuing a `run` command. The project for this chapter is configured as a multi-module SBT project. Because of this, the `run` command has to be prefixed by the module name so that it is fully spelled as `http4s/run` as shown in the next screenshot:

```
slasch@packt:~$ cd Learn-Scala---Fundamentals-of-Scala-2.13/ch14
slasch@packt:~/Learn-Scala---Fundamentals-of-Scala-2.13/ch14$ sbt
[info] Loading settings for project ch14-build from plugins.sbt ...
[info] Loading project definition from /home/slasch/Learn-Scala---Fundamentals-of-Scala-2.13/ch14/project
[info] Loading settings for project root from build.sbt ...
[info] Set current project to root (in build file:/home/slasch/Learn-Scala---Fundamentals-of-Scala-2.13/ch14/)
[info] sbt server started at local:///home/slasch/.sbt/1.0/server/5feabd4374d0fc31ffb8/sock
sbt:root> http4s/run
d[info] Running ch14.Server
19:52:45.105 [run-main-0] INFO org.flywaydb.core.internal.util.VersionPrinter - Flyway Community Edition 5.1.4 by Boxfuse
19:52:45.131 [run-main-0] DEBUG com.zaxxer.hikari.HikariConfig - HikariPool-1 - configuration:
19:52:45.152 [run-main-0] DEBUG com.zaxxer.hikari.HikariConfig - allowPoolSuspension............false
19:52:45.157 [run-main-0] DEBUG com.zaxxer.hikari.HikariConfig - autoCommit.....................true
19:52:45.157 [run-main-0] DEBUG com.zaxxer.hikari.HikariConfig - catalog........................none
19:52:45.158 [run-main-0] DEBUG com.zaxxer.hikari.HikariConfig - connectionInitSql..............none
19:52:45.160 [run-main-0] DEBUG com.zaxxer.hikari.HikariConfig - connectionTestQuery............none
19:52:45.161 [run-main-0] DEBUG com.zaxxer.hikari.HikariConfig - connectionTimeout..............30000
19:52:45.161 [run-main-0] DEBUG com.zaxxer.hikari.HikariConfig - dataSource.....................none
19:52:45.161 [run-main-0] DEBUG com.zaxxer.hikari.HikariConfig - dataSourceClassName............none
19:52:45.161 [run-main-0] DEBUG com.zaxxer.hikari.HikariConfig - dataSourceJNDI.................none
19:52:45.162 [run-main-0] DEBUG com.zaxxer.hikari.HikariConfig - dataSourceProperties...........{password=<masked>}
19:52:45.165 [run-main-0] DEBUG com.zaxxer.hikari.HikariConfig - driverClassName................none
19:52:45.165 [run-main-0] DEBUG com.zaxxer.hikari.HikariConfig - healthCheckProperties..........{}
19:52:45.165 [run-main-0] DEBUG com.zaxxer.hikari.HikariConfig - healthCheckRegistry............none
19:52:45.165 [run-main-0] DEBUG com.zaxxer.hikari.HikariConfig - idleTimeout....................600000
19:52:45.165 [run-main-0] DEBUG com.zaxxer.hikari.HikariConfig - initializationFailTimeout......1
19:52:45.166 [run-main-0] DEBUG com.zaxxer.hikari.HikariConfig - isolateInternalQueries.........false
19:52:45.166 [run-main-0] DEBUG com.zaxxer.hikari.HikariConfig - jdbcUrl........................jdbc:h2:mem:ch14;DB_CLOSE_DELAY=-1
19:52:45.167 [run-main-0] DEBUG com.zaxxer.hikari.HikariConfig - leakDetectionThreshold.........0
19:52:45.167 [run-main-0] DEBUG com.zaxxer.hikari.HikariConfig - maxLifetime....................1800000
19:52:45.167 [run-main-0] DEBUG com.zaxxer.hikari.HikariConfig - maximumPoolSize................10
19:52:45.167 [run-main-0] DEBUG com.zaxxer.hikari.HikariConfig - metricRegistry.................none
19:52:45.167 [run-main-0] DEBUG com.zaxxer.hikari.HikariConfig - metricsTrackerFactory..........none
19:52:45.167 [run-main-0] DEBUG com.zaxxer.hikari.HikariConfig - minimumIdle....................10
19:52:45.167 [run-main-0] DEBUG com.zaxxer.hikari.HikariConfig - password.......................<masked>
19:52:45.167 [run-main-0] DEBUG com.zaxxer.hikari.HikariConfig - poolName......................."HikariPool-1"
```

Different components of our API will output lots of information. The application is started after the address of the HTTP server is shown. You can see how this looks on the bottom of the next screenshot:

```
19:52:46.799 [run-main-0] DEBUG org.flywaydb.core.internal.database.Table - Lock acquired for table "PUBLIC"."flyway_schema_history"
19:52:46.845 [run-main-0] INFO org.flywaydb.core.internal.command.DbMigrate - Current version of schema "PUBLIC": << Empty Schema >>
19:52:46.867 [run-main-0] DEBUG org.flywaydb.core.internal.database.ExecutableSqlScript - Parsing V1__inventory_table.sql ...
19:52:46.878 [run-main-0] DEBUG org.flywaydb.core.internal.database.ExecutableSqlScript - Found statement at line 1: CREATE TABLE art
icle (
  name   VARCHAR PRIMARY KEY,
  count INTEGER NOT NULL CHECK (count >= 0)
)
19:52:46.879 [run-main-0] INFO org.flywaydb.core.internal.command.DbMigrate - Migrating schema "PUBLIC" to version 1 - inventory tabl
e
19:52:46.883 [run-main-0] DEBUG org.flywaydb.core.internal.database.ExecutableSqlScript - Executing SQL: CREATE TABLE article (
  name   VARCHAR PRIMARY KEY,
  count INTEGER NOT NULL CHECK (count >= 0)
)
19:52:46.891 [run-main-0] DEBUG org.flywaydb.core.internal.database.ExecutableSqlScript - Update Count: 0
19:52:46.902 [run-main-0] DEBUG org.flywaydb.core.internal.command.DbMigrate - Successfully completed migration of schema "PUBLIC" to
version 1 - inventory table
19:52:46.959 [run-main-0] DEBUG org.flywaydb.core.internal.database.Table - Locking table "PUBLIC"."flyway_schema_history"...
19:52:46.968 [run-main-0] DEBUG org.flywaydb.core.internal.database.Table - Lock acquired for table "PUBLIC"."flyway_schema_history"
19:52:46.971 [run-main-0] DEBUG org.flywaydb.core.internal.schemahistory.JdbcTableSchemaHistory - Schema History table "PUBLIC"."flyw
ay_schema_history" successfully updated to reflect changes
19:52:46.979 [run-main-0] DEBUG org.flywaydb.core.internal.database.Table - Locking table "PUBLIC"."flyway_schema_history"...
19:52:47.003 [run-main-0] DEBUG org.flywaydb.core.internal.database.Table - Lock acquired for table "PUBLIC"."flyway_schema_history"
19:52:47.050 [run-main-0] INFO org.flywaydb.core.internal.command.DbMigrate - Successfully applied 1 migration to schema "PUBLIC" (ex
ecution time 00:00.567s)
19:52:47.357 [run-main-0] INFO org.http4s.blaze.channel.nio1.NIO1SocketServerGroup - Service bound to address /0:0:0:0:0:0:0:0:8080
19:52:47.358 [run-main-0] INFO org.http4s.server.blaze.BlazeBuilder - 
19:52:47.361 [run-main-0] INFO org.http4s.server.blaze.BlazeBuilder -   | |_| |_| |_ _ __| | |  ___
19:52:47.361 [run-main-0] INFO org.http4s.server.blaze.BlazeBuilder -   | ' \ _| _| '_ \_  _(_-<
19:52:47.361 [run-main-0] INFO org.http4s.server.blaze.BlazeBuilder -   |_||_\_|\__| .__/ |_|/__/
19:52:47.361 [run-main-0] INFO org.http4s.server.blaze.BlazeBuilder -              |_|
19:52:47.520 [run-main-0] INFO org.http4s.server.blaze.BlazeBuilder - http4s v0.18.9 on blaze v0.12.13 started at http://[0:0:0:0:0:0
:0:0]:8080/
19:53:15.716 [HikariPool-1 housekeeper] DEBUG com.zaxxer.hikari.pool.HikariPool - HikariPool-1 - Pool stats (total=10, active=0, idle
=10, waiting=0)
```

After that, the API should serve HTTP requests, for example, issued with curl in another terminal window as the following screenshot demonstrates:

```
slasch void: $ ## Get Inventory
slasch void: $ curl "http://localhost:8080/inventory"
{}slasch void: $ ## Create Chocolate
slasch void: $ curl -X "POST" "http://localhost:8080/articles/chocolate"
slasch void: $ ## Create Eggs
slasch void: $ curl -X "POST" "http://localhost:8080/articles/eggs"
slasch void: $ ## Restock
slasch void: $ curl -X "POST" "http://localhost:8080/restock" \
>       -H 'Content-Type: application/json; charset=utf-8' \
>       -d $'{
>    "stock": {
>      "chocolate": 10000,
>      "sugar": 10000,
>      "flour": 10000,
>      "eggs": 10000
>    }
> }'
curl: (18) transfer closed with outstanding read data remaining
slasch void: $ ## Reinventory
slasch void: $ curl -X "POST" "http://localhost:8080/restock" \
>       -H 'Content-Type: application/json; charset=utf-8' \
>       -d $'{
>    "inventory": {
>      "chocolate": 10000,
>      "sugar": 10000,
>      "flour": 10000,
>      "eggs": 10000
>    }
> }'
{"chocolate":10000,"eggs":10000}slasch void: $ ## Get Inventory
slasch void: $ curl "http://localhost:8080/inventory"
{"chocolate":10000,"eggs":10000}slasch void: $
```

As our example uses in-memory database, it will lose its state after restart.

Building microservices with Akka-HTTP and Akka Persistence

Now that we've seen how the principle functional approach to the implementation of the microservice works, let's change our technological stack and implement the same shop with Akka-HTTP and Akka Persistence. The flow of the discussion for this example will be similar to the one we had about the functional approach—we will start with looking at the way to persist the state of the service and the configuration needed for that. We'll then address the task of actually persisting the data and providing access to it via the HTTP service. As before, we'll conclude our journey by testing the implementation we'll come up with.

Project structure

The project structure, in this case, will be almost the same as we had before.

We'll have an API layer responsible for the interaction with HTTP clients. We'll also inevitably have some configuration and a database initialization code that will be implemented in a similar, or identical, way to what we did as we've built the previous microservice.

The persistence layer will be represented by a persistent actor. This will affect the definition of the model as well as the structure of the database tables.

Akka Persistence introduces different paradigms of how the state of the system is stored and represented. The approach is called **Event-Sourcing** and it makes sense to take a minute to discuss it.

Event-Sourcing and CQRS

Event-sourcing is about how the state of the system is stored. Normally the state of the system is persisted into the database as a number of related tables. Changes to the state are reflected in the database by modifying, adding, or deleting table rows. The database contains the current state of the system with this approach.

Event-sourcing provides an alternative method. It handles updates of the state very much like functional programming handles effects. Instead of executing a computation, it just describes it so that it is possible to execute it later. Descriptions of computations can be combined, as we saw in the second section of this book. The same way the changes of the state can be combined in an event-sourced approach to produce current state. In essence, event-sourcing is to the state what functional programming is to the computations and effects.

This description of the state change is called **event** and it usually (but not necessarily!) corresponds to some user action, called **command**. The system receives commands, validates them, and if the command makes sense in the context of current system state, respective event(s) is created and persisted into the event journal. The event is then applied to the in-memory representation(s) of the state and the required side-effects are executed.

When the event-sourced system is restarted, the events are read from the journal and applied to the initial state one by one, modifying it but not executing side-effects. At the end, after all events are applied, the internal state of the system should be the same as it was before the restart. Hence, *events* are the *source* of the state representation of the system in this scenario. The reconstructed state often represents only one aspect of the whole system and is called **view**.

The event journal is used only for appending events. Because of this, it is usually seen as an append-only storage, and often solutions other than relational databases are used.

CQRS is another name that goes hand in hand with Event-Sourcing. This is an abbreviation for Command Query Responsibility Segregation, which in turn is just a fancy way to name a principle of *Command–Query Separation* implemented with Command and Query entities (as opposed to the method calls). The CQS principle states that every method should be either *command*, which modifies the state, or *query*, which returns the state, and these responsibilities should not be mixed. With Event-Sourcing, this separation comes naturally from the definition of the *Event* (which is the Command in the CQS definition) and the concept of internal state as a *View* that needs to be queried separately.

Event-Sourcing has a lots of advantages over the traditional database-mutating approach:

- Append-only approach to store data scales much better than traditional relational databases.
- Events provide audit, traceability, and in the case of special storages, security for free.
- No need to use an ORM.
- The domain model and event model can evolve at a different pace.

- It is possible to recover the state of the system to any specific moment in the past.
- Events can be combined in different ways, allowing us to construct different representations of state. Combined with the previous advantage, it gives us the ability to analyze past data in ways that weren't known at the time of the event's creation.

Of course, there are some drawbacks as well:

- The state does not exists until it is reconstructed from events. Depending on the format of the journal, it might even impossible to analyze the events without writing special code for this purpose. In any case, it requires some effort to build the state representation from events.
- Explosion of domain model in complex projects. Implementing new use-cases always requires the introduction of new commands and events.
- Changes in the model as the project evolves. Changes in existing use-cases often mean changes in the structure of existing evens, which need to be done in the code because the event journal is append-only.
- The number of events can grow rapidly. In actively-used systems, there may be millions of events produced daily, which can affect the time needed to build the state representation. Snapshotting is used to work around this issue.

Configuring Akka Persistence

Akka Persistence allows us to store and replay messages sent to `PersistentActor` and thus implements an event-sourcing approach. Before going into the details of the actors implementation, let's look at the arrangements we need to make in the project configuration.

We're going to use the H2 relational database for this project. Akka Persistence supports many different storage plugins, including a local filesystem for storing snapshots, and in our case, it appears to be a good idea to use the same database we used with doobie to underline the differences in the architectural style.

Again, we're using Flyway to create the structure of the database. The tables will be different though. This is the table that will store events:

```
CREATE TABLE IF NOT EXISTS PUBLIC."journal" (
  "ordering" BIGINT AUTO_INCREMENT,
  "persistence_id" VARCHAR(255) NOT NULL,
  "sequence_number" BIGINT NOT NULL,
  "deleted" BOOLEAN DEFAULT FALSE,
  "tags" VARCHAR(255) DEFAULT NULL,
```

```
    "message" BYTEA NOT NULL,
    PRIMARY KEY("persistence_id", "sequence_number")
);
```

`persistence_id` is an ID of a specific persistent actor, which needs to be unique for the whole actor system (we'll see in a minute how this maps to the code), the `tags` field holds tags assigned to the events (this makes constructing views easier). `message` holds an event in serialized form. The serialization mechanism is decoupled from the storage. Akka supports different flavours, including Java serialization, Google Protobuf, Apache Thrift, or Avro and JSON. We'll use the JSON format in order to keep the example small.

The snapshots table is even simpler:

```
CREATE TABLE IF NOT EXISTS PUBLIC."snapshot" (
    "persistence_id" VARCHAR(255) NOT NULL,
    "sequence_number" BIGINT NOT NULL,
    "created" BIGINT NOT NULL,
    "snapshot" BYTEA NOT NULL,
    PRIMARY KEY("persistence_id", "sequence_number")
);
```

Basically, it's just a snapshot in serialized form, with a timestamp and the `persistence_id` of the actor it belongs to.

With these tables in the migrations file, we now need to add following dependencies to `build.sbt`:

```
"com.typesafe.akka"  %% "akka-persistence"       % akkaVersion,
"com.github.dnvriend" %% "akka-persistence-jdbc" % akkaPersistenceVersion,
"com.scalapenos"     %% "stamina-json"           % staminaVersion,
"com.h2database"     %  "h2"                     % h2Version,
"org.flywaydb"       %  "flyway-core"            % flywayVersion,
```

The `akka-persistence` dependency is obvious. `akka-persistence-jdbc` is an implementation of the JDBC storage for the h2 database. `Flyway-core` is used to set up the database like in the previous example. `stamina-json` allows for schema migrations—it gives us a way to describe how the events stored in the old format in the database should be converted to the new format used in the code if needed.

We also need to put quite a bit of configuration for the Akka persistence
in `application.conf` to configure journals. This configuration is quite verbose, so we will
not discuss it here in full, but we will take a look at one part of it that describes
serialization:

```
akka.actor {
    serializers.serializer = "ch14.EventSerializer"
    serialization-bindings {
      "stamina.Persistable" = serializer
    }
}
```

Here, we configure serialization for the stamina. Let's take a look at `EventSerializer`:

```
class EventSerializer
    extends stamina.StaminaAkkaSerializer(v1createdPersister,
                                          v1deletedPersister,
                                          v1purchasedPersister,
                                          v1restockedPersister,
                                          v1inventoryPersister)
```

Here, we tell stamina which serializers to use. The serializers are defined as follows:

```
import stamina.json._

object PersistenceSupport extends JsonSupport {
  val v1createdPersister = persister[ArticleCreated]("article-created")
  val v1deletedPersister = persister[ArticleDeleted]("article-deleted")
  val v1purchasedPersister = persister[ArticlesPurchased]("articles-
purchased")
  val v1restockedPersister = persister[ArticlesRestocked]("articles-
restocked")
  val v1inventoryPersister = persister[Inventory]("inventory")
}
```

In the `PersistenceSupport` object, we define persisters for our events. We don't need any
migrations yet, but in the case we would, the migrations would be described here. Persister
requires implicit `RootJsonFormat` to be available and we provide them in
the `JsonSupport` trait:

```
import akka.http.scaladsl.marshallers.sprayjson.SprayJsonSupport
import spray.json.{DefaultJsonProtocol, RootJsonFormat}
import DefaultJsonProtocol._

trait JsonSupport extends SprayJsonSupport {
  implicit val invJF: RootJsonFormat[Inventory] =
    jsonFormat1(Inventory)
```

```scala
    implicit val createArticleJF = jsonFormat2(CreateArticle)
    implicit val deleteArticleJF = jsonFormat1(DeleteArticle)
    implicit val purchaseJF = jsonFormat1(PurchaseArticles)
    implicit val restockJF = jsonFormat1(RestockArticles)

    implicit val createdJF = jsonFormat2(ArticleCreated)
    implicit val deletedJF = jsonFormat1(ArticleDeleted)
    implicit val pJF = jsonFormat1(ArticlesPurchased)
    implicit val reJF = jsonFormat1(ArticlesRestocked)
}
```

We extend `SprayJsonSupport` and import `DefaultJsonProtocol._` to get implicit formats for basic types already defined by `spray-json`. Then we define `RootJsonFormat` for all of our commands (these formats will be used by the API layer to un-marshall request bodies), events (which will be used by both the API layer to marshall responses, and the persistence layer to serialize events), and an Inventory (which is required for snapshots to be serializable). Here we're not relying on circe's auto-derivation and hence describe each case class individually.

Now we have persisters and formats for the model, but what is that model? It reflects the event-sourcing approach!

Domain models

With event-sourcing, we want to store changes of the state as events. Not every interaction with the client is an event. Until we know that we can comply, we're modeling it as a command. Specifically, in our example it is represented as sealed traits:

```scala
sealed trait Command
sealed trait Query

object Commands {
  final case class CreateArticle(name: String, count: Int) extends Command
  final case class DeleteArticle(name: String) extends Command
  final case class PurchaseArticles(order: Map[String, Int]) extends
Command
  final case class RestockArticles(stock: Map[String, Int]) extends Command
  final case object GetInventory extends Query
}
```

In the spirit of CQRS, we model incoming data as four commands and one query. The commands can be made into the events if the current state allows that:

```
object Events {
  final case class ArticleCreated(name: String, count: Int) extends Event
  final case class ArticleDeleted(name: String) extends Event
  final case class ArticlesPurchased(order: Map[String, Int]) extends Event
  final case class ArticlesRestocked(stock: Map[String, Int]) extends Event
}
```

In our simple case, commands and events correspond to each other, but in the real project, this won't always be the case.

We also have a representation of the current state of the store:

```
final case class Inventory(state: Map[String, Int]) extends Persistable {
... }
```

`Inventory` extends `Persistable` so that we can make snapshots later. We will keep the business logic separate from the actor-related code. Because of this, our inventory should be able to handle events itself:

```
def update(event: Event): Inventory = event match {
  case ArticleCreated(name, cnt) => create(name, cnt).get
  case ArticleDeleted(name)      => delete(name).get
  case ArticlesPurchased(order)  => add(order.mapValues(_ * -1))
  case ArticlesRestocked(stock)  => add(stock)
}
```

The `create` method adds an article to the store and assigns some initial counts to it if possible. It returns an inventory in the new state in the case of success:

```
def create(name: String, count: Int): Option[Inventory] =
  state.get(name) match {
    case None => Some(Inventory(state.updated(name, count)))
    case _    => None
  }
```

The `delete` method tries to delete an article from the inventory:

```
def delete(name: String): Option[Inventory] =
  if (state.contains(name))
    Some(Inventory(state.filterKeys(k => !(k == name))))
  else None
```

The `add` method sums the count of articles from another inventory with counts of all articles existing in this inventory:

```scala
def add(o: Map[String, Int]): Inventory = {
  val newState = state.foldLeft(Map.empty[String, Int]) {
    case (acc, (k, v)) => acc.updated(k, v + o.getOrElse(k, 0))
  }
  Inventory(newState)
}
```

Now our inventory can accept events and return itself in an updated state, but we still have to deal with commands first. One possible implementation of the logic for command-handling could look like this:

```scala
def canUpdate(cmd: Command): Option[Event] = cmd match {
  case CreateArticle(name, cnt) =>
    create(name, cnt).map(_ => ArticleCreated(name, cnt))
  case DeleteArticle(name)      => delete(name).map(_ =>
ArticleDeleted(name))
  case PurchaseArticles(order) =>
    val updated = add(order.mapValues(_ * -1))
    if (updated.state.forall(_._2 >=  0)) Some(ArticlesPurchased(order))
else None
  case RestockArticles(stock)   => Some(ArticlesRestocked(stock))
}
```

The `canUpdate` method takes a command and returns a corresponding event in the case that it is possible to apply the command successfully. For creating and deleting articles, we're checking that the operation will produce a valid result; for purchases, we're checking that there are enough articles in stock, and restock should always succeed.

Our Inventory is not synchronized and hence it is not safe to work within a concurrent scenario. Moreover, if one thread makes modifications to the inventory at the time another thread already called `canUpdate`, but has not called `update` yet, we might end up with the incorrect state because of this race condition. But we don't need to worry about that because we're going to use our inventory inside of an actor.

The persistent actor

The persistent actor in Akka extends the normal `Actor` and mixes in a `PersistentActor`. `PersistentActor` implements the `receive` method but requires a few other methods to be implemented by us:

```
class InventoryActor extends Actor with PersistentActor {
  private var inventory: Inventory = Inventory(Map.empty)

  override def persistenceId: String = InventoryActor.persistenceId

  override def receiveRecover: Receive = ???

  override def receiveCommand: Receive = ???
}
```

Besides the `inventory` that we need as a representation of state, we need to define a unique `persistenceId` and two methods: `receiveRecover` and `receiveCommand`. The former is called during the recovery time, for example at startup or if the persistent actor is restarted, and it receives all events from the journal. It is expected to modify the internal state but not to execute any side-effects. The latter is called during the normal lifetime and it receives all the commands. It is supposed to convert valid commands to events, persist the events, modify the internal state, and execute side-effecting code after that.

In our example, `receiveRecover` just delegates the event processing to `inventory`:

```
override def receiveRecover: Receive = {
  case SnapshotOffer(_, snapshot: Inventory) => inventory = snapshot
  case event: Event => inventory = inventory.update(event)
  case RecoveryCompleted => saveSnapshot(inventory)
}
```

Additionally, it handles instances of `SnapshotOffer` by restoring the inventory as a whole from the latest snapshot. `SnapshotOffer` will be the first message the actor receives if there are snapshots available, and it will contain the latest snapshot so it is safe to restore the inventory from it. The events in the journal before the snapshot will not be replayed. Finally, after receiving the `RecoveryCompleted` event, we save the current state as a snapshot for use after the next restart.

The `receiveCommand` implementation is a bit more involved:

```
override def receiveCommand: Receive = {
  case GetInventory =>
    sender() ! inventory
```

```
        case cmd: Command =>
          inventory.canUpdate(cmd) match {
            case None =>
              sender() ! None
            case Some(event) =>
              persistAsync(event) { ev =>
                inventory = inventory.update(ev)
                sender() ! Some(ev)
              }
          }
      }
    }
```

We handle the `GetInventory` query by sending a current state to the sender. Inventory is a wrapper over an immutable map, so it is safe to share.

We handle all `Commands` the same way, by letting Inventory do the actual work. If a command cannot be applied, we respond to the sender with `None`. In the opposite case, we asynchronously persist corresponding events and provide a callback that will be executed after the event is persisted. In the callback, we apply the event to the internal state and send the new state to the sender. In contrast to the normal actor, it is safe to use `sender()` in an async block.

And this is it, we now have a persistent actor that will restore its state after the restart. Time to make it available for HTTP clients.

Akka-HTTP

Akka-HTTP provides a nice DSL to describe a server-side API similar to doobie. But Akka's language flows a bit differently. Instead of pattern-matching the request by applying rules one by one, it works more like a sieve. It filters requests by providing a number of directives, each matching some aspect of the request. The directives are nested so that each request travels deeper and deeper into matching branches until it reaches the processing logic. Such a combination of directives is called route. This is the inventory route:

```
    lazy val inventoryRoutes: Route =
      path("inventory") {
        get {
          ???
        }
      } ~
        path("purchase") {
          post {
            entity(as[PurchaseArticles]) { order =>
              ???
```

```
            }
          }
        } ~
        path("restock") {
          post {
            entity(as[RestockArticles]) { stock =>
                ???
            }
          }
        }
      }
```

This route contains three smaller routes, one matching GET /inventory, another POST /purchase, and the third POST /restock. The second and third routes also define that the request entity must be parseable as PurchaseArticles and RestockArticles respectively and provide the result of the parsing as a parameter to the body. Let's see how the internals of these routes are implemented. We know that the inventory route should return the current state so we ask the inventory actor about that:

```
complete((inventory ? GetInventory).mapTo[Inventory])
```

The complete method takes ToResponseMarshallable, and we rely on the Akka-HTTP and JSON serializers we defined earlier to do the implicit conversion from the Future[Inventory] that we're getting as the result of the application of the ask pattern here.

inventory is provided as an abstract field for now. This is how it looks in the definition of Routes:

```
trait Routes extends JsonSupport {
  implicit def system: ActorSystem
  def inventory: ActorRef
  def config: Config

  implicit lazy val timeout: Timeout = config.timeout
  implicit lazy val ec: ExecutionContext = system.dispatcher
```

We define an abstract config that we then use to define an implicit timeout for the ask. We also define ExecutionContext in order to be able to map over Future in other routes.

The implementation of the other two routes is similar. This is the purchase route:

```
val response: Future[Option[ArticlesPurchased]] =
  (inventory ? order).mapTo[Option[ArticlesPurchased]]
onSuccess(response) {
  case None        => complete(StatusCodes.Conflict)
  case Some(event) => complete(event)
```

The logic is almost the same with differences related to the situation we can't satisfy the requirements. In this case, we return the `409 Conflict` error code.

The restock route is even simpler because it always succeeds:

```
val response: Future[Option[ArticlesRestocked]] =
  (inventory ? stock).mapTo[Option[ArticlesRestocked]]
complete(response)
```

The definition of `articleRoute` for article creation and deletion is very similar and is available on GitHub so we will omit it here.

The routes are combined together using ~, the same way we already did inline:

```
lazy val routes: Route = articlesRoutes ~ inventoryRoutes
```

Bringing it all together

Having the routes implemented, we can now go on with the server definition:

```
object Server extends App with Routes with JsonSupport {

  val config = Config.load()

  implicit val system: ActorSystem = ActorSystem("ch14")
  implicit val materializer: ActorMaterializer = ActorMaterializer()

  DB.initialize(config.database)

  lazy val inventory: ActorRef = system.actorOf(InventoryActor.props,
InventoryActor.persistenceId)


  Http().bindAndHandle(routes, config.server.host, config.server.port)
  Await.result(system.whenTerminated, Duration.Inf)
}
```

We mix together the `Routes` and `JsonSupport` traits and define abstract fields. The actor system is needed in order to instantiate the materializer, and a materializer is a machine driving Akka-HTTP. Then we initialize the database, instantiate our persistent actor (which starts to receive events from the journal and restore its state), bind and start the server, and wait for the termination of the actor system.

 The way we injected dependencies by defining abstract members and then mixing traits together is called trait-based DI or the thin cake pattern. Usually, in simple cases, we would prefer constructor-based DI, like in the http4s example.

Compared to the http4s implementation, this server is eager. Every statement is executed the moment it is defined (with respect for laziness).

Now we have another version of our store done and can test it as well.

Testing

Of course, Akka would not be Akka if it did not provide a nice DSL for testing HTTP routes. The DSL allows us to test routes in a way that it is not needed to start a real server. It is possible to provide a mock implementation of the business logic to test routes in isolation. In our case, the logic is so simple that it actually makes sense to test the app as a whole, the same way we did in the http4s case.

The definition of the specification should not be surprising:

```
class RoutesSpec extends WordSpec with Matchers with ScalaFutures with
ScalatestRouteTest with Routes {

  override lazy val config: Config = Config.load()

  DB.initialize(config.database)

  override lazy val inventory: ActorRef =
system.actorOf(InventoryActor.props, "inventory")
    ...
}
```

The good news is that `ScalatestRouteTest` already provides a definition for the actor system and `materializer` so we don't need to initialize them before the test and close after the test. The `Routes` are the same `Routes` we defined earlier and are about to test now. We still have abstract definitions of `config` and `inventory` here, so provide an implementation for them.

And this is how we can test a route:

```
"Routes" should { "be able to add article (POST /articles/eggs)" in {
  val request = Post("/articles/eggs")
  request ~> routes ~> check {
    status shouldBe StatusCodes.Created
    contentType shouldBe ContentTypes.`application/json`
    entityAs[String] shouldBe """{"name":"eggs","count":0}"""
  }
}}
```

First, we define the `request` we want the route to be checked against. Then we transform it with the `route` to the response, which in turn gets transformed into `check`. In the body of `check`, we can refer to the properties of the response in a simple way.

The `routes` in `request ~> routes ~> check` refer to the field defined in the `Routes` trait.

Similarly, it is possible to create a request with a body and use it to test a route that expects such request:

```
"be able to restock articles (POST /restock)" in {
  val restock = RestockArticles(Map("eggs" -> 10, "chocolate" -> 20))
  val entity  = Marshal(restock).to[MessageEntity].futureValue
  val request = Post("/restock").withEntity(entity)
  request ~> routes ~> check {
    status shouldBe StatusCodes.OK
    contentType shouldBe ContentTypes.`application/json`
    entityAs[String] shouldBe """{"stock":{"eggs":10,"chocolate":20}}"""
  }
}
```

Here we `Marshal` the restock case class to `Entity` the same way it worked on routes. `.futureValue` is from the ScalaTest's `ScalaFutures` helper. The rest of the snippet is very similar to the previous example.

Running the application

To run the Akka-HTTP API, we have to use the same approach as we used for the http4s version. The name of the module will be, well, `akkaHttp`, but the principle is the same. The next screenshot shows the output in the console after `akkaHttp/run` was entered in the SBT shell:

```
slasch@packt:~$ cd Learn-Scala---Fundamentals-of-Scala-2.13/ch14
slasch@packt:~/Learn-Scala---Fundamentals-of-Scala-2.13/ch14$ sbt
[info] Loading settings for project ch14-build from plugins.sbt ...
[info] Loading project definition from /home/slasch/Learn-Scala---Fundamentals-of-Scala-2.13/ch14/project
[info] Loading settings for project root from build.sbt ...
[info] Set current project to root (in build file:/home/slasch/Learn-Scala---Fundamentals-of-Scala-2.13/ch14/)
[info] sbt server started at local:///home/slasch/.sbt/1.0/server/5feabd4374d0fc31ffb8/sock
sbt:root> akkaHttp/run
[info] Updating akkaHttp...
[info] downloading https://repo1.maven.org/maven2/com/typesafe/akka/akka-slf4j_2.12/2.5.14/akka-slf4j_2.12-2.5.14.jar ...
[info]   [SUCCESSFUL ] com.typesafe.akka#akka-slf4j_2.12;2.5.14!akka-slf4j_2.12.jar (1167ms)
[info] Done updating.
[warn] There may be incompatibilities among your library dependencies.
[warn] Run 'evicted' to see detailed eviction warnings
[info] Packaging /home/slasch/Learn-Scala---Fundamentals-of-Scala-2.13/ch14/akka-http/target/scala-2.12/akka-http_2.12-1.0-SNAPSHOT.j
ar ...
[info] Done packaging.
[info] Running ch14.Server
20:26:48.713 [ch14-akka.actor.default-dispatcher-5] INFO  akka.event.slf4j.Slf4jLogger - Slf4jLogger started
20:26:48.991 [run-main-0] INFO  o.f.c.internal.util.VersionPrinter - Flyway Community Edition 5.1.4 by Boxfuse
20:26:49.559 [run-main-0] INFO  o.f.c.i.database.DatabaseFactory - Database: jdbc:h2:file:./ch14 (H2 1.4)
20:26:49.856 [run-main-0] INFO  o.f.core.internal.command.DbValidate - Successfully validated 1 migration (execution time 00:00.065s)
20:26:49.931 [run-main-0] INFO  o.f.core.internal.command.DbMigrate - Current version of schema "PUBLIC": 1
20:26:49.933 [run-main-0] INFO  o.f.core.internal.command.DbMigrate - Schema "PUBLIC" is up to date. No migration necessary.
```

The application outputs a few lines and then waits for incoming requests. It is now safe to play with it the same way we did with the http4s version:

```
slasch void: $ curl "http://localhost:8080/inventory"
{"state":{"eggs":935,"flour":1000,"sugar":1000,"chocolate":995}}slasch void: $ curl -X "POST" "http://localhost:8080/purchase" \
>     -H 'Content-Type: application/json; charset=utf-8' \
>     -d $'{
>   "order": {
>     "chocolate": 5,
>     "eggs": 65
>   }
> }'
{"order":{"chocolate":5,"eggs":65}}
slasch void: $ curl "http://localhost:8080/inventory"
{"state":{"eggs":870,"flour":1000,"sugar":1000,"chocolate":990}}slasch void: $ _
```

One subtle but important difference is that the Akka version persists the database into the filesystem and retains the state between restarts, as shown by the first request on the previous screen.

Summary

In this chapter, we briefly discussed the pros and cons of the microservice-based approach.

We've built two small examples with similar functionality but different technological stacks.

The first project was built using a purely functional approach with wrapping effects in IO monad and functional streams. This allowed us to describe a system as a computation that is only started at the *end of the world*. We used the ORM approach in this case by mapping the state of the system to the database table and modifying it in response to the required changes. Finally, we demonstrated how to use the http4s client to test the system as a whole by building an integration test.

The basis for the second project was the *"official"* Lightbend stack. We looked at how well Akka-HTTP and Akka Persistence play together. We demonstrated that the event-sourced approach allows us to reconstruct state in memory by recombining it from persistent events. This helped us to avoid writing any SQL statements. We also looked at how the Akka-HTTP test kit can be used to test routes without the need to start the real HTTP server.

Questions

1. What is a database migration?
2. Describe what could be an alternative approach to discard an order completely in the case of insufficient stock for some articles.
3. Describe the conceptual difference between http4s and Akka-HTTP with regard to defining routes.
4. Name a reason why event-sourced data storage can scale better than traditional relational databases.
5. Implement a `GET /articles/:name` call with http4s and doobie.
6. Implement a `GET /articles/:name` call with Akka-HTTP and Akka Persistence.

Further reading

- Vinicius Feitosa Pacheco, *Microservice Patterns and Best Practices[Explore the concepts and tools you need to discover the world of microservices with various design patterns.*
- Jatin Puri, Selvam Palanimalai, *Scala Microservices: Design, build, and run microservices elegantly using Scala.*

- Héctor Veiga Ortiz, Piyush Mishra, *Akka Cookbook: Learn how to use the Akka framework to build effective applications in Scala.*
- Rambabu Posa, *Scala Reactive Programming: Build fault-tolerant, robust, and distributed applications in Scala.*
- Christian Baxter, *Mastering Akka: Master the art of creating scalable, concurrent, and reactive applications using Akka.*

15
Project 2 - Building Microservices with Lagom

The final part of this book goes into the details of the Lagom framework by discussing its philosophy, the way Lagom applications are structured, and available APIs and how to use them.

In this chapter, we will build, once again, our bakery project, this time structured as a number of microservices.

After reading this chapter, you will be able to do the following:

- Understand the advantages of using Lagom
- Set up Lagom and use it to create projects
- Structure an application as required by the framework
- Efficiently use provided APIs
- Unit test Lagom services

Technical requirements

Before we begin, make sure you have the following installed:

- JDK 8+
- SBT 1.2+

The code for this chapter is available at GitHub: `https://github.com/PacktPublishing/Learn-Scala-Programming/tree/master/Chapter15`.

Why Lagom?

In the previous chapter, we discussed the benefits and downsides of a microservices-based approach. We named the main architectural properties of microservices such as autonomy, isolation, and data ownership. We also noted that, compared to the traditional monolithic approach, microservices reduce the complexity of a single service but the complexity of the system as a whole does not disappear. In a sense, it just moves from the internals of a single microservice into the space between them. We looked at the implementation of the shop as a RESTful microservice, and we admitted that we would avoid this additional complexity by focusing on a single service.

As we worked through the Akka-based solution, we also chose the proper database to store events as well as defining and applying migrations to have a proper database schema. The choice of the configuration mechanism was predetermined by Akka but we still had to read and verify the configuration manually. We also needed to decide how to pass dependencies as we constructed runnable applications and properly implemented this passing.

The Lagom framework builds on top of a few existing technologies and utilizes the "convention over configuration" approach to reduce the burden of these repetitive mechanical tasks and to deliver some additional functionality specific to the microservice systems. It does so by providing a kind of "template" for projects.

The preconfigured features include the following:

- Use of event sourcing as a mechanism for distributed persistence. The recommended database is Apache Cassandra because of its exceptional scalability and natural support for the read side of the CQRS principle.
- Support for asynchronous communications by making use of reactive streams with Akka Streams as an implementation and message-passing style with Apache Kafka as a broker.
- Transparent support for different communication protocols, which allows you to abstract complex API calls behind simple method calls.
- Expressive-service-description DSL, which allows you to define APIs in a flexible and concise way.
- Dynamic scalability with Akka Cluster.
- A choice of dependency injection frameworks to wire the application at compile or runtime.

- Development mode with hot code reload and an ability to start all services and required infrastructure components, including a special development service registry and a service gateway with a single command.
- Default configuration for the infrastructure and preconfigured logging.

Let's see how these features will help us to re-implement our bakery project.

Project overview and setup

We already implemented our bakery project three times using different technologies in Chapter 11, *An Introduction to the Akka and Actor Models,* to Chapter 13, *Basics of Akka Streams.* Let's recap what this is about for the readers who aren't familiar with the third section of this book.

The bakery project

The bakery contains a few employees working together to produce delicious cookies. The structure of their communication is represented in the following diagram:

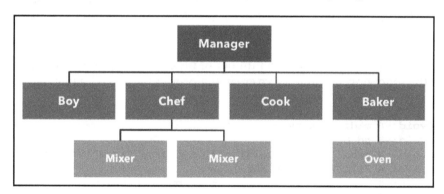

Each of the employees is skilled in a specific area:

- The **Manager** drives the process by taking the results of the work of each of the participants and giving them to the next step in the flow. They also create initial shopping lists.
- The **Boy**, if given a shopping list, will run to the grocery store and return with groceries.

- The **Chef**, if given groceries, will make dough. They do so by creating a couple of **Mixers** of limited capacity so that bigger amounts of groceries can be processed in parallel.
- The **Cook**, if given dough, makes some raw cookies.
- The **Baker**, if given raw cookies, will bake them for some time using the **Oven**, hence producing delicious cookies.

This time we're going to model each worker as a microservice. The **Mixers** and the **Oven** will become implementation details of the owning service.

Project setup

It goes without saying that we'll implement our microservices using the Lagom framework. Lagom supports both Maven and SBT as build tools but SBT provides a much better user experience so we will ignore Maven as it is less relevant for Scala projects.

 Further, in this section we're going to create a Lagom project from scratch. We could utilize a slightly different approach by creating an example project with Giter8 and then modifying and extending it as needed. The command is similar to the one we mentioned in Chapter 11, *An Introduction to the Akka and Actor Models*: sbt new lagom/lagom-scala.g8.

As before, our SBT setup will contain a number of files describing different aspects of the project. For the following, assume we've created a project folder and navigated to it in the Terminal:

```
slasch@void:~$ mkdir bakery
slasch@void:~$ cd bakery
slasch@void:~$ echo 'addSbtPlugin("com.lightbend.lagom" % "lagom-sbt-
plugin" % "1.4.7")' > plugins.sbt
slasch@void:~$ echo 'sbt.version=1.1.5' > build.properties
slasch@void:~$ cd ..
slasch@void:~$ echo '-J-Xms1024M
> -J-Xmx4096M
> -J-Xss2M
> -J-XX:MaxMetaspaceSize=1024M' > .sbtopts
```

Here, we define that our project requires a Lagom SBT plugin, the version of SBT to be used, as well as few SBT options in the .sbtopts file. The first two lines define the initial and maximum amount of memory SBT is allowed to consume. We're going to start quite a lot of microservices and supporting infrastructure components so it is necessary to have enough memory available. The -Xss parameter defines a stack size of 2M per thread. It is generally useful in Scala projects to prevent non-tail-recursive functions from overflowing the stack too soon. The last parameter, -XX:MaxMetaspaceSize, defines the size of the metaspace that is used (starting from the JVM 8) to store class metadata. Because of the Lagom's hot reloading, we're going to create and load many classes during development so we need to have a metaspace of significant size.

build.sbt will contain a number of submodules so it is easier to create with a text editor. This is what the (partial) final result looks like:

```
organization in ThisBuild := "packt"
version in ThisBuild := "1.0-SNAPSHOT"

scalaVersion in ThisBuild := "2.12.6"

val macwire = "com.softwaremill.macwire" %% "macros" % "2.3.0" % Provided
val scalaTest = "org.scalatest" %% "scalatest" % "3.0.5" % Test
val defaultDependencies = Seq(lagomScaladslTestKit, macwire, scalaTest)

lazy val `shared-model` = (project in file("shared-model"))
  .settings(libraryDependencies += lagomScaladslApi)

lazy val bakery = (project in file("."))
  .aggregate(
    `boy-api`, `boy-impl`,
    `chef-api`, `chef-impl`,
    `cook-api`, `cook-impl`,
    `baker-api`, `baker-impl`,
    `manager-api`, `manager-impl`)

lazy val `boy-api` = (project in file("boy-api"))
  .settings(libraryDependencies += lagomScaladslApi)

// other APIs defined the same way

lazy val `boy-impl` = (project in file("boy-impl"))
  .enablePlugins(LagomScala)
  .settings(libraryDependencies ++= defaultDependencies)
  .dependsOn(`boy-api`)

// other implementations defined the same way
```

```
lazy val `chef-impl` = (project in file("chef-impl"))
  .enablePlugins(LagomScala)
  .settings(
    libraryDependencies ++= Seq(
      lagomScaladslPersistenceCassandra,
      lagomScaladslKafkaBroker,
      lagomScaladslTestKit,
      lagomScaladslPubSub,
      macwire
    )
  )
  .settings(lagomForkedTestSettings: _*)
  .dependsOn(`chef-api`)

lazy val `manager-impl` = (project in file("manager-impl"))
  .enablePlugins(LagomScala)
  .settings(libraryDependencies ++= defaultDependencies)
  .dependsOn(`manager-api`, `boy-api`, `chef-api`, `cook-api`, `baker-api`)
```

We've cut the repetitive definitions so please refer to the GitHub repository (https://
github.com/PacktPublishing/Learn-Scala-Programming/tree/master/Chapter15) for the
full source code. Here, we define general properties of the project, a shared model, and five
microservices.

Each microservice consists of two modules, an API definition, and an implementation. Most
of the API definitions in our case require just a single lagomScaladslApi dependency and
the implementation—just macwire in the main scope. We've defined
defaultDependencies including the test scope to keep further definitions concise.

For chef-impl, we include three other compile-time dependencies:

- lagomScaladslPersistenceCassandra
- lagomScaladslPubSub
- lagomScaladslKafkaBroker

The Chef will take some time to mix the dough and because of this we aim to implement
communication with the Manager via a message broker to decouple both from each other.

Another deviation is the definition of `manager-impl`. The Manager will communicate with each of the other services, so it needs to know the API definitions of other workers. We also created a folder for each of the defined microservices in the filesystem. This is what our file structure with multiple modules looks like in the end:

```
slasch@void:~/ch15 [ch15-lagom]$ tree --dirsfirst
.
├──── baker-api
├──── baker-impl
├──── boy-api
├──── boy-impl
├──── chef-api
├──── chef-impl
├──── cook-api
├──── cook-impl
├──── manager-api
├──── manager-impl
├──── project
│     ├──── build.properties
│     └──── plugins.sbt
└──── build.sbt
```

As we go on with the implementation, we'll define a project structure as required by SBT for each of the modules:

```
slasch@void:~/ch15/cook-api [ch15-lagom]$ tree
.
└──── src
      ├──── main
      │     ├──── resources
      │     └──── scala
      └──── test
            ├──── resources
            └──── scala
```

By having this structure, we're done with the preparation of the project infrastructure and can move on to implementing the services.

The next diagram outlines the communication flow between modules:

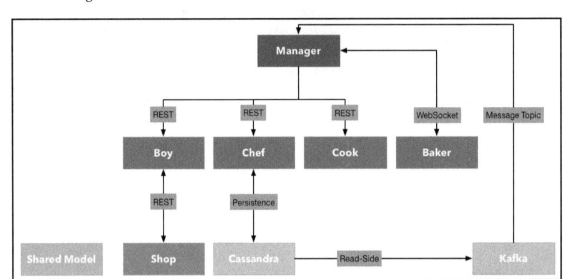

In order to simplify our example a bit, we will violate the rule that each microservice should own the definition of its model. We'll define a module containing definitions of all of the case classes used by the services we're going to build. We will add this module as a dependency to every other module we've defined before.

The module itself will contain definitions already known to us from previous chapters:

```
package ch15

object model {
  final case class ShoppingList(eggs: Int, flour: Int, sugar: Int,
chocolate: Int)
  final case class Groceries(eggs: Int, flour: Int, sugar: Int, chocolate:
Int)
  final case class Dough(weight: Int)
  final case class RawCookies(count: Int)
  final case class ReadyCookies(count: Int)
}
```

Our objects will be sent in serialized form between services. This means we also need to define serialization rules for them. We'll do this by relying on Play's macros, similar to Circe, which we used in the http4s example project:

```
import play.api.libs.json._

implicit val dough: Format[Dough] = Json.format
```

```
implicit val rawCookies: Format[RawCookies] = Json.format
implicit val readyCookies: Format[ReadyCookies] = Json.format
implicit val groceries: Format[Groceries] = Json.format
implicit val shoppingList: Format[ShoppingList] = Json.format
```

These formats go into the same `object model` instance along the case classes.

Lagom's APIs

As before, we will start with an implementation of the simplest of our workers, which just performs basic mathematical operations in order to do its work with `Cook`, which makes `RawCookies` out of `Dough`.

Service API

In order to define our Cook as a service we need to implement a special interface called a service descriptor. The service descriptor defines two aspects of a Lagom service:

- The service signature: How the service should be called and its return type
- The service meta data: How the service call is mapped to the transport layer, for example to the REST call

The service descriptor extends Lagom's `Service` trait and in its simplest form just needs to override the `descriptor` method. This is what it looks like in our `Cook` definition, which we place into the `cook-api` module:

```
import com.lightbend.lagom.scaladsl.api._
import ch15.model._

trait CookService extends Service {
  def cook: ServiceCall[Dough, RawCookies]

  override def descriptor: Descriptor = {
    import Service._
    named("CookService").withCalls(call(cook))
  }
}
```

Here we define a descriptor that connects the single call of the service, the `cook` method, to the service identifier `"CookService"` which will be needed for the routing later. For the call, we use the simplest identifier which just takes the name of the method. The configuration will result in the call mapped to the `/cook` REST URL.

The call itself is defined to be of the `ServiceCall[Dough, RawCookies]` type. Let's take a look at `ServiceCall` in more detail. The definition in the Lagom's source code looks like this:

```
trait ServiceCall[Request, Response] {
  def invoke(request: Request): Future[Response]
}
```

`ServiceCall` is typed by the request and response and can be invoked at the moment the request is issued by the client producing a response asynchronously.

The request and response types in Lagom can be strict or streamed. There are four possible combinations ranging from both sides being strict to both sides being streamed. Strict means that the request or response is fully buffered in the memory at the method boundary. The combination of both the strict request and response results in the synchronous semantics of the call. A streamed request or response is of the `Source` type, which is known to us from `Chapter 13`, *Basics of Akka Streams* where we looked at Akka streams. For the streaming calls, Lagom will try its best to choose the appropriate semantics. Typically, this will be WebSockets, and we will see how it works later in this chapter.

Our `Cook` instance is very quick so it is appropriate to define the service in synchronous terms.

The implementation of `Cook` goes in another module, `cook-impl`. This separation is essential in order to give microservices a possibility to refer to the definitions of each other without having any knowledge about implementation details.

The implementation is somewhat more involving, but not because of the service definition itself. The code should be very familiar by now:

```
package ch15

import ch15.model._
import com.lightbend.lagom.scaladsl.api._

import scala.concurrent.Future

class CookServiceImpl extends CookService {
  override def cook = ServiceCall { dough =>
    Future.successful(RawCookies(makeCookies(dough.weight)))
  }
  private val cookieWeight = 60
  private def makeCookies(weight: Int): Int = weight / cookieWeight
}
```

The only new part here is the definition of the service call wrapper. It is done by using the constructor defined in the `ServiceCall` companion object:

```
def apply[Request, Response](call: Request => Future[Response]):
ServiceCall[Request, Response]
```

We provide a function that converts `Dough` (request) into `Future[RawCookies]` (response) and the constructor builds a proper `ServiceCall` from it.

The previously mentioned complexity is related to the fact that we also need to wire together and start our service. For those who read `Chapter 14`, *Project 1 - Building Microservices with Scala,* the approach will look very much like a combination of both approaches we looked at there: mixing traits and providing concrete implementations for abstract members and passing dependencies as constructor parameters. But this time, we'll get the Lagom's help for this task. First, we define `LagomApplication`:

```
abstract class CookApplication(context: LagomApplicationContext)
  extends LagomApplication(context) {
  override lazy val lagomServer: LagomServer =
serverFor[CookService](wire[CookServiceImpl])
}
```

The application extends `LagomApplication` and needs `LagomApplicationContext`, which is just passed over via a constructor. No doubt you recognize the thin-cake pattern we used to connect together the components of our `Akka-HTTP` example. `lagomServer` is an overridden method, which is used by Lagom to provide correct wiring for the service calls. Another wiring happening here is the binding of `CookServiceImpl` to `CookService` with the help of Macwire.

 Macwire (`https://github.com/adamw/macwire`) is a dependency injection framework that implements constructor-based DI. It does so by generating calls to the class constructors with appropriate parameters found in scope. In a sense, it provides proper constructor calls behind the scenes the same way Circe or Play provide proper mapping to JSON structures. It would be very useful in projects of significant size.

Now our application can be used in the application loader, which does the real work of starting the service in a development or production environment:

```
class CookLoader extends LagomApplicationLoader {

  override def load(context: LagomApplicationContext) =
    new CookApplication(context) with AhcWSComponents {
      override def serviceLocator: ServiceLocator = NoServiceLocator
    }

  override def loadDevMode(context: LagomApplicationContext) =
    new CookApplication(context) with AhcWSComponents with
LagomDevModeComponents
}
```

`CookLoader` can be started by Lagom as needed. It overrides two `load` methods for respective environments. Please note how we extended `CookApplication` with `AhcWSComponents`. The latter is needed in order to provide `wsClient`, which in turn is required by `LagomApplication` we defined as a base class for our `CookApplication`. For the development mode, we also mix in `LagomDevModeComponents`, which gives us a development mode service locator.

Now we need to configure the application loader by providing a corresponding play setting in the well-known by now `application.conf`:

```
play.application.loader = ch15.CookLoader
```

And that is it—now we are ready to start our application. The easiest way to do this is by using Lagom's `runAll` command in the SBT console. It will try to start all of the services we've defined so far as well as the components of the underlying infrastructure—the development mode service locator, Cassandra database, and Kafka message broker:

```
sbt:bakery> runAll
[info] Starting Kafka
[info] Starting Cassandra
[info] Cassandra server running at 127.0.0.1:4000
[info] Service locator is running at http://localhost:9008
[info] Service gateway is running at http://localhost:9000
[info] Service cook-impl listening for HTTP on localhost:57733
[info] Service baker-impl listening for HTTP on localhost:50764
[info] Service manager-impl listening for HTTP on localhost:63552
[info] Service chef-impl listening for HTTP on localhost:56263
[info] Service boy-impl listening for HTTP on localhost:64127
```

The logs witness that the logging is working alongside other infrastructure components.

 At this stage, the log will contain a lots of stacktraces (not shown here) because of missing loader configurations for all but the `boy-impl` modules. We will fix this during this chapter, as we will implement the services one after another.

We can also see that our service is running on port 57733 and can try to communicate with it:

```
slasch@void:~$ curl -X POST http://localhost:57733/cook -d '{ "weight": 100
}'
{"count":1}
```

Congratulations, we just talked to our first Lagom microservice!

 We communicated to the service directly without using a service registry and service locator. It is safe to put the port number into the code listing for reference because despite their random appearance, ports are assigned to the services by Lagom in a deterministic manner (basically by using a hash of a project name). Hence, the services are assigned the same port numbers (with respect to port conflicts) in any environment.

Now we can move on to the implementation of the `Boy` service, which is similarly simple in its functionality. It is expected to forward incoming shopping lists to external services and forward groceries it will get in return to the initial caller.

The definition of the service should look familiar, except that we're using the `namedCall` method to map the `shop` call to the `go-shopping` name in order to have a nicer URL:

```
trait BoyService extends Service {
  def shop: ServiceCall[ShoppingList, Groceries]

  override def descriptor: Descriptor =
    named("BoyService").withCalls(namedCall("go-shopping", shop))
}
```

The implementation is a bit more complex then the `Cook` service because the `Boy` service needs to call an external HTTP service to make an order. The following template should not raise any questions:

```
class BoyServiceImpl extends BoyService {
  override def shop = ServiceCall(callExternalApi)
  private val callExternalApi: ShoppingList => Future[Groceries] = ???
}
```

How do we call the external API though? We could, of course, use an HTTP client library and do the call the same way as before, issuing the HTTP request, getting the HTTP response, and handling marshalling and unmarshalling. But this would lower the abstraction level of our solution and hard-wire the implementation to the external service's location.

We will do the following instead. First, we will register our externally running service with the service locator by adding the service's URL to `build.sbt`:

```
lagomUnmanagedServices in ThisBuild := Map("GroceryShop" ->
"http://localhost:8080")
```

Then, we will define an API for the grocery store as if we were about to implement it:

```
trait ShopService extends Service {
  def order: ServiceCall[Order, Purchase]
  override def descriptor: Descriptor = {
    named("GroceryShop").withCalls(restCall(Method.POST, "/purchase",
order))
  }
}
```

Here, we specify a service descriptor for the service with the same name as we just registered with the service locator. The API call is registered with a `restCall` descriptor to be sure that both the HTTP method and the path are correctly mapped to the existing service. We also need to wrap and unwrap `ShoppingList` and `Groceries` into proper `Order` and `Purchase` as expected with the existing shop service. Luckily, the JSON representation of our case classes is the same as for `Map[String, Int]` so we can safely just reuse the existing model along with serializers and add the wrappers on top of it:

```
object ShopService {
  final case class Order(order: ShoppingList)
  final case class Purchase(order: Groceries)
  implicit val purchase: Format[Purchase] = Json.format
  implicit val order: Format[Order] = Json.format
}
```

We don't need to provide an implementation for `ShopService`; we just want Lagom to apply all existing machinery to represent an existing REST service as if it were one made with Lagom.

The shop service is ready to use with `Boy` now:

```
class BoyServiceImpl(shopService: ShopService)
                (implicit ec: ExecutionContext) extends BoyService {
  override def shop: ServiceCall[ShoppingList, Groceries] =
```

```
ServiceCall(callExtApi)

    private val callExtApi: ShoppingList => Future[Groceries] = list =>
        shopService.order.invoke(Order(list)).map(_.order).recover {
            case _ => Groceries(0, 0, 0, 0)
        }
}
```

Note that we provide the `shopService` client and an execution context. The latter will be used to transform the future result we'll get from the service invocation. The `callExtApi` function shows how this is done: we refer to the `order` method from the `ShopService` definition, which returns `ServiceCall`, which we happily invoke with `Order` we created from the shopping list. The result is `Future[Purchase]` so we unwrap an order out of it. Finally, we define that, if anything wrong happens with the external service, for example, the service is not available or there is insufficient inventory to fulfill the order, the Boy should just return back with empty hands.

Now `Boy` is able to communicate with `ShopService` we built in `Chapter 14`, *Project 1 - Building Microservices with Scala* using `Akka-HTTP`.

 The shop service must be running and must have sufficient inventory in order for further examples from this chapter to work properly.

Our `Boy` and `Cook` services are stateless. The `Cook` service just returns the result immediately so there is no point having any state in it. `Boy` is unsophisticated and just comes back for instructions if anything unexpected happens. But `Chef` and `Baker` are different because they are supposed to represent processes taking some time. For this reason we can't implement them in a synchronous manner.

The Baker has `m:n` semantics in the sense that it can respond with zero, one, or many response messages to a single incoming message. Let's use Lagom's possibility to define asynchronous services to implement it. This will allow us to reuse the flow definition for `Baker` we constructed in `Chapter 13`, *Basics of Akka Streams*.

We first need to define the service as we already did, but this time with asynchronous semantics:

```
import akka.NotUsed
import akka.stream.scaladsl.Source

trait BakerService extends Service {
    def bake: ServiceCall[Source[RawCookies, NotUsed],
```

```
                          Source[ReadyCookies, NotUsed]]

    override def descriptor: Descriptor =
    named("BakerService").withCalls(call(bake))
    }
```

Here, we define `BakerService` to have a request of the `Source[RawCookies, NotUsed]` type and the response of the `Future[Source[ReadyCookies, NotUsed]]` type. This should allow us to just write `RawCookies` at the moment they are available and get `ReadyCookies` back after they are baked.

The implementation is straightforward because it is literally wrapping the flow taken from `Chapter 13`, *Basics of Akka Streams*:

```
    import play.api.Logger

    class BakerServiceImpl extends BakerService {

      private val logger = Logger("Baker")

      override def bake: ServiceCall[Source[RawCookies, NotUsed],
                          Source[ReadyCookies, NotUsed]] =
        ServiceCall { dough =>
          logger.info(s"Baking: $dough")
          Future.successful(dough.via(bakerFlow))
        }

      private val bakerFlow: Flow[RawCookies, ReadyCookies, NotUsed] =
        Baker.bakeFlow.join(Oven.bakeFlow)
    }
```

We reuse the definition of the `Baker` and `Oven` flows and return the combined flow as the result of the call. In this snippet, we also demonstrate the use of `Logger` available from the underlying Play framework.

Persistence API

`Chef` in our scenario takes some time to complete the mix process. Because of this, we would like to store the work in progress so that, in case the service is restarted, it does not get lost and the process just continues from where it was interrupted after recovery.

We will use persistence facilities provided by the framework in order to implement this. The recommended way to persist data in Lagom is by utilizing an event sourcing approach, which we already used to implement an example project in Chapter 14, *Project 1 - Building Microservices with Scala*. Lagom automates data schema creation with Cassandra and also provides a Cassandra instance for development purposes. Therefore, we can start directly with the definition of the data model. As in the previous chapter, we need to provide a set of commands and events and also have an internal representation of the state. The following few snippets show one of the possible ways to represent these parts. As this model is just an implementation detail of Chef, it goes into the chef-impl module.

First, we need to have a bunch of imports in scope:

```
import ch15.model._
import java.util.UUID
import akka.Done
import com.lightbend.lagom.scaladsl.persistence._
import PersistentEntity.ReplyType
import com.lightbend.lagom.scaladsl.playjson.JsonSerializer
import play.api.libs.json._
```

Having these, we can define our commands:

```
sealed trait ChefCommand
final case class MixCommand(groceries: Groceries) extends ChefCommand with
ReplyType[Done]
final case class DoneCommand(id: UUID) extends ChefCommand with
ReplyType[Done]
```

MixCommand represents an incoming request to mix some groceries. Commands in Lagom define the expected response type and we are using Akka's Done for the response. The reason for this is that we'll always accept MixCommand (because there is no reason not to), but at the moment the command is accepted it is not possible to predict which effect it will have.

DoneCommand represents a state transition from "mixing in progress" to "mixing done". It will be an internal command sent by Chef to itself. Technically we don't need a response type here but we have to use Done again in order to make the compiler happy. id represents the unique identifier of the mixing job. Where does it come from? It is generated at the moment we're creating an event from the command:

```
sealed trait ChefEvent
final case class Mixing(id: UUID, groceries: Groceries) extends ChefEvent
final case class MixingDone(id: UUID, dough: Dough) extends
  ChefEvent with AggregateEvent[MixingDone] {
    override def aggregateTag: AggregateEventTag[MixingDone] =
```

```
ChefModel.EventTag
  }
```

The `Mixing` event is created in response to the `MixCommand` and the `MixingDone` event—in response to the `DoneCommand`. Both events relate to each other via the `id` property. At the recovery time both events with same `id` will annihilate: presence of both events means that in the past a mixing job was started and then finished. In contrast, if there is only single event we can conclude that the job was not finished. Having unbalanced `Mixing` events after the recovery will mean we need to restart the mixing processes for them. Having unbalanced `MixingDone` events can only mean programming errors.

To provide this functionality, we'll define the state as follows:

```
sealed trait ChefState {
  def batches: List[Mixing]
}
final case class MixingState(batches: List[Mixing]) extends ChefState
```

We'll take a look at how it is used in the service implementation in a moment, after discussing the final bit of the model definition:

```
object ChefModel {
  import play.api.libs.json._
  implicit val mixingFormat = Json.format[Mixing]

  val serializers = List(
    JsonSerializer(mixingFormat),
    JsonSerializer(Json.format[MixingDone]),
    JsonSerializer(Json.format[MixingState]))

  val EventTag: AggregateEventTag[MixingDone] =
AggregateEventTag[MixingDone]("MixingDone")
  }
```

Here, we provide serializers for our events and commands the same way we did in the previous chapter. The Lagom's recommended serialization format is JSON so we're utilizing the same approach we already used for the shared model definition.

We also define `EventTag` which we'll need to implement the read-side of the event journal in order to notify `Manager` about the completed mixing jobs.

The final piece of configuration we need is a definition of Cassandra's key space for `Chef`. This is done in the usual way in `application.conf`:

```
user.cassandra.keyspace = chefprogress

cassandra-journal.keyspace = ${user.cassandra.keyspace}
cassandra-snapshot-store.keyspace = ${user.cassandra.keyspace}
lagom.persistence.read-side.cassandra.keyspace =
 ${user.cassandra.keyspace}
```

The definition of the service reflects the fact that the communication is synchronous on the request side and message based on the response side:

```
trait ChefService extends Service {
  def mix: ServiceCall[Groceries, Done]

  def resultsTopic: Topic[Dough]

  override def descriptor: Descriptor = {
    named("ChefService")
      .withCalls(call(mix))
      .withTopics(topic(ChefService.ResultsTopic, resultsTopic))
      .withAutoAcl(true)
  }
}
object ChefService {
  val ResultsTopic = "MixedResults"
}
```

The `mix` call accepts `Groceries` and returns `Done` (compare this with the return type of the commands we've just defined). The implementation of the service is also reasonably concise because it delegates state management to `ChefPersistentEntity`:

```
class ChefServiceImpl(persistentEntities: PersistentEntityRegistry,
                      as: ActorSystem) extends ChefService {

  private lazy val entity = wire[ChefPersistentEntity]
  persistentEntities.register(entity)

  override def mix: ServiceCall[Groceries, Done] = ServiceCall { groceries
=>
      val ref = persistentEntities.refFor[ChefPersistentEntity]("Chef")
      ref.ask(MixCommand(groceries))
  }

  override def resultsTopic: Topic[Dough] = ???
}
```

First, we need to pass two dependencies, `PersistentEntityRegistry` and `ActorSystem`. We pass the actor system, `as`, to `ChefPersistentEntity` at the moment of wiring and use the persistent entity registry to register our, well, persistent entity as required by Lagom. The `mix` call then just uses the registry to look up a reference to the entity and uses an `ask` pattern to send it an incoming command and get a response the same way we did with actors.

We're omitting the implementation of `resultsTopic` for now to focus on the persistence aspect of the service.

`ChefPersistentEntity` is a bit longer, so let's take a look at it in smaller chunks. We start with overriding Lagom's `PersistentEntity`:

```
final class ChefPersistentEntity(
    persistentEntities: PersistentEntityRegistry, as: ActorSystem
) extends PersistentEntity { ... }
```

The persistent entity can be accessed from anywhere in the cluster. Because of this, using persistence in Lagom automatically means using clustering (which is definitely a good idea). The persistent entity needs to override a few fields:

```
override type Command = ChefCommand
override type Event = ChefEvent
override type State = ChefState
override def initialState: ChefState = MixingState(Nil)
```

The `Command`, `Event`, and `State` types refer to those we defined earlier. We also define an initial state to be empty `MixingState`.

For simplicity, we won't implement the mixing behavior in its full complexity as we already did this three times in previous chapters. Instead, we'll mock it:

```
private def dough(g: Groceries) = {
  import g._
  Dough(eggs * 50 + flour + sugar + chocolate)
}
```

Now we can finally define the behavior of our entity which will accept commands, persist events, and modify states. Again, this is done similarly to how we did in the previous chapter, but Lagom adds its five cents by providing an `Actions` constructor, which allows us to define command and event handlers in a builder-like manner:

```
Actions()
  .onCommand[MixCommand, Done] {
    case (MixCommand(groceries), ctx, _) if groceries.eggs <= 0 =>
      ctx.invalidCommand(s"Need at least one egg but got: $groceries")
```

```
        ctx.done

    case (MixCommand(groceries), ctx, _) =>
      val id = UUID.randomUUID()
      ctx.thenPersist(Mixing(id, groceries)) { evt =>
        as.scheduler.scheduleOnce(mixingTime)(
          thisEntity.ask(DoneCommand(id)))
        ctx.reply(Done)
      }
  }
```

The command handler must return a `Persist` directive, which describes what should be persisted with an optional callback for side-effecting code, which should be executed after an event was successfully written to the storage.

In the preceding snippet, we're handling two commands. `MixCommand` with a negative amount of `Dough` is marked as invalid (which is modelled by sending `InvalidCommandException` to the caller), and calling `ctx.done` returns `PersistNone` with the meaning that nothing needs to be persisted.

The second handler is for valid commands. With it, we first generate random `id` for the event we're going to persist, then we construct the event and return `PersistOne` with the event and a callback. The callback schedules send a command to the persistent entity itself meaning the mixing is done and sends `Done` back to the caller.

In order to be able to dereference an entity, we need to use a registry as we did in the service earlier:

```
lazy val thisEntity =
persistentEntities.refFor[ChefPersistentEntity](this.entityId)
```

Please note that our persistence callbacks are only executing side effects and not modifying the state. For the state modifications, another constructor, onEvent, should be used. This separation is done in order to gain the possibility to reconstruct the state during the recovery as many times as required, but to have side effects executed only once after the actual event had happened and was persisted:

```
Actions()
  .onCommand[MixCommand, Done] { ... }
  .onEvent {
    case (m: Mixing, state) =>
      MixingState(state.batches :+ m)

    case (MixingDone(id, _), state) =>
      MixingState(state.batches.filterNot(_.id == id))
  }
```

Here, we've just put new mixing jobs into the queue and we remove them from the queue after they are complete. Now we have to define how to react to the `DoneCommand` our entity sends to itself:

```
Actions()
  .onCommand[MixCommand, Done] { ... }
  .onEvent { ... }
  .onCommand[DoneCommand, Done] {
    case (DoneCommand(id), ctx, state) =>
      state.batches
        .find(_.id == id)
        .map { g =>
          ctx.thenPersist(MixingDone(id, dough(g.groceries))) {
            _ => ctx.reply(Done)
          }
        }
        .getOrElse(ctx.done)
  }
```

We're looking in the current state for `MixingCommand`, which we created before by using `id` as an equality criteria, just to have a reference to `groceries`. The groceries will be required later; at the moment we will read the event on the read side. Then we construct and persist an event and return `Done` to make the compiler happy. You probably noticed that we haven't defined any side-effects for the `MixingDone` event. We don't need to because these events will be streamed to `resultsTopic` we specified earlier.

To conclude the implementation of `Chef`, we need to wire all components together. `ChefLoader` is not any different from other loaders we've defined so far. In contrast, `ChefApplication` deviates a bit:

```
abstract class ChefApplication(context: LagomApplicationContext)
  extends LagomApplication(context) with CassandraPersistenceComponents
with LagomKafkaComponents {
  override lazy val lagomServer: LagomServer =
serverFor[ChefService](wire[ChefServiceImpl])
  override lazy val jsonSerializerRegistry = new JsonSerializerRegistry {
    override def serializers = ChefModel.serializers
  }
}
```

We need to provide an implementation of `JsonSerializerRegistry` for Lagom to be able to pick up our serializers. Our application also needs to extend `CassandraPersistenceComponents` as we're using persistence and also `LagomKafkaComponents`—by publishing our events we're effectively using messaging as well. Unfortunately, currently Lagom can't check at compile time whether messaging is used by the application, so it is easy to forget to extend Kafka components, which will lead to runtime errors at the moment the application is started.

We have defined the persistent side of the `Chef` service' `MixingDone` events, so let's turn to the messaging side.

Message Broker API

When we implemented persistence in `Chef` we skipped the definition of `resultsTopic` we provided in the API definition. Let's take a look at the definition of `resultsTopic` now:

```
class ChefServiceImpl(...) extends ChefService {

  ...

  override def resultsTopic: Topic[Dough] =
    TopicProducer.singleStreamWithOffset { fromOffset =>
      persistentEntities
        .eventStream(ChefModel.EventTag, fromOffset)
        .map { ev => (convertEvent(ev), ev.offset) }
    }

  private def convertEvent(chefEvent: EventStreamElement[ChefEvent]): Dough
  = {
    chefEvent.event match {
      case MixingDone(_, dough) => dough
    }
  }
}
```

We're using the `singleStreamWithOffset` constructor of the `TopicProducer` factory to construct a topic to which all of the events marked with `ChefModel.EventTag` will get published. Before publishing happens, we convert `ChefEvent` into `Dough` as expected by the downstream services. This is done in the `convertEvent` method.

The receiving side is `Manager`. Lagom provides all of the infrastructure so that the consumption of the events boils down to the following one-liner:

```
val sub: Future[Done] =
chefService.resultsTopic.subscribe.atLeastOnce(cookChefFlow)
```

Here, we're using `chefService resultsTopic` to subscribe to the events. We provide `cookChefFlow` as a callback which will be called at least once for each of the published events. The `atLeastOnce` method expects `akka.stream.scaladsl.Flow[Payload, Done, _]` as a parameter with Payload referring to the type of the message. We'll define our flow of the `Flow[Dough, Done, _]` type in a moment.

Service API from the client side

We have defined all of our worker services so let's take a look at `Manager` and how it drives the baking process by calling other services in the right order. Let's start with the service definition:

```
trait ManagerService extends Service {
  def bake(count: Int): ServiceCall[NotUsed, Done]
  def sell(count: Int): ServiceCall[NotUsed, Int]
  def report: ServiceCall[NotUsed, Int]

  override def descriptor: Descriptor = {
    import Service._
    named("Bakery").withCalls(
      restCall(Method.POST, "/bake/:count", bake _),
      restCall(Method.POST, "/sell?count", sell _),
      pathCall("/report", report)
    )
  }
}
```

We define three methods:

- `bake`, for initiating a baking process for a number of cookies
- `sell`, for selling cookies if there is enough stock
- `report`, for checking the number of cookies currently in stock

We map them to two rest calls and a path call. We're using one path and one query parameter just to demonstrate the possibilities offered by the Lagom's descriptor DSL.

Let's get on with the service implementation:

```
class ManagerServiceImpl(boyService: BoyService,
                         chefService: ChefService,
                         cookService: CookService,
                         bakerService: BakerService,
                         as: ActorSystem)
    extends ManagerService {

  private val count: AtomicInteger = new AtomicInteger(0)

  private val logger = Logger("Manager")

  ...
}
```

We have to provide all of the services we're about to call as constructor parameters so that we can wire them together later in the definition of the application. We also define `logger` and `count`, which will hold the current number of cookies. In a real project, we would implement an event-sourced approach to the internal state of the Manager, but here we're just keeping it in memory for simplicity.

The `report` and `sell` methods are implemented by checking the internal state and modifying it if appropriate:

```
override def sell(cnt: Int): ServiceCall[NotUsed, Int] =
  ServiceCall { _ =>
    if (cnt > count.get()) {
      Future.failed(new IllegalStateException(s"Only $count cookies on
sale"))
    } else {
      count.addAndGet(-1 * cnt)
      Future.successful(cnt)
    }
  }

override def report: ServiceCall[NotUsed, Int] = ServiceCall { _ =>
  Future.successful(count.get())
}
```

The `bake` method is implemented by actually calling other services:

```
override def bake(count: Int): ServiceCall[NotUsed, Done] = ServiceCall { _
=>
  val sl = shoppingList(count)
  logger.info(s"Shopping list: $sl")
  for {
    groceries <- boyService.shop.invoke(sl)
    done <- chefService.mix.invoke(groceries)
  } yield {
    logger.info(s"Sent $groceries to Chef")
    done
  }
}
```

Here, we generate a shopping list based on the number of cookies we requested to be baked. Then, in a for-comprehension, we're calling `boyService` and `chefService`. With the call of the chef service, we need to return because it is going to take some time for the chef to make the dough.

We already defined the listener for `Dough`, which is sent back by `Chef` via the message topic, so we just need to define the flow to handle the incoming messages:

```
private lazy val chefFlow: Flow[Dough, Done, NotUsed] = Flow[Dough]
  .map { dough: Dough =>
    val fut = cookService.cook.invoke(dough)
    val src = Source.fromFuture(fut)
    val ready: Future[Source[ReadyCookies, NotUsed]] =
      bakerService.bake.invoke(src)
    Source.fromFutureSource(ready)
  }
  .flatMapConcat(identity)
  .map(count.addAndGet(cookies.count))
  .map(_ => Done)
```

Here again, we're representing the possible one-liner as a couple of statements so that it is easy to spot what is going on: we define `Flow`, which transforms dough into `Future[RawCookies]` by calling `cookService`. `bakerService` is a streaming one so it expects `Source[RawCookies, _]` and we create it from `Future`. The invocation of `bakerService` returns `Future[Source[ReadyCookies, _]]` so we convert `Future` into `Source` again and then flatten `Source[Source[ReadyCookies, _]]` with `flatMapConcat`. Finally, we change the service's internal state and return `Done` as expected by the subscription method.

It's time to build `ManagerApplication` together! We need to provide references to all of the services we've used in `ManagerImpl`. Of course, we'll use `serviceClient` for this:

```
abstract class ManagerApplication(context: LagomApplicationContext)
    extends LagomApplication(context) with LagomKafkaClientComponents {
  lazy val boyService: BoyService = serviceClient.implement[BoyService]
  lazy val chefService: ChefService = serviceClient.implement[ChefService]
  lazy val cookService: CookService = serviceClient.implement[CookService]
  lazy val bakerService: BakerService =
serviceClient.implement[BakerService]
  override lazy val lagomServer: LagomServer =
    serverFor[ManagerService](wire[ManagerServiceImpl])
}
```

`ManagerServiceImpl` itself is constructed using the Macwire as before.

Running the application

Now, we have all of our services built together and can run the project as a whole using the `runAll` command as before. We also need to have an `Akka-HTTP` example from the previous chapter running and have enough inventory so that the boy can get some groceries from it:

```
slasch void:              $ cd Learn-Scala---Fundamentals-of-Scala-2.12/ch15    slasch void:              $ cd Learn-Scala---Fundamentals-of-Scala-2.12/ch14
slasch void:                                                   [mas    slasch void:                                                   [mas
ter]$ sbt                                                             ter]$ sbt
[info] Loading settings for project ch15-build from plugins.sbt ...    [info] Loading settings for project ch14-build from plugins.sbt ...
[info] Loading project definition from /Users/slasch/Dropbox/packt/Learn-Scala    [info] Loading project definition from /Users/slasch/Dropbox/packt/Learn-Scala
---Fundamentals-of-Scala-2.12/ch15/project                            ---Fundamentals-of-Scala-2.12/ch14/project
[info] Loading settings for project bakery from build.sbt ...         [info] Loading settings for project root from build.sbt ...
[info] Set current project to bakery (in build file:/Users/slasch/Dropbox/pack    [info] Set current project to root (in build file:/Users/slasch/Dropbox/packt/
t/Learn-Scala---Fundamentals-of-Scala-2.12/ch15/)                     Learn-Scala---Fundamentals-of-Scala-2.12/ch14/)
[info] sbt server started at local:///Users/slasch/.sbt/1.0/server/1b265a88e47    [info] sbt server started at local:///Users/slasch/.sbt/1.0/server/8034325e153
ace241bb7/sock                                                        80d474f63/sock
sbt:bakery> runAll                                                    sbt:root> akkaHttp/run
                                                                      [info] Running ch14.Server
                                                                      21:06:56.474 [ch14-akka.actor.default-dispatcher-2] INFO  akka.event.slf4j.Slf
                                                                      4jLogger - Slf4jLogger started
                                                                      21:06:56.693 [run-main-0] INFO  o.f.c.internal.util.VersionPrinter - Flyway Co
                                                                      mmunity Edition 5.1.4 by Boxfuse
                                                                      21:06:57.395 [run-main-0] INFO  o.f.c.i.database.DatabaseFactory - Database: j
                                                                      dbc:h2:file:../ch14 (H2 1.4)
                                                                      21:06:57.685 [run-main-0] INFO  o.f.core.internal.command.DbValidate - Success
                                                                      fully validated 1 migration (execution time 00:00.056s)
                                                                      21:06:57.774 [run-main-0] INFO  o.f.core.internal.command.DbMigrate - Current
                                                                      version of schema "PUBLIC": 1
                                                                      21:06:57.778 [run-main-0] INFO  o.f.core.internal.command.DbMigrate - Schema "
                                                                      PUBLIC" is up to date. No migration necessary.
```

The previous screenshot shows two Terminal windows: on the right the Akka HTTP shop from Chapter 14 is running and on the left the `runAll` command is ready to be executed. The `runAll` command takes some time to start all of the subsystems and produces a lot of output in the console.

At the moment of this writing the processing pipeline stopped just before returning baked cookies to the manager. We reported this issue as a Lagom bug (`https://github.com/lagom/lagom/issues/1616`) but unfortunately got no feedback from Lagom team yet. We left the example as it is with the hope that the issue will be fixed in upcoming version of the framework. In the unlikely case if this is not a but we will update the example immediately after getting corresponding reaction to the bug report.

After everything settles down, we can call our `Manager` service with an `http` client from another window:

```
curl -X "POST" "http://localhost:58866/bake/10"
```

This should produce output similar to the following in the Lagom Terminal:

```
20:55:58.666 [info] Manager [] - Shopping list: ShoppingList(10,300,100,50)
20:55:59.735 [info] Manager [] - Sent Groceries(10,300,100,50) to Chef
20:56:11.570 [info] Baker [] - Baking: Source(SourceShape(Map.out(882804106)))
20:56:11.582 [info] BakerFlow [] - Extracting: RawCookies(15)
20:56:11.583 [info] Oven [] - Baked: RawCookies(12)
```

Looks like it is time to enjoy the cookies! Well, not quite yet!

Testing

As before, we would like to conclude our journey by testing the implementation we came up with. Luckily, Lightbend follows the same approach to testing as it did with other libraries. There is a test kit that allows us to test services and persistent entities easily. We'll demonstrate how to test services in this section and leave testing persistent entities as an exercise for the reader.

It makes sense to start by testing the simplest service we defined—`CookService`. Here is a test for it, placed in the test scope of the `cook-impl` module:

```
import ch15.model.Dough
import com.lightbend.lagom.scaladsl.server.LocalServiceLocator
import com.lightbend.lagom.scaladsl.testkit.ServiceTest
import org.scalatest.{AsyncWordSpec, Matchers}
import play.api.libs.ws.ahc.AhcWSComponents

class CookServiceSpec extends AsyncWordSpec with Matchers {
```

```
  "The CookService" should {
    "make cookies from Dough" in
ServiceTest.withServer(ServiceTest.defaultSetup) { ctx =>
    new CookApplication(ctx) with LocalServiceLocator with
AhcWSComponents
    } { server =>
      val client = server.serviceClient.implement[CookService]
      client.cook.invoke(Dough(200)).map { cookies =>
        cookies.count should ===(3)
      }
    }
  }
}
```

Lagom provides a `ServiceTest` object whose purpose is to support testing of a single service. Its `withServer` constructor takes two parameters: an application constructor and a block of test code. It looks similar to the approach we used while testing the `Akka-HTTP` implementation in the previous chapter, but it behaves differently. `ServiceTest` actually starts the real server with the service. In our example, we mix it with `LocalServiceLocator`, so that we can get a service implementation from it in the test block. Here, we can invoke the service and verify that it works as expected.

Our specification extends `AsyncWordSpec`, which gives us the freedom to formulate our expectations by mapping over `Future` returned by the service.

Testing a synchronous service such as `CookService` is very easy. But how about testing the asynchronous (streaming) service? We've built an example using `BakerService`. Here is one possible implementation of the unit test for it:

```
class BakerServiceSpec extends AsyncWordSpec with Matchers {

  "The BakerService" should {
    "bake cookies" in ServiceTest.withServer(ServiceTest.defaultSetup) {
ctx =>
    new BakerApplication(ctx) with LocalServiceLocator
    } { server =>
      val client = server.serviceClient.implement[BakerService]
      implicit val as: Materializer = server.materializer
      val input: Source[RawCookies, NotUsed] =
        Source(List(RawCookies(10), RawCookies(10), RawCookies(10)))
          .concat(Source.maybe)

      client.bake.invoke(input).map { output =>
        val probe = output.runWith(TestSink.probe(server.actorSystem))
        probe.request(10)
        probe.expectNext(ReadyCookies(12))
```

```
        probe.expectNext(ReadyCookies(12))
        // because the oven is not full for the 6 other
        probe.cancel
        succeed
      }
    }
  }
}
```

The definition of the test, the test server, and the client is the same as before. The only difference is that, instead of our normal domain types we need to provide Source and get Source back. So we reach out for the Akka-Streams test kit and use our knowledge gained in Chapter 13, *Basics of Akka Streams* to formulate the expectations against the streams. We create an input Source from List and use TestSink to confirm that the output of the service meets our expectations.

Now it's the time to enjoy the cookies!

Summary

Lagom framework is a Lightbend's solution aiming to streamline and simplify building microservices with Scala and Java. It is build on top of existing libraries and frameworks such as SBT, Akka, and Play and provides additional functionalities such as a rich development environment with hot code reload, a service registry and service locator, an embedded database, and a message broker.

Lagom has three useful APIs:

- Service APIs, which allow you to represent remote service calls as local function calls
- Persistence API, which provides additional structure and some useful defaults for Akka-Persistence
- Message broker API, which makes public/subscribe communication and working with the read-side of the journal a breeze

Lagom comes with a test kit that helps to test services or persistent entities in isolation. Combining Lagom's test kit with the Akka-Streams test kit and AsyncWordSpec from ScalaTest makes it possible to write concise and expressive test expectations.

In this chapter, we just touched briefly upon possibilities provided by Lagom for development of microservice-based systems. This area of software engineering is still quite immature and Lagom is one of the first attempts to address the new challenges.

We hope with our example project we could spark your interest in Lagom and highly recommend you look at the official Lagom documentation at `https://www. lagomframework.com/documentation/1.4.x/scala/Home.html` for further inspiration.

Questions

1. How do you map an endpoint with a query parameter to a REST call?
2. What is the recommended serialization format for persistent entities?
3. Can you explain why clustering is required in order to use persistence in Lagom?
4. Describe one possible data model which could be used to make the Manager a persistent entity.
5. Outline an alternative way to implement the Baker service.
6. Can you identify a design bug in current implementation of the Chef?
7. The Manager implementation stores a number of cookies in memory and this number will be lost at the moment the service restarts. Can you name another reason why it is a bad idea to hold the number of cookies in a local variable?

Further reading

- Rambabu Posa, *Scala Reactive Programming: Build fault-tolerant, robust, and distributed applications in Scala*
- Jatin Puri and Selvam Palanimalai, *Scala Microservices: Design, build, and run Microservices using Scala elegantly*

Preparing the Environment and Running Code Samples

The instructions in this chapter are based on our experience of installing JDK and SBT and running code samples in late 2018. Installation instructions like this usually become outdated as soon as they are published because of the rapid pace at which the software is updated; please bear this in mind as you work through this chapter.

Installing software

The recommended way to install JDK, Scala, and SBT is by using the SDK manager available at `https://sdkman.io`. Please refer to the instructions on the web page to complete the installation.

Further, we'll describe the process of manual installation for Java and SBT. For your convenience, we've packaged the commands represented in further screenshots as scripts for OS X and Linux and made them available in the `Appendix` folder in the GitHub repository at: `https://github.com/PacktPublishing/Learn-Scala-Programming/tree/master/Appendix`.

Installing Java Virtual Machine (JVM)

At the moment, as of writing this, the last available JDK version available at `http://jdk.java.net` was 11. Scala 2.13 requires Java 1.8+.

It is possible to install Java on Linux or macOS X platforms by using one of the existing tools, such as `apt` or `yum`, using the package manager for Linux or `brew` for an OS X environment. Please use the help pages and guides available for the respective tools if you intend to install the JDK this way.

The manual installation of Java consists of three steps:

1. Downloading the package from the internet. The choice of distribution files for different platforms is offered at `http://jdk.java.net/11/`.
2. Extracting the installation file.
3. Updating the environment.

With Linux or OS X, you can use the following sequence of shell commands to perform all these steps, as shown in the next two screenshots:

Installing JDK 11 in OS X

The installation flow in Linux is so similar that we have even refrained from putting arrows into the screenshot:

The same steps in Linux

On Windows, you'll need to use the web browser to download the installation package, the file navigator to unpack it, and system settings to update the path variable. Please be aware that Java 11 is only available as a 64-bit version, so if you have a 32-bit system you have to install one of the previous versions of the JVM.

Please follow the steps outlined in the following screenshots to perform the setup:

1. First, download the installation file from the internet:

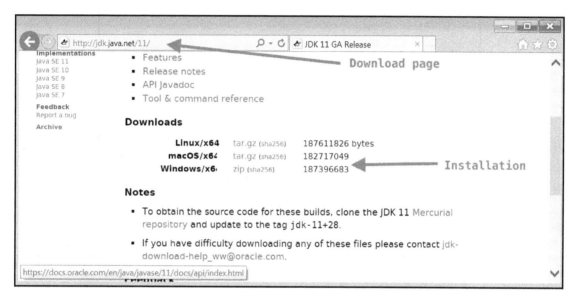

Step 1. Downloading the installation with the web browser

2. Then, extract the Java runtime from the archive:

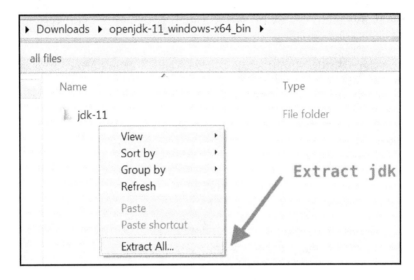

Step 2. Extracting binaries from the downloaded bundle

3. Next, the system path needs to be extended by altering the corresponding property:

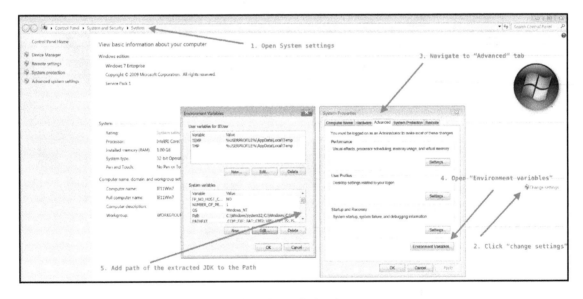

Step 3. Five actions to update the environment

4. Finally, the version of Java can be checked:

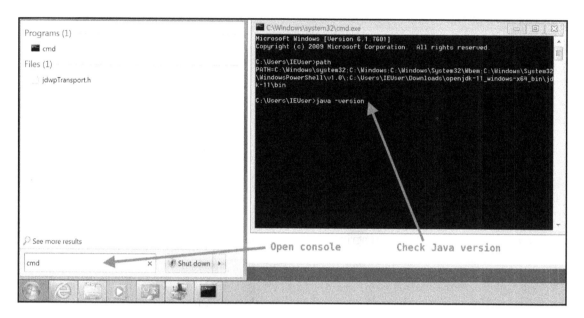

Finishing the installation and checking the Java version

The next step after installing Java is the installation of SBT. You are not required to have Scala installed separately to be able to work with the sample code for this book.

Installing SBT

For the SBT, the simple build tool, there are installation options: using tools such as `apt-get`, `brew`, or `macports`, or doing it manually. First, we'll cover the manual setup.

For Linux and macOS, the procedure is the same as with JDK:

1. Obtain the installation package.
2. Unzip the downloaded file.
3. Update the environment.

The latest version of the SBT can be found on the respective website at `https://www.scala-sbt.org/download.html`.

On Linux or macOS, you can use the command line in a way shown in the next screenshot to perform these three installation steps:

```
slasch void: $ wget https://piccolo.link/sbt-1.2.3.tgz          ◄──────────── Download the installation bundle
--2018-09-29 15:59:14--  https://piccolo.link/sbt-1.2.3.tgz
Aufl"osen des Hostnamens piccolo.link (piccolo.link)... 159.8.72.228
Verbindungsaufbau zu piccolo.link (piccolo.link)|159.8.72.228|:443 ... verbunden.
HTTP-Anforderung gesendet, auf Antwort wird gewartet ... 301 Moved Permanently
Platz: https://sbt-downloads.cdnedge.bluemix.net/releases/v1.2.3/sbt-1.2.3.tgz [folgend]
--2018-09-29 15:59:16--  https://sbt-downloads.cdnedge.bluemix.net/releases/v1.2.3/sbt-1.2.3.tgz
Aufl"osen des Hostnamens sbt-downloads.cdnedge.bluemix.net (sbt-downloads.cdnedge.bluemix.net)... 23.37.48.60
Verbindungsaufbau zu sbt-downloads.cdnedge.bluemix.net (sbt-downloads.cdnedge.bluemix.net)|23.37.48.60|:443 ... verbunden.
HTTP-Anforderung gesendet, auf Antwort wird gewartet ... 200 OK
L"ange: 46849530 (45M) [application/gzip]
Wird in <<sbt-1.2.3.tgz.1>> gespeichert.

sbt-1.2.3.tgz.1            100%[===================================================================================>]  44.68M  2.26MB/s    in 19s

2018-09-29 15:59:35 (2.38 MB/s) - <<sbt-1.2.3.tgz.1>> gespeichert [46849530/46849530]

slasch void: $ tar -xzf sbt-1.2.3.tgz              ◄──────────── Extract sbt files
slasch void: $ export SBT_HOME=`pwd`/sbt/bin    ◄
slasch void: $ echo 'PATH=$PATH':$SBT_HOME >> .bashrc    ◄──────── Update environment
slasch void: $ export PATH=$PATH:$SBT_HOME       ◄
slasch void: $ sbt version                  ◄──────────── Verify installation
[info] Loading project definition from /Users/slasch/project
[info] Set current project to slasch (in build file:/Users/slasch/)
[info] 0.1.0-SNAPSHOT
slasch void: $
```

We have included an installation script in the `appendix_a` folder in the GitHub repository to save you some typing.

On Windows, the installation is done a bit differently. The website will offer you an MSI package for download, which can be installed after downloading by double-clicking on it, as shown in the next screenshot:

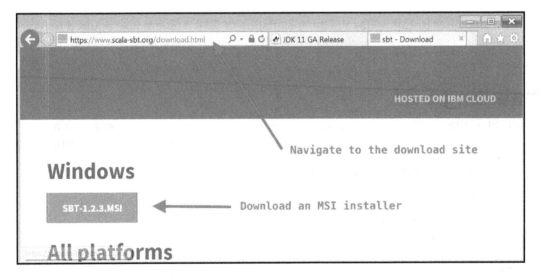

Downloading an SBT installation package

After the SBT installer is downloaded, it can be executed:

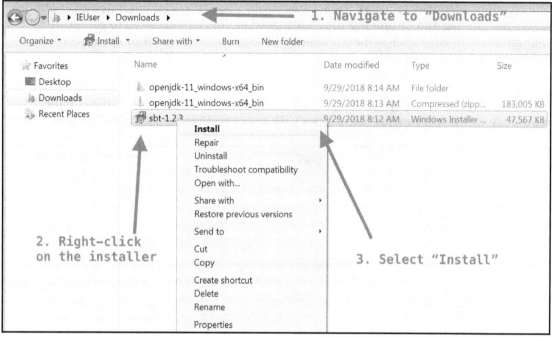

Steps to start the SBT installation

After the installation has started, just follow the steps in the wizard to finish the setup.

Working with the code

The code examples for this book can be found in the GitHub repository under the following URL: `https://github.com/PacktPublishing/Learn-Scala-Programming`.

In this section, we will give you a short introduction to how to download and work with the source code using the SBT console and Scala REPL.

Getting the code

The recommended way to install the accompanying code is by cloning it using Git utilities. As we're updating and improving the code if needed, this will allow us to get future changes easily. Please refer to the installation instructions for the Git tools for your operating system.

In this case, there are no Git tools available; the source code can be downloaded using a web browser or other download tool. There is a **Download ZIP** button in the GitHub repository which will generate the proper URL to be used for the download, as shown next:

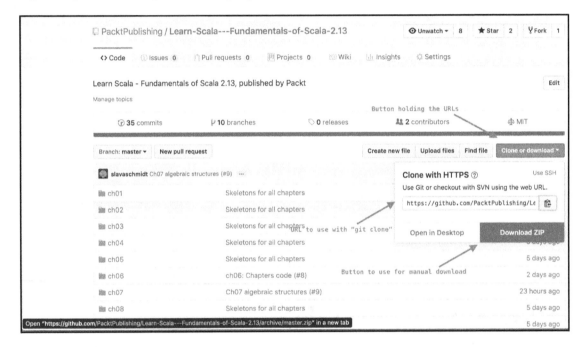

The following screenshot demonstrates both approaches for cloning and downloading the source code:

```
slasch void:~/code$ git clone https://github.com/PacktPublishing/Learn-Scala---Fundamentals-of-Scala-2.13          cloning with git
Cloning into 'Learn-Scala---Fundamentals-of-Scala-2.13'...
remote: Enumerating objects: 93, done.
remote: Counting objects: 100% (93/93), done.
remote: Compressing objects: 100% (61/61), done.
remote: Total 602 (delta 11), reused 80 (delta 8), pack-reused 509
Receiving objects: 100% (602/602), 108.48 KiB | 793.00 KiB/s, done.
Resolving deltas: 100% (119/119), done.
slasch void:~/code$ wget https://github.com/PacktPublishing/Learn-Scala---Fundamentals-of-Scala-2.13/archive/master.zip          Downloading
--2018-09-29 17:51:28--  https://github.com/PacktPublishing/Learn-Scala---Fundamentals-of-Scala-2.13/archive/master.zip
Aufl"osen des Hostnamens github.com (github.com)... 192.30.253.113, 192.30.253.112
Verbindungsaufbau zu github.com (github.com)|192.30.253.113|:443 ... verbunden.
HTTP-Anforderung gesendet, auf Antwort wird gewartet ... 302 Found
Platz: https://codeload.github.com/PacktPublishing/Learn-Scala---Fundamentals-of-Scala-2.13/zip/master [folgend]
--2018-09-29 17:51:29--  https://codeload.github.com/PacktPublishing/Learn-Scala---Fundamentals-of-Scala-2.13/zip/master
Aufl"osen des Hostnamens codeload.github.com (codeload.github.com)... 192.30.253.120, 192.30.253.121
Verbindungsaufbau zu codeload.github.com (codeload.github.com)|192.30.253.120|:443 ... verbunden.
HTTP-Anforderung gesendet, auf Antwort wird gewartet ... 200 OK
L"ange: nicht spezifiziert [application/zip]
Wird in <<master.zip>> gespeichert.

master.zip                         [ <=>                              ] 146.22K    388KB/s    in 0.4s

2018-09-29 17:51:30 (388 KB/s) - <<master.zip>> gespeichert [149728]

slasch void:~/code$ unzip master          Unzipping downloaded bundle
Archive:  master.zip
400449748f4fed56c817b7c046aa80c7aa64cece
   creating: Learn-Scala---Fundamentals-of-Scala-2.13-master/
  inflating: Learn-Scala---Fundamentals-of-Scala-2.13-master/.gitignore
  inflating: Learn-Scala---Fundamentals-of-Scala-2.13-master/LICENSE
  inflating: Learn-Scala---Fundamentals-of-Scala-2.13-master/README.md
  inflating: Learn-Scala---Fundamentals-of-Scala-2.13-master/build.sbt
   creating: Learn-Scala---Fundamentals-of-Scala-2.13-master/ch01/
  inflating: Learn-Scala---Fundamentals-of-Scala-2.13-master/ch01/build.sbt
   creating: Learn-Scala---Fundamentals-of-Scala-2.13-master/ch01/project/
 extracting: Learn-Scala---Fundamentals-of-Scala-2.13-master/ch01/project/build.properties
   creating: Learn-Scala---Fundamentals-of-Scala-2.13-master/ch02/
  inflating: Learn-Scala---Fundamentals-of-Scala-2.13-master/ch02/build.sbt
   creating: Learn-Scala---Fundamentals-of-Scala-2.13-master/ch02/project/
 extracting: Learn-Scala---Fundamentals-of-Scala-2.13-master/ch02/project/build.properties
   creating: Learn-Scala---Fundamentals-of-Scala-2.13-master/ch02/src/
   creating: Learn-Scala---Fundamentals-of-Scala-2.13-master/ch02/src/main/
   creating: Learn-Scala---Fundamentals-of-Scala-2.13-master/ch02/src/main/scala/
   creating: Learn-Scala---Fundamentals-of-Scala-2.13-master/ch02/src/main/scala/ch02/
  inflating: Learn-Scala---Fundamentals-of-Scala-2.13-master/ch02/src/main/scala/ch02/Contravariance.scala
```

Cloning or downloading the source code concludes the first-time setup procedure.

Working with the source code

The source code is organized in such a way that each chapter has its own folder, named by convention as Chapter 1, *An Introduction to Scala 2.13*, to Chapter 15, *Project 2 - Building Microservices with Lagom*. You can experiment with examples by navigating to the appropriate folder and starting SBT. It is recommended to occasionally issue the git pull command for the cloned repository to get recent updates and bug fixes, shown as follows:

```
slasch void:~/code$ cd Learn-Scala---Fundamentals-of-Scala-2.13  ◄─────────── Changing into the project folder
slasch void:~/code/Learn-Scala---Fundamentals-of-Scala-2.13 [master]$ git pull ◄─── Getting latest updates
Already up to date.
slasch void:~/code/Learn-Scala---Fundamentals-of-Scala-2.13 [master]$ cd ch02  ◄──── Stepping into the chapters folder
slasch void:~/code/Learn-Scala---Fundamentals-of-Scala-2.13/ch02 [master]$ sbt  ◄──── Starting SBT
[info] Loading project definition from /Users/slasch/code/Learn-Scala---Fundamentals-of-Scala-2.13/ch02/project
[info] Updating ProjectRef(uri("file:/Users/slasch/code/Learn-Scala---Fundamentals-of-Scala-2.13/ch02/project/"), "ch02-build")...
[info] Done updating.
[info] Loading settings from build.sbt ...
[info] Set current project to ch02 (in build file:/Users/slasch/code/Learn-Scala---Fundamentals-of-Scala-2.13/ch02/)
[info] sbt server started at local:///Users/slasch/.sbt/1.0/server/37d37da6e4699d80ac89/sock
sbt:ch02>
```

Each chapter has its own configuration files, project/build.properties and build.sbt. The former configure the version of the SBT to be used, the latter the required version of Scala and other dependencies. The SBT will download and cache all configured versions as required. This is why we don't need a separate installation of Scala.

Using the SBT console

After starting SBT, one lands in the interactive mode or SBT **shell**. The shell allows for the issuing of different commands to drive SBT to test, execute, or do something else with the source code. The most important for our purposes are the following commands:

- exit: Closes the SBT and exits into the Terminal shell
- test: Runs all test suites in the current project (if there are any in the src/test/scala folder)

The next screenshot shows how SBT compiles and runs tests for `Chapter 11`, *An Introduction to the Akka and Actor Models*:

```
slasch void: /code/Learn-Scala---Fundamentals-of-Scala-2.13/ch11 (master)$ sbt  ◄──────────────────  Start SBT
[info] Loading project definition from /Users/slasch/code/Learn-Scala---Fundamentals-of-Scala-2.13/ch11/project
[info] Loading settings from build.sbt ...
[info] Set current project to akka-bakery (in build file:/Users/slasch/code/Learn-Scala---Fundamentals-of-Scala-2.13/ch11/)
[info] sbt server started at local:///Users/slasch/.sbt/1.0/server/fd41eff9682461385ed3/sock
sbt:akka-bakery> test  ◄──────────────────────────────────────────────────────────────  Enter "test" command
[INFO] [09/29/2018 18:07:55.548] [pool-5-thread-4] [akka.remote.Remoting] Starting remoting
[INFO] [09/29/2018 18:07:55.548] [pool-5-thread-5] [akka.remote.Remoting] Starting remoting
[INFO] [09/29/2018 18:07:55.856] [pool-5-thread-5] [akka.remote.Remoting] Remoting started; listening on addresses :[akka.tcp://BakerySpec@127.0.0.1:2552]
[INFO] [09/29/2018 18:07:55.860] [pool-5-thread-4] [akka.remote.Remoting] Remoting started; listening on addresses :[akka.tcp://Store@127.0.0.1:2553]
[INFO] [09/29/2018 18:07:55.864] [pool-5-thread-5] [akka.remote.Remoting] Remoting now listens on addresses: [akka.tcp://BakerySpec@127.0.0.1:2552]
[INFO] [09/29/2018 18:07:55.865] [pool-5-thread-4] [akka.remote.Remoting] Remoting now listens on addresses: [akka.tcp://Store@127.0.0.1:2553]
[INFO] [09/29/2018 18:07:56.335] [BakerySpec-akka.actor.default-dispatcher-2] [akka://BakerySpec/user/$a] Message [scala.Symbol] from Actor[akka://BakerySpec/system/testActor-1#1103
913486] to Actor[akka://BakerySpec/user/$a#-1814815196] was not delivered. [1] dead letters encountered. If this is not an expected behavior, then [Actor[akka://BakerySpec/user/$a#-
1814815196] may have terminated unexpectedly, This logging can be turned off or adjusted with configuration settings 'akka.log-dead-letters' and 'akka.log-dead-letters-during-shutd
own'.
[INFO] [09/29/2018 18:07:56.895] [BakerySpec-akka.remote.default-remote-dispatcher-13] [akka.tcp://BakerySpec@127.0.0.1:2552/system/remoting-terminator] Shutting down remote daemon.
[INFO] [09/29/2018 18:07:56.897] [BakerySpec-akka.remote.default-remote-dispatcher-13] [akka.tcp://BakerySpec@127.0.0.1:2552/system/remoting-terminator] Remote daemon shut down; pro
ceeding with flushing remote transports.
WARNING: An illegal reflective access operation has occurred
WARNING: Illegal reflective access by org.jboss.netty.util.internal.ByteBufferUtil (file:/Users/slasch/.ivy2/cache/io.netty/netty/bundles/netty-3.10.6.Final.jar) to method java.nio.
DirectByteBuffer.cleaner()
WARNING: Please consider reporting this to the maintainers of org.jboss.netty.util.internal.ByteBufferUtil
WARNING: Use --illegal-access=warn to enable warnings of further illegal reflective access operations
WARNING: All illegal access operations will be denied in a future release
[INFO] [09/29/2018 18:07:56.942] [BakerySpec-akka.remote.default-remote-dispatcher-4] [akka.remote.Remoting] Remoting shut down
[INFO] [09/29/2018 18:07:56.944] [BakerySpec-akka.remote.default-remote-dispatcher-5] [akka.tcp://BakerySpec@127.0.0.1:2552/system/remoting-terminator] Remoting shut down.
[info] BakerySpec:
[info] The boy should
[info] - should forward given ShoppingList to the seller
[info] - should ignore other message types
[info] The baker should
[info] - should bake cookies in batches
[INFO] [09/29/2018 18:07:59.328] [Store-akka.remote.default-remote-dispatcher-15] [akka.tcp://Store@127.0.0.1:2553/system/remoting-terminator] Shutting down remote daemon.
[INFO] [09/29/2018 18:07:59.329] [Store-akka.remote.default-remote-dispatcher-15] [akka.tcp://Store@127.0.0.1:2553/system/remoting-terminator] Remote daemon shut down; proceeding wi
th flushing remote transports.
[INFO] [09/29/2018 18:07:59.334] [Store-akka.actor.default-dispatcher-6] [akka.remote.Remoting] Remoting shut down
[info] StoreSpec:
[info] A seller in store
[info] - should do nothing for all unexpected message types
[info] - should return groceries if given a shopping list
[info] Run completed in 4 seconds, 760 milliseconds.
[info] Total number of tests run: 5
[info] Suites: completed 2, aborted 0
[info] Tests: succeeded 5, failed 0, canceled 0, ignored 0, pending 0
[info] All tests passed.
[success] Total time: 8 s, completed 29 Sep 2018, 18:07:59
sbt:akka-bakery> _  ◄──────────────────────────────────────────────────────  SBT is ready for the next command
```

- `run`: Runs the main class if there is a single main class in the project. This command will throw an exception in the case that it fails to detect the `main` class. If there are multiple main classes, the SBT will ask you to pick one of them to run. This behavior is represented by the following screenshot:

```
sbt:akka-bakery> run  ◄────────────────────────────────────────────────────────  Enter "run" command
[warn] Multiple main classes detected.  Run 'show discoveredMainClasses' to see the list

Multiple main classes detected, select one to run:

 [1] ch11.Bakery
 [2] ch11.Store
[info] Packaging /Users/slasch/code/Learn-Scala---Fundamentals-of-Scala-2.13/ch11/target/scala-2.12/akka-bakery_2.12-1.0.jar ...
[info] Done packaging.

Enter number:  ◄────────────────────────────────────────────────────────  Choose one of the two main classes
```

- `console`: Starts scala REPL

Using REPL

REPL is a tool for evaluating expressions in Scala. It can be started from the command line by entering `scala` or directly from the SBT session. The nice thing about starting it from the SBT shell is that all of the dependencies configured for the project will be available, as shown in the next screenshot:

```
>>> slasch void:~/code/Learn-Scala---Fundamentals-of-Scala-2.13/ch07 [master]$ sbt ◄────────── Start SBT
[info] Loading global plugins from /Users/slasch/.sbt/0.13/plugins
WARNING: An illegal reflective access operation has occurred
WARNING: Illegal reflective access by sbt.ivyint.ErrorMessageAuthenticator$ (file:/Users/slasch/.sbt/boot/scala-2.10.7/org.scala-sbt/sb
t/0.13.17/ivy-0.13.17.jar) to field java.net.Authenticator.theAuthenticator
WARNING: Please consider reporting this to the maintainers of sbt.ivyint.ErrorMessageAuthenticator$
WARNING: Use --illegal-access=warn to enable warnings of further illegal reflective access operations
WARNING: All illegal access operations will be denied in a future release
[info] Loading project definition from /Users/slasch/code/Learn-Scala---Fundamentals-of-Scala-2.13/ch07/project
[info] Set current project to ch07 (in build file:/Users/slasch/code/Learn-Scala---Fundamentals-of-Scala-2.13/ch07/)
[info] Found 1 dependency update for ch07
[info]    org.scala-lang:scala-library : 2.13.0-M4 -> 2.13.0-M5
[success] Total time: 1 s, completed 29 Sep 2018, 18:18:16
[ch07] ⑂ master ✔
>>> console ◄────────── Start REPL
[info] Compiling 6 Scala sources to /Users/slasch/code/Learn-Scala---Fundamentals-of-Scala-2.13/ch07/target/scala-2.13.0-M4/classes...
[info] Starting scala interpreter...
[info]
Welcome to Scala 2.13.0-M4 (OpenJDK 64-Bit Server VM, Java 11).
Type in expressions for evaluation. Or try :help.

scala> org.scalacheck.Gen.posNum[Long].sample ◄────────── Use dependencies from build.sbt
res0: Option[Long] = Some(95)

scala> :q ◄────────── Exit REPL

[success] Total time: 19 s, completed 29 Sep 2018, 18:18:39
[ch07] ⑂ master ✔
>>> _ ◄────────── Next command
```

Please refer to the Scala documentation at `https://docs.scala-lang.org/overviews/repl/overview.html` to learn how to use REPL efficiently.

To exit REPL and return to the SBT shell, enter `:q`.

Assessments

Chapter 1

1. **Describe two ways to make it possible for some resource, `R`, to be used together with the `scala.util.Using` resource management utility.**

   Let `R` extend `java.lang.AutoCloseable`. This will allow existing implicit conversion from `AutoCloseable` into `Resource` to be applied to `R`.

   Provide an implicit implementation of `Resource[R]`.

2. **How can `Set` and `List` be compared?**

   Equality is not defined between `Set` and `List`, hence we have to use the `sameElements` method in one of two ways, directly on `List` or on the iterator of `Set`, as shown in the following snippet:

   ```
   val set = Set(1,2,3)
   val list = List(1,2,3)

   set == list // false

   set.iterator.sameElements(list) // true

   list.sameElements(set) // true
   ```

   Another possibility is to utilize the `corresponds` operation in combination with the equality checking function. This works similar in either direction:

   ```
   scala> set.corresponds(list)(_ == _)
   res2: Boolean = true
   scala> list.corresponds(set)(_ == _)
   res3: Boolean = true
   ```

3. **Name the default concrete implementation for an immutable `Seq`.**

   ```
   scala.collection.immutable.List
   ```

4. **Name the default concrete implementation for an immutable indexed** Seq.

   ```
   scala.collection.immutable.Vector
   ```

5. **Name the default concrete implementation for a mutable** Seq.

   ```
   scala.collection.mutable.ArrayBuffer
   ```

6. **Name the default concrete implementation for a mutable** IndexedSeq.

   ```
   scala.collection.mutable.ArrayBuffer
   ```

7. **It is sometimes said that** List.flatMap **is more powerful than it is expected to be. Can you try to explain why?**

   flatMap is defined on IterableOnce and hence takes a function returning IterableOnce as its argument. Because of this, it is possible to mix different types while flatMap pings. Consider the following example where List is able to flatMap the collection with Set[Int] and as its elements:

   ```
   scala> List(1,2,3,4,5,6).flatMap(i => if (i<3) Set.fill(i)(i) else
   Seq.fill(i)(i))
   res28: List[Int] = List(1, 2, 3, 3, 3, 4, 4, 4, 4, 5, 5, 5, 5, 5,
   6, 6, 6, 6, 6, 6)
   ```

8. **Describe a way to map over a collection multiple times using different functions but without producing intermediate collections.**

   Create a view, map over the view as required, and force conversion back to the original representation type:

   ```
   scala>
   List(1,2,3,4,5).view.flatMap(List.fill(_)("a")).map(_.toUpperCase).
   toList
   res33: List[String] = List(A, A, A, A, A, A, A, A, A, A, A, A, A,
   A, A)
   ```

Chapter 2

1. **Which type constraints can you name?**

   There are two constraints: the lower bound or subtype relation and the upper bound or supertype relation.

2. **What implicit type constraints are added to a type if there are no type constraints defined on it by the developer?**

   For missing upper bound, the compiler adds `Any` as a constraint, and, for missing lower bound–`Nothing`.

3. **Which operators can be used to refer to the nested type of some type?**

   There are two operators. The notion `A#B` refers to the nested type of the `A` type. The notion of `a.B` refers to the `B` subtype of the instance `a`.

4. **Which type can be used as an infix type?**

   Any type which is parameterized by exactly two type parameters.

5. **Why is the use of structural types discouraged in Scala?**

   Use of structural types often leads to generated byte code, which accesses methods via reflection, which is slower than normal method calls.

6. **What is expressed via variance?**

   The correlation between subtyping relations of parameterized and parameterizing types.

Chapter 3

1. **What will be a type of the following function in curried form:** `(Int, String) => (Long, Boolean, Int) => String`**?**

   `Int => (String => ((Long, Boolean, Int) => String))` or simplified `Int => String => (Long, Boolean, Int) => String`

2. **Describe the difference between a partially applied function and a partial function.**

   A partial function is not defined for some of the possible input values. A partially applied function has some of its parameters fixed to specific values.

3. **Define a signature and implement a function,** `uncurry`, **for a curried function of three arguments,** `A => B => C => R.`

```
def uncurry[A,B,C,R](in: A => B => C => R): (A,B,C) => R =
(a,b,c) => in(a)(b)(c)
```

4. **Implement a head-recursive function for the factorial calculation (n! = n * (n-1) * (n-2) * ... * 1.**

```
def factorial(n: Long): Long = if (n < 2) n else n *
factorial(n-1)
```

5. **Implement a tail-recursive function for a factorial calculation.**

```
def factorial(n: Long): Long = {
  def f(n: Long, acc: Long): Long = if (n < 2) acc else f(n-1, n *
acc)
  f(n,1)
}
```

6. **Implement a recursive function for a factorial calculation using trampolining.**

```
import util.control.TailCalls._
def factorial(n: Long): TailRec[Long] = if (n<2) done(n) else
tailcall(factorial(n-1)).map(_ * n)
```

Chapter 4

1. **Describe a case where an implicit parameter is also an implicit conversion.**

   This is the case if an implicit parameter is a function: `def func[A, T](a: A)(implicit adapter: A => T): T = adapter(a)`.

2. **Replace the following definition that uses view bounds with one using context bounds:** `def compare[T <% Comparable[T]](x: T, y: T) = x < y.`

```
type ComparableContext[T] = T => Comparable[T]
def compare[T : ComparableContext](x: T, y: T) = x < y
```

3. **Why are type classes sometimes said to separate behavior and data?**

   Because type class instances define logic to work and the data comes from the values the type class is applied to.

It is easy to change the example of possible conflicts in lexical scope so that one of the implicits wins over others and all others can be uncommented without having conflicts anymore. Make this change. For example, it can be done by changing one of the definitions of `vals` to the definition of an object:

```
package object resolution {
  // change // implicit val a: TS = new TS("val in package object")
// (1)
  // to      //
  implicit object TSO extends TS("object in package object") // (1)
}
```

Then, the TSO will be more specific than the rest of the values because of static resolution rules and will be selected by the compiler for the application.

Chapter 5

1. **Define an invariant property for sorting a list.**

```
def invariant[T: Ordering: Arbitrary]: Prop =
  forAll((l: List[T]) => l.sorted.length == l.length)

scala> invariant[Long].check
+ OK, passed 100 tests.

scala> invariant[String].check
+ OK, passed 100 tests.
```

2. **Define an idempotent property for sorting a list.**

```
def idempotent[T: Ordering: Arbitrary]: Prop =
  forAll((l: List[T]) => l.sorted.sorted == l.sorted)

scala> idempotent[Long].check
+ OK, passed 100 tests.

scala> idempotent[String].check
+ OK, passed 100 tests.
```

3. **Define an inductive property for sorting a list.**

```
def inductive[T: Ordering: Arbitrary]: Prop = {
  def ordered(l: List[T]): Boolean =
```

```
        (l.length < 2) ||
          (ordered(l.tail) && implicitly[Ordering[T]].lteq(l.head,
l.tail.head))
    forAll((l: List[T]) => ordered(l.sorted))
}

scala> inductive[Int].check
+ OK, passed 100 tests.

scala> inductive[String].check
+ OK, passed 100 tests.
```

4. **Define a generator for** `List[Lists[Int]]` **so that elements of the nested list are positive.**

```
val genListListInt = Gen.listOf(Gen.listOf(Gen.posNum[Int]))

scala> genListListInt.sample
res35: Option[List[List[Int]]] = Some(List(List(60, 99, 5, 68, 52,
98, 31, 29, 30, 3, 91, 54, 88, 49, 97, 2, 92, 28, 75, 100, 100, 38,
16, 2, 86, 41, 4, 7, 43, 70, 21, 72, 90, 59, 69, 43, 88, 35, 57,
67, 88, 37, 4, 97, 51, 76, 69, 79, 33, 53, 18), List(85, 23, 4, 97,
7, 50, 36, 24, 94), List(97, 9, 25, 34, 29, 82, 59, 24, 94, 42, 34,
80, 7, 79, 44, 54, 61, 84, 32, 14, 9, 17, 95, 98), List(4, 70, 13,
18, 42, 74, 63, 21, 58, 4, 32, 61, 52, 77, 57, 40, 37, 54, 11),
List(9, 22, 33, 19, 56, 29, 45, 34, 61, 48, 42, 56, 64, 96, 56, 77,
58, 90, 30, 48, 32, 49, 80, 58, 65, 5, 24, 88, 27, 44, 15, 5, 65,
11, 14, 80, 30, 5, 23, 31, 38, 55, 1, 94, 15, 89, 69, 23, 35, 45,
38, 96, 11, 35, 22, 90, 46, 39, 69, 11, 26, 53, 18, 23, 8, 85, 22,
12, 49, 79, 63, 39, 1, 89, 68, 91, 24...
```

5. **Define a generator for** `Map[UUID, () => String]`.

```
val pairGen = for {
  uuid <- Gen.uuid
  function0 <- Gen.function0(Gen.asciiStr)
} yield (uuid, function0)

val mapGen = Gen.mapOf(pairGen)
mapGen: org.scalacheck.Gen[Map[java.util.UUID,() => String]] =
org.scalacheck.Gen$$anon$1@16ca4e8d

scala> mapGen.sample
res36: Option[Map[java.util.UUID, () => String]] =
Some(Map(31395a9b-78af-4f4a-9bf3-c19b3fb245b6 ->
org.scalacheck.Gen$$$Lambda$2361/1400300928@178b18c, ...
```

Please note that `Gen.function0` generates a function of zero arguments that just return random values generated by the provided generator.

Chapter 6

1. **What would be the proper effect to represent getting each of the following:**

   - **The first element of some** `List`: `Option[?]` with `None` representing an empty list does not have a head element
   - **A list of tweets**: `Future[List[Tweet]]` as the operation will probably take some time as it goes over the network
   - **User information from the database for a given** `userId`: `Future[Option[?]]` with `Future` denoting the network call and `Option` denoting no user account for a given `userId`

2. **What is a range of possible values of the following expression:** `Option(scala.util.Random.nextInt(10)).fold(9)(_-1)`

   An inclusive [-1;9]

3. **What will be the result of the following expression:**

   ```
   Try[Int](throw new OutOfMemoryError()).filter(_ > 10).recover {
     case _: OutOfMemoryError => 100
   }(20)
   ```

   The `Try` constructor will not catch an `OutOfMemoryError`, hence the given expression will throw the `OutOfMemoryError`.

4. **Describe the result of the following expression:**

   ```
   Future[Int](throw new OutOfMemoryError()).filter(_ > 10).recover {
     case _: OutOfMemoryError => 100
   }
   ```

   The result of the expression will be `Future(<not completed>)` which will eventually throw an `OutOfMemoryError`, as in the previous case.

5. **Given the following function:**

```
def either(i: Int): Boolean =
  Either.cond(i > 10, i * 10, new IllegalArgumentException("Give me
more")).forall(_ < 100)
```

6. **What would be the result of the following call:** `either(1)` ?

The result will be `true` because `Either.cond` evaluates to `Left` for `i == 2` and `Left.forall` evaluates to `true` for any `Left`.

Chapter 7

1. **Why is the property of associativity essential for the monoid to be useful in a distributed setup?**

   In a distributed setup, we're usually talking about folding and reusing datasets with parts of the data being processed by different computers. Monoidal operations are applied on remote machines. Regardless of the order in which they were sent from the master machine, network delays, different load patterns, and hardware settings will influence the order in which they will be returned. It is important to be able to apply an operation on the intermediate results already at hand without waiting for the first operations to complete.

2. **Implement a monoid for** `Boolean` **under** `OR`.

   The implementation is as follows:

   ```
   implicit val booleanOr: Monoid[Boolean] = new Monoid[Boolean] {
     override def identity: Boolean = false
     override def op(l: Boolean, r: Boolean): Boolean = l || r
   }
   ```

   The property is as follows::

   ```
   property("boolean under or") = {
     import Assessment.booleanOr
     monoidProp[Boolean]
   }
   ```

3. **Implement a monoid for** `Boolean` **under** `AND`.

   The implementation is as follows:

```
implicit val booleanAnd: Monoid[Boolean] = new Monoid[Boolean] {
  override def identity: Boolean = true
  override def op(l: Boolean, r: Boolean): Boolean = l && r
}
```

   The property is as follows:

```
property("boolean under and") = {
  import Assessment.booleanAnd
  monoidProp[Boolean]
}
```

4. **Given** `Monoid[A]`, **implement** `Monoid[Option[A]]`.

   The implementation is as follows:

```
implicit def option[A : Monoid]: Monoid[Option[A]] = new
Monoid[Option[A]] {
  override def identity: Option[A] = None
  override def op(l: Option[A], r: Option[A]): Option[A] = (l, r)
match {
    case (Some(la), Some(lb)) =>
Option(implicitly[Monoid[A]].op(la, lb))
    case _ => l orElse r
  }
}
```

   The property is as follows:

```
property("Option[Int] under addition") = {
  import Monoid.intAddition
  import Assessment.option
  monoidProp[Option[Int]]
}

property("Option[String] under concatenation") = {
  import Monoid.stringConcatenation
  import Assessment.option
  monoidProp[Option[String]]
}
```

5. **Given** `Monoid[R]`, **implement** `Monoid[Either[L, R]]`.

   The implementation is as follows:

   ```
   def either[L, R : Monoid]: Monoid[Either[L, R]] = new
   Monoid[Either[L, R]] {
     private val ma = implicitly[Monoid[R]]
     override def identity: Either[L, R] = Right(ma.identity)
     override def op(l: Either[L, R], r: Either[L, R]): Either[L, R] =
   (l, r) match {
       case (l @ Left(_), _) => l
       case (_, l @ Left(_)) => l
       case (Right(la), Right(lb)) => Right(ma.op(la, lb))
     }
   }
   ```

   The property is as follows:

   ```
   property("Either[Int] under multiplication") = {
     import Monoid.intMultiplication
     implicit val monoid: Monoid[Either[Unit, Int]] =
   Assessment.either[Unit, Int]
     monoidProp[Either[Unit, Int]]
   }

   property("Either[Boolean] under OR") = {
     import Assessment.booleanOr
     implicit val monoid: Monoid[Either[String, Boolean]] =
   Assessment.either[String, Boolean]
     monoidProp[Either[String, Boolean]]
   }
   ```

6. **Generalize two previous implementations for any effect parameterized by** `A` **or describe why it is not possible.**

   Unfortunately, it is not possible to implement such a monoid in general because the implementation would require two aspects:

   - An identity element for the new monoid
   - A possibility to check whether an effect is empty and retrieve an element if it is not

   It is possible to pass an identity element as an argument to the constructor, but then there is no way to work with existing effects as required by the second point.

Chapter 8

1. **Implement** `Functor[Try]`.

```
implicit val tryFunctor: Functor[Try] = new Functor[Try] {
  override def map[A, B](in: Try[A])(f: A => B): Try[B] = in.map(f)
  override def mapC[A, B](f: A => B): Try[A] => Try[B] = fa =>
map(fa)(f)
}
```

2. **Implement** `Applicative[Try]`.

```
implicit val tryApplicative: Applicative[Try] = new
Applicative[Try] {
  override def apply[A, B](a: Try[A])(f: Try[A => B]): Try[B] = (a,
f) match {
    case (Success(a), Success(f)) => Try(f(a))
    case (Failure(ex), _) => Failure(ex)
    case (_, Failure(ex)) => Failure(ex)
  }
  override def unit[A](a: => A): Try[A] = Success(a)
}
```

3. **Implement** `Applicative[Either]`.

```
implicit def eitherApplicative[L] = new Applicative[({ type T[A] =
Either[L, A] })#T] {
  override def apply[A, B](a: Either[L, A])(f: Either[L, A => B]):
Either[L, B] = (a, f) match {
    case (Right(a), Right(f)) => Right(f(a))
    case (Left(l), _) => Left(l)
    case (_, Left(l)) => Left(l)
  }
  override def unit[A](a: => A): Either[L, A] = Right(a)
}
```

4. **Implement** `Traversable[Try]`.

```
implicit val tryTraversable = new Traversable[Try] {
  override def map[A, B](in: Try[A])(f: A => B): Try[B] =
Functor.tryFunctor.map(in)(f)
  override def traverse[A, B, G[_] : Applicative](a: Try[A])(f: A
=> G[B]): G[Try[B]] = {
    val G = implicitly[Applicative[G]]
    a match {
```

```
        case Success(s) => G.map(f(s))(Success.apply)
        case Failure(ex) => G.unit(Failure(ex)) // re-wrap the ex to
change the type of Failure
      }
    }
}
```

5. **Implement** Traversable[Either].

```
implicit def eitherTraversable[L] = new Traversable[({ type T[A] =
Either[L, A] })#T] {
  override def map[A, B](in: Either[L, A])(f: A => B): Either[L, B]
=
    Functor.eitherFunctor[L].map(in)(f)
  override def traverse[A, B, G[_] : Applicative](a: Either[L,
A])(f: A => G[B]): G[Either[L, B]] = {
    val G = implicitly[Applicative[G]]
    a match {
      case Right(s) => G.map(f(s))(Right.apply)
      case Left(l) => G.unit(Left(l)) // re-wrap the l to change
the type of Failure
    }
  }
}
```

6. **Implement** Traversable.compose.

```
trait Traversable[F[_]] extends Functor[F] {
  def traverse[A,B,G[_]: Applicative](a: F[A])(f: A => G[B]):
G[F[B]]
  def sequence[A,G[_]: Applicative](a: F[G[A]]): G[F[A]] =
traverse(a)(identity)

  def compose[H[_]](implicit H: Traversable[H]): Traversable[({type
f[x] = F[H[x]]})#f] = {
    val F = this
    new Traversable[({type f[x] = F[H[x]]})#f] {
      override def traverse[A, B, G[_] : Applicative](fa:
F[H[A]])(f: A => G[B]) =
        F.traverse(fa)((ga: H[A]) => H.traverse(ga)(f))

      override def map[A, B](in: F[H[A]])(f: A => B): F[H[B]] =
        F.map(in)((ga: H[A]) => H.map(ga)(f))
    }
  }
}
```

Chapter 9

1. **Implement** `Monad[Try]`.

```
implicit val tryMonad = new Monad[Try] {
  override def unit[A](a: => A): Try[A] = Success(a)

  override def flatMap[A, B](a: Try[A])(f: A => Try[B]): Try[B]
= a match {
    case Success(value) => f(value)
    case Failure(ex) => Failure(ex)
  }
}
```

2. **Prove the right identity law for the** `State` **monad.**

   Let's start with the property definition we had in this chapter:

```
val rightIdentity = forAll { (a: A, f: A => M[B]) =>
  M.flatMap(M.unit(a))(f) == f(a)
}
```

   Let `f(a) = a => State(s => (b, s2))`

   First, we substitute the definition of unit with the result of the call.
   Hence, `M.flatMap(M.unit(a))(f)` becomes `M.flatMap(State(s => (a, s)))(f)`.

   Next, we substitute `M.flatMap` with `compose`, which gives us `State(s => (a, s)).compose(f)`.

   Next, we'll use the lemma proved in this chapter to substitute the `compose` call with the definition of it:

```
State(s => {
  val (a, nextState) = (a, s)
  f(a).run(nextState)
}
```

   By application of `f`, the previous code can be simplified to `State(s => State(s => (b, s2)).run(s)` and further to `State(s => (b, s2)`. **(1)**

The right side of the equation, `f(a)`, is by definition equal to `State(s =>
(b, s2))`. **(2)**

We have (1) == (2) and hence proved the right identity law for the state
monad.

3. **Pick one of the monads we defined in this chapter and implement
   the `go` function that will encode the notion of sinking the boat with a 1%
   probability.**

   `Option` will represent the notion of the sunk boat:

   ```
   import Monad.optionMonad
   ```

   ```
   def go(speed: Float, time: Float)(boat: Boat): Option[Boat] =
     if (Random.nextInt(100) == 0) None
     else Option(boat.go(speed, time))
   ```

   ```
   println(move(go, turn[Option])(Option(boat)))
   ```

4. **Please do the same but encode the notion of a motor breaking in 1% of the
   moves, leaving the boat immobilized.**

   Both `Try` and right-biased `Either` can be used to encode the case of the
   broken motor.

   Following is the implementation with `Try`:

   ```
   import Monad.tryMonad
   ```

   ```
   def go(speed: Float, time: Float)(boat: Boat): Try[Boat] =
     if (Random.nextInt(100) == 0) Failure(new Exception("Motor
   malfunction"))
     else Success(boat.go(speed, time))
   ```

   ```
   println(move(go, turn[Try])(Success(boat)))
   ```

   Following is the implementation with `Either`:

   ```
   import Monad.eitherMonad
   type ErrorOr[B] = Either[String, B]
   ```

   ```
   def go(speed: Float, time: Float)(boat: Boat): ErrorOr[Boat] =
     if (Random.nextInt(100) == 0) Left("Motor malfunction")
     else Right(boat.go(speed, time))
   ```

   ```
   println(move(go, turn[ErrorOr])(Right(boat)))
   ```

5. **Describe the essence of monads we defined in this chapter using (loosely) the following template: The state monad passes state between chained computation. The computation itself accepts the outcome of the previous calculation and returns the result along with the new state.**

   The option monad allows the chaining of computations which might return no result. The computations are carried over until the last one or until the first one returns no result.

   The try monad does the same as the option monad but instead of having a special *no result* value, which aborts the whole computation chain, it has a notion of *failure* represented by a `Failure` case class.

   Either monad has similar semantics to the option and try monads but, in this case, the notion of aborting the sequence of steps is carried on by the Left type and the notion of continuing the sequence, by the `Right` type.

6. **Define a** `go` **method that both tracks the boat's position and takes the possibility of sinking the boat using the structure with the following type:** `type WriterOption[B] = Writer[Vector[(Double, Double)], Option[Boat]].`

```
object WriterOptionExample extends App {
  type WriterOption[B] = Writer[Vector[(Double, Double)],
Option[B]]
  import WriterExample.vectorMonoid

  // this implementation delegates to the logic we've
implemented in the chapter
  def go(speed: Float, time: Float)(boat: Boat):
WriterOption[Boat] = {
    val b: Option[Boat] = OptionExample.go(speed, time)(boat)
    val c: WriterTracking[Boat] = WriterExample.go(speed,
time)(boat)
    Writer((b, c.run._2))
  }

  // constructor - basically unit for the combined monad
  private def writerOption[A](a: A) =
    Writer[Vector[(Double, Double)], Option[A]](Option(a))

  // we need a monad of the appropriate type
  implicit val readerWriterMonad = new Monad[WriterOption] {
    override def flatMap[A, B](wr: WriterOption[A])(f: A =>
WriterOption[B]): WriterOption[B] =
      wr.compose {
```

```
            case Some(a) => f(a)
            case None => Writer(Option.empty[B])
        }

      override def unit[A](a: => A): WriterOption[A] =
    writerOption(a)
      }
      // tracks boat movement until it is done navigating or sank
      println(move(go, turn)(writerOption(boat)).run)
    }
```

7. **Compare the answer to Question 6 and the way we combined applications in the previous chapter.**

   In Chapter 8, *Dealing with Effects*, we implemented a generic combinator for applications. In this implementation involving monads, we needed to know how to dissect the options effect in order to be able to implement the combination logic. Please read Chapter 10, *A Look at Monad Transformers and Free Monad*, for more details.

Chapter 10

1. **Why does the type of monad transformer reflect the type of the stack "upside-down"?**

   It is impossible to define a monad composition in general, only in a way specific to the internal effect of the stack. Because of this, the name of the effect is fixed in the name of the transformer and the outer effect becomes a type parameter.

2. **Why is it possible to reuse existing monads for the top layer of the stack?**

   The return type of the Kleisli arrow fits well with the type of the stack. For this reason, it is possible to produce the result of the proper type by utilizing the flatMap method of the outer monad.

3. **Why is it impossible to reuse existing monads for the bottom layer of the stack?**

   The argument type of the arrow expects a plain argument. Consequently, we need to extract the effect-free value from the context of internal effect. This is only possible in a specific way but not in general.

4. **Implement the** `TryT` **monad transformer.**

```
private def noResultTryT[F[_] : Monad, T](ex: Throwable):
F[Try[T]] =
  Monad[F].unit(Failure[T](ex))

implicit class TryT[F[_] : Monad, A](val value: F[Try[A]]) {
  def compose[B](f: A => TryT[F, B]): TryT[F, B] = {
    val result = value.flatMap {
      case Failure(ex) => noResultTryT[F, B](ex)
      case Success(a) => f(a).value
    }
    new TryT(result)
  }

  def isSuccess: F[Boolean] = Monad[F].map(value)(_.isSuccess)
}

def tryTunit[F[_] : Monad, A](a: => A) = new
TryT(Monad[F].unit(Try(a)))

implicit def TryTMonad[F[_] : Monad]: Monad[TryT[F, ?]] = new
Monad[TryT[F, ?]] {
  override def unit[A](a: => A): TryT[F, A] =
Monad[F].unit(Monad[Try].unit(a))
  override def flatMap[A, B](a: TryT[F, A])(f: A => TryT[F,
B]): TryT[F, B] = a.compose(f)
}
```

5. **Use the** `TryT` **monad transformer instead of** `EitherT` **with the example functions from this chapter.**

```
object Ch10FutureTryFishing extends FishingApi[TryT[Future, ?]]
with App {
  val buyBateImpl: String => Future[Bate] = ???
  val castLineImpl: Bate => Try[Line] = ???
  val hookFishImpl: Line => Future[Fish] = ???

  override val buyBate: String => TryT[Future, Bate] =
    (name: String) => buyBateImpl(name).map(Try(_))
  override val castLine: Bate => TryT[Future, Line] =
    castLineImpl.andThen(Future.successful(_))
  override val hookFish: Line => TryT[Future, Fish] =
    (line: Line) => hookFishImpl(line).map(Try(_))

  val result: Future[Try[Fish]] = goFishing(tryTunit[Future,
String]("Crankbait")).value
}
```

6. **Implement another take on the monad transformer stack, this time with this layers placed upside-down:** `EitherT[OptionT[Future, A], String, A]`.

```
type Inner[A] = OptionT[Future, A]
type Outer[F[_], A] = EitherT[F, String, A]
type Stack[A] = Outer[Inner, A]

object Ch10EitherTOptionTFutureFishing extends FishingApi[Stack[?]]
with App {

  val buyBateImpl: String => Future[Bate] = ???
  val castLineImpl: Bate => Either[String, Line] = ???
  val hookFishImpl: Line => Future[Fish] = ???

  override val castLine: Bate => Stack[Line] =
    (bate: Bate) => new
OptionT(Future.successful(Option(castLineImpl(bate))))

  override val buyBate: String => Stack[Bate] =
    (name: String) => new OptionT(buyBateImpl(name).map(l =>
Option(Right(l)): Option[Either[String, Bate]]))

  override val hookFish: Line => Stack[Fish] =
    (line: Line) => new OptionT(hookFishImpl(line).map(l =>
Option(Right(l)): Option[Either[String, Fish]]))

  val input: EitherT[Inner, String, String] = eitherTunit[Inner,
String, String]("Crankbait")
  val outerResult: Inner[Either[String, Fish]] =
goFishing(input).value
  val innerResult: Future[Option[Either[String, Fish]]] =
outerResult.value

}
```

7. **Add an action to release the caught fish to the free monad example we developed in the chapter.**

Only the changed parts of the example are shown here. Please see the accompanying code to see the example with incorporated changes:

```
final case class ReleaseFish[A](fish: Fish, f: Unit => A) extends
Action[A]

def releaseFish(fish: Fish): Free[Action, Unit] =
Join(ReleaseFish(fish, _ => Done(())))

implicit val actionFunctor: Functor[Action] = new Functor[Action] {
```

```
    override def map[A, B](in: Action[A])(f: A => B): Action[B] = in
match {
    ... // other actions as before
    case ReleaseFish(fish, a) => ReleaseFish(fish, x => f(a(x)))
  }
}

def catchFish(bateName: String): Free[Action, _] = for {
    bate <- buyBate(bateName)
    line <- castLine(bate)
    fish <- hookFish(line)
    _ <- releaseFish(fish)
} yield ()

def goFishingLogging[A](actions: Free[Action, A], unit: Unit): A =
actions match {
    ... // the rest as in the chapter code
    case Join(ReleaseFish(fish, f)) =>
      goFishingLogging(f(()), log(s"Releasing the fish $fish"))
}

def goFishingAcc[A](actions: Free[Action, A], log: List[AnyVal]):
List[AnyVal] = actions match {
    ...
    // the rest as in the chapter code
    case Join(ReleaseFish(fish, f)) =>
      goFishingAcc(f(()), fish.copy(name = fish.name + " released")
:: log)
}
```

We need to extend the action model and a function, add a helper lifting method, add the additional step to the definition of the process, and augment both interpreters to support the new action.

Chapter 11

1. **Name two ways in which an actor can change itself in response to the received message.**

   An actor can mutate its internal state using a var field. This is a classical object-oriented approach.

Another way is to use context and become close over some value which will become part of the new state. The context.become can also be used to change the behavior of the actor completely. This is a more functional approach because both state and behavior are in fact immutable.

2. **What is the purpose of** `ActorRef`**?**

The ActorRef provides a means to address an actor via the actor path. It also encapsulates an actor's mailbox and a dispatcher. Actors in Akka communicate via ActorReference.

3. **Look up in the official documentation the description of the system guardian. What is the main purpose of it?**

The main purpose of the system guardian is to supervise system level actors. It is also used to ensure a proper shutdown order so that system level actors are available for user-defined actors until the user guardian is terminated.

4. **Describe the advantages and disadvantages of using Akka FSM.**

Akka FSM allows for the modeling of actor behavior as a state machine defining separate state transitions and data for these states.

Akka FSM couples business logic to the particular implementation and makes it hard to test and debug.

5. **In how many ways can an actor in another actor system be accessed? Describe them.**

There are two ways to access an actor in a remote system – remote deployment and remote lookup. With remote deployment, a new actor is created in the remote system. The remote deployment can be done explicitly in the code or by providing a deployment configuration. Remote lookup allows for the selection of an existing actor in a remote system using the same approach as used for the lookup locally.

6. **Why does testing actors require a special toolkit?**

Actors are highly non-deterministic. The state of the actor is inaccessible. The only way to properly test an actor is by sending messages to it and waiting for its responses. Sometimes a whole actor hierarchy needs to be created for this purpose.

Chapter 12

1. **What is the meaning of the** `Behavior[Tpe]` **definition?**

   `Behavior[Tpe]` explicitly specifies that this actor is capable of handling messages that are subtypes of `Tpe`. By recursion, we can conclude that the returned behavior also will be `Behavior[Tpe]`.

2. **How do you get access to the scheduler in the actor's behavior?**

   The schedule is accessible via the behavior constructor, `Behaviors.withTimers`.

3. **Describe possible ways an actor can be stopped.**

   An actor can be stopped by the parent using the parent's actor context: `context.stop(child)`.

   An actor can also stop itself by returning respective behavior: `Behaviors.stopped`.

   An actor can also be stopped if an exception was thrown by the actor's logic and the `SupervisorStrategy` defined for this actor is `stop`.

4. **What is the difference between a local and a cluster receptionist?**

   There are different implementations but there is no noticeable difference for the developer.

5. **What supervision possibilities exist and how are they defined?**

   There are three supervision strategies: stop, restart, and resume. They are defined by wrapping an actor in supervising behavior using `Behaviors.supervise`.

6. **Why should stashing be used judiciously?**

   Current stashing implementation buffers messages in memory and can lead to `OutOfMemory` or `StashOverflowException`, depending on the stash size. If messages are unstashed, the actor will not produce other incoming messages until all stashed bits are processed, which might make it unresponsive.

7. **What is a preferred way to test actor logic in isolation?**

Synchronous testing using BehaviorTestKit provides better possibilities to test actor logic in isolation.

Chapter 13

1. **Name two different modes associated with "classic" streams. Why are they problematic?**

The two modes are push and pull. Push is problematic in the case of a slow consumer because it can lead to dropped stream elements or memory overflow. Pull is suboptimal in the case of a slow producer because it can lead to blocking or extensive resource consumption.

2. **Why are Reactive Streams considered to work in dynamic pull-push mode?**

Reactive Streams introduce the notion of non-blocking back pressure. The consumer reports the demand it has and the producer pushes data in batches according to this demand. When the consumer is faster, the demand is always there so the producer is always pushing data as soon as it is available. If there is a producer which is faster, there is always data available and the consumer just pulls it as soon as it has some demand. The flow automatically switches between these modes.

3. **What are the typical building blocks of Akka Stream's graph?**

A flow is a stage with exactly one input and one output. Fan-In has multiple inputs and one output. Fan-Out is the opposite with multiple outputs and one input. BidiFlow represents bi-directional flow with two inputs and two outputs.

4. **How do you convert a graph into a runnable graph?**

A graph can be connected into a runnable graph by connecting a source and a sink to it.

5. **What is the main goal of having materialization as a separate explicit step?**

   Before the materialization step, any graph can be considered to be just a blueprint of the stream and hence can be freely shared and reused.

6. **Describe the effects of applying different supervision strategies.**

   There are three different supervision strategies.

   Stop interrupts the stream in the failed processing stage. The failure propagates downstream and cancellation propagates upstream.

   Resume drops the current element and continues streaming.

   Restart drops the current element, cleans the internal state of the processing stage (usually by re-creating it), and continues steaming.

7. **Which main abstractions provide Akka Streams TestKit? Why are they useful?**

   Two main abstractions provided by Akka Streams TestKit are TestSink and TestSource. They allow the control and verification of assumptions about stream flow on different levels, for example, a high messaging level or low reactive-streams level. They also make it possible to use a nice DSL to drive the test and to formulate expectations about the outcomes.

Chapter 14

1. **What is a database migration?**

   The database migration (or schema migration) is the automatic management of updates to the database schema. The changes to the schema are incremental, usually reversible, and applied in the moment the database schema needs to be changed in order to reflect changes in the application code.

2. **Describe what could be an alternative approach to discarding an order completely, in the case of insufficient stock for some articles?**

   One of the alternatives could be to satisfy orders for all articles for which there are sufficient stock. This could be implemented by running each inventory update in a separate transaction and combining the results of all of them that succeeded.

Yet another alternative would be to satisfy orders as fully as possible. This approach would require selecting rows for update, calculating new possible states, and applying them in the same transaction.

3. **Describe the conceptual difference between http4s and Akka HTTP in regard to defining routes.**

   http4s defines routes as a partial function that pattern matches over the request. Akka HTTP route definition is constructed from nested directives. The requests follow the path through matching directives top-down.

4. **Can you name a reason why event-sourced data storage can scale better than a traditional relational database?**

   Concurrent updates require much more locking and synchronization than append-only operations.

5. **Implement a** GET /articles/:name **call with http4s and doobie.**

   1. Add new route definition:

   ```
   case GET -> Root / "articles" / name =>
   renderInventory(repo.getArticle(name))
   ```

   2. Extend the repository getArticle method:

   ```
   def getArticle(name: String): Stream[IO, Inventory] =
       sql"SELECT name, count FROM article where name = $name"
         .query[(String, Int)].stream.transact(transactor)
         .fold(Map.empty[String, Int])(_ + _)
   ```

   See the source code in GitHub for the refactored version, which reuses the parameterless definition of getInventory.

6. **Implement the** GET /articles/:name **call with Akka HTTP and Akka Persistence.**

   1. Add a new query definition:

   ```
   final case class GetArticle(name: String) extends Query
   ```

   2. Add a query handler in InventoryActor:

   ```
   case GetArticle(name) =>
     sender() ! Inventory(inventory.state.filter(_._1 == name))
   ```

3. Add the route definition:

```
pathPrefix("articles") {
    path(Segment) { name =>
        get {
            complete((inventory ?
GetArticle(name)).mapTo[Inventory])
        }
    }
}
```

The GitHub repository contains this route definition embedded in the previously defined `lazy val articlesRoutes: Route`.

Chapter 15

1. **How do you map the endpoint with the query parameter to a REST call?**

```
def answer(parameter: Int): ServiceCall[NotUsed, Done]

override def descriptor: Descriptor = {
  import Service._
  named("Answer").withCalls(
    restCall(Method.POST, "/answer?parameter", answer _)
  )
}
```

2. **What is the recommended serialization format for persistent entities?**

Lagom's recommended serialization format is JSON.

3. **Can you explain why clustering is required in order to use persistence in Lagom?**

Lagom's persistence is implemented on top of Akka persistence. Akka requires each persistent actor to have a unique persistence ID. In a microservice landscape, each service is supposed to have multiple instances at the same time. Without clustering, there will be multiple persistent actors with the same ID storing events into the same database, which will corrupt data. By utilizing clustering and cluster sharding, Akka makes sure there is only one persistent actor in the cluster across all instances of the service.

4. **Describe one possible data model that could be used to make the** Manager **to the persistent entity.**

```
trait ManagerCommand
final case class AddCookies(count: Int) extends ManagerCommand with
ReplyType[Int]
final case class RemoveCookies(count: Int) extends ManagerCommand
with ReplyType[Int]

trait ManagerEvent
final case class NumberOfCookiesChanged(count: Int) extends
ManagerEvent with AggregateEvent[NumberOfCookiesChanged] {
  override def aggregateTag:
AggregateEventTag[NumberOfCookiesChanged] =
AggregateEventTag[NumberOfCookiesChanged]("NumberOfCookiesChanged")
}
sealed trait ManagerState {
  def cookies: Int
}
final case class MixingState(cookies: Int) extends ManagerState
```

5. **Outline an alternative way to implement the Baker service.**

   The Baker service could also be implemented message passing style similar to the Chef service.

6. **Can you identify a design bug in the current implementation of the Chef?**

   The Chef does not trigger mixing for unbalanced mixing events after recovery.

7. **The** Manager **implementation stores a number of cookies in memory and this number will be lost at the moment the service restarts. Can you name another reason why it is a bad idea to hold the number of cookies in a local variable?**

   In a production environment, there will be multiple instances of the service running. Each of them will have its own internal state.

Other Books You May Enjoy

If you enjoyed this book, you may be interested in these other books by Packt:

Scala Reactive Programming
Rambabu Posa

ISBN: 9781787288645

- Understand the fundamental principles of Reactive and Functional programming
- Develop applications utilizing features of the Akka framework
- Explore techniques to integrate Scala, Akka, and Play together
- Learn about Reactive Streams with real-time use cases
- Develop Reactive Web Applications with Play, Scala, Akka, and Akka Streams
- Develop and deploy Reactive microservices using the Lagom framework and ConductR

Scala Design Patterns - Second Edition
Ivan Nikolov

ISBN: 9781788471305

- Immerse yourself in industry-standard design patterns—structural, creational, and behavioral—to create extraordinary applications
- See the power of traits and their application in Scala
- Implement abstract and self types and build clean design patterns
- Build complex entity relationships using structural design patterns
- Create applications faster by applying functional design patterns

Leave a review - let other readers know what you think

Please share your thoughts on this book with others by leaving a review on the site that you bought it from. If you purchased the book from Amazon, please leave us an honest review on this book's Amazon page. This is vital so that other potential readers can see and use your unbiased opinion to make purchasing decisions, we can understand what our customers think about our products, and our authors can see your feedback on the title that they have worked with Packt to create. It will only take a few minutes of your time, but is valuable to other potential customers, our authors, and Packt. Thank you!

Index

www.ingramcontent.com/pod-product-compliance
Lightning Source LLC
Chambersburg PA
CBHW060641060326
40690CB00020B/4479